OUTLAWS IN VIETNAM

Hello you2 —
See you next time!
Dave
OL 23-24

OUTLAWS IN VIETNAM

The story of the 175th Aviation Company (AML)
1966-1967

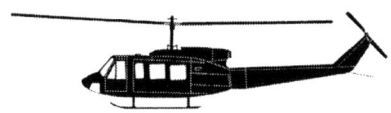

DAVID L. EASTMAN
(Outlaw 23, 24)

Peter E. Randall Publisher
Portsmouth, New Hampshire
2001

©Copyright 2000. by David l. Eastman
All rights reserved

Petert E. Randall Publisher
Box 4726
Portsmouth, NH 03802

To contact the author directly, write
Dave Eastman
Box 59
Center Sandwich, NH 03227
(603) 323-2907
OUTLAW WEB SITE:
http://home.members.net/JARW/175th.htm

*To the helicopter flight crews of the Vietnam War.
Their comraderie, competence, and fellowship is an untold story.*

U.S. ARMY HELICOPTER CREWS
VIETNAM

"The aviation units were the sole combat element of the U.S. Army that did not come apart under the stress of the war in Vietnam. Nearly 6,000 helicopter pilots and crew members perished, but the Army airmen never cracked. Whether it was the oneness of man and acrobatic flying machine, whether it was the equally shared risk of officer pilot and enlisted crew member, whatever the reason, the men of the helicopters kept their discipline and their spirit. As the French parachutists became the paladins of that earlier war, so the U.S. Army aviators became the dark knights of this one. Almost all career aviators served two tours in Vietnam..."

Neil Sheehan
A Bright Shining Lie

Contents

Prologue	1
Chapter 1: Orders to Vietnam	9
Chapter 2: Can Tho and Vinh Long	23
Chapter 3: Receiving Fire	32
Chapter 4: Formation Flying	40
Chapter 5: Wives and the Picture	50
Chapter 6: Savelli's Thanksgiving	59
Chapter 7: "Negative Suppression"	65
Chapter 8: Tay Ninh	71
Chapter 9: A Christmas Present	83
Chapter 10: Christmas at Vinh Long	93
Chapter 11: Mortar Attacks	102
Chapter 12: "FNGs"; Ski and the Rigging Crew	110
Chapter 13: Johnson	118
Chapter 14: Vi Thanh	130
Chapter 15: A Close Call Upon My Life	141
Chapter 16: Platoon Hooch Life	147
Chapter 17: Outlaw 6's Luau	154
Chapter 18: Major Juri Poometuu	160
Chapter 19: Tay Ninh Again	170
Chapter 20: The Mavericks Get a New Lead	181
Chapter 21: Meehan Becomes Outlaw 6	189
Photo Gallery	199-220
Chapter 22: The Battle of Easter Sunday	221
Chapter 23: All Are Saved, Save One	238
Chapter 24: R&R and the Silver Star	258
Chapter 25: A Month with the Mavericks	271
Chapter 26: Back with the Slicks Again	285
Chapter 27: Outlaw 24	294

Chapter 28: Defense Counsel	308
Chapter 29: Lightning Bugs	320
Chapter 30: Platoon Parties and Other High Jinks	335
Chapter 31: Tommy McCarthy and I Have a Mission	348
Chapter 32: The Colonel Has Chieu Hois	356
Chapter 33: Special Forces Operations	361
Chapter 34: Jim Hardbeck's Lightning Bug	369
Chapter 35: Knight 6 Gets Fooled	376
Chapter 36: Outlaw 24 Flies Lead	384
Chapter 37: That Mang Thit Canal Outpost	390
Chapter 38: The Magnificent Seven Are Going Home	400
Chapter 39: "DEROS"	406
Chapter 40: Epilogue	410
Glossary	428

Prologue

The Delta night rang out with sounds and muzzle flashes from the firefight being waged far below our circling Huey. The Viet Cong were in a treeline next to a cleared area immediately under the ship. At 2,500 feet, we were safely watching the forces engaged below. As usual, the cool air at altitude relieved us from the tepid, 80-to-90-degree temperature on the ground, where troops traded fire with the VC element they were in contact with. I smoked another cigarette, a menthol-laced Salem, as Andy, my copilot, turned the ship in another racetrack turn, using up time at our assigned place in the sky until the brass told us to go in for the medevac for which we'd been called out. For a new guy, my peter pilot was handling the bird well, and I could tell, even across the cockpit, that he felt my acknowledgment of his growing skills with this D-model.

"Take it a little farther over by the river on this pass," I said.

"OK. Will we drop down from here, or closer to their position?" he asked.

"I don't know yet, but I'd rather have the room to do what I want when they do call," I replied.

The rear doors were open and Johnson was sitting back there, somewhat alert but also relaxing for the moment, like a lot of the crews did whenever they got the chance in flight. Sp/4 Ron Johnson was my crew chief, and I knew he was thinking about all the maintenance he'd have to pull once this mission was over, whenever we got back on the ground at the end of the evening. The enlisted men had to think about that all the time; it was their job. The crew chief's work was never done, it seemed. The kids had to stay out on the flight line far longer than we pilots ever had to. It made for a long day in the platoon. With luck, we might get four or five hours of sleep tonight if they released us pretty soon.

I turned around in the armor-plated seat to see what the door gunner was doing on the right side of the ship. In the dark, I could make out his form—hunched over, peering at the ground to see what he could make of the action far below. He wasn't my usual door gunner, but someone new to the unit that Johnson had yanked along at the last moment. Apparently he had transferred into the Outlaws because he wanted to be a door gunner in the 175th, which he'd heard was a romantic assignment. Some former infantry types couldn't get enough of all this. By his manner and actions, I guessed he had been in country for at least a year, probably with the 25th Infantry Division or the "Big Red One" northwest of Saigon. I hadn't caught his name but could catch up with this info later when I needed to fill in the green logbook after landing. He seemed intent as he looked down, and I could also tell this was all new to him, and fairly enjoyable. I thought I might break the ice.

"What are your thoughts looking at an infantry engagement from the air, up here in the middle of the night, from your experiences up north?" I inquired.

He jumped slightly at being addressed, and so casually, by an officer. Especially in the same ship. Probably he'd just been a grunt in that unit above Saigon and had never spoken to an aviator flying the ship in which his squad was being transported. At least I figured all that out, intuitively and quickly.

"Well . . . they're doing things a little differently than we would have. I can't quite get what they think they're doing, but then I've never watched from a plane before. This *is* different!"

I smiled and turned forward again. At any moment, the C&C ship covering this show was going to give us a call and we'd have to go into action. Apparently an advisor was down there getting first aid from taking a hit, and after his buddies arrested his bleeding, we had to get him out quickly before the VC knew what we were up to. It was another reason to fly out over the Mekong River so we could act like we were just watching the show and were here only for surveillance. Every minor pretense helped. No sense broadcasting we were about to descend from the sky in a high-speed circling approach, landing literally in the midst of both parties. In the Delta, one went from relative safety to immediate contact in the blink of an eye, and we helicopter pilots were all used to that fact.

The muzzle flashes below now seemed more static, coming from the same positions both sides had held for a while. I knew our guys were trying to stabilize things for our medevac attempt, so they could recommend which direction we should approach from and maximize our security. They would soon tell us so. It was a nice effort. I could appreciate their thoughts, if nothing to that end even occurred while gliding up to the wounded man's position with all the speed we could maintain. The trick was to do it very well, without being dangerously inept. Suddenly the UHF radio erupted with Outlaw 5's voice. He was flying up here tonight, it seemed, while the old man got some sleep. Good experience for the XO, I thought; I'll bet he's feeling his oats. He wants to act like the company commander for a change.

"Outlaw 23, this is Outlaw 5, over," came the major's voice.

"This is 23, go," I replied.

"They're ready for you down there now; are you ready?"

"Roger. That's affirmative."

I prepared to take over the controls after glancing over at my competent friend in the other seat. He wordlessly nodded up and down and silently released the stick into my hands as he felt the pressure come on it.

"OK, you guys in the backseat better be ready to assist this man on board once we get there. And let me know if there are any bushes I don't know about as we come to a hover, all right?" They confirmed they got it. They didn't need a tail rotor mishap, either. We all had to get this thing home.

Outlaw 5 came back on the horn again. He had been talking with the gunships as well as the MACV advisors leading the Vietnamese troops downstairs.

"The Mavericks will be laying down suppressive fire to the south side of this man's position as you come in, Outlaw 23. They want you to drop down at your discretion from west to east on your approach. They'll try to stay out of your way and ask that you do the same," Outlaw 5 said.

"Roger that!" I called back.

"This man is doing OK and will be holding a red-lensed flashlight in his armpit to guide you in. That's the best they can do, as they don't want to let Charlie know where he's located and give you away, too. The flashlight will be shown only toward your flight path. They hope this will be enough . . . ," said Outlaw 5.

I could tell he was waiting for my reply and also to see if I could do this. I figured I was capable of it but hoped the D-cell batteries in that standard Army-issue flashlight were not weakening by the minute in the humid Delta night. This would be a new enterprise. I thought to myself, "I've never made a high-speed approach in the night darkness to a less-lit target; oh, boy, another first."

"Just tell him to keep it in the same exact position and stay constant with his concentration on where he thinks the helicopter is coming from," I radioed.

Everything was rogered and I was ready to go in. The gunships started with their rockets and miniguns and as usual targeted that treeline where the unlucky VC were hunkered down; it began to look like the Fourth of July. In a minute, they would catch on to what we were doing, and I had to hurry before that realization sank in.

I noticed Andy had already beeped down some of the RPM as I decreased the pitch stick, and I silently thanked him for being such a good, conscientious copilot and thinking ahead. The rotor stayed in the green, as I dumped the power. I'd been momentarily holding 60 knots before doing so, and now I dumped the nose into just above 80 on the airspeed indicator for the dive to commence. Down we went, losing lift suddenly until it started building back on the blades again. Our vertical-speed indicator (VSI) was rapidly descending toward 2,700 feet a minute; very soon, it would climb back up to 2,300 feet a minute or so. We needed to come out of the sky as much as we could; we were used to doing this. We knew these ships well, and I appreciated the fact that Outlaw 23 always did what it was told. Some ships sail in a descent, and I was always glad I didn't have that problem.

We had been coming around from the west toward a southerly direction and I had planned the orbit down to finish the approach precisely where the soon-to-be-rescued man was holding his flashlight with great, patient fortitude. I was coming fast out of the darkness while the gunships continued to do their thing in their two Charlie models, strafing the treeline and firing rocket bursts. At least they looked helpful.

But I was getting worried; we were halfway through the maneuver and I still couldn't see the red flashlight beam. I directed my crew to start looking hard for the thing.

"Anybody see that red flashlight yet?" I was beginning to sweat.

"*There* it is! I *see* it! Over there, about one o'clock!" Johnson cried.

"Yeah!" the new guy yelled, "I see it *too!* Can you see it, sir?"

And I did. It was nowhere near as bright as I'd have liked, but there it was, dimly muted by the armpit of the soldier holding it. I wished he weren't being so careful! The lens was almost buried in his fatigue shirt, it seemed. I slowed the speedy descent and pursued that precious little red light right up to his location. He wasn't alone; he had some friends with him, and they all seemed to be lying belly-down behind a rice paddy dike.

"GET HIM IN! Get him in, goddamn it!" I yelled, not caring at the moment whether or not I was keeping my cool.

Figures lunged up and at the Huey, dragging the wounded man between them. They threw some gear on board the aircraft, too; it looked like a sawed-off carbine and a few canteens they'd been using to give him water. The new door gunner helped them, and I noticed he seemed very experienced at it—probably had helped a lot of wounded American soldiers aboard a Huey. Lucky me; a break for our side. Good man. He climbed back into the ship and signaled to Johnson that the task was complete and we were OK to depart. I noticed him strapping in; this guy learned fast.

My attention went back outside the aircraft again, and I noted the Mavericks putting down some excellent suppressive fire for me, God bless 'em. They always did a good job, and I was proud to know them as friends and to work with them as pilots. Now we had to keep those VC from shooting up a perfectly good helicopter and putting us back on the ground with the rest of the troops.

The new door gunner had the treeline on his side and reported incoming fire at the ship. He was fingering the M-60, which had been brought up and leveled, and I knew he was wondering if he should start shooting and return fire.

"OK! OK! I see it too," I replied. The gun started firing in steady bursts.

The VC had heard and seen the bird, and they wanted to start placing rounds on us before we'd gotten away. Their tracers started zipping above and past the darkened machine like bright, bronze-needled lights searching for the fuselage. I kept hoping they were shooting at the sound of the Huey and couldn't see too well. I figured that letting the new kid mark some of the machine-gun positions firing at us would be helpful to the Mavericks, so I instructed him what to do.

"Just shoot level at where those muzzle flashes are coming from, but keep it low. Just try to indicate the enemy positions so the gunships can put some accurate rounds on them, get it?" I asked hurriedly, while getting airborne at the same time.

"Yessir," he responded enthusiastically. These kids loved teamwork and the chance to fire.

No lights for takeoff, just steady-dim on the red and green nav lights. I knew we had cleared the damp rice paddy mud safely when we were skimming along at a four-foot hover and simultaneously increasing altitude and airspeed. We were going to do just fine and would be out of here soon! Andy was watching the gauges, and my attention was outside the aircraft as I whirled away in my high-speed departure. At 80 knots, I pulled the nose up and we soared into the welcoming sky as a few errant tracers zoomed past us in frustration. "So sorry about that," I whispered to myself, as I passed through 1,000 feet, then 1,500 feet, and we were still climbing.

"You out of there OK, 23?" came the voice of the Maverick fire team leader.

"Yeah. Great job taking care of us. Really love your protection," I chortled a bit, and unexpectedly. But what the hell, they knew me, and my sense of humor.

"Rog. Glad to be of service. See you back at Victor Lima [Vinh Long]," said Jack Mankin's bulldog voice. He always did enjoy his work.

Suddenly, there were aircraft lights in front of the window over the instrument panel, and Outlaw 5 went veering over to his right and my left as he careened by. Jesus! I had forgotten his whereabouts and apparently had zoomed right up to his flight path in my climb out.

"What the hell . . . ?! Watch it, 23!" said the rankled exec.

"Yessir," I said. I could tell he was sweating over that one!

"You're released after you get that wounded man on the ambulance awaiting him at the airstrip. That's all we need you for tonight." Outlaw 5 seemed relieved to be alive instead of being the victim of a midair collision—maybe even more thankful than completing the rescue. We quickly put him astern as we headed easterly.

"Gawd. That was really something," Andy said. "We nearly got killed hitting our own ship. That's not being very cool," he snickered at his own joke.

"Yeah. And after making that great approach, sir," said Johnson, who'd been quiet up to now. Which was unusual.

"Johnson! I thought you might have left us back there. Maybe gotten out on the ground for a little nighttime stroll or something," I jested. We were close, maybe too close for an officer and an enlisted man, but that's the way our relationship was.

"Fat chance! I like riding in this thing too much, even if you do try to kill me half the time," Johnson bellowed back over the intercom. "CHRIST! Did you forget about *him* or what?" He went off the intercom, but I could still hear him guffawing back there in his crew chief's seat all by himself, and loudly.

"Well, you know, I'm still working at being perfect, you guys. . . . " More laughter. I turned the controls over to Andy, tuned in the Vinh Long airfield tower frequency on the UHF, and let him take us in. Another night's work, and "good night, Irene," was my statement for it all. Jeez, that was close . . . .

It had been nine months now—close to 10, actually—of my tour in Vietnam. It had been really, really good. Vinh Long and the 175th Outlaws had been great, almost too good to be true. A better tour than I could ever have expected for a young Army aviator fresh out of flight school and immediately sent to Vietnam. I never thought this would be such an exacting experience, or that I would become so good at it. Knowing at this point that there was a possibility of maybe surviving this experience, I filled out the green logbook and thought back on my initial moments of coming over here after my flight school graduation. The kids were tying down the blade, walking it around to the tail boom.

"What's your name again?" I had to ask the new gunner. Embarrassing.

1

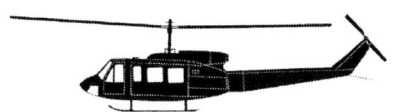

ORDERS TO VIETNAM

FRED STETSON AND I had just returned from our "pack trip." Six days of hiking in the backcountry of the Pemigewasset Wilderness of New Hampshire's White Mountain National Forest had gone well; we were out OK but tired. I said now that that was over, all we had to do was wait for our travel orders to Vietnam. Stets responded that he already had received his—in fact, the plane ticket had arrived even before he had come from Vermont to join me in New Hampshire.

"What?" I said. "What do you mean?!" (We actually had not spent time discussing our forthcoming departure to Vietnam at all during our hike in the mountains; we'd already had nearly a year covering that subject.)

"The orders came my first week or so of leave. I've already got my ticket. We're supposed to fly out of Fort Dix at McGuire Air Force Base."

"Hmmm," I said to myself, pondering what could have happened. We had just finished eight months of flight school at Fort Wolters, Texas, and Fort Rucker, Alabama, and now we were new, young Army aviators en route to Vietnam. Thirty days of leave were almost over, and we had just completed the week of backpacking as my good-bye to the Appalachians I so loved. Deep down, I didn't think I would be coming back from Southeast Asia, so the White Mountains trek with Fred at the height of fall foliage had been meant as a final farewell to these forested mountains that so enthralled me. My wife, Karen, would develop the film from our trip, and the prints would cover the table/desk in my hooch in the year to come.

I finally got around to calling the Army and asking why I had not received my expected travel orders and flight assignment. They told me that the orders and ticket had indeed been sent—to a David Eastman in North Conway, New Hampshire. They had been received, so why was I calling them? Finally, all my inquiries produced the answer: The orders had been mailed to another David Eastman (with a different middle initial: H), and apparently he had been sitting with *my* Vietnam travel orders! I could well imagine the funk this guy was in—10 days to departure and what to do? Someone in his immediate family finally must have told him that the Army usually does somewhat more to prepare somebody for combat than just send his ass an airline ticket to Vietnam! I mean, first you get drafted and then there's basic training, and advanced infantry schooling, before you get sent overseas. That's sort of a bare minimum of training, for instance! The rest of the details fail me at this late date, but I eventually got my plane ticket, and off to Fort Dix went this young second lieutenant in his Army greens, displaying airborne and aviator wings for the big assignment for which a year's worth of Army instruction had prepared me.

I flew out of Boston's Logan Airport and noticed another lieutenant from my flight school class at one of the windows; I think his name was Flynn. He nodded and briefly noted that the only thing he knew about this aircraft was that it burned JP-4 fuel like our Hueys did, and that was the extent of his aviation knowledge about it. I knew exactly how he felt and admitted so. Meanwhile, the man next to me was complaining that the plane was 15 minutes late taking off and that meant he would be that much later in Los Angeles. I was stunned, and told him it still beat walking. That was my attitude after going from the infantry into Army Aviation. I had a good deal. He looked at me in astonishment; what a world of difference between us!

I believe I landed in New York and took a bus to Fort Dix. I shared a seat with a polite, friendly young black soldier who was off to some assignment with as much mystery as mine held. We were both just green kids with no knowledge of what the future months would hold for either of us. It produced a sort of kinship on the ride, despite my attempts to keep a proper officer "aloofness." I wondered about his past, his education and upbringing, and what had brought him into the service. I really wondered when he produced a comic book to read, and then another, and said to me, "Comic book, sir?" I declined and said I didn't like to "read" on a bus. It made me think about what level of intelligence and schooling I might find among the troops in my assigned unit in Vietnam.

Upon arrival at Dix, the first big surprise was seeing almost half of my flight school classmates. The Army had flown everyone who lived east of the Mississippi to this big base, and all those who lived west of the river had been flown to California. So, we had plenty of company, and this policy of sending aviators en masse was to prove a very different matter much, much later for Vietnam veterans surviving the traumas of the conflict. We aviators always stuck together, much as the World War II troops had done. Many of these guys had been with me not only during the eight months in U.S. Army Aviation School (January 1966 to September 1966), but also in Airborne school at Fort Benning and the Infantry Officer's Basic Course before that. We had gotten married together, searched for our first apartments together, witnessed the wives' pregnancies and first births, and a lot else. We were a very close group of young people, just out of college, going through a tremendous life experience. The lifelong friendships that resulted had a lot to do with the fact that not many of these Army aviators would ever suffer from post-traumatic stress disorder (PTSD), which consumed so many men's postwar lives. We would go over as a group, serve together in many units, and know how well each was performing. Those who came home would often be sitting together on the airliner headed back to the land of the big PX. We began and finished the Army together.

While we were spending those last hours Stateside on the east coast, some of the guys from the Midwest decided to go see New York City—a big deal to them. So they loaded themselves in taxis to see the Empire State Building, the Statue of Liberty, and more. I almost told them to check out Rockefeller Center and the Rockettes, too. I had spoken of my joke of nearly not getting my travel orders, and this tied in with an event that had appeared in the media at that time. Some guy from the World War II era had recently showed up before the authorities and asked if he was now out of the service, so the story went. After boot camp during World War II, according to *Life* magazine, he apparently had been told to go home and await his orders for embarkation. After many a year (until 1966, to be accurate), this guy wandered into some official place and asked if he was "out of the Army, now"! It seems that they never sent him his orders, and the old soldier was not guilty of desertion or being AWOL because he had actually followed his last orders to "go home and wait." He sure had. We were all mirthfully contemplating the chances of a similar event happening to us, so I told my classmates of my near miss. Typical of my life's stories up to that point—and, I was beginning to suspect, of our upcoming experience with Vietnam. What provided the capstone to this hilarity was that the next morning, the guys who had gone to New York reported that their taxi driver had had the same experience in World War II! He had finished basic training and then sat out the war on his own porch, waiting one day at a time for the orders to show up. The humor needed to outlast Vietnam had set in. Something should have told me at this point that many more such sagas would follow.

My friends and I had spent that last night in our class-A greens at the officers' club, reminiscing about the good-byes and tearful farewells from our individual families. We figured the Italians among us would have had the most emotional partings, and this proved so. Joe Mirabella sat on my right at the bar and told of his uncles and father advising him of what to do in this fast-approaching future. All of us had World War II veterans in our families, and it wasn't unusual to hear about Uncle Joey, and then Uncle Ken, as well as our own fathers, doing the best they could to come up with information that would be helpful to us from their own history. They all showed surprise, too, realizing that their own relatives were going off to war the way they had gone in their generation. Somehow, America was not quite ready to deal with this fact. It was numbing. My grandmother had said to me at our last embrace, "Oh, Dave, I had to watch your father go off to two wars. I never thought I'd be seeing you do the same." Being sons of that generation, we had always known we might go, too, and now, yup, here we were.

We packed up the class-A officers' greens we had received from our ROTC uniform allowance, sent them off to our homes, and donned the short-sleeved Army tans that would be our tropical dress uniforms for the next year.

The big Trans World Airways 727 was waiting for us on the runway. Stets and I were ready to go for whatever this Vietnam experience had to show us.

Fred Stetson and I sat alongside Ray Snoddy in our three-abreast airline seats. We had about a 36-hour flight ahead of us, with refueling stops in California, Hawaii, and Okinawa. As I recall, the flight across the Pacific was 18 hours in itself. Snoddy was a well-known rascal—from the University of Missouri, a nationally ranked party school—and had already established himself among us as a notorious nut. He was oblivious to all of it, of course. His magnesium-blue Stingray, for instance, had gotten him in a lot of trouble at Fort Bliss in his Air Defense Artillery officer's branch course. Seems he didn't feel the need to follow all those signs on the post that said "15 mph." The Army has those all over the place on most posts so you don't run over the troops. The Army is pedestrian, to say the least. Makes second lieutenants really want to get back to those hot GTO-type cars they're prone to buying with those green paychecks. Snoddy had nearly received two Article 15s while at Bliss, and the word was that they were glad to get him to flight school and away from the Air Defense Artillery school. The Army was a rough transition for this Delta Tau Delta, who had been chairman of Greek Week in 1965 and the organizer of many other campus events. Surprisingly, he had also been a Distinguished Military Graduate, which brought with it a Regular Army commission, but the Army had been a far different piece of turf than he ever could have imagined.

"So, what did you two guys do on your leave, huh? Huh?" said Snoddy.

"We went camping in the White Mountains with the packboards we built at the post woodshop while we were at Rucker," said Stets. "East here took me around the mountains on the trails and shelters for a week like he said he would. We had it planned for the last six months. It was really pretty, and a lot of fun."

"Sounds great. This is what I did," said Snoddy.

"*What?*" I asked.

"This. I just took my orders and flew around the country on airlines. I really like this stuff. I've just been flying and flying and flying. Lots of good meals on these planes, too. I've been on airliners nonstop for 30 days. This is really cool—this was my vacation!"

We sat there stunned, but we always felt nonplussed when it came to Snoddy. Somehow he had convinced various ticket sellers at airline desks that each flight was the one to the military hop he was supposed to get to for his Vietnam departure, and he had just kept going from one destination to another.

"Oh," was the only response we could muster.

During the last phase of flight school, when we were flying like we supposedly were in Vietnam, and also thoroughly out of attitude in this last part of training, Snoddy had found a way to beat the heat of the Alabama summer. There were quartermaster showers installed à la Vietnam—outdoors canvas enclosures around showerheads, with pallets as floorboards. Ah, realism. Snoddy determined that it was cooler to stand under the constantly flowing water, and then, only at the last minute, board a Huey helicopter when everyone was called out for a mission. "You guys ought to try this, too," he'd preach. Everyone else had planned the assigned mission and attended briefings, but this didn't bother Snoddy much. He kept entreating the others to remain in the showers with him, but everybody else was well prepared for him and knew when to call Snoddy out of the showers as we all went to the ships.

Bob Vandel had to fly with Snoddy on a low-level cross-country exercise and had a few joyful anecdotes about the experience. One was that Snoddy just took off his officer's fatigue shirt and whipped it into the back of the B-model Huey they were flying at the time. Flying bare-chested, Snoddy kept saying, "This is much cooler; you ought to try it, too!" Another time they were with an instructor pilot who was sitting in the jump seat between the two students. Vandel was flying and Snoddy was navigating. For navigation, we were issued obsolete state highway maps—to simulate the quality of maps we might expect to find upon arriving in a foreign country. Snoddy was clowning around with their limitations. He'd peer over the small, 12-inch-by-12-inch chart, giving Vandel instructions as he was supposed to, but he would also add his own special touches. He'd say things like, "And here comes a little schoolhouse with a red roof! Yeah, there it is. Now comes a bunch of kids playing at a road intersection. Yeah! There they are! Now, ..." Vandel said the look on the old warrant officer's face was amazing. Probably no flight instructor had ever before encountered a character like Lieutenant Snoddy.

Later, after we had survived our class's formation flight just prior to graduation, we were picking up our duffel bags at the completion of TAC-X training. Snoddy drove his big blue Stingray out onto the parade field, where the Army had insisted on dropping off our gear from its olive-drab, canvas-canopied trucks. This was typical, and always a minor irritation, but as tired as we were, we got used to the Army's doing stupid, inconvenient things like that. The deuce-and-a-half trucks had driven out across the grass to deposit all our stuff, and we had to walk out from our parked cars to get it. Not Snoddy. Out he came, driving that big blue snout of a car with chrome tailpipes behind that rocket-ship fuselage, along with his usual admonition, "Hey, you guys should try this, too. I mean, why not, think about it. Hey, you guys!" He lived in a different world. I always enjoyed him.

We stood around wherever we landed for refueling at some airport unknown to us in Hawaii. It was dark but smelled lovely. We at least could say we had experienced Hawaii, even if we never really saw it beyond this moment. Our next stop after many an air mile was Okinawa. There, for the first time, in the minuscule PX at the airfield, I saw a Nikon-F with a Photomic "T" device. This was the first big development of a through-the-lens light-metering device in that photographic age, and it was the most-in-demand color camera in the world at that time. The press loved this heavy, old dinosaur of a camera; it was built like a truck and almost indestructible, as well as being of the highest quality. Truly, I felt like I was headed for Vietnam for no other higher purpose than to purchase that camera whenever I could. At the counter, I was allowed to lift it up and play with the precision of it. Wow. What a difference from the old Argus C-3 that I had been carrying around and using for learning all this time. Watching me, Snoddy said it looked like I was going to "come" just touching it. I said, "Hey, do you know what this camera is?? This is the best in the world!" He said, "Why don't you buy it, then?" I replied I really didn't have the money at the moment, but I would surely capitalize on this investment at the earliest opportunity. At the time, American PX prices in that part of Asia for fine Japanese workmanship were about 40 percent below world market prices. And here was this Nikon-F, sitting there with a price tag of about $215 on it. I would have to wait.

Back on the 727, on the last leg of our journey, we fidgeted. The guys were of course reflecting various stages and styles of tension. Many had been playing endless games of cards on top of small suitcases they had set up as card tables between them. I kept feeling that many were trying to convey the message they weren't scared. I think most were trying to project in their minds what this experience was going to be like, and what it was going to do to them—well beyond what it might do to their bodies. Nobody ever mentioned being in harm's way and not coming back in one piece. It seemed taboo to discuss such things, even with your best buddy. There was considerable tension in the airliner.

Suddenly someone yelled, "There it is!!" Everyone ran over to one side of the jet, and I thought it would at least lean over with all their weight shifting to the right like that. But it didn't, and the excited young officers were leaning over those seated, gawking at the green foliage, fog, and mountain passes below. I snapped two or three shots quickly and marveled at the lushness of the primitive land below us. I wondered just how much we would become used to it, each in our way, as we developed the skills needed to survive the year. I had a premonition that all of us would be considerably changed as we became combat aviators negotiating the wild terrain we were seeing. The tension in the plane seemed to disappear with a "whoosh," as we all now knew we had something definite to react to. We would be landing quite soon, and the guys were getting ready to experience that event. Suddenly, everyone seemed exhilarated, wearing beaming smiles with eyes glistening at the thought of the forthcoming experience. Nobody now seemed too worried. We just had to wait for touchdown.

The TWA 727 landed without event on Tan Son Nhut's main runway, and we were about to smell Saigon—without being prepared for that invasive moment. The aircraft door opened and intense, humid heat raced in at us. The most horrible scents accompanied that hot, moist rush of air as we became acquainted with the odors of open, raw sewage, unwashed bodies' sweat, cooked pork, rancid fish, poorly cleaned streets, the sorry pollution of hundreds of cyclo-bikes' exhaust pipes, and all else that Saigon had to offer the olfactory sense. My first reaction was, "I have to endure *this* for a year? How can I do it?" All the guys tumbled out, carrying their small bags and kits.

We hurried down the steps, and just as I reached the tarmac, Russ LeGrow on my right muttered something. He was a tall, dark-haired lieutenant from Northeastern University. I had known of him from ROTC summer camp at Fort Devens but had somehow never gotten close to him. He was in the platoon barracks next to mine at the old Massachusetts post, whose only purpose was to act as a facsimile of boot camp for all of us New England college boys each year.

"What did you say?" as I leaned over to him.

"I'm going to die here. Oh, my God, I just realized I'm going to die here!" the young LeGrow said, with a look of stark horror in his eyes.

"Come on," I said. "How can you know that?"

"I just do. I just do. It came to me as soon as my feet hit the pavement. I'll never see my family again. I'm going to die here." His eyes remained downcast.

I looked at him in amazement and decided to leave him alone with his perplexing thoughts as I quickly snapped a picture of Snoddy and Stets ahead of me. Snoddy gave a hand wave as if he were a wealthy tourist landing in some Central American beach resort. Stets was laughing at this obvious buffoonery. Two contrasting images right off as we arrived in Saigon.

Our group assembled just off the parking apron, and when things quieted down, some bureaucrat of a Saigon warrior said that we were not allowed to carry private weapons into the country, and if we had them on our person, they would be confiscated *right now!* Everyone was silent, of course, and the fellow repeated himself to no avail. Some of the guys had spent their own money acquiring small pistols, such as a .25-caliber magnum, for personal defense outside what the military would arm us with, and they were carrying these handguns at this moment. Nobody was going to relinquish these weapons to this Saigon warrior, so the group remained quiet until the questioning was over.

Stets and I suddenly realized we had to pee like crazy, so we took off to find a men's room while the rest of the crowd waited for a bus to Camp Alpha, the depot for assignments in this country. We figured we were at best skillful enough to find an airport restroom, even if this was a foreign country on the level of Vietnam. We joyously rushed into a very wet, smelly but available facility. As we ripped open our flies to take relief, we realized we had rushed past a little old Vietnamese man squatting on the water-covered floor. He had a small board in his hand about three inches wide and 20 inches long. With it, he was industriously sweeping the water in broad strokes from one direction to another, seemingly to no avail. It seemed curiously pointless. At this moment, as our overwhelmed bladders felt some comfort again, I suddenly noticed I was peeing all over my well-shined shoes. I had tried to step back gingerly through the water with my Army low-quarters, but I was still urinating all over my own legs and feet. There were no pipes connected to the urinals! All release just went straight to the floor through the hole. The wiry old man was squatting in a small ocean of urine that had no place to go. He was just endlessly sweeping it from side to side as he looked up at us with a toothless grin, dipped his head, and said, "Yah!" I jumped back from the urinal, as Fred was doing simultaneously, and said, "Stets, we're in Vietnam!"

We rejoined the group, laughing in sidesplitting mirth about the joke we had just played on ourselves. Fred Stetson and I realized almost immediately that this event portended many similar episodes to come. We then told the other guys about it, warning them to expect more of the same.

In those days, newly arrived troops in Saigon were always billeted at Camp Alpha until their orders came through. Only a few newcomers had orders already cut for them, so most of us had to wait and experience some mystery about what our assignments would be. The typical overnight facility at Camp Alpha was a pretty standard military hooch, which for Vietnam meant wooden sides up to the screening, and then a roof of galvanized metal sheeting. These screened buildings were built in rows. Sandbags piled up to where the window screening began (to restrain shrapnel damage from mortar attacks) completed the decor. A door at each end provided access. Inside were lots of Army cots with the standard thin mattresses over metal springs. A few groupings of these buildings duplicated each other, with a walking lane between. Here we would remain for a few days until all the units in short supply of Army helicopter pilots had been replenished with members of our class. In fact, we were the first large class produced for this war, amounting to about 120 with the officer/aviators. I don't know how many warrant officer/pilots were in the graduating class, but it was close to the same number. We had been the "Blue Hats" throughout our training. The Army had become accustomed to producing one flight class a month during this period, with four in session at any given time, but each class normally had had about 40 to 50 graduates. Vietnam needed helicopter pilots fast, and the need was still growing. We wondered what would become of us.

Trying to look a bit into our uncertain future, we also wanted to be savvy with our last days of somewhat civilized living in Saigon. As military men, we worried about when we would have clean uniforms again, and some thought we should check out the Vietnamese laundry services being advertised right outside the gates of Camp Alpha. Med Ruehle and John Roland decided to take the plunge, and they turned in the fatigues they had worn the first day to see if they could get a good Stateside starch job before heading out on whatever assignment might come in. You never know . . . . It was at the end of the rainy season, and things were quite flooded, so the two guys walked across boards spread across the mud puddles to the old mama-san beneath her sign. They handed over the fatigues, gave her the equivalent of fifty cents, and waited. Watching from afar, I was shocked to see her come out of the back door of her shanty and pummel John and Med's uniforms into the rusty brown flood water surrounding her place of business. She smacked them around in the muddy water for a while and then took them back inside! After a while, they were dry, and the two chastened lieutenants got their clothing back—worse, in my opinion, than when they had given them over to her professional services.

By the second day, orders had come through for quite a few of us, so we knew where in Vietnam we would be stationed. The majority of my classmates were to go to the First Air Cavalry Division as replacements for all the guys who had probably brought the division over from Fort Benning a year earlier. Bill Jenkins and the others were pretty glum as they contemplated the next year's living conditions. They would be lucky even to sleep in cots; the First Cav lived with the troops. "At least we'll have that big horse blanket to wear on our shoulders when we get back home," he said. The others commiserated: "Yeah, that's true." And, I thought, that will be about it—that and a lot of glory for enduring the Cav. The shoulder patch was indeed an old cavalry emblem, and the horse's head, like a chess piece, had been added when the unit went airmobile. I still had not received my orders, nor had Snoddy.

Stets then came up and told me that our orders had just come through. After watching my flight school classmates try to reconcile themselves to their fate, I needed a mood shift. The shack where the orders were handed out was just beyond the latrine, so we headed there. Snoddy and I approached the high desk inside, behind which two enlisted men were sitting. Did they have our orders yet?

"Yessir. Lieutenant Snoddy, you are going to the Cav. Lieutenant Eastman, you are going to the Delta," said the young clerk.

"What!? You can't send me up there! You don't want a guy like me with the Cav—send Eastman here!" blurted out Snoddy. "Come on, Eastman, show them what you got!"

He held up my slim arm and pointed to my airborne and aviator's wings as if having one more capacity made me more applicable than he. I was sure hoping my crossed rifles weren't more qualifying than his artillery crossed cannons with the tiny Nike missile on display overriding them. I felt things were getting close here; I was immediately tense. The small enlisted man looked stunned and said, "Lieutenant Snoddy, I don't write the orders; I just hand them out. There's nothing I can do about your wishes."

"Phew!" I thought to myself. "He's right, he's right!" with great relief. Snoddy's head drooped with resignation. I felt reborn; that was my emotional reaction.

Orders in hand, I emerged from the shack to look for Stets. I found him and relayed my good news. He too had gotten orders for the Delta, so we both exulted. This meant we would most likely be seeing quite a bit of each other throughout the coming year, and we could keep our friendship going. We were overjoyed with our feelings of good luck. We would be fighting the old war, staying out of the American units' efforts with all their bravado and hopes of fighting the VC with red-blooded American boys under career-minded Army regulars. I for one wanted to be stationed in the populated Delta with all its Vietnamese traditions, archaic customs, and style. Anything I'd heard about the "new war" didn't sit with me too well, and I was all too happy not to have to fight it. We kept quiet with our opinions and didn't broadcast our feelings to others, but we both agreed we were in luck. At this point, we only entertained the notion that we would be in the same battalion of four aviation companies, and we didn't speculate further. Later that day, we would have a briefing by a burly, jocular major who had just been promoted to lieutenant colonel, and he let us know what we were in for as far as flying conditions down there. This robust aviator seemed like the old-school type and was about to go home; he told us he was a happy person for having experienced the Delta Aviation Battalion. Along the way, he'd had some good times. We were ready to start feeling very good ourselves. This was going to turn out all right.

2

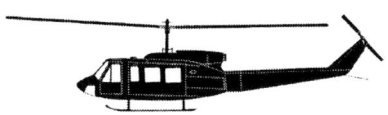

CAN THO AND VINH LONG

THE HUEY SPED ON TO CAN THO. The four of us in the back seat stared ahead at the backs of the two pilots seated before us as if *they* were still the real Army aviators we sought to be and we were just raw replacements in the cabin area behind. They didn't turn around and talk to us, and we didn't expect them to. The flight to the Delta battalion headquarters city would take us nearly two hours in the gray end of the rainy season, and there wasn't much to do but sit quietly and be grateful for an experience that was yet to develop. Troy Tison, Jimmy Redmond, Stets, and I were the passengers. Although I knew Troy quite well from being with him at Benning, and our wives were the best of friends, I didn't know Jimmy Redmond except by sight. He was from one of the other sections in the flight-school class called 66-14; he seemed a pleasant, blond kid, even handsome. Jimmy was obviously glad to have escaped the Cav, too, and he was openly friendly in what chatter we could make over the noise inside the helicopter.

When we landed at Can Tho, we had some time before getting briefed by the CO, the first sergeant, intelligence, and the like, so we headed for the street. There, in the dusk of the early Delta evening, we were treated to what appeared to be an endless stream of motorbikes, attractive Vietnamese women in *ao-dai* pant-suits that seemed like dresses attached to a blouse, lots of tanned-skin kids with jet black hair, different street trees than we'd ever seen, and what Stets pointed out as French architecture. The lampposts and telephone poles were all made of concrete, and everywhere we saw mold and stain on the walls. The tropical air was fetid with the cyclo-bikes' exhaust—all part of this noisy Third World activity we had never experienced firsthand.

The brass called us back inside, where we tried to absorb our first briefing about how smart the VC were and weren't, the geography of the Delta and its peoples (about which I can't recall a thing), and the fact that there were Special Forces camps up around the Cambodian border, "but they didn't account for much." "Huh?!" my brain said. "I thought these guys were the real masterminds behind the Vietnam War and were kick-ass types. What's this guy saying to me?" I let it go and decided there were probably many things I'd have to find out for myself now that I was finally *here*. We were allowed to stroll around again after all this informative discourse, and we were told a helicopter would be coming from Vinh Long to pick us up. It now became increasingly obvious to Stets and me that we wouldn't even be separated across the Delta, but actually together at the same posting. Boy, choice not chance was paying off, which is the U.S. Army buddy system. (This is an inside joke, but you get the idea.)

We walked outside where there was an archway, a Delta honor roll that listed all the recipients here of medals the Army gives for combat heroics. Suddenly it occurred to me that this *was* a place where one might get some, and I wondered if there was any chance something I might do would put me in the numbers up there. There was no Medal of Honor winner, but from the Distinguished Service Cross on down, there were quite a few numbers below each ribbon. The Silver Star had only a few more than the DSC, but a considerable number of Distinguished Flying Crosses had been handed out, as well as Bronze Stars and Air Medals, of course. It was a pretty and gallant sight, but we sure didn't think we were in that membership just yet. Still, we knew we were in a theater where all this sort of stuff happened and was the main order of business. The sun had been out now for a while and was brightly shining on the wet arch and the compound behind it. We were finding out that even though it rained heavily every day, it did break—just as the old Delta battalion aviator briefing us in Saigon had said—and made for some adequate flying weather even in the monsoon season.

After night fell, the rain came down in buckets again. We were informed that a flight was now waiting for us down on the apron below the tower. We scampered through the downpour to the waiting Huey, and *this one* looked like the real thing. A genuine combat-ready aircraft. Lights were flashing and reflecting on the wet fuselage, guns seemed to be hanging everywhere, and when the EM crew opened the sliding cargo door and motioned us inside, it was with a well-rehearsed grace that I knew I had never seen in Stateside soldiers. These were the real troops in a real combat unit, and we were about to go on board with them. We sat on the back seat again, and this time the pilots in the front seats took off their helmets and joyously yelled back to us.

"Are you guys pilots?" Terry McDowell inquired from the left seat.

We looked down at the satiny silver wings embroidered on our chests, then looked back up and said, "Yup," without the greatest of authority in our voices.

"That's great, we need you guys!" said Jon Myhre in the right front seat.

We couldn't believe that somebody wanted us green "f—-ing new guys"; it was amazing to feel that we could somehow be of some worth right off, and welcomed. It relieved us somewhat as the helmets went back on. As the aircraft lifted off, the capable EM crew members smiled warmly at us to confirm that we really were needed. About 25 minutes later, we reached Vinh Long, and a Jeep took us from the airstrip to our quarters. We learned that Troy and Jimmy were going to the Knights and Stets and I would be with the Outlaws, each of us assigned to one of the platoons. The two sister companies had been at Vinh Long for a very long time, with the 114th Knights being one of the oldest companies in Vietnam. The Outlaws had come later, and until recently had been called the A/502nd, but that unit in Germany had wanted its name back, so now it was the 175th Aviation Company (Airmobile Light). So, gee whiz, after a whole year of schooling and training, we were actually with a real unit! As we showered together and shot the bull, we all determined that from the looks of things, the guys going to the Knights seemed to have gotten the better deal; Stets and I would have to get along with the Outlaws as best we could. This opinion would change over the next few months, but guys gotta gripe, right?

Next morning, we met the CO, Maj. Roger LaCourse, who looked tired. The first sergeant had been the chauffeur of the Jeep the night before, so we recognized him. While Major LaCourse was introducing us to the unit and its operations, Maj. Robert Blake, the executive officer, interrupted our conversation to inquire if it was OK to let the good sergeant get some emergency leave to go home and take care of some personal problems Stateside. "Some sonofabitch is fooling around with his wife, Suh," Blake said in his most gentlemanly southern accent, "and Ah think we should let him go home and kill that no-good scum!" LaCourse casually replied, "Yeah, sure, whatever . . . go do it." I was amazed at the exchange, but even more so at the fact that they let someone go *home* after getting to this place?! What trust! It was the first sign that I was in one of the most affectionate units in the whole United States Army. Yes, the sergeant did go home, take care of business, and did return. No sweat.

Major Blake then replaced the kindly CO with his own round of briefing, during which he informed me that Major LaCourse ran the company in the air, "and Ah run it heah on the ground." I had run into these types before, and I nearly dozed off during his soliloquy. He abruptly awakened me, and I had to explain quickly that flying through all those time zones over the previous few days had me fatigued. He replied, "Oh, yes, Ah see. It all takes some adjustment being twelve hours different than yore home time zone, of course, Lieutenant." Blake was one of those guys who got flight pay on five hours a month and needed a good warrant officer on the controls while he did it. I didn't want to get in trouble with this guy right off.

He did say we had a nice town in downtown Vinh Long and

that if I caught the clap there, he wouldn't write home about it the first time, but if it happened again, there could be a letter to the wife telling of my errant doings. A word to the wise should be sufficient for an officer, he informed me. I got the message.

Next came assignment to the second platoon and a check ride with Mike Rheihofer, probably the best pilot in the company and a person who had just extended for six months following his first year's tour. I quickly learned that Mike liked to do things like that—which was ultra-cool Vietnam helicopter jock stuff—anywhere and anything like "it was written" somehow. He loved being in Vietnam. He knew all about the stereo equipment we soon would be buying in the PXs, courtesy of the expanding Japanese electronics industry. He had the Super-8 movie camera gear for shooting movies of us out the helicopter window. And he had *Air Force* headphones instead of the standard Army flight helmet the rest of us had to wear. Mainly, though, the "Snake," as he was called, knew all about the Huey. He was now a maintenance test pilot, which meant he was supposed to iron out all those one-to-one vibrations all the helicopter pilots insisted were coming through the controls of their fine ships, and they wanted them fixed so it was always smooth flying in their birds. Mike flew by night and slept by day, soaking up the sun's rays, right out in front of everybody on a vinyl-covered chaise longue of the type the Vietnamese sold downtown. Made all the new guys wonder what that guy did at all, for crying out loud. Mike said nothing; he was ever aloof while getting a tan.

So this is the guy I have to take my check ride with, demonstrating that I have forgotten everything the Army thought it taught me in eight months of flight school. Thirty days of leave absents one from control touch as well as knowledge of the starting procedure, which seems lengthy at first in a Huey. The Snake was fairly kind, though, and he didn't eat me alive despite my ineptness. As we labored through the ride, finally he rolled off throttle and set me up for a forced landing in a rice paddy. I almost did all the right things, but he informed me at the bottom—with the power back on after completing the autorotation while we hovered around—that the Huey was pretty forgiving, but I shouldn't take chances slewing around in the mud. Sliding in it during an emergency landing would take the skids off and then we'd cartwheel and crash and burn. All this made sense to me, but I was having a hard time devoting all my attention to him because the poor rice paddy farmer who owned the place we were hovering over was having his newly planted crop blown all to hell. I tried telling Mike that this really concerned me, and he kept saying rather emphatically, "Don't worry about it!" I let him know that I only could do so with my forestry background and other things, but he just kept repeating himself. The Vietnamese simply stood there, nearby, while the rotor wash blew delicious patterns in the newly planted rice seedlings—as if he and Mike knew what was common practice and I didn't. This was my first thought about how insensitive we Americans could be in the country we had come to liberate—or whatever we were doing. Over the next few weeks, there would be many more incidents that would make me ponder over what happened to people after they'd been over here for a while.

Over the next few days that stretched into weeks, Stets and I would fly peter pilot with all the experienced aircraft commanders (ACs) in our respective platoons and then meet each other after dark to discuss what we were going through with these ACs. Some were good guys like Jack Smith and Mark Howell, and a Lt. Dave Alexander in his platoon. Others were just plain gooney. We made up our minds never to behave like some of them when we had our own ships, and never to be the assholes some of these men could be, which was way out of the book for good officer conduct. Many of the warrants were former enlisted men such as chief petty officers in the Navy or sergeants, looking for an upward mobility boost in their careers any way they could get it, as if lifers deserved it. These were just high-grade EM-lifers to us, and people we would never have to meet again once we got out of the military.

They weren't necessarily better pilots than the commissioned officers, either, nor did they possess outstanding courage. It was just a bad day any time you were assigned as copilot for one of their missions. They all worshiped the Snake, however—as if they could even start to match his skills and mentoring.

Mainly, they did not want to respect the commissioned officers who filled up many of these aviation platoons until realistic assignments could be made up for them. During 1966, the need for helicopter pilots had become critical. Department of the Army had issued an order that all aviators of major rank and below would be assigned to a flying position, regardless of that rank being filled. Aviation platoons in Vietnam initially had tons of high-ranking officers acting in the role of warrant-officer pilots. Those of this latter rank who were senior in flight time and experience lorded it over these newly arrived captains and majors. Eventually, flight-school classes would be as big as mine or larger to produce the young pilots for the air war in Vietnam. In the meantime, the high-flight-time guys with months in the unit were just plain rude, acting like this situation would go on forever. I tried to follow the example of those officers more senior in rank than I, who'd had a lifetime of living with these warrant officers in aviation platoons, and were good sports about it. Being a copilot was mostly a life of endurance.

Some of the young warrant officer pilots had thrown away "the book" in Vietnam, and they encouraged me to do the same. Everything was to be hot, overloaded, and sassy. It was "cool" to strain the ship, do dangerous takeoffs, flare up into high-airspeed climbs, and more. They taught me how to do all of this, and I thought I was making real progress. "You're in Vietnam now, Dave!" John Savelli would say. After a few weeks of gaining experience like this, one day I flew with Major O'Kane. He was new to the unit, so of course, the warrants casually called him "Old Dusty," because they had not taken to his enthralling speeches on how to fly the Huey, even though he was a school-trained instructor pilot (IP) out of Germany. He had quieted down after that and assumed a low profile until things got better. He was paternally friendly.

I flew with O'Kane one morning out of Vinh Long, and after we had cranked, he smiled over at me on my side of the cockpit, and said, "Take her up." I said, "Yes, sir!" and after hovering out to the runway, nosed the bird over and quickly built up to about a 100-knot airspeed while still skimming quickly over the ground at three feet. Then I quickly pulled the stick back and started a "cyclic climb" rapidly to our flying altitude. I was getting pretty good at this hot-dog stuff, but when I glanced over at him to see how he was taking my performance, his eyes were bugging out like hard-boiled eggs. I wondered if I was doing something wrong; but what?? As we began to level off after this maneuver, O'Kane breathed into the mike: "Don't ever do something like that again." I was stunned, but listened. "At no time during that entire takeoff could I have recovered the ship and saved you and myself from anything that could have happened." This was curious to me, and he went on to say that come that night, he would take out the "-10," the manual for the helicopter's performance, and show me what he meant. I said, granted, this could be interesting. No AC had spoken like this.

Maj. Bob O'Kane changed my life forever that evening by his bunk as he endeavored to explain the graphs in that manila-colored manual. He was patient and he was informative. This man should never have been mocked, and I was his from that moment on. I kept a lot of pilots alive the rest of that year by telling them that many people had operated "out of the envelope" and killed themselves, instead of being done in by enemy fire. Between the two aviation companies stationed at Vinh Long, we lost 18 men in the time I was in Vietnam, and only two that I knew of were killed by enemy rounds. The rest did themselves in, flying in extreme conditions that they and the bird couldn't handle. "Pilot error" was written as their cause of death. When I finally got my own ship, I became a real hard-ass about flight safety, and I put a lot of copilots through the wringer following my insistent directions as I gained experience. What the hell, they're still alive to hate my guts, if that's the way they want to feel about it; but most of them are still my friends. However, that was much later than this moment when I was a green copilot trying to develop the control touch it would take to fly the Huey like it was called for in this extreme tropical environment so close to the equator. O'Kane became my example to follow for the whole year.

3

RECEIVING FIRE

LOOKING BACK OVER LETTERS to my mother and other family members from the time of my initial experiences in Vietnam, I find I was telling them not to worry about me because I was in a safe unit, which had a great maintenance record, extensive time in-country, etc. It seems laughable now that I was trying to placate *anyone's* anxiety about my situation in those early months, because in later letters, I surely was not worried about how they received my news. I laid it right on the line. We just changed over time. The first quarter of my year in Vietnam saw the last of the person I was when I started out—before I became the different person who finished out the year. And those first few months were like a few years of development in various other areas of life.

I took hits the first few days in-country, starting with the episode that quickly earned me the designation of "magnet ass." John Savelli and I were flying Outlaw 26, his ship, up by the Seven Mountains area near the Cambodian border. The pilots also called these mountains the "Seven Sisters." This was a dangerous but beautiful place—rather like the image of Bali Hai or some such place in the South Pacific. Rice fields were livid green amid the lush pastoral scene of well-placed coconut palms and banana trees. Thatched village roofs completed the picture, with the mountains spread across the verdant terrain and meeting the sky—the perfect landscape artist's dream of a tropical firmament filled with bountiful, multihued clouds.

We had been flying from Chau Doc, the Special Forces "B" camp serving the outlying "A" teams along the border. This boundary wasn't well marked, being only a long, river-like canal between the two countries. Just across this small waterway was Cambodia—which, of course, was a very bad place to wind up by mistake. It had the radio code name of "Stormy Weather"—a congenial way for one airman to tell another that he was about to enter terrain where he could only get shot up. (The proper response to be so alerted was not to reply with, "Not a cloud in the sky!")

If you ever get over there, the river is called Kinh Vinh Te, and the small town over which we got lost was Tinh Bien. Here's how it happened. We had just finished lunch at Chau Doc when Savelli gave me the map before takeoff and said he wanted me to navigate to a Special Forces camp and not get him lost. I said, "OK," but wondered where we were going that we had not already been to that morning. He took off, going low-level, and I kept him located on the map as best I could. He then started making erratic maneuvers, banking left and right and continuing on a new course for a while before resuming our southwest heading. He'd ask, "Still got us on the map OK, Dave?" And I would say, "Yuh," and we'd continue. I had no clue why he was doing this, because we were heading across the same territory over which we'd flown before we broke for lunch. Then, as we came up over pretty little Tinh Bien, we streaked over the peasant huts and went over and behind a slight hill just to the south of the village. Savelli came zooming back over the little town, with the kids looking up from their perches on water buffaloes, and headed right into Cambodia, a scant few hundred yards away over these rice paddies. Whoever was waiting for us on the other side knew where he was on the map, because he fired off three rifle rounds very rapidly. Two of them went through our tail boom, and all hell broke loose. I had been trying to warn John for the previous few minutes that he had drifted across the border, but he thought that he knew where he was and that I didn't. The two black crew members in the back started shooting their M-60s all over the place and screaming loudly at the same time. Savelli was yelling over the intercom, "Are you hit? Are you hit?" The kids were yelling back over the gunfire, "No, sir! The ship is hit, we're not hit!" This went on for a few minutes until things calmed down enough for real communication. As a new pilot in-country, I was flabbergasted to see these guys lose it so quickly, with near-panic. They were so frightened they were actually panting. I thought I would be the one to be the most scared, but not so. I got John to turn the ship around, and he glanced quickly over at me to see if he could trust my directions. At that point, it was obvious that he still thought I had fouled up and directed *him* across the border.

Since this was a two-ship area during missions, Savelli tried calling up Outlaw 21, being flown by Major O'Kane and Jack Smith. There was no response—one of the rounds had severed our FM radio's antenna cable to the whip antenna at the end of the tail boom. The antenna was OK at the top of the tail, but it was no longer connected to us. John then tried another radio, the UHF, and Smitty and O'Kane came back at us pretty quickly. We decided we'd all land at Tinh Bien and inspect the damage.

Sitting on the ground, with everyone making a big fuss over the bullet holes in the fuselage, I was approached by John, who was still coming down from his adrenaline high. He was trying to be forgiving, and I was getting exasperated. Shrugging off his "It's OK now, Dave, you frigged up, but we're all OK and that's what matters!" I said, "John, come over here and let me show you on the map what you just did to us. You got lost, John. Look!" He then watched while I traced the route on the chart; then he blushed. His fooling around, trying to get me disoriented, had put all of us in jeopardy, and I wasn't about to let this pass. He needed to know what he had done. We kept the truth from O'Kane and Smitty.

Now came a short, little ceremony for getting shot up. The "hit button" was removed from the top of my fatigue hat, and I became a combat veteran in the unit—now that I had taken "a hit." Maybe so, but this was getting ridiculous! This was the first I knew of units having some token nostalgic ritual marking what happened once you had received fire and actually gotten some holes in the ship. It was cute, almost on a folklore level. Sort of a freshman beanie thing.

Other such incidents occurred during those early days, but what was becoming consistently evident was that if you flew with me, you were likely to take fire that day, just by my being along as your copilot. All this just convinced me that I surely would not be going home from this experience. My premonitions of several years seemed to be coming true, and I felt once again that I just needed to accept them. It made no sense to worry about it, and after a while, I didn't. I just went on the assumption that it was inevitable that some time during this year I would be shot dead. Accepting such a foregone conclusion is probably the best way to get through combat, but I only learned that much later, when examining this period of my life.

As much fun as the single-ship missions were, we all knew we would have to go back to formation work pretty soon, flying the military operations. These were large lifts in the number of ships gathered together because in the Delta, the expansive rice paddies created wide-open opportunities for helicopters to land troops in all at once. A whole battalion of ARVN (Army of the Republic of Vietnam) could be dropped close to the objective even if they were in plain sight of the enemy and quite a target themselves once they landed. That scenario didn't bother their brass very much, and our advisors, called cadre, had to ensure that the Vietnamese military *did not* land us too close to a fortified situation and create a virtual suicide mission for us aviators. The formation of anywhere from 10 to 20 Hueys needed to keep a distance of a few hundred yards between the touchdown point in the landing zone and the objective. The point for the Vietnamese officers to push was that if you could land right in the thick of it, then their troops *would have to fight*, as they would be engaged immediately with the enemy.

Much of the work at the Vietnamese division headquarters with the American advisors went into finding the Viet Cong. After extensive planning, on the day of the operation, senior advisors and Vietnamese generals and colonels had their own Command and Control ship loaded with radios to keep in touch with the troops on the ground as they moved out across the flat terrain and through the Delta's treelines. These were along canals the French had built to drain this place years earlier. This is also where most of the Vietnamese peasantry lived.

I wondered how I would react to combat—trying to fly the helicopter, listen to the radios, and also avoid getting shot at. I pondered how one could do all this at once, and how I would perform. Getting used to flying the Huey and doing intelligent things with it were hard enough for this green copilot. There were major extenuating factors related to flying this aircraft in Vietnam. Due to the high heat and humidity, the helicopter faced a phenomenon known as *density altitude,* causing it to labor on takeoff when well loaded. That meant the Huey, as great a machine as it was, "thought" it was flying at a higher elevation than the zero sea level of the Delta. In fact, the thinned tropical air made the aircraft perform *as if* it were operating at as much as 3,000 to 4,000 feet of altitude on some days. It was as if you were flying in the mountains instead of down at the sweltering rice paddy level of a country near the equator. So, flying loads was precarious; it took considerable skill on the cyclic, the stick in one's right hand. The left hand held the collective stick, which was all the power we had from the turbine and also controlled the angle of the blades at liftoff. Once you had pulled all you had, you had to be rock-steady on the cyclic to get off the ground at all. The saying was, "If you can hover, the thing will make it on takeoff." But you had to be steady on the controls.

So, once you loaded 10 ARVN "each," as the military likes to say, in the cabins of the D-model Hueys, the entire flight would lift off at once after sitting on the runway in a straight line, one behind the other. Each aircraft would become airborne as best it could, sucking the guts out of the Lycoming engine; you'd try not to bleed off RPM as you did your best to depart. Experienced pilots could take off much better than new ones; this was not only a matter of great pride and the essence of helicopter flying, but also a capability of great necessity. Individual ships varied in power, too.

My first RF (Reaction Force, but we always called it a Rat F-k) that experienced some combat was over in Go Cong Province, very near the South China Sea. This one-lift operation was supposed to be pretty peaceful, and probably not of much consequence, because it was known that the VC hung out in this province only for rest and recuperation; they didn't want any war in this location. Nor did they conduct any. The American advisors assigned there had a pretty boring time of it and really chafed at the posting, because after a year in Vietnam, they had nothing to show for it, not even Vietnamese decorations. Nothing ever went on in Go Cong, even when you wanted to scare up trouble—the Viet Cong just didn't want you to bother them. Over the year I flew missions there, it was almost funny to watch this scene. A good place to practice breaking in copilots, though.

Smitty had become an aircraft commander, and I enjoyed flying with him. He taught you all he could, and on this particular day he enabled me to make takeoffs with loads. Under Jack's tutelage, I was instructed to hold the stick like I was pulling it straight up out of cement and not to move it even a squiggle, to get the aircraft to take off. Otherwise, lift was shaken off the rotor blades and the Huey would settle back down on the ground and scrape along on the skids. Bad. Gradually, through the day, I gained confidence in making loaded takeoffs and felt that maybe I might become an experienced helicopter pilot after all.

Landing was another thing. After flying in a V-formation of five aircraft, followed by an identical flight right behind us, we had to land in the rice paddies the same way, holding our position and separation as airspeed changed and we approached the ground. You had to watch your own gauges and the place of intended landing, and at the same time notice what people were doing adjacent to you and off to your side. The novice pilot's tendency was to overshoot and slide slightly forward of where you should terminate. As the troops hurriedly got out, the aircraft immediately lost 1,000 pounds of human beings. That took some quick adjustment on the power. A ship that could just barely land would become light as a feather within seconds, with too much power in. Jack Smith was being patient with me, in his own style. This tall, black-haired Texan had a way of always being cool, quiet, and gathered—as he wanted to be. I didn't think I could ever behave that way with somebody like me on the controls, but we were working it out together this day.

Suddenly the radios reported contact with the enemy, and it became a shooting war. I wondered where to duck, but there was no place to do that. We were very vulnerable when setting down, as we kept putting in troops on both sides of the objective, with a lot of thin air between our aircraft and the action. The West Pointers were all abuzz on the FM frequencies, realizing they actually had a battle on their hands in little ol' Go Cong Province. Even with this frightening chaos, the morning light colored the scene beautifully, lighting up the LZ serenely but surrealistically as we landed on one side of the firefight and then the other. Vietnam could be startlingly beautiful at the same moment that it was terrifying you. I was scared, wondering where all the bullets were going, but it quickly moved to the back burner my problems of flying with loads and making landings correctly. I had never before felt such stimulation and found myself trembling all over with awareness.

The advisors thought that they had accidentally surprised a VC unit stuck between their two bodies of troops that we had inserted. The sounds of a lot of rifle fire came over the microphones as they transmitted their progress while they felt they were closing in for the kill. They were very elated about how well the mission was going. Here was an opportunity at last to prove how effective they could be, given the chance. We sat around the runway between lifts, listening to the transmissions and keeping up with the day's unfolding events. It was the real thing, the first time I had ever heard something like this.

Suddenly the tone of the voices on the ground-pounder's radios changed. The mood shifted from elation to despair. There was obvious confusion here, and questioning back and forth. If they were closing in on all sides with the enemy they had been firing at and into all day, where was he? They were now within sight of each other, and the troops on both sides had been taking casualties during the closure, so how could there be a victory and no VC? Gradually it dawned on the advisors that they had been playing war with themselves all morning long and into the afternoon; there never had been any Viet Cong present. Worse, one American was now dead—a young captain who they thought had lost his life heroically in battle until this moment of terrible reckoning. The atmosphere was like that of a baseball game rained out in the eighth inning, with both teams being in an exciting contest until the cloudburst. Nothing to do now but go home and feel mournful. I saw the recently killed U. S. Army advisor under a poncho, with one bloodstained arm hanging out, after his still body had been transported back to our runway via a Huey. He was the first battlefield corpse I'd experienced, a tragic enough event, but he was now surrounded by all his surviving room-mates who had killed him.

The ARVN troops had all been airlifted back to the strip, and our day was nearly done. The soldiers disembarked from the Hueys and went over to the standing water along the runway to clean their weapons. These diminutive men, the size of Cub Scouts, wore our Defense Department's cast-off uniforms, helmets, and other gear as if they were. One squad let me take a photo, and as they dispersed, one of them casually went over and dunked his M-60 in the tepid water, swishing it back and forth down his machine gun's barrel. Once it drained away, he slung it over his shoulder like a baseball bat and merrily smiled at me as he sauntered his way toward the town. This day of battle was over. The whole operation was certainly nothing like I'd expected.

4

FORMATION FLYING

ON A SUNDAY MORNING, I found myself assigned to a "milk run" to Saigon for ice cream. I had to ask incredulously if what I was hearing was real, and I was told that it certainly was. We were headed to an ice cream factory up in Cholon on the southeast side of Saigon. Two Hueys were to load up this desert cargo for the whole Vinh Long compound, as though this were a fairly serious mission. Each Huey had cost the Army half a million dollars, and I could imagine the number-crunching Secretary of Defense Bob McNamara pondering this one. Later, I would learn that this task was usually reserved for majors trying to make the minimum five hours of flight time for their Army aviator pay. This was the first and last time I would have the experience of going for the ice cream.

Mike Rheihofer flew one ship and I was Denny Haugen's copilot on his helicopter, Outlaw 24. From the air, Saigon looked like a pillar of smog rising from the surrounding rice paddy terrain. Auto exhaust and cyclo-bikes spewed a constant stream of carbon monoxide into the air. It's been said that the United States used to be like this prior to World War II, and that military aviators were told that if they wanted to find a city when lost, look for the column of smog and fly to it. Then they could identify what large town or city it might be. These were back in the days when Arthur Godfrey was a super pilot and now long gone. At least Saigon showed me that the old myth probably was true. I snapped a picture of all the sampans in the Saigon River in the Cholon district.

From our altitude, it looked as though they had totally congested every inch of parking space on the water's surface. It made me think of a Conrad novel, maybe *Lord Jim*.

After loading the two Hueys to the roofs with unmarked boxes of ice cream, we departed for the Delta. I was flying OK and trying to pay attention not only to what I was doing but also to the landscape below. I figured I'd be becoming well acquainted with this route over time, so I wanted to start identifying significant terrain features. In addition to Highway 4, which ran southwesterly to My Tho, we crossed two rivers. The first had a small town named Ben Luc on the Saigon side of it, and the next was at Tan An. This second river flowed into the first, and I always called it the "wiggly river," because of its many oxbows and twists and turns. Its real name was the Song Vam Co Tay, if you're interested. It originated in the Plain of Reeds near Cambodia, up beyond Moc Hoa, another Special Forces "B" team headquarters town. The two rivers converged into the Saigon River and soon flowed into the South China Sea. The transport ships carrying American supplies into this part of Vietnam were often anchored in this area for months before they could unload. This great delay also explains why our beer cans were always rusty and the contents were flat. There was always plenty of the canned beverage, but the cans were in such bad shape that you couldn't even read the label to see if it was Pabst or Schlitz.

While I was absorbed memorizing the pleasantly green but wet terrain far below our altitude of 2,500 feet, Haugen came on the mike and hissed over the intercom, "Don't do anything stupid or abrupt; Rheihofer is overlapping rotor blades with you right now . . . ." As I glanced back over my left shoulder, it looked like the Huey was coming in the cargo door! The sliding doors were in their locked-back position while we were en route, and I had a full view of the Snake with his Air Force headphones, intently focused on his angle with my aircraft, but *he was CLOSE!* I paled and said to Denny, who didn't much like us butter-bar new lieutenants, "Look why don't you take the controls while he is doing this, so I can get a picture?" He did so, and I got out the old Argus C-3 that

I'd received at my wedding and snapped a few shots of Rheihofer trying to come in the door. In the pictures, the crew is sitting nonchalantly, surrounded by piles of manila-colored ice cream boxes, as if it was no big deal. Here is what Mike was doing:

The rotating blades of the helicopter are not visible to the human eye as independent whirling wings. You can capture them at 1/125 of a second on the camera, but the effect is like looking at the rotating spokes of a wagon wheel on an old Concord stagecoach in the Western movies. You are aware of the speed and shape, but the human eye can't discern the actual spokes. That's the way it was to perceive the disc of the rotor blades. The sight picture for flying formation in terms of the vertical alignment was to put this disc on the horizon. This gave you about three feet of separation to keep your aircraft clear, height-wise, from the helicopter you were flying on. The horizontal clearance was supposed to be about two rotor discs from the ship on which you had a position. Mike wasn't doing that. Overlapping the two rotor-blade discs was about as dangerous as anything, trusting one's flying skills to quickly prevent a midair collision. The angle we flew on each other any time we joined up like this was 45 degrees. This was achieved by lining up the cross tubes leading down from the cabin area of the Huey to where they joined the skids. Where the right one of the front seemed to visually touch the left one of the rear did the trick. This was called "maintaining a 45," and it was important for experienced ACs to insist on this with newly arrived green copilots. It gave unity to the whole formation when it was a large one, making us a stable, cohesive flying military unit for both safety and deployment. Quickly gaining these formation flying skills early in the game was deeply important. After "performing" for a while, Mike moved off to a normal flying distance, and I felt quite relieved when he did so. No matter how good we all became, we all did some dumb, arrogant things flying over there.

Over time, we got used to flying a lot of lifts and became acclimated to the potential of combat while flying, but I was becoming increasingly dismayed by the lack of standardization throughout the units when we were linked up in big formations. The situation reached a peak one day, and something had to change. Major O'Kane had become platoon leader, and as we were on short final to the Tra Vinh airstrip, he radioed ahead to Capt. Ray Leuty, who was flying Outlaw Lead, that he felt it was time for some ground school when we landed—on formation-flying procedures. "I think we need it," said O'Kane, and there wasn't much Leuty could respond, except "OK." I felt better already and took a deep breath; I had seen quite enough of supposedly seasoned pilots doing anything but what we had been taught in flight school at Rucker. Coming over to Vietnam, I had assumed we were all in agreement on what we were supposed to do in the air in these formations. I had learned differently, and this was becoming increasingly dangerous among the units.

As he did with everything, O'Kane took matters well in hand and discussed what we should be doing in each of the various formations we had to undertake for performing different tasks as an aviation unit. He went over all the rules on which we needed to establish consensus. Not doing so was like square dancing without a caller or without knowledge of a partner's moves. Some mid-air collisions were inevitable if our present confusion continued. It was beyond embarrassing.

After this intensive day on the ground, we flew our formations beautifully, and I was proud of us. We didn't like getting involved with the Soc Trang people, however, and it took some politicking before we could insist that we only wanted to fly with each other in *our* platoons in each "V" of five. The Tigers and Warriors making up the other half of the aviation battalion said it didn't really matter; we said we thought it did. It always was easier to keep units together so that you knew whom you were flying near, and whom you could trust. You had to know all the pilots' idiosyncrasies like they had to learn those of their individual aircraft. As much everyone worked at standardization, we very much had to understand what any individual would do when employing his best talents or abilities in combat. Why work with a complete stranger? This was no place to learn about somebody for the first time under life-threatening conditions. After this moment, there were no more mixed formations of Delta Aviation Battalion aircraft in my slides sent home.

The first platoon flew together as a unit under Leuty, and the second platoon did so under O'Kane. The two platoon leaders swapped off flying Lead every other day to give each other a break. The commander flying Trail played "tail-end Charley" and provided a backseat perspective for the guy up front who was in charge of the operation that day. We soon became more comfortable with who we were.

We had to get used to three basic formations: the standard "V" of five, the straight trail, and the staggered trail. The first involved aircraft flying on 45-degree angles to the right and left of the lead aircraft. If it was first in position of a large formation—say, of 20 to 30 ships, which the Delta's landing zones could sustain—then it was called the "gold flight." The next one was the "white flight," and the one beyond that was the "green flight." I don't know if we ran out of colors after that, or just didn't care, but the tiny colored placards could be inserted just behind the front door on the side of the Huey. The battalion brass liked to see us adjust these throughout the day of an operation, but we didn't get around to that very much. Mostly, we just kept these designations in our heads as positions, and answered the call of "Gold 2" or "White 3" if the platoon leader wanted to call us up about something without recalling our tail number or call sign in the unit. When we answered, then he could determine which individual ship it was and use its call sign. Many times, missions would come up while we were flying around en route to somewhere, and a typical conversation might go something like, "Gold 3, can you handle that?" The reply was, "Yessir, Outlaw 25 breaking down and to the right, right NOW." The ship so dispatched then would lose some altitude as he broke down and away from the formation as it continued on its way. Cool stuff, boy.

If the formation could not land in this "V" of five, such as on a runway, or in the field to pick up troops ready to go home, we went to a "straight trail," meaning we broke out of the "V" shape into a linear formation that placed us one behind the other for landing. This way, we could each pick up "sticks" of troops (10 in a "stick"); they would be standing on the rice paddy dikes as if they were waiting for a crosstown bus to take them home at the end of a working day. We would hover up to each group of ARVNs and load them up with their stinking rice paddy mud all over their boots and pants. They'd be smiling, carrying all their ducks and chickens, and even small puppies, which they had looted from the populace for their evening meals. There were times when I felt the ARVN's military operations were entirely for the "liberation" of foodstuffs from their country's civilians.

When all the ships were loaded, Trail would acknowledge this over the FM to Outlaw Lead. He would then transmit to the gunships protecting us that we were ready for departure and the platoon Lead would give us the command to commence takeoff. We would do so, one at a time, the water draining out of our skids and the now-full Hueys laboring up into the sky. Once up there, we would regroup into the "V" formation once again, which was our usual method of getting around.

The last formation we would employ in very similar circumstances was the "staggered trail," which meant we flew 45-degree angles on the ship to our side, *and* directly behind the ship in front of us. We didn't worry much about that latter sight picture as we directed our attention to the guy at our side. This produced a "column of twos," in Army jargon, and was utilized when the troops to be picked up were in two long groupings spread across the rice paddies. Sometimes, but not often, this formation was used for flying at higher altitude. It took too much effort for a long period of time en route. We might hold it, for instance, if we had to set down the troops fairly quickly at a nearby location in the same conformation.

The only other formations besides these three were much more complicated and undesirable, although we did experience them from time to time. They were a "right oblique" and a "left oblique." These involved a strand of aircraft all on 45-degree angles to each other, extending in one direction to the right or left of the lead aircraft. It was very unwieldy, not nice at all, but sometimes the shape of a landing zone in the trees below demanded this wing-shaped echelon. We only did these formations if it was important to keep the flight together under gunship protection. Their platoon leaders thought up the directions for us in choosing these formations, because they had to shepherd us in and out of these situations, being responsible for our safety from enemy fire. You had to have a noggin on your shoulders to be a gunship platoon leader in the Delta. These guys were as busy as a Stateside air traffic controller.

The most impressive aspect of performing these aerial maneuvers was the artistry of it all. When we went from the "V" formation to the straight trail, Lead would flick on his anti-collision light; that red flashing beacon was a visual signal accompanying the radio transmission commanding it. Otherwise, we never saw this light on, whereas it is common practice to fly with it on in the States. In Vietnam, it was too dangerous to have the anti-collision light on; it made you a better target. But the light was a backup in case you didn't hear the radio call, for instance if you were involved in a discussion with your crew and had not been paying attention. Going to "trail" was the only time the light was used. The lead aircraft in the middle of the "V" would then dip his nose and gain an additional five knots of airspeed. That enabled the second aircraft in "Gold 2" position to move laterally, straight across, without backing off from our 80-knot cruising speed. The third aircraft, "Gold 3," over on the far side of the formation (on Lead's left), had to taper his airspeed a bit until "Gold 2" settled in place directly behind him. Then "Gold 4" on the right came over and filled in. Finally, "Gold 5" took up the last position in line. Meanwhile, the "white flight" had zipped slightly to the right while this was going on, and that grouping did the same as the above. When the linear arrangement was complete, the Lead on the second flight swung over and lined up to be a 10-ship formation, all in tandem. We often were descending to the runway at the same time, so a lot of coordination and faith went on here. The repetition of months of flying together by the individual ACs allowed this to be done quite well, and even became monotonous, but that's the way it was and we were.

In the straight-trail formation, the sight picture was to split the turbine's exhaust port with the tail fin of the Huey's tail boom. Putting the tail rotor gearbox on the "swash plate" of the main rotor system was the rest of the story. Pilots hung in there on tight turns and descents throughout this maneuver, at the same time keeping a distance of two aircraft lengths. When you came home after 800 to 1,400 hours of this stuff, you could fly effortlessly all day and amaze your students with your ability as an instructor demonstrating these maneuvers in flight school. We used a lot of stick and very minute power changes enabling us to be incredibly fluid with the aircraft just in front of us or to our side, whatever the sight picture was. "You don't move!" my students would exclaim. It did look pretty, and I think I never ceased taking pictures of it all. At least my wife thought so—she handled the developing of all the slides I sent Stateside.

After a month or so, I was getting better at all the flying we were doing. One morning, I flew copilot with O'Kane in the lead aircraft. Getting this assignment at least showed I was getting smoother on the controls. Usually the best warrant officer/copilot flew with Lead so that the commander could talk on the radios and work off the operations map while the kid flew. We needed somebody smooth and consistent on the controls of the first aircraft; otherwise, everything done there would ripple through the flight like a snap-the-whip game. And complaints would come through pretty quickly on the platoon FM radios: "Hey, Lead, that was too tight a bank back there!" and other comments that were equally emphatic.

I took off and did the flying, feeling smug that I was doing OK. When I looked over at O'Kane, he was fast asleep, slumped up against the armor-plated seat's sliding plate. The platoon leaders often flew nearly 200 hours a month at that time, while we averaged 120 to 140. They were always pooped and at times looked like zombies. I guessed I had to do a good job and not let anyone down while we flew on to Moc Hoa for a lift. I looked back and Mark Howell in Outlaw 22 smiled back at me from the left seat in his ship; I knew he was trying to give me confidence. Oh, boy.

The sky to the north, where we were headed, was very gray, with no horizon. It was a murky dawn, so it was tough to tell what kind of day was ahead. Between the morning blahs, not enough sleep, and just boring, uneventful flying, I was getting pretty dozy myself. "C'mon," I said to myself, "get alert; some people are depending upon you here." I glanced over at O'Kane, and he was still sleeping like a babe. Pretty trusting, I thought.

It was at about this point that I suddenly had an attack of vertigo. The red lights on the gauges, the false gray light of the dawn, the lack of a discernible horizon, and the sleepiness all put me into it. I got on the instruments. I knew from flight school that I always went into a right-hand turn when I had this condition, so I had to start guarding against that. Sure enough, I'd look down at the attitude indicator and a sneaky little 1.5- to 2.5-degree turn was starting, so I'd correct. I'd hold the appropriate heading for a while, and then that turn would start again. This was going to take work. I kept shaking my head like some old trucker after six days on the road, finishing his run on bennies he had to take every once in a while. There was no way I could say to the flight of 10 ships behind and around me, "Hey, go somewhere else! I've got vertigo up here!" Glancing back at Mark, I saw that he was still hanging tight on me in the perfect position he always flew. I couldn't wave him off, either. I wanted to say, "Not today, good friend, not today. Trust me another time!" But sending those telepathic messages didn't work either. I labored on, staying painfully on the instruments and trying hard not to screw this up anymore than I already was doing.

A few miles short of the runway, Major O'Kane woke up and stretched. "Everything OK?" he inquired. "Sure," I replied. After all my hard work, maybe nobody had caught on. Now O'Kane could take over and give me a break, going on to land the thing. He took the controls and I reached for the Argus in my flight helmet bag. I photographed Outlaw 22 still holding on precisely where he was supposed to be. On the ground after shutdown, Mark Howell walked over to me and said in his froggy voice, "You did pretty good, except you were in a constant right-hand turn the whole time! What was that about?" I told him that's what happens to me when I get vertigo, and that's where I had been most of the flight up. "Vertigo?!" he yelled. "See if I fly close on you anymore!" Oh, well . . . .

5

WIVES AND THE PICTURE

GRADUALLY IT BEGAN TO DAWN ON US how long it would be before we would be with our wives again. Some of the guys planned to reunite with their loves on R&R in Hong Kong or Hawaii, but that could be as much as six months away, at the earliest. People wrote, of course, and a few tried to use a new, modern gizmo—the battery-powered tape recorder. Many couples bought matching sets before the men departed for Southeast Asia. The idea was to send vocal letters back and forth for the realism of hearing your loved one's voice during the long period of separation. The small sets ran on D-cell batteries, and that's where this idea ran into trouble. The power supply was erratic; likewise the pitch and timbre of the recorded voices. Some of this got pretty funny.

A guy would need privacy, of course, to tell his woman what he was feeling for her. You would see men walking out behind the hooch and talking in total darkness, or sitting even farther out than that—where they could even be mistaken for a foe—while speaking into the little handheld mike. Just when the one-way conversation would begin in earnest, the recorder would run out of tape and spin round and round, hissing. The spool then would be rewound and sent Stateside through the mail to the mate. Hers would come back about the same time yours was en route. Then you'd have to walk back out toward the rice paddies again to hear the comments your loving wife made about your poor use of the machine.

Before I gave up on all this, one tape my wife sent me went like so: "Your last tape sounded just awful! What did you do?! It made horrible slurring sounds and groans, and then speeded up and made screeching noises like your voice was really high or something. I mean it was just awful. Did you switch on the machine like you were supposed to? Did you break the thing already? Gawd, it was really awful. I kept playing it back and it didn't get better. You sounded terrible and not like yourself at all. Can you fix this? Can you find some way to make it better?" She was still talking like that when her tape ran off the reel at the end. Hey, some of her tapes sounded just as bad. "W-w-whunnn-hooounnnn-innn-eeeeey, unn—oohnh." A whole tape of gibberish, and sounds you didn't want to share with anyone in the platoon, I'll tell you.

A man would come back out of the darkness and the rest of the guys would ask. "Hey, did you get a tape from your wife?" And he'd reply, "Sure, right, uh-huh." Then, "Well, what did she say?" "Oh, nuthin'." After a while, we just told our wives to drop the whole thing.

Sometimes, though, we'd goof around and send a message with three of us zinging lines to one of our wives, letting her know who we were over here. "We love you, we love yoo-o-o!" I'm sure this vaudevillian routine was well received back home, too. . . . Harvey Persyn and Dickie Hyde joined me one time for a real chuckler to Karen.

While I was becoming an experienced copilot, at least in my opinion, I had the chance to fly Harvey to Saigon so he could meet his wife in the Philippines for a week. Manila wasn't a usual R&R destination, but it was where he had somehow made arrangements to meet Tollie, and he was going. The trouble was, he was sick as a dog, but he was bound and determined to get on that big silver bird in Saigon and go see his wife. Since I would have to fly back to Vinh Long solo after dropping him off, this was a real test as far as I was concerned, to see if I could do things right, and arrive home safe and sound. Harve was in his khakis and coughing and hacking in the left seat, while I did all the work getting us there, radio calls to flight following and everything. I didn't mind that too much, because I figured it was good practice for the return trip, doing everything in reverse. Sneezing and wheezing, Harvey thanked me for all the effort and for flying him up there in his own ship, Outlaw 27.

Harvey was a kick and a half. He looked like an Aussie but was from a farming family near San Antonio, Texas. He had graduated from Texas A & M, which was a joke to everyone except the people who had attended this institution of higher learning. A few years later, there would be a fad of telling jokes about Texas A & M, in the vein of: "Did you hear? The Texas A & M library burned down last night." "Yeah, both books burned up!" Things like that. Harvey wasn't at all dumb; he was simultaneously pompous and affable. He once showed me a photo of himself in jodhpurs, holding a saber, in his A & M military corps uniform. A bad thing for a first lieutenant in Vietnam surrounded by the kind of rank-disrespecting warrant officers we had. Before Stets and I had arrived, he had told Rheihofer, Savelli, and Haugen: "One second lieutenant can stand 10,000 warrants up against the wall!" Well, he didn't have that many, and they weren't up against any wall. Instead, they were rolling around the floor laughing. The warrants didn't let him off this point either, and they harassed him pretty badly ever after. As senior pilots with the most flight time in the unit, they were doing a power trip on Harvey and declared open season on him. The guy was comical in his quirks, but certainly nobody to punish as much as they did. That bunch did like to get mean on commissioned officers.

When Stets and I had first arrived, Smitty and Dickie Hyde had pulled us off to the side and said, "Don't be like this guy. I don't know what you guys are like, but do not get on the bad side of these men." We didn't know just exactly what had occurred, but it sounded pretty negative to us. Inwardly, we felt we had weathered worse storms in the athletic and fraternity worlds of our New England school backgrounds, but who knows? So Harvey was tempered by this onslaught, and all the other commissioned officers kept a low profile before the warrants. Not good for morale.

I dumped Harvey off in Saigon at the "Hotel-3" heliport, where he said good-bye after thanking me for the ride. Now I was on my own. I made the calls for the tower and we were ready. Two crew members were on board, so I asked one to fly with me in the right front seat. The one who came forward was named Rhodes, I think. We had two of them in the platoon at that time, as I remember. He had glasses and was a nice-mannered kid. I told him I'd teach him to fly on the way home as best I could. He said, "All right, I'll try to do that, sir." We took off, and darkness had fallen.

The moon was full, lighting up the ground far below us. More so than I had ever seen, I thought. Overhead, it glowed brightly in the night sky. Below us, more tracer fire was coming up than I had experienced during any night flying up to this point. Not very soothing for my first experience on my own. I was making the right radio calls to Paris Radar, our flight following service, squawking "Ident" on the transponder and the like, and feeling fairly professional. Except those tracers kept coming up. Rhodes was on the stick by now, sitting in that well-rehearsed slouch typical of Huey aviators. The EM would pick up on things like that, watching us fly from their seats in the back alongside the transmission. When one would come forward and try flying, he always looked as though he'd been doing it for a while. He would even hold the cyclic stick loosely in his right hand, in a claw fashion, with his index finger just so on the mike button. It was always interesting to see, and worth remarking about. The masterful control would not last for long, though, and before too many minutes passed, the aircraft would go careening over to one side or the other. Now the look of stark fear would come into his eyes. Then the lesson would begin. "Look out over the console, pick up the horizon, keep that space firmly in mind, don't look at the gauges much, just glance at them, and get back 'outside' the aircraft." Just like our flight instructors in primary helicopter training had said to us in our first few hours. When we survived our tour in Vietnam, we would be right back there at Wolters or Rucker as instructor pilots for our next duty assignment, so we were curious as to just how competent we would be at doing that coaching. These token flights with our crew tested that capability, as well as giving us all some life insurance in case both pilots got shot up and the kids had to come forward and fly this thing home. Unfortunately, that had actually happened more than a few times. Why should they die just because we had? So, this was a morale builder and a joy, as well as just plain good planning.

Rhodes was flying well and gaining confidence, and I was feeling OK, but there had to be a way to make those tracers stop coming up at us. I looked over the cockpit layout and checked things over. Suddenly I realized that the landing light was still on. We had never turned it off after takeoff. I should say, *I* had never turned it off. After a quick correction on that element I had overlooked, those pesky tracers tapered off fairly fast. For all those miles, the VC had had their choice of two moons to shoot at—ours was just a bit smaller and nearer. After I shut off the light, there was less "moonlight" reflecting off the rice paddy water, too. That was a joke on us; we shared it and continued on toward Vinh Long.

When I switched the UHF to the airstrip's tower frequency, I made the call for "extended left base" as we approached, and I let Rhodes continue on the controls. We worked the aircraft down from altitude and turned final. I didn't take the ship from him until just before touchdown, and after giving it over to me, he said he really did think he could have gotten the bird down safely the rest of the way. He thanked me for the experience and beamed proudly that he had done so well on his first attempt. The last part of the approach in getting a helicopter down is most dangerous for the novice, because there is a moment when the airflow around the fuselage stops stabilizing the aircraft, and you have to start using the tail rotor pedals to control yaw. That's another whole set of controls to comprehend, and an inexperienced person would *have* to fly the thing onto the ground, maintaining some airspeed, keeping it light on the skids to prevent rolling over at that point. It would be nothing short of miraculous for an EM crew chief or door gunner to be able to accomplish this. Once in a while, however, legends were made of Huey crew members who had managed to do just that.

In the next few days, a mission up in the Long Xuyen area had me waiting around while the advisors we were carrying talked to their Vietnamese counterparts inside the compound. Killing idle time like this meant either staying right at the helicopter and catching a few winks or walking around checking out the sights. This day, I was inside the barracks and saw a *Playboy* centerfold I had seen a few summers back. What was remarkable about this particular pinup was that it was almost an exact duplicate of *my* wife's body. Don't jump to conclusions and immediately assume that she had the stereotypical centerfold's form, because she didn't. This picture was the exception to the rule of big-boobed women. In August 1965, I had seen that issue of the magazine at Cressey's Pharmacy in North Conway, New Hampshire. I went home and said, "You won't believe this, but you are in *Playboy* this month!" She looked at the model, peered intently at the photograph, and said, "Naw, she still has slightly bigger breasts than mine." We are talking nearly flat-chested here. Anyway, I thought she was beautiful, and I came up with an inspiration while looking at the centerfold on that barracks wall. I needed that centerfold. I asked around to see whose pinup it was, and they found the sergeant who owned it. When I asked him for it, telling him it looked just like my wife, he said, "Yeah, sure, go ahead and take it."

I had a wallet-size copy of Karen's photo in the Phi Mu sorority composite from the University of New Hampshire yearbook, and I carried that with me everywhere. This is what my idea was. The Vietnamese artists could actually take a *Playboy* centerfold and paint a near-photographic likeness; that could be ordered enlarged to three by six feet, or any dimension suitable for placing over the bar of an officers' club or platoon day room. This was considered really cool stuff, creating an aura something like a Victorian era men's club. It suited our post-adolescent minds superbly. These things abounded around the places where alcohol was served in the military compounds of South Vietnam. At this point, after seeing quite a few of these excellent renditions, the only conversation when reviewing them was just how good our local artist was in comparison to others, and which centerfold the guys had chosen by consensus as being special enough to be so rendered.

I took the foldout Playmate and my wife's head cameo down to "Oscar the artist" in downtown Vinh Long. He did all our "nose art" on the cowlings of our Hueys, and sometimes the tail numbers and other decorative insignia, too. He was very good. Many a Maverick gunship and Outlaw shield had been done by him, either in his shack or on the airstrip itself. I walked into where he was working at his easel, with his wife and kids in attendance, and spoke to him. Through sign language, some smattering of Vietnamese, and gesturing, I tried to describe what I wanted. He didn't get it. I was getting frustrated and kept attempting to explain what I considered a simple task—putting my wife's face over the girl's in the centerfold to unite them both as one painting. He still couldn't understand. Nor could his wife, sitting on a stool with numerous children playing on the earthen floor. Finally, a MACV enlisted man, who had come there with his own order, said to me, "Do you want me to interpret what you want?" I said, "Yeah!" The young red-haired man inquired, "What do you want him to do and I will tell him exactly." I explained.

The American turned and spoke fluent Vietnamese very quickly and concisely to Oscar and his wife. Upon hearing what he told them, they burst into shrieking, hysterical laughter. The kids rolled around the floor in peals of glee, and the wife had tears in her eyes as she howled. Oscar seemed in considerable mirth himself. The woman pointed at the centerfold, and asked, "Wye, you?" I said, "Yes, she's my wife." More peals of laughter. I was really making their day. When the humor died down and some composure was restored, Oscar said, "Yes, I can do." I left after being told the work would be done within the week.

I returned at the appointed time and strolled into Oscar's workshop. There was my wife in stunning full color, but with a light sunburn, in downtown Vinh Long, Vietnam. Naked. Holding her small red bikini top in one hand. Other than some touches that were needed around the eyes, it was a nearly perfect facsimile of the real thing. Oscar corrected some of the portrait's imperfections and we were done. I paid him something like $15 or $25 and left, with the large painting in a plain brown wrapper. Now, I had to get this thing through the compound gate and home.

The sentry at the Vinh Long airfield compound's front entrance passed me through and then asked, "Is that one of those paintings?" I said, "Yeah!" The young EM inquired, "Can I see it?" I replied, "NO!" I could see by the expression on his face that he wondered why, but I moved on. I got to the second-platoon hooch and uncovered the thing. Geez, more than 10 and a half months to go, and there is my erotic wife in all her pulchritude staring back at me. Maybe this wasn't such a good idea. I immediately got pretty horny. I installed it on the wall, next to the closet with my uniforms.

At supper that night, I told Stets and Troy Tison to come by and see what I done to myself. They asked what it was. I told them never mind; just come and see for yourself. Stets was like a third member of my marriage and knew Karen quite well.

Later that evening, he came in the door first and said, "East, what did you have me come over for?" Then he saw the painting and burst into uncontrolled laughter. He fell down and rolled back and forth, holding his ribs. Then Troy came in and said, "What's up, Eastman? What did you want? What's wrong with Stetson, here?" Then he looked and saw Karen all naked there on the wall, and he repeated Stets's performance. The two of them were rolling around in stitches, occasionally colliding with each other, and I was beginning to get worried they might hurt themselves. Beet red in the face, as was Fred, Troy said to him, "Can you believe he did that to his wahf?!" Stets shook his head for a "No," because he couldn't talk. Troy continued in his Georgia accent, saying "I can't believe you, Eastman, I just can't believe you did that!" Stets just kept guffawing. They were confusing me. I'm thinking, "How about some strokes, here?" I thought I had done a pretty clever thing, and this was a real salute to my mate's physical beauty. They finally got up off the floor, their eyes still crinkled up with tears, and made their way out the door. They remained pretty much in agreement on their views of the whole thing. I eventually got the reputation around the compound as "the guy who had *that paint-*

ing of his wife." Some of the other guys in the second platoon wrote home asking their wives for appropriate photos, but no luck. Never happened. My wife was absolutely furious with me and asked, "How would you like it if I showed a picture of you completely naked around North Conway, with just a hanky around your wrist?!" I didn't get the hanky part.

6

SAVELLI'S THANKSGIVING

As WE WERE APPROACHING one of our big holidays away from the home folks, we all began to ponder how we would emotionally handle the separation from family and friends on this significant holiday. We were in the tropics, there were no turkeys, and there weren't going to be any such fowl around—not as a part of this agriculture. Just some rice paddy ducks, and that wouldn't cut it. We figured it would just be a no-go for this rich holiday all of us had unconsciously enjoyed since childhood days. But John Savelli had a different plan.

In the box of C-rations that so often accompanied our lift missions, there were several canned goods whose contents were fairly OK, and there were others that definitely weren't. "Ham and Lima Beans" was in the latter category; when it got that bad, we called it "gunner food." The door gunner ranked lowest of the four people necessary to crew a Huey, with the AC at the top end of the pecking order. Crew chief and peter pilot were about dead even here. There was a chili beef selection that was saucy and all right; I preferred that myself. "Beef with Spice Sauce" was its name, if I remember correctly. The olive-drab cans had black markings describing the ingredients, and we would heat them over an ingenious diminutive cooking stove we invented. We took a can of "White Bread," cut off one end, squashed it inwardly a bit on two sides, then went under the Huey and filled this sordid pale mass—which I don't think *anyone* ever ventured to eat—with JP-4 fuel from one of the fuel cocks there. These devices on the Huey's belly were meant to bleed water from the fuel tanks—I doubt the Army ever thought we would be cooking with the same fuel we flew on. JP-4 was very much like kerosene anyway. The little can became a "sterno stove," and the bent-in sides made a pretty good cooking surface for the other cans. We would rotate our meal preparation, and all four of us eventually would have a hot meal. The first time I saw this clever process, I cracked up. The crews had been doing it so often during breaks between lifts that they thought nothing of it; it was just mealtime. Something like this becomes so habitual that it evolves as part of the background moves and lore for combat troops in a particular conflict. War is funny; in World War II, at the end of the day, the infantry would put potatoes in the exhaust tubes of an M-1 Sherman tank to cook them. Finding a tank crew putting their machine to bed for the night meant hot chow for any infantry troops accompanying them. By the time the engine had cooled down, the potatoes were adequately cooked. American GIs *are* inventive.

Ingeniously, Savelli instructed his crew of Outlaw 26 to save the cans of "Turkey Loaf" during the weeks preceding Thanksgiving. He'd say, encouragingly, "Now you guys agreed we'd all have our Thanksgiving dinner no matter where we were or what we were doing, and you're going to stick to that, right?" And the guys in the rear would nod their heads, in what looked to me like dumb accommodation. Over several weeks, I watched them hoard their "Turkey Loaf" C-rations and couldn't believe they were serious. This was pitiful. "We're going to have Thanksgiving dinner as planned, OK, guys?" Savelli would entreat. I thought I'd watch from the sidelines on this one. This was sad, perhaps even desperate. Better to forgo the holiday meal than perform this charade.

Come Thanksgiving Day, we had an operation up at Moc Hoa, and, disgruntled as we were, we went out the door after breakfast at the club that morning and formed up the flight of Hueys, 10 or 15 or more. We didn't feel good making war on this feast day, and it didn't seem right to go looking for the enemy on this day of traditional rest and thankfulness. Almost a violation of some kind.

The operation commenced after loading up the Vietnamese at Moc Hoa's strip. We flew our ships to the Plain of Reeds and dropped off the RF/PF troops whom the Special Forces had trained. It was somehow a serenely beautiful sight landing in these wet grasslands, and I snapped a few pictures of the lift hovering there, and then taking off in a big, broad circle to the left. We looked like we were square dancing over the lush beds of grass.

We returned to the airstrip at Moc Hoa and waited for further instructions. None came, and none came after that, either. We sat around and waited. This was demoralizing. Then Savelli got out the C-ration box and put it on the ground to act as a table for eating the saved canned food. One of the crew even went out in the deep grass growing alongside the airstrip and paralleling it, where the rice paddies began, and picked some flowers to make a centerpiece. We all watched. Savelli's personnel then brought out their hallowed "Turkey Loaf" and commenced to feast. For the first time, we all envied their foresight. It was with sad emotion that we watched the four-member crew of Outlaw 26. Feeling low, we inwardly paid attention to our own personal observations and determined to operate better in the future in a similar event. Nobody said much, but all eyes up and down the line of parked Huey "slicks" were on Savelli's banquet.

Suddenly news came down that we were released. There was some good in this world after all. Decency had won out, it seemed, and we could go home to Vinh Long and commiserate with ourselves for the rest of the day that remained. Anything would be better than playing war on this holiday. What a relief.

We flew home, somber and quiet. When we landed at our Vinh Long airfield, it was mealtime, so we went directly to the club. As we entered through the usual door to the officers' mess area, we got a big surprise. There were tables covered with white linen tablecloths and loaded with browned turkeys, cranberry sauce, green peas, mashed potatoes, plenty of gravy, stuffing and all the fixings. More than adequate for all of us. The Hawaiian mess sergeant had a big grin for us, and we knew we all had been had. We turned around to the majors and other senior officers, looking at those who had kept this quiet all morning while with the air crews. "Why didn't you tell us?" we asked. They just smirked. As our faith in the unit was restored, we felt slightly sheepish for our dark thoughts. Wherever we all were was home in the Outlaws. I started loving my company that day. I also found out—being so far removed from our culture on the other side of the world—how powerful our religious and national holidays were to us.

Thinking back on it, I should have known this affectionate treat was coming. Harvey had a role in all this after returning from Manila. One day at the end of flying, I found him getting a beer out of our smallish refrigerator and slumping up against the wall of the operations board as he popped open the top.

"You wouldn't believe what I did today," he stated, needing a breath.

"No. What did you do today, Harve?" I responded.

"I flew to every outpost in the Delta!" he gasped as he took a swig.

I quickly ran out of numbers trying to estimate how many that might be, and said, "What were you doing? That's a lot of flying!"

"I was flying turkeys!" Harvey gasped again, and took another gulp of beer.

He looked exhausted. Then he told me the story of how he'd flown Outlaw 27 to the Saigon heliport, where he had met a bull colonel standing by with a whole truckload of frozen turkeys. I don't know why they always assigned a full colonel, displaying his silver eagles and all, to such an important task, but there he was waiting for Harvey. He addressed the tall aircraft commander:

"Lieutenant Persyn, if *one* of these turkeys thaws, melts, or gets spoiled, some man out there is not going to have *Thanksgiving!* Do you understand?"

With Harvey, they had found their man. I can see him now, stumbling back a step or two, staggered by the comprehension of this responsibility just imposed upon him. The bird colonel wagged his finger a time or two in front of Harvey's face for emphasis, and he drove off once the truckload of turkeys had filled up the Huey's cabin. Harvey got the job done magnificently and "flew fast," as we used to say. I was seeing him at the completion of this important morale-boosting mission. He took another belt of the beer.

"I deserve a medal. They should give me a medal!" he exclaimed.

"Harve, they don't give medals for turkeys!" I said.

"They should! Morale, you know. There's nothing more important than morale!" Harvey quoted, still slumped against the board, spiritually exhausted.

I just shook my head and walked away laughing.

We had it pretty good at Vinh Long. Adjacent to the compound, and just down the main road to the town of Vinh Long itself, was the Irish missionary nuns' convent. About six or seven of these white-robed ladies spent their entire lives there, which was impossible for us newly arrived aviators even to comprehend as a destiny. They made for very polite company when we appeared as visitors. Their brogue was intense, and they let us know they knew an awful lot about the political reality of Vietnam; it wasn't going to end soon, this "war." Encountering them was part of our continuing education of acclimating to Vietnam; there was always something new to learn about this experience.

Some of the guys enjoyed the swimming pool with a couple of Army air mattresses floating around in it. The water was too warm for me, and the plentiful clumps of floating algae didn't make me relish it much. The whole place looked like some Hollywood villa. Some of the guys really needed this place for their sanity; it had a long history of being there for the Vinh Long officers. Just behind the pool and the open, estate-looking areas was the facilities building for doing our laundry. Here lots of little orphans cleaned our uniforms and other clothing. Each man was assigned a petitely threaded laundry mark identifying his clothes, and they did a fairly creditable job of keeping it all straight. Each hooch had a laundry officer, and a three-quarter-ton truck went around on a regular basis to all the unit's living quarters and picked up the clothing.

From time to time, though, we would have to object to their removing the elastic stretch bands from our Jockey shorts. They would use the elastic for their black pajama waistbands. They would take out just a little bit at a time, until finally, the leg holes of your undershorts were baggy and funny looking. "They're doing it again . . . !" Then Tommy McCarthy, the platoon laundry officer, would complain once again that the orphans were up to this mischief, and the problem would stop for a short while. You would think that a country that grew rubber trees would have no shortage of elastic, but think again.

We had Vietnamese hooch maids or house boys to make our beds, change sheets, clean the rooms, and polish our boots, too. It was the first time in the Army that I had had *that* kind of help, especially the latter task! So, we were always spit-shined and starchily well dressed and pressed in our jungle fatigue uniforms. Only in the Delta and other developed areas did the troops constantly look so spiffed up. We were lucky for these amenities, and we knew it.

7

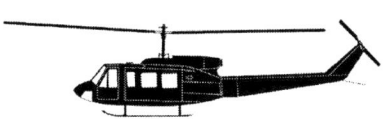

"Negative Supression"

Sometimes the Vietnamese brass up above with Outlaw 6 actually let us shoot at the enemy. This was always looked forward to, because the Viet Cong sure took delight at shooting at us. Flights of slicks often took fire while the gunships escorting us into LZ's hadn't taken a round all day. The guerrillas knew who to shoot at for effectiveness and who to leave alone for their own safety. Back home in the good ole USA, we felt most of the American citizenry thought we were shooting up everybody in Vietnam. The way the media portrayed us on TV, bloodthirsty GI's were slaughtering anybody oriental that came into our vision. It made good footage covering the grunts in a firefight, and with all the automatic-weapons firepower now inherent with the American troops, we looked pretty overwhelming on film. You could actually feel sorry for the indigenous Vietnamese fighters of the National Liberation Front. They just had rusty old French and Czechoslovakian rifles of World War II vintage and some ancient machine guns. Pretty pitiful armament.

The truth was, both the American and Vietnamese brass were pretty tentative about letting us use our M-60 machine guns hanging on the sides of the D-models for our protection. We often demurely took fire from the VC while pleading with the powers-to-be, who were overhead, to allow us to shoot back. Tracer fire would envelop us from surrounding tree lines and sometimes the gunships could detect the actual targets themselves, running around with web belts, canteens, the little green pith helmets the

Vietnamese insurgents wore, and even identifying the weapons by their make, while presently being used in the VC's hands. This came as a shocking truth to new pilots just coming into the unit, but it was a reality for the older ACs who had become accustomed to this advisor war in Indochina. We were here as guests, to be useful, not to totally take the battle to the enemy for the Vietnamese— who would not close with and destroy their foe. The Americanization of the war probably resulted from such frustration. So, we got shot at a lot and couldn't do a thing about adequately firing back without suitable permission. The denying command became known as "Negative Suppression." Military jargon; which still brings a smirk to all those who experienced such absurdity in the midst of a shooting war, where the helicopters and their crews were very vulnerable targets. Summing up our hostility at being so used in this non-declared war, one first platoon aircraft commander even named his ship with the derogative term. "Negative Suppression" was emblazoned just above the Outlaw shield on the radio compartment's cowling cover.

The Mavericks had just killed two men. Friendlies, it turned out. All day long in this operation out of Moc Hoa, the gunships of the 175th had reported two men way out in front of the advancing RF/PF troops being led by their Special Forces advisors. Constantly inquiring about these Vietnamese skirting just ahead in a comfortable distance from the militia forces, the Maverick gun platoon ships had not been able to ascertain if these men were scouts for the Americans on the ground, or in fact, the bad guys. This went on for some time, and the confusion did not get cleared up. Finally, late in the day, someone gave them the authority to fire on these two men who seemed intent on scurrying away from impending danger. The Special Forces seemed relieved, and almost bored, of being finished with the tiresome question-and-answer process that had gone on all day. The matter had been laid to rest. Or, so it seemed.

It quickly turned out that the two had been scouts, and the Special Forces troopers should have known better, much better.

They were immediately beat up by their Vietnamese counterparts; in fact, their lives were in danger. We had to go in and pick up the RF/PF troops now at the end of the operation, and we were told we'd better not bother them in any way. Let them get in the aircraft any old way they wanted to, and try not to anger them, so maybe they wouldn't also shoot us up. Leuty told us all this over the radio, and we were tense. Really scared. We landed in the Plain of Reeds landing area where the troops were gathered, and held our breath, waiting for something to happen. Suddenly rifle fire broke out, and machine gun bursts roared out of the back cabin area of the Hueys. Awaiting whatever was happening, we crawled deep within our respective skins, and hunched down ridiculously in our armored-plated seats. Any explanation of what was occurring behind our backs would be quite adequate. Were we still alive? Then the EM crews spoke up. Someone said they weren't shooting anyone, just the sampans they had been sitting in when we picked them up. So that the VC wouldn't have them either, they were destroying these native craft with their weapons. A collective sigh of relief was expelled by all of us. We actually broke into giggles, relaxing from the tension.

After living through this day, there was still a price to pay. Out came the message from the IV Corps: the gunships now could not fire unless they were fired upon. This policy was not going to do us any good, because we already knew the VC commonly never fired at the guns anyway; it was literally suicidal to do so. Shooting at the slicks transporting the troops was the game; they had the soldiers on board who were to search for the VC. So, we were always the target and the gunships the frustrated predators. The revised policy would make us even more vulnerable to enemy ground fire was the upshot. It left us all with a bad taste in our mouths; we did not blame the Mavericks for the mistake. They had taken precautions all that day to confirm their suspicion that the scouts were enemy; the error had been elsewhere. But, they were crestfallen, knowing the blunder would hurt all of us over the next few weeks. We slicky pilots knew we would be the ones on the receiving end.

I was flying copilot with Dickie Hyde in Outlaw 25 down by Ben Tre. An operation had been going all day; now the troops were collecting themselves for the pick-up. Terry McDowell had been flying overhead with old Pappy Martin in the Mavericks' battered old B-models. The dapper, mustached Martin was a distinguished senior warrant with already several tours in Vietnam. They had been watching well-outfitted VC track back into the operational area as the ARVNs retreated towards the PZ. Pappy had been instructing the young warrant on the gear and uniforms being displayed by these VC, giving Terry quite an education on just how dangerous these particular guerrillas were. As they both observed these constant appearances, while overflying their targets, they could not get permission to engage these rascals since the VC would not fire upon the gunships passing by overhead. Again and again, we heard the Mavericks request permission to fire, and be denied by the brass in the C & C ship.

"Outlaw 6, we have suspects in the tree lines surrounding the PZ. Request permission to commence firing on same, over."

"Maverick One, have you been fired upon by these suspects, over?"

"Negative; we just keep watching them close in behind the troops and they are armed and seem to be on the way to attack soon, sir,. . . over."

"Well, until they fire at you, you may not fire at them, over."

And so it went on through the afternoon. At least, Terry got a close-hand view of real VC troops as they passed through the sparsely vegetated areas, while learning about their web belts, helmets, and other apparel. It was a real intelligence-gathering day for him, as Pappy lectured on. He was duly impressed with the strict discipline the VC soldiers had for withholding fire, and not compromising their safety. Somebody had clued them in on the game. They seemingly knew about the Delta-wide policy.

As for us coming into the PZ, the Vietnamese were lined up on the rice paddy dikes in sticks of ten, as if they were waiting for a cross-town bus to take them home at the end of the working day.

They stood casually, in spaced out lines, their weapons held at their legs, and empty of tension. We descended in straight trail, tail low, killing off airspeed as we approached to a hover alongside each squad's column. The green jungle they had exited was off to our left, filled with coconut palms and hooches. The PZ was out in the rice paddies for our ships' arrival. The Mavericks buzzed over this treeline to our left, keeping a ready eye on the small dangerous men infiltrating through the greenery below.

Suddenly, like bronze darning needles, tracer fire erupted out of the green treeline and over the heads of the ARVNs needing a ride home. They didn't flinch or squat down quickly, as most infantry are prone to do, but remained calmly upright and kept waiting for their bus service. Bullets grazed through the flight, and some struck home in the fuselages. As the troops loaded onto the ships and pilots screamed "receiving fire," the Mavericks wanted to help out by suppressing the treeline and killing our attackers. "Negative," came the voice from above. Why? Because the gunships still had not been fired upon; therefore, they couldn't execute their reason for being there.

The Maverick gunnies were getting mad. We were getting frustrated, even feeling foolish. Somewhere up ahead, tracers licked into the cab area of one of the front aircraft.

"This is Gold 2. I just got shot in the head!"

I looked over at Dickie Hyde, and said, "If someone just got shot in the head, how can he talk?" Dickie just giggled back, nodding. It turned out to be Captain Bridle in the first platoon, who had been able to maintain consciousness after the round bounced off his helmet.

As flight after flight went into that pick-up zone, each time taking hits, we realized we were the butt end of a very bad joke. It just became a matter of who was going to get hit this time. Becoming hilarious about our outrageous predicament, we began fatefully cracking jokes with each eventful approach into that PZ. Seemingly oblivious to the danger we faced, the ARVN still stood calmly upon the dikes, listlessly awaiting their ride out of the place. By now, about half the flight had received hits. Five out of ten ships. We wondered out loud who would be next. So far, it had not been Dickie and myself. We tensely waited.

Then Willie Stout got his, up forward in Outlaw 19. An old water-cooled machine gun on a tripod was suddenly facing him out of a straw-covered hooch. A bamboo-camouflaged covering had abruptly flipped-down, and there was Captain Stout looking right down the barrel of the archaic WW I machine gun. Stout said to himself, "Be cool. Be cool. Your crew is counting on you; you've got to maintain your composure. They need to see you holding it together. Stay brave!" Later, I asked him what he did then. . . . "I sat there and got shot!" Willie Stout said. And he wasn't trying to be funny either! Nine bullet holes through his tail boom were the result.

The Mavericks never did get to fire; nor did we fire back. We limped home bravely, in humorous defeat, and further disgusted at the way this war was being conducted. Wouldn't our moms and dads back home be proud of their boys? Was anyone covering this story on the networks? We thought not. Those bastard ARVNs spent the whole day out in the bush, ransacking their own people's supplies of rice, pigs, and ducks, and we get shot at picking them up? What was this! How did this happen? What got us into this anyhow? The only thing we seemed to be teaching these Vietnamese was how not to spend a night out there, and to get home by six o'clock to have dinner with their families, sharing the loot they had picked up. We were just their taxi's, with our lives at stake while doing the ferrying.

8

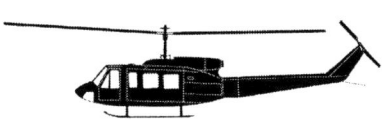

Tay Ninh

About this time, we were "invited" to the real war "up north," in III Corps. We participated as an aviation company in two major operations in the vicinity of Tay Ninh, northwest of Saigon. One was perhaps Operation Attleboro and the other was Operation Junction City. I don't remember which one was first, but the other was months later, in February. Another big show was Operation Cedar Falls, which some Outlaws remember as having been in between the other two. Operation Hastings is yet another one, but nobody told us any of these names at the time—we just went up to Tay Ninh. The names of operations that you probably saw on your TV screen were never revealed to us, nor were the names of the NLF or VC regiments they were designed to trap. It wasn't even common knowledge what these operations were intended to do; we just went where we were sent. (I always wondered whose hometowns these large American operations were named after; it seemed weird to hear their names later as part of the history of the Vietnam War.) We flew up to join many other airmobile aviation units that routinely followed the American troops around and flew in these huge search-and-destroy missions. They were Corps-size schemes, exemplifying Gen. William Westmoreland's strategic dream of destroying the VC infrastructure concentrated near the Cambodian border.

We were to see fellow flight school buddies who knew nothing of the activities we enjoyed in the Delta. They flew these American troop lifts all the time—pretty much the only thing they did. No

Vietnamese peasants with their chickens and ducks hopping aboard our UH-1Ds at any chance they could get for safe transportation around to the population centers in the IV Corps. This whole scene was what we had been escaping by being assigned to the 13th Aviation Battalion, whose four companies covered the Delta and its Vietnamese divisions. These were to be our only times flying the American infantry and working with their commanders. Experiencing jet strikes and numerous artillery fire missions was also brand new to us. There was plenty of that!

Tay Ninh was beyond the area known as "the Iron Triangle" and in War Zone C. To get there, we had to fly around the "Parrot's Beak," an intrusion of Cambodia into Vietnam; this meant we couldn't fly directly from Vinh Long to this installation. Here we found tent city galore, and a very real, massive American presence. It seemed as if they had imported a Stateside Army installation and covered up the real Vietnam like a giant rug. They quickly made things look ugly. Seeing these compounds, I sometimes even felt that they had brought the red clay of Fort Benning with them. Upon landing in the red dust, we were told where to park the Hueys, and then we strolled over to where we would be sleeping during this two-week–plus enterprise. Our unit had put up the standard eight-man Army tents and, inside these, put up the canvas cots we all associate so well with the Army. We would be "camping" like Boy Scouts for a while. Immediately we started contemplating how long this would last. All of us Outlaws instantly realized this was the lifestyle we were missing, and we didn't need it one bit. As we bumped into guys from other units that we recognized, they told us this was the only life they knew, and they had been doing since we had last seen them in Saigon at Camp Alpha. Sometimes, if they were with the troops for the night, they even slept alongside their helicopters in the field. They couldn't believe stories of our comfort level, with hooch maids, mosquito netting, fans, our own stereo equipment, and the like. Vinh Long was like an air-conditioned country club compared to the living conditions of the majority of American units in the rest of the country. Nobody had it like us, and I checked that out for sure during the whole year I was there.

Our gunship platoon, the Mavericks, didn't have much to do for a mission in Tay Ninh. The third platoon of the 175th was famous for its work in the Delta, but it did not have much to do up here. The first and second platoon slicks surely did, however. Once we flew in the big, burly American soldiers—who seemed to fill up our ship with only six or seven, compared to the 10 slightly built Vietnamese we customarily carried—we had to resupply them all day long. The individual ARVN was self-sufficient with one small bag of rice he kept with him that day. He usually carried it in an empty M-60 machine-gun ammo bag he had pilfered somewhere along the way. We were used to putting them in the LZ's and then taking them out at the end of the day. They cooked in the field. When we inserted the Americans, we were only getting started with our working day. Pathfinders in their black baseball hats had us for the rest of the day's flight time, as our formation's lifts approached them with their arms raised as a landing signal, and we hovered up to their presence. They would come up to the window of the Huey and tell us where we should ferry the stuff, and we would nod and comply as we checked out the map. That was the hard part, figuring out which unit in the field was supposed to get the stuff. That was enough to drive us bonkers, and tempers became short. Still, we would never be able to comprehend the oversupply of these American units. Not only did they get hot chow in the foxhole, literally, but they also received iced soft drinks, bundles of the Army's Stars and Stripes newspaper, and all kinds of gear from the Army inventory. Nothing missing there. This was an affluent war, and unlike anything anyone in Korea or World War II had ever experienced. Later reports would say the United States spent $25 million on Operation Junction City alone; some model operation. We were bushed at the end of each day, having spent two hours putting in the troops and six to eight hours supplying their needs.

We flew two hours at a time, because that was all the flight time the Huey could do between refuelings. We could refuel running at the Tay Ninh airstrip, with big hoses from the giant black rubber refueling bladders, or shut down at the landing area adjacent to our billets. One morning, while the other pilot rolled off throttle and let the turbine cool down for the appropriate time, I got out and shot pictures of the nose art of the other units settling down around us, doing the same thing. After seeing the Hornets, Little Bears, and an aircraft from the Big Red One, there weren't too many to catch. They just didn't have the artists we had among the Vietnamese in the Delta. I spontaneously took a picture of Stets desperately peeing in the dried-out grassy open area, trying to embarrass him, which I did. Sometimes we had to go so badly after two hours of flying that there was no holding back when you leapt out of that Huey for relief. It was funny seeing guys sprint away from the aircraft in such need. I laughed and went back to the left side of the ship to put away the camera.

When I looked up again, there was Major LaCourse himself, our CO. I wondered why he was approaching me: "What's he gonna do? Confiscate my film for taking a picture of Stets peeing? Naw." He then told me that the two of us had been promoted and were now first lieutenants, after slightly more than a year in the Army. This was a nice surprise, because it previously had taken 18 months, but Vietnam was exterminating young officers so fast that they had moved up the time element, as they often do in wartime. He produced a facsimile of a silver first lieutenant's bar from some downtown Vietnamese shop and pinned it on my collar: "You can get a real one when you return to Vinh Long. Congratulations!" This little ceremony was very meaningful to me, and it made me respect him even more as a commander for taking this time. I was delighted to get rid of my second lieutenant's butter bar. It had always made me feel like Ensign Pulver in *Mister Roberts.* I was glad that phase of my life was over. Now I could feel like a real officer.

While we were flying these "ashy trashy" missions of supplying the troops, listening to their conversations on their FM frequencies was enlightening as well. We would have to call in to them not only to find out their location but also to avoid the artillery fire protecting them—which was quite constant. You didn't want to get in the trajectory between all those fired rounds from the 155s and the 105mm howitzers and their intended destination. We flew routes that encountered these fire missions and tried to avoid being in front of the tube's work, both on the ground when landing their stuff and in the air, with the shells en route. I did have one airburst go off to the left side of the ship one day, and I must say it was a one-of-a-kind experience; I preferred to keep it that way.

The ground-pounders never had brief radio transmissions like we aviators did; they used the whole call sign every time, over and over again. We pilots were used to each other's voices and needed to keep calls to a minimum, with so many ships and conversations going on among all the parties on that frequency. We often acknowledged instructions by just clicking twice on the mike switch for "affirmative." No need to waste airtime. The infantry companies have four platoons, which had four squads, each with a handheld radio, or a radio carried on the back of the RTO, the platoon radiotelephone operator. It seemed to us that the commanders in the sky needed to call their troops constantly to visualize where they were in the dense jungle below them, and the guys on the ground needed to talk on that thing to make their situation less "lonely." Babble was going on all the time. It was part of the background noise of an operation. We got into the habit of remembering some of these inane conversations and would repeat them daily at dinner time, vying to see who could report the most ridiculous ones we had heard while flying that day. It was quite important to make the sounds like the FM radio made, like "sh-h-h-h," hissing between the calls . . .

"Sliding Circles 6, this is Sliding Circles 6A, Over." Sh-h-h-h-h.

"Sliding Circles 6A, this is Sliding Circles 6, Over." Sh-h-h-h.

"Uh Roger, Sliding Circles 6, Go ahead, Over." Sh-h-h.

"Roger, Sliding Circles 6A, how do you read this transmission, Over." Sh-h-h.

"Sliding Circles 6, this is Sliding Circles 6A. Read you loud and clear, how me, Over." Sh-h-h.

"Uh Roger, Sliding Circles 6A, read you five by five. This is Sliding Circles 6, Out."

That could go on all day long. I still don't understand how doing this down there in the bush kept you in a safe tactical situation with the VC or NVA all around you. It had to be somewhat noisy. With my infantry crossed rifles and airborne wings, I was very glad I had chosen a better assignment than this jungle-fighter work. Any Army aviator has nothing but solace for all those grunts down there who have to go through this miserable stomping around, the Army's traditional job for its ground forces. Why the Marines think this is glory stuff, I'll never figure out. It's just hot, miserable, tiring, slogging it out, and forever the ultimate fatigue.

And of course, there were the wounded. The dead were worse. This was the first time we would see American boys in body bags. The bags were rubber, with a big zipper running the length of the sack. Putting a few of those in the back seat sure made you think. Flying these deceased boys back to the base camp at Tay Ninh was like flying a hearse, and we felt pretty glum contemplating who was inside. You never felt a bit of the war was worth it when you flew those poor dead soldiers in the black rubbery bags.

Another first-time experience in Tay Ninh Province was seeing the effects on the landscape of Agent Orange, the now-infamous defoliant that contained dioxin. C-123s ("Providers") were used like crop-dusting aircraft to spray wide swaths of this chemical on the triple-layered jungle. This was called Operation Ranch Hand and billed as "modern technological area-denial." What a mouthful of doublespeak. They would proceed on one bearing for miles and miles, and it was strange to see the dead branches on these compass headings extending to the horizon. I never thought the operation was very effective for what it was intended to do, because it only killed the tops of the jungle, and there was still greenery below—at least in this area of the country. Around Tay Ninh, wide savannas contrasted with 200-foot-tall teak-forested areas surrounding them. We landed in the openings and climbed laboriously with our heavy loads of Americans over the tall, dead trees.

One particular time, Harvey and I in Outlaw 27 nearly didn't make it. The aircraft had to climb so severely with our heavy load, compared to the long, level takeoffs in the Delta, that it seemed that we were just not going to get over those trees this time. Over the intercom, Harvey anxiously said to me, "Look for a forced landing area." I said, "I am, I am!" mostly just to make him feel better. There wasn't one. Both our mouths were dry; I didn't think we could pull it off. All those dead clawing branches were reaching out to us, and I knew only his flying skills and experienced control touch could get us through this one. A few more months of flying time than mine on his side of the aircraft were all we had going for us at that moment. RPM was bleeding off and we were sinking through, but we were keeping this precarious 200-foot tree height above the ground while barely making it over those browned treetops. I was praying inside and at the same time trying to look confident for his sake. Finally he got us over the last deadened crown and picked up airspeed, and I relaxed a bit. "That was goddamn close," he said. "Yup," and a nod was all I could contribute. Agent Orange didn't do us any favors.

One of the things that really did surprise us about the Americans on the lifts was that they fired their weapons while on short final going into one of these LZs. I mean, *shooting at a would-be enemy!* We were used to the ARVNs sometimes being asleep in the aircraft until touchdown—to the point that my crew chief had to wake them during the last parts of the approach by dinging them on their helmets with an aluminum tube from the seat backs. These American grunts would lean out of the aircraft and put some firepower into the treelines like they really wanted to participate in this thing. Gee whiz. We were impressed, even took some pictures of them—these later made us look like combat photographers back home!

Watching the Air Force put in jet strikes for the troops on the ground was a show. We would stay off to the side as the "fast-movers" would come right on in under the forward air controller. "Mac the FAC," as he was called, would be doing lazy-eights in his delicate-looking, gray push-pull prop Cessna, which replaced the L-19 Bird-Dog. He had some rockets under the wings, so he could mark the intended target pretty well. The F-4s would come zooming in, drop their load, go around in a 20-mile circle, and return for another try. One time, when I was flying a mission with Rheihofer, the Snake said, "Ooh, ooh! Take the controls, take the controls!" He then produced a Super-8 movie camera to film the whole thing. Anything for the folks back home. Harvey reported that on a similar mission he was overseeing, the Air Force jocks were singing their way in on a bombing run, "We all live in a yellow submarine, a yellow submarine, a yellow submarine!" right out over UHF. Everybody is macho here . . . .

Then there were the colonels. I think the lieutenant colonels were the worst. They had their command slots and were trying to look promotable. Token, little green-felt command tabs on their shoulder straps and crisp, starched uniforms. They were the great "Squad Leaders in the Sky." One got in my aircraft and delivered this opening line: "Lieutenant, I want you to keep that LZ my troops are just landing in on my side of the aircraft at all times, is that clear?" Since I also had to stay on the southerly side of that clearing at the same time to avoid enemy fire, I quickly did some visual calculations in my head and saw this wasn't going to work. However, I had the sense to draw a picture on my clipboard of a racetrack-shaped ellipse while the other pilot flew, because I knew what was coming. As soon as I went into a left turn and left the LZ to my right rear, I could hear the lieutenant colonel screaming: "Lieutenant, I told you to keep that LZ on my side of the ship, what *are* you doing? WHAT ARE YOU DOING?" I quickly waved him up forward and showed him my diagram. As we came down the backstretch of the oval, he studied it for a moment while I tried to convince him I could only keep the clearing on his side of the aircraft *half the time*. "OK, I see," he said. Whew, close one there.

One of the more ridiculous conversations we monitored went about like this. One commander said he had some walking wounded who needed to be picked up and flown back for medevac. The brass he was reporting to was up in a helicopter as always and asked if they were "ambulatory." (I'll leave out the call signs.)

"I Roger your "walking wounded"; are they ambulatory? Over." Sh-h-h-h.

"Negative, negative ambulatory—-these are walking wounded, Over." Sh-h-h.

"Roger, walking wounded, but are they ambulatory?? Over." Sh-h-h.

"I say again I have walking wounded, walking wounded; negative ambulatory, Over." Sh-h-h.

This went on for burlesque minutes, with the dialogue being repeated again and again. I felt like finding out who these two parties were and landing with a dictionary for their perusal. We were often shaking with mirth while flying over these guys, listening to these comedy acts.

Toward the end of the campaign came one of the funniest episodes. The American units had all pushed through the area of contention, always driving the VC before them. Some of our gunships saw them crossing the river into their Cambodian strongholds, as they usually did in this war. Jack Payne from my flight school class watched them fording the river that was the border between the two countries, holding their weapons above their heads to avoid getting them wet. We could only watch the retreat from on high, as the whole reason this operation was conducted was voided by the neutrality of Cambodia. Gave you a real distaste for policy. It was much, much later that we would discover that the VC always would break down from larger military units into platoon-size groupings to disengage when things were going badly with superior-strength American units. They would systematically retreat into their Cambodian sanctuaries, but we did not know much about their military strategies then.

Anyway, we had landed in a landing zone that for some reason looked like a golf course, with ideally clipped grass all over it. Had water buffaloes eaten here? Armored personnel carriers were parked on it in various places, and as I recall, we were mostly resupplying them with water in jerry cans. The scene was so verdantly country-clubbish that it seemed incongruous except for the

10 VC bodies lying at one end of the LZ, their hair and clothing being ruffled by our rotor wash as we flew by them. They were proof that there actually was a war going on here. The APC crews were taking it easy and wrapping up their time and effort as things closed down. Somewhere else was not so relaxed.

Over the radio came an excited, frustrated voice wondering why he was being so overly supplied at this point of the operation. It was always important to plan things just right, so you could use up things exactly on time and retreat into base camp without having to leave things out in the bush. Commanders didn't want to supply the Viet Cong with American ammo, petrol, foodstuffs, etc. All of this was the mark of a good military officer—and noted as such.

What became obvious here was that some rival officer in the position of S-4 (which means supply at the battalion level) was dumping waves of helicopter-borne military goods on this guy at this crucial moment of closing down the campaign, ruining his execution at precisely the right point. I could see "Vs" of Hueys continuously coming down out of the sky at this guy's position while he screamed over the radio: "I didn't order this stuff! Why are you sending this stuff? Take it all back, stop sending this stuff! You always do this to me! You've been doing this to me since the Point! Stop, Stop!" It was absolutely great burlesque. What made matters even worse is that the S-4 way back at headquarters was laughing back over the radio, sounding like the kind of laughing teeth you buy for a joke at a pawn shop. "Ah-Hah-ha-ha-ha-ha!" in a nasal tone of voice like he was part of a carnival fun house. "Hah-ha-ha-ha-ha!" over and over as the guy on the ground continued to plead to shut off this supply lift. And there we were at altitude, giggling as we listened to this radio traffic; until that moment, I didn't think wars were conducted this way.

When we were packing up to go home to Vinh Long and get out of the Tay Ninh circus, Stets and I decided to get our footlockers out to the ships early and ahead of the others—when we really should have been acting more like young officers, helping out and directing. We were not being treated very much like respected lieutenants at this point, so we had not started acting appropriately, either. We got one of those small trucks one step up from a Jeep, called a "three-quarter," since the Army insists on calling all its vehicles by their tonnage. (That's where a "deuce and a half" gets its name.) As we drove our loaded trunks around the tail boom of the Huey we had in mind, we went smack dab into an old foxhole where the former perimeter had been some place back in time. Just as we hit the thing with a big "clump!" O'Kane snarled as he appeared right behind us: "This is exactly what happens to guys who only care about themselves instead of assisting others as their rank calls for! Get back in there and start acting like lieutenants!" He actually liked us and was showing us his disappointment in our self-seeking behavior. He was also very canny about being in the right place at the right time, as in this instance, and his chewings-out usually had a positive effect on our actions. Stets was completely embarrassed, but I was beginning to learn about the ways of O'Kane. He could make a good officer out of you.

When all the 175th's stuff was loaded on the Hueys, we were ready to begin our flight back to Vinh Long. Somebody thought of tying smoke grenades to the skids with W2 commo wire (that's the black covered wire used with field telephones). Some of the wire held the grenades on the skids, and another three- or four-foot section was wired to the pin to pull it out, igniting the secured canister in flight. We all hoped the things would stay tied on en route until we got over the Vinh Long airstrip. We would see. The idea was to come on like the Blue Angels for a homecoming pass over the compound to celebrate our return. Jon Myhre told me that some of the grenades fell off during takeoff and ignited tents that we flew over on departure. I'll bet they were glad to see us go after that! Bye-bye, Tay Ninh.

I was flying with Outlaw 3, Major Casper, who was so long-legged and stringy that he had to have the left seat of the Huey shoved all the way back in its tracks in order to fly at all. He was the only person I ever saw who was so tall that he couldn't rest his flying hand on his right thigh to stabilize his control touch. We all needed to do that. I was amazed at his smoothness despite not being able to use this technique we'd all thought up for steady helicopter flying. His right arm just had to hang out there in thin air. He was a good guy to get along with and at that time he was serving as the operations officer for the Outlaws. Before that period on the Vinh Long compound, whoever was the more senior of the aviation company commanders also had to run the airfield through his operations officer. The tall major would eventually become the airfield commander as well, but this was later, in January and February, as a separate job. Don Casper was about to make lieutenant colonel within the year; he was fairly senior to everybody else I knew at Vinh Long, but we just knew these field-grade officers as "the majors."

We had a good time flying home, and when we got over the airstrip, everyone popped their smoke grenades as planned for the show. Plumes of purple smoke, green and red smoke, and probably even yellow, trailed behind the skids of the numerous Hueys as we flew over the strip in a series of "Vs." Wowee, pretty cool. In our minds, we looked like the Lafayette Escadrille or the Red Baron's "Flying Circus" for a while. Gradually the smoke grenades fizzled out and we went to straight trail for our landing formation and finally put down on our home turf again. We had had enough for a while of the big American war up north.

9

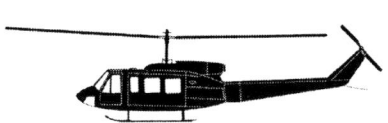

A Christmas Present

EVEN THOUGH WE WERE NOW FLYING a lot of lifts, it was something of a relief being with the Vietnamese again down in the Delta, after participating in the big American Tay Ninh operation. For the first time, we admired the fact that they *didn't do anything,* including needing a lot of massive resupplying. It sure made life easier on us after we'd put them in first thing in the day. One morning, while preparing for takeoff on the Ben Tre runway, loading ARVN troops, I saw the big haunch of an American advisor about to settle down on the radios between me and the AC in the left seat. Well, a big haunch compared to the tiny butts of the Vietnamese men. This would not work, because the console was not as solid as it looked—with its black, lettered metallic surface. The whole partition was a case comprising only thin metal plaques between the radio boxes, with nothing but wiring and space underneath the panel. It wasn't anywhere near as substantial as it appeared. We couldn't have anything heavy park here; the person in question would just cave in the whole box-like affair, and we'd be ruined for communications. As the MACV advisor continued to lower his butt, facing aft at the same time, I grabbed the back of his webbed belt and heaved. He went tottering back toward the transmission as I intended him to, then crashed amid the ARVN squad he was accompanying—steel pot helmet all wrapped around his neck and looking silly. Then I noticed he had a major's black embroidered leaf on his collar, and I thought, "Uh-oh . . . ." However, something about his face looked familiar, and it wasn't only the confused expression from being heaved into the rear of the Huey. I realized I knew him! I took off my sunglasses and hollered:

"Hey, Captain LaTour! I mean Major LaTour! It's me—Dave Eastman! One of your ROTC cadets from UNH! Come on up and talk to me after takeoff!"

We got the loaded ship airborne, then I waved him forward. It was LaTour, all right, out here with the RF/PF, the lowest echelon of Vietnamese troops. He was air defense/artillery for his branch, and they sure didn't have any Nike sites or Hawk missile batteries in this period of "the Vietnam War." That was his job. So, here he was playing infantry advisor, with a light carbine in his hand and about to get rice paddy mud on his feet for the first time. I took off my flight helmet and apologized for throwing him on his can. In a most earnest fashion, I tried to explain why I had had to do so. He got it, and he promised never again to try to sit on the radio console. We talked all the way to the LZ, as he squatted between the two armor-plated pilots' seats, catching up with his former ROTC student.

What was really humorous here was that this guy had been in charge of the ROTC flying program back at UNH. The abbreviated course of 35 flying hours at the local airport could get you your private pilot's license if you were really good, which I wasn't, but they checked out your ability to fly an airplane before the Army wasted a lot of money on you in flight school. It was a pretty clever way to thin out prospects, and a big come-on for recruiting into ROTC the guys who thought they maybe wanted to be military aviators when they entered the service after graduation. I had been terrible in the Cessna 172, but I found my true niche flying the Huey. Interestingly, and thankfully, there was a phenomenon that many aviators could fly either rotary-wing or fixed-wing, but only a few could fly both. My hopelessness with fixed-wing had not carried over to the helicopters I loved. Even years later, with a lot of FAA ratings, I couldn't fly fixed-wing aircraft like I could zip a Jet Ranger or a Huey around the sky.

On this first lift transferring the troops from Ben Tre to wherever they were going for the province chief's military operation, Bob LaTour and I kibitzed back and forth about what had occurred since we had last seen each other at UNH, at least a year and a half earlier. We were pretty much caught up on personal news when my AC indicated I ought to get my helmet back on and rejoin the war effort. The newly promoted major said, "OK, see ya again!" and resumed his place out in the back of the Huey, ready to go in with the ARVNs. I wondered, as I watched him jump off the aircraft after we touched down in the mud, how many career-oriented officers in armor or artillery would be running around these rice paddies with ARVN soldiers. What do you write to the wife back home?

After two months in-country, I was more than ready to make aircraft commander. Flying in the right seat with all the ACs in the various ships of the second platoon had taught me a great deal, but there comes a moment in every first pilot's life that he cannot stand another day as a copilot. He wants freedom, like some jailbird wishing for blue sky. It's nothing against the guys with whom he's flying, but there has to be a day when he can spread his own wings and fly solo or be the pilot in command. This is an attitudinal thing, and one becomes very impatient for this day to arrive.

I was flying with Dickie Hyde in Outlaw 25 out of Long Xuyen, where the Cao Dai sect kept the VC from doing anything in their sector. Since we were close, I petitioned him to "champion" me to be set up for an AC checkride. He said, "You're not ready yet, East, you need more time." "Aaaagh!" I replied. "If *you* truly feel that way, I'll never get put up; the other guys must feel even worse about my possibilities!" I tried to demonstrate needed abilities to present myself in the best manner feasible. I needed to get my own ship and gain autonomy.

When I first joined the Outlaws, the second platoon had more new UH-1Ds than pilots. They had just traded in their old B-models over at Vung Tau, on the coast, for these birds right out of the Bell Helicopter plant in Fort Worth, Texas. Some of the aircraft had almost zero flight time, and you darn near could take your pick of which one you wanted to claim as your personal ship for the tour. D-models were called "slicks," because they were not armed with rockets or flexible minigun kits like the gunships were outfitted with. Nor was the crew allowed to have "free guns" either—the M-60 machine guns handheld by the gunship door gunners. Our "60s" were on upright pylons attached to the fuselage of the ship, with a machine-gun ammo bag on the left side of the gun for the 7.62mm belts of ammo. In the movies made about the Vietnam War, those things might have looked fearsomely effective, but it was not much weaponry for these ships, nor enough to throw back some of the firepower extended toward us. It was almost like packing a sidearm and not much more; hence the slang term, "slicks." We were slicked down compared to real military aircraft armament in "the guns." In real language, we were also known as "transports."

An aviator in need of stepping up becomes a bit grouchy and sullen. At last, one day Major O'Kane said he was taking me out for a day of flying around Ben Tre Province for my AC checkride. This was actually Kien Hoa Province, and it had a lot of VC. The Mekong River split into quite a few deltaic channels here, and some areas of the province were always hotspots and under VC control throughout the war. I suppose some American advisory headquarters thought they knew why, but nothing ever happened to change the situation from the beginning to the end of the decade-long war. This flight was a good idea to show what I knew about tactical flying as well as to getting the job done, visiting and resupplying the outposts here.

The Hueys were the workhorses of the Vietnam War. It was impossible to move men and supplies safely down these Delta roads without an armed convoy, which could takes weeks of preparation for a trip of maybe 12 miles. Thus, the helicopters were in high demand, so we had to operate efficiently during the day we were assigned to help out these men in their isolated outposts. Everything went to these sites through us. If there were a lot of troop lifts going on, they had to wait weeks for supplies they had requisitioned. They made it pretty clear to us what their needs were and how long they had been earnestly, even desperately waiting. We tried to satisfy their demands as best we could and earned a lot of respect and friendship while doing so. It also provided great strokes when they recognized individual ships and crews who delivered the goods better than another aircraft did. After a while, you developed a reputation that made you feel good about your call sign and crew identification. In a way, it was like feeling famous. The MACV advisors couldn't swap for things, as the Special Forces outposts up by the Cambodian border were able to do, but they were grateful for a well-ordered day taking care of their requests. When you did a good job, you had everyone pulling for you—from the top of the command structure on down—and if you needed help and a bit more support that day than you had been getting, you could get on the horn to headquarters and get results quickly. We did not mind being seen as prestigious, I'll tell you.

A big part of the work was radio usage, both on the FM to the individual MACV outposts and on the UHF to "Paddy Radar." This Air Force flight-following service was located in the central part of the Delta. We were always on the scope, and we identified ourselves by the use of the transponder. Paddy would request that we "squawk flash," and we would hit the ident toggle switch on the face of the device. That would "paint" about five lines, all close together, on the face of the radarscope and present a different appearance for a moment from any other aircraft he was displaying on the screen. He would tell us he had us and monitor our flying across the skies for an instant recognition of that helicopter's flight path over the ground. If we went down, we could squawk "emergency" by throwing a switch and showing our aircraft in much the same way as with the ident "flash." That, and going to the "guard" channel on the UHF radio for our "mayday" broadcast, could get us found pretty quickly by anyone flying nearby. If you really needed a speedy rescue, it was important to make that call on 243.0 megahertz as you lost altitude and plunged toward the earth. Closer to the ground lost line-of-sight communication between your radio and someone else's. (The curvature of the earth limits the distance of certain types of radio transmissions.) The ability to keep your cool and make that transmission while in a physical emergency situation with the aircraft was a quality demanded of a pilot that bordered on the heroic, but you had better possess it when the demand came. We had to be ready constantly to radio our position as well as go through emergency procedures; every pilot has to know instinctively about his aircraft if it fails to operate as it is designed to do. An AC had to stay on his toes all the time, including monitoring what his copilot, new in-country, was doing on the controls. This was a demanding position.

All this was what O'Kane was checking out that day out of Ben Tre. I made the calls to Paddy Radar out of the SOI, our secret code book for all the outposts so that we wouldn't reveal where we were landing. This was changed almost monthly for security reasons, but I suspect the VC got a copy of the little booklet almost as fast as we did. The copilot on the ship would transmit, "Outlaw 801 off Lima-one, en route Lima-two, will call landing," and Paddy would roger. Meanwhile, the AC would be talking to that outpost on the FM for further instructions and letting that radio operator know we were coming toward his location. We wanted and needed things to be crisp on the ground and have people available and waiting for us. Time was of the essence in conducting these flights. Minutes lost in the morning hours could not be recouped in the afternoon's flight time, and we had to train these advisory teams to accept this. "Come on in for a cup of coffee," offered first thing in the morning, was not to be tolerated, and only a green crew thought this was a good idea and a friendly overture. All utilization of the aircraft had to be well executed.

As the day progressed with O'Kane, I didn't feel I was doing these things to the best of my ability. In my own estimation, I was looking like a dork. He wasn't saying much of anything, which is how he was supposed to react, but I felt awkward. I tried to smooth out procedures but continued giving the impression I was pretty rough around the edges. I hadn't made any big mistakes, but I could have performed better, I thought. By lunchtime, I was beginning to wonder about ever making AC. My confidence was slipping away. We shut down at the Ben Tre airstrip and got a Jeep ride into the MACV compound headquarters. This was the nice part of flying duty around the Delta, because sometimes the cooks they hired in these places were pretty good at preparing American chow.

As luck would have it, over walked Major LaTour, whom I knew was stationed here. He just had to be all friendly and everything, and he asked Major O'Kane how I was doing: "Is he straight? Does he fly well? Is he a good officer?" and on and on. Gawd, not today. O'Kane just grimaced and said, "Yeah, sure, sure." I informed LaTour that this was my AC checkride, and, "No, I'm not looking especially good this day." He finally got the message and pushed on. I was in a tough spot, and this was not the time to discuss socially what a great pilot UNH ROTC had produced. O'Kane remained noncommittal, and after finishing lunch, we returned to the aircraft.

For the rest of that day, we accomplished what we had set out to do, even though I didn't think I was improving my performance. I decided to let that go and inquired of O'Kane how he was taking missing his family back in the States. With Christmas approaching, we were all missing our young wives, but he responded that he missed the kids the most. I looked over at him in astonishment. "Missing the kids?" How did one miss children? I wondered. He nodded painfully, making me realize that there was probably more to this family thing than I knew about at this point in my young manhood. At that stage in our lives, we tended to think of matrimony as just a more advanced phase of "going steady" or "being pinned." The wives seemed to enjoy this whole marital institution more than we did. He was teaching me a lot about paternal life.

Later that night, as I passed by his bunk, he said, "Park." I grabbed a chair and admitted sheepishly that I had not done as well as I'd wished. He said, "You did well enough. I'm going to turn you loose." I gasped. You could have knocked me over with a feather. "Just one thing, though, that you ought to do better," O'Kane suggested. Here it comes, I'm thinking. "What's that?" I inquired. "Don't do too many things the same way. Vary your approaches so the VC can't expect you to come in on the same flight path you used the last time. That sometimes means you're landing crosswind with a heavy load over barbed wire and minefields, but so be it. Just don't do things the same way every time." I could understand that, and I agreed to do so.

"I'm giving you Outlaw 23 for a ship," O'Kane then said.

"Oh, no! That's the dog of the platoon! Give me 29, that's still available!"

"Nope. I hear what you're saying, but I need someone to shape up that aircraft and cease making it the dog of the platoon. I want to see what you can do with it."

Oh, goody, another Boy Scout task for good ol' Eastman. Story of my life. "OK," I replied. "If that's what you want, I'll do the best I can with that ship." I got up feeling mixed emotions—relieved that I would be getting my AC orders but let down about the ship those orders would get me.

By this month, many of the guys from my flight school class had gotten their own aircraft in the first and second platoons. Just before my arrival to Vinh Long, the older B-models had been traded in for 1965 D-models over at Vung Tau. There was a good chance to get a brand-spanking-new ship that still had the smell of the factory throughout it; the new birds were in "show-room" condition. The Army serial numbers of helicopters delivered from Bell at that time were in fairly consecutive order for the second platoon aircraft: 65-09796, -797, -799, -800, -801, -802, -805, etc. Although this presented a feeling of order, they weren't given out to the ACs in any consistent numerical sequence when designating them as second platoon ships. And, outside of company airmobile operations, the tail number's last three digits were always used for radio transmissions. Outlaw 23 was "800" as a call sign to an airfield tower or when contacting flight following. (An experienced tower operator could identify you by the sound of your voice even as you spoke your tail number; sometimes they prematurely made the wrong aircraft identification if you were flying someone else's bird while yours was briefly in maintenance.)

Of the warrants from 66-13, Norris Marshall got Outlaw 24

when Denny Haugen went to Maintenance to be with Rheihofer. Tommy McCarthy, all 19 years of him, got Outlaw 29. He was from Maury High School in my old high school town of Norfolk, Virginia. He was probably the youngest pilot there; we called them "boy-pilots" when they were this incredibly young. O'Kane respected him a lot and "Mister Mac," as he was called by his crew, was also respected by them. So I had Outlaw 23, Harvey had 27, Mark Howell had 22, Savelli continued with Outlaw 26, and the platoon leader's aircraft was 21. O'Kane felt that assigning each of the platoon's aircraft to a specific AC made him totally familiar with the eccentricities of his bird, which was true. Even though all the aircraft were only one serial number apart as delivered from Bell, each flew just a bit differently. Outlaw 23 was gutless, while Outlaw 24 was powerful. Outlaw 29 sailed on descent, while others sank. Flying Dickie Hyde's Outlaw 25 made me feel I was scrunched over a bit to the left, and not sitting in a chair straightforwardly, and while we all admitted that, nothing could be done about it. After a while, it was strange to fly another guy's bird, when yours was perhaps in maintenance, and feel these subtle differences. In our book, having one's own Huey was like having the U.S. government give you a Ferrari or a Maserati, and being responsible for a half-million-dollar aviation machine brought tremendous self-esteem into our young lives. Dreams do come true! Two weeks before Christmas and I already had my Christmas present—I was to be an AC *and* have my own bird!

Now that I had Outlaw 23 for my own aircraft, I also inherited its crew chief, MacDougal, a red-haired southern cracker type who was nearly at the end of his tour in Vietnam and the U.S. Army as well. We got along OK, but I think I felt he'd seen his allotted amount of pilots-in-command. He seemed to know the aircraft fairly well, and there wasn't much I could do to improve his knowledge any further. We actually didn't have too much contact for my first command, except when he asked me for a contribution for the new nose cowling over the radio compartment. He'd chosen "Cat Ballou" as the new name for the ship, as we were supposed to come up with some "outlaw" names for the ships after there had been a rash of "cab" names for a while, such as "Yellow Cab," or "Checker Cab." This had all ended when someone had adorned his aircraft's front with "Slope Cab," and the brass didn't like this racist epithet one bit. So they made us change all the previous names and we complied. "Slope" was the pejorative term for the Vietnamese with their "slanted-eyes" in this war; "Gook" was used up north. The military at higher echelons didn't like us taking such a dim view of the people we were supposed to be aiding.

The other thing I remember about this young man from the South was that both he and Stets's crew chief on Outlaw 11 were locked in a dead heat for how many times they had caught the clap downtown. Gonorrhea strains in Vietnam were very potent, and I've often wondered since that time if all the young EM who caught these virulent infections were rendered sterile for the rest of their lives. It amazed us officers to see how often young crew members caught these diseases in their favorite bars downtown and kept returning for more of the same thing. At times, I thought MacDougal in his pain would twist the tail boom off back there. (When one has the clap, urinating produces an extreme burning sensation due to the infection of the urinary tract in the penis.) I think Stets's crew chief won the contest (the tally was kept to ourselves), with a total of 19 doses! Both soon would be rotating out, and we would get new EM soon. One day, MacDougal came up to me with a piece of paper and asked for my recommendation on his Air America application. I signed and wished him well. He would be living in Saigon as a civilian with the CIA's own private aviation arm; I couldn't comprehend anyone wanting to stay on in Vietnam after their tour was up. This had become a lifestyle, I suppose, and even a chance to make a lot of money. I would see MacDougal only a few more times after that, wearing the white shirt and blue pants that employees of Air America wore. I said hello to him at Can Tho once or twice; one time, he introduced me to the two pilots dressed the same way, standing by their blue-and-white Air America B-model Huey. I never saw him again after that.

10

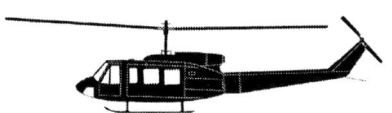

CHRISTMAS AT VINH LONG

WE FLEW ALL SORTS OF MISSIONS continuously for the remainder of December 1966; they tended to blur together after a while. As those first few months progressed, it was mostly the incidental events and humorous moments that set something apart from the routine experiences. I remember a day with O'Kane, before I became aircraft commander, when we had stopped at an outpost in Kien Hoa Province. This well-fortified compound actually had about five artillery pieces that had never been used. We proposed giving them some practice, as in, "How'd you like to have us call in a fire mission?" The Vietnamese soldiers looked at us like we were crazy. They knew that if they used these 105mm howitzers *at all*, the VC would storm the place and ruin them quickly! Annihilation within a fortnight. Not only did they have concrete bunks for sleeping, they slept *under them!* Talk about a morale problem. I think the outpost's name was Mo Cay, although I could be wrong. Later in my tour, the XO of the 114th Knights did try calling in a fire mission, and the artillery rounds went "Kersplash!" dead center into the river. He couldn't believe it, so he called in again, saying, "Drop 1,000," as a correction. They put the shells right into the river again. No fools here. Exasperated, the artillery branch senior major tried again. The third attempt went right into the exact middle of the river channel. He gave up then. I could have saved him some time . . . .

Another day, down by Rach Gia, a major climbed into the Huey with a preteen Vietnamese girl who had some kind of wild disease; her whole face was falling down her throat! He peered at our staring expressions, registering our disbelief, and said in a twangy southern accent, "Ain't that awful? We're going to fix that!" I went, "Oh, yeah! Well, good luck! Right." Wow. Apparently all the calcium in her jawbone was disappearing, and there was nothing left to stop her mouth and cheeks from going down inside. That was a sight that made you twist your head forward—*quickly!*

We were constantly reminded that we were in a foreign country rooted firmly in the past, stuck back somewhere in the time frame of our own tenth to twelfth centuries' culture. This undeveloped world was a complete historical throwback, and one for which we were totally unprepared. Some handled it better than others, and assisted the rest of us with viable explanations, but you never knew what was going to hit you next, the sick little kids or whatever. Tropical diseases were rampant and obvious.

Then there was the war's danger, ever-present, which could occur out of nowhere, and you had to cope with that. On one morning's mission with Harvey before I became AC, we were down at "new Camau" (versus "old Camau," an airstrip the Japanese had left behind during World War II). Just as we were shutting down at the beginning of the tropical dawn's beautiful sunrise, suddenly there was a big explosion. We had flown down from Vinh Long to join the Soc Trang "Tigers" and their sister company, the "Warriors." We performed those Vinh Long takeoffs in the dark in order to arrive at the appointed airstrip at the break of dawn. When the blast occurred immediately after landing, everybody freaked. Ships' crews cranked up hysterically. Gunships getting airborne plowed the treelines across the way with rocket fire and machine guns. Suspecting mortar fire, everyone thought the first explosion would be followed by many more. Talk about "jump-through-your-ass" protocol. After nothing further happened, things eventually settled down, and we got out of the ships and went back to look at the hole the sabotage had made. We had not been fired upon; a satchel charge apparently had been inserted under the new runway planking and went off when some aircraft made it do so, or maybe it had been a time bomb. A big, black, earthy hole was the result, and not much more. The VC were awfully smart, and they probably had figured out what our reaction would be. They had calculated accurately that in our terror we would lace the nearby populated treeline, suspecting the fire was coming from the peasant hooches over there. More enemies for Uncle Sam. One satchel charge like that could ruin our whole day, even if no one was hurt and no aircraft was damaged. Just a psychological insult in its impact, but one that obviously worked to the other side's advantage.

Of course, there were the problems associated with too much flying and just plain fatigue. After the predawn takeoffs out of Vinh Long, we often would have to fly for an hour to get to the southern parts of the Delta, and guys would fall asleep at the controls. You would see a ship drifting about, getting pretty sloppy in its position, and know the guy was dozing off. You could only pray that his copilot could focus and wake him up, or take the controls. One time, I saw a ship go right over the top of the formation. The EM crews would always grab some shut-eye during these flights on the way down. (They'd been up half the night maintaining the ships.)

Encountering fog or low clouds, you would be aware that the running lights on the aircraft you were flying formation on had suddenly become quite fuzzy. This was nature's way of telling you that one had suddenly gone into the scud. That could get alarming if the loose cloud cover didn't break quickly. You could only hope you happened to be hitting just a few of these patches in your travels. We didn't need the whole flight going IFR (instrument flight rule conditions).

One time, Savelli's running lights went out completely as he was on my left, and suddenly I was flying formation on the red lights of his cockpit's instrument panel. I had to call him up and inform him he had nothing for nav lights on the outside. He fiddled around and they came back up, "steady-dim," the way they were supposed to be. That was interesting for a while . . . .

In those dark morning hours, we sometimes were over the airstrip where the operation would be taking place that day, and couldn't find it. We would have the ground forces continue transmitting to us so that our homing devices could lock in on their communicating efforts. The ILS (instrument landing system) needles would show where the FM transmitter was relative to the nose of the aircraft, and as long as the guy kept talking, we could fly down in a straight line and find the runway. This FM homing worked only when the man's mike switch was depressed; it found the signal. We had to use all these things ingeniously. I often pondered what we'd do without them. We could have been wandering about the Delta for several miles on both sides of the airstrip, waiting for the sun to come up in order to find it. The extraordinary thing was we got used to all this stuff. It was all part of the learning and growth curve. We used everything the aircraft had to give us.

One of the most memorable sounds in the darkness in which we preflighted was the boisterous sound of the Saigon Armed Forces Radio coming on the air. The enlisted men would have the volume knob on their "ghetto blaster" radios already turned on, and when the station opened in the morning, it broadcast Adrian Cronauer's famous raucous salutation, "Good morning, Vietnam!!" the way he always had done in the earlier days of the war. Sort of famous by then. It was downright freaky to hear this loud, startling exclamation emerge from the Delta's predawn stillness as we groped around the aircraft, looking over the fuselage and the engine components with a red-lensed flashlight. It never ceased to spook me when it happened, and it always produced some surprised laughs somewhere on the ramp when the station signed on in this Third World rice paddy environment. The effect was like a rooster crowing.

There was always the unexpected in other areas of the humor department, too. One fall morning when I was still a peter pilot, Denny Haugen and I had to pick up two full colonels at the Can

Tho parking apron. Since there were no American generals in the Delta, these two had to be senior-senior, and on the same team. After climbing out of their Jeep, they shook our hands and were especially friendly, attempting to relax us in spite of their rank. Those eagles on the collars do tend to be a bit intimidating. It was nice of them to relieve our awkwardness at seeing such high rank; showed good command stature on their part, too. They told us where they wanted us to take them. This had been the heaviest rainy season in 20 years, and many parts of the Delta were still flooded, sometimes to depths of 10 feet or more. They met a Vietnamese man in a sampan, holding onto a stake in deep water, and waved us off after getting in with him. They had given us a time to return to pick them up after the completion of whatever this mission was. That must have been one important peasant.

We arrived at the appointed time, and the two fat bird colonels started paddling their sampan toward the Huey like they were reminiscing about Boy Scout camp quite a few years back. Problem was, that particular summer camp probably had not had a Huey for canoeing merit-badge practice. As the two older men nearly made it to the floating Huey, hovering so low that its skids were immersed in the water, the rotor wash would blow them back repeatedly, and in circles, like leaves on a pond's surface. A Chinook helicopter can create hurricane-force winds when it hovers, and I'd seen that at Rucker, but we had no bragging rights close to that. Still, as much as we tried to lower pitch and float the ship lower and lower in the water, the two now distraught men could not make it back to the ship. Not only was this getting pathetic, but it was fast becoming a comedy routine. We were trying to keep straight faces, but these two were putting us in stitches. We knew we dared not laugh, but that wasn't working either. Sooner or later, these frustrated senior officers would think we were doing this on purpose, holding in a small amount of pitch just to make their day a little tougher. Red-faced and exhausted, they were beginning to look like potential heart attack candidates—either one of them, take your pick.

Denny had a plan. If we moved away, maybe they would have

the good sense to grab the same stake the lone Vietnamese had been holding onto earlier. We did that. The two bird colonels apparently thought we were leaving them; their faces showed the fear of abandonment. Now, things were getting really tense. The two portly fellows were exhausted, had given it their best, and were bent over in the shallow sampan with their sides heaving, just floating around, looking apoplectic. God only knew what they would do to us *if* they ever did get back on board the aircraft. Suddenly, we could see they had a brainstorm. They pointed back at the stake and looked at it questioningly. "Yes, Yes!" we indicated, nodding our heads vigorously from a distance of a few hundred feet or so. We wanted to assure them that was exactly what we had in mind. We remained at a low hover, still even at the water's surface with the skids underwater, the flooded paddy's water nearly coming in over the cabin's floor, and cruised up to the pooped colonels, struggling to hold onto that stake despite the effect of the strong rotor wash. They were bent over like flood victims getting picked up by a rescue helicopter, but this time we were going to do it! They crawled into the cabin space, which was only about five inches above the waterline—we could control the ship that well. Both rolled in, spent. Immediately they examined our faces to see if the gag was on them. Haugen quickly took off his flight helmet and told the more senior officer quite forcefully that we had tried everything we could to pick them up, and this problem had just happened; he was awfully sorry. As I watched him do this while I was on the stick, I decided, Maybe it *is* good to have *some* former EM experience behind you for a ticklish situation like this! The colonels read his face and believed him. They nodded painfully, and I could see they needed a real rest on the flight back to Can Tho. When you cranked in the morning, you never knew what humor you'd find on these missions. My sides ached from laughing, as I kept shaking in quiet mirth while flying back. When the two colonels looked us steadily in the eyes one more time before releasing us at noontime, I think they still thought we had put one over on them.

Christmas provided a welcome break, and many of the men's families went gloriously overboard sending everyone everything that could be shipped in time. We received many, many packages and certainly didn't feel forgotten. We were looking forward to quiet personal time on Christmas morning, opening up all these welcome gifts and experiencing very precious thoughts while we were overseas on this date.

After witnessing Thanksgiving, I had been wondering what this important holiday would mean to us. I knew it would be overwhelming on an emotional level, and I was curious just how it would play out. We visited each other's hooches and wished each other the sentiments of the season, but the Outlaws' first platoon hooch took the prize for creating the greatest impact on all of us Christmas Eve. Ray Leuty's wife and the other officers' wives of that platoon had gotten together and sent over a silver tinsel tree made out of shiny aluminum—the kind of fake artificial tree you wouldn't be caught dead with outside of a store's decorated window or an office party. Some wives had sent red balls, the others lights and icicles, and so on. There it stood in the Vietnamese night, in all its metallic splendor. All of us stood there speechless, drinks in hand, and just kept looking at that ornamental tree. It was quite the stand-in for Christmases past and easily could have become a religious shrine at that moment. I'd never before seen men so transfixed by a silver tinsel tree, and joined them in silently gaping at is quiet impressiveness. The only lights in the day room were the tree's bulbs, and the wrapped gifts under the tree seemed to need this artificial ornament to make things right. Various men came by the first platoon hooch, stood mute, stared at the decorated tree, and then quietly moved on. Their deeply felt, unspoken testimony was an understated salute to the wives who had joined together and thought up this Christmas gift for their men. It was a very good idea.

After that, we went to the Protestant service over at the chapel that Vinh Long was so proud of—a cute little chapel that itself almost resembled a Christmas card image. The small, white building with a steeple had been well designed by someone; it was a meaningful religious place. After the Protestant ceremony, we all went to the Catholic midnight mass. We had become visibly emotional, and men were openly bawling by this time of the night. At the conclusion of the mass, we linked arms and sang Christmas carols at the tops of our lungs as we marched in wide lines down the company street. Loud, and scarcely in tune, weeping and embracing, we felt no embarrassment, as we couldn't restrain our homesick emotions and didn't even think to do so. There was nothing else to do but *care*. Unabashed tears and embellished good will reigned. I have never seen such a deluge of caring, feeling, and well-wishing—and guys missing home.

Christmas morning, we quietly opened our presents, each in his own personal living space in the platoon hooches. Each tiny room had a bunk, desk and chair, footlocker and closet space, with some drawers and shelving. In mine, I had built a hutch-type room divider, painted green, with bookshelves and storage space below. Not much was said as the guys tended to their gifts from back home. One gift was universal among all of us, however: Christmas cookies. Tons of them. All in crumbs and stale; broken to smithereens and reduced to powder in some cases. The red and green sugar spackles and sprinkles were in there, too, as well as other well-intentioned, elaborate cookie decor that had not survived the trip. It was almost as though busted-up cookies had been gathered by everyone's family and used for shipping material to cushion the other presents. Some of the men tried, out of goodwill, to scoop up the crumbled, powdery mess and eat the remains, but it was a lost cause. The tropics had finished off any remaining freshness, and these former cookies were moldy. We all wondered why the folks back home had not forecast this more predictably. It made me think of my mother sending 78 RPM records to my father at the Naval Academy back around 1940. They remembered for a lifetime that not one had arrived in a piece bigger than a broken saucer. This was definitely in the same category. As the guys finished unpacking and opening their families' gifts, we started to cluster to check out what everyone had received from loved ones.

The biggest conversation, however, centered on the broken-cookie matter. Someone would have to clue in the folks Stateside that this was a hopeless endeavor, and they should never, ever, send cookies to the troops overseas. We all made a mental note of that, but no one had any idea about whom to inform in official channels on this issue. It perplexed us.

11

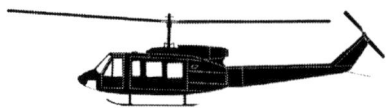

Mortar Attacks

Roughly once a month, the VC harassed us with mortar attacks. Since they usually targeted the runway, we weren't bombed in our sleep where we lived. Everyone reacted every time, however, as though we had been. There might be a first time. . . . Complete pandemonium would break out at the first sound of an explosion, and wherever people were, they sprinted for the nearest bunker. For bunkers we used steel CONEX containers that ships had used for sending us materiel from the States. Vietnamese laborers—usually women, since all the men had been conscripted into military service—filled up sandbags and piled these around the exterior of the metal container. Some were placed just outside in front, too, so the doorway to the container also had some protection for an entrance. Sandbags also covered the roof of the steel box, and when finished, the whole bunker had a very tidy appearance, if only for a short while. The military effect of the finished product did not last long in the monsoon rains and tropical rot, as the sandbags deteriorated within a month or two. Partially completed bunkers abounded in the Vinh Long compound, and nobody seemed to care too much until the next mortar attack. Then work began earnestly again to refill the sandbags and stack them neatly. Later in my tour, they started using fiberglass sandbags with a green tint; I can't say they lasted much longer. I'm sure the steel surfaces of the containers would have performed adequately without the sandbag exterior, but who knows? We never took a direct hit on one of these things to find out. It just remained an anxiety. When panic-stricken people poured into one of these steel boxes during an attack, they didn't seem to mind the disheveled condition of the sandbags. Some bunkers just looked like kids' sandpiles were playfully built up against them. Vietnam was full of personnel bunkers in various states of disarray.

Mortar attacks could be either just that, or from rockets. They both made the same bang and blew things up just as well. The only way we knew what had been used against us was when duds hit on the runway and did not explode. Joe Gammon of the Mavericks hit the deck when one of these landed immediately alongside him one night as he was running to his gunship. (He had heard the whine of the incoming projectile, and dived to the runway's surface.) Both he and the missile rolled around together for a short while on the PSP, the new metal planking on the runway. He was within kissing distance of the bum mortar round that had not survived the trek down from North Vietnam. Some of these munitions might have spent two years on the Ho Chi Minh Trail before getting to us. Joe reported that "his" dud hit with a clank; after that, he didn't want to go the runway anymore, but of course he continued to do so, as the Mavericks had to do when the rounds were incoming.

Wherever personnel were on the compound—in hooches or in the officers' club—when the first explosions were heard, all except the gunship pilots scooted for the nearest bunker, The gunship drivers of the Lancers, Cobras, and Mavericks headed for the runway on a dead run to crank up their B-models and Charlie models and get airborne. This took some bravery, to say the least, and complete dedication. You could not be in the "guns" if you weren't willing to do this task, because getting gunships in the air, and locating the mortar tubes, was the only thing that stopped the attack. If the guys could see the flash as the round left the tube, then they could fire on the position and put it out of commission. The VC understood this, of course, and would cease firing almost as soon as the helicopters became airborne. Very infrequently was there any sort of battle between the attackers and the gunships. The VC did not want to get hosed by the gunships' available firepower, so they were ready to pack it in as soon as they saw the ships rise up into the night. All this worked to motivate the gunship crews to perform as valiantly as they did, but it was still scary every time they dashed for that runway.

When the gunship fire teams did have the good luck to engage the enemy still in the act of firing those incoming rounds, a nice little firefight could ensue. Tracer fire from any automatic weapons the attackers were using allowed the pilots to place their flex-kit machine-gun firepower directly on the mortar positions, plus they could use the rockets from their pods on the sides of the Huey gunships. If a 221st "Shotgun" pilot in his 01E Bird-Dog was up flying that night, he could guide the gunships on an azimuth to the tube that was the source of the mortar fire. These little fixed-wing planes could stay up for three and a half hours, and if they happened to be on patrol that night for airfield security, observing the field and the compound perimeter, they could be quite helpful once an attack commenced. If they were airborne, they also fired rockets from their wings to the target area. The tower operator could provide some visual assistance, too. He had a device that could sight on the muzzle flash from mortars and the exhaust flame from rockets. When the gunships got aloft, he often contacted them with an azimuth to the target. But the usual VC firing positions were down in the treeline of the canal on the west end of the Vinh Long runway, so this wasn't news. Earthen ramps were also used for rocket attacks launched from here. These were built up to about a 120-degree angle and the rockets were supposedly touched off with batteries. Pretty primitive, but effective.

Gunships often were left on their pads with the whole starting procedure complete—everything done except for throwing the battery switch forward for cranking the turbine. Even the throttle was in the indent position or near to it, so the left hand just had to pull the start trigger under the collective. Helmets were left on board, and overhead on a clip. If a pilot could get to the ship, he was supposed to start the machine and fly it by himself, even if no one else joined him in time. This happened a lot. He was supposed to pull pitch and get up there as quickly as possible; time was of the essence. There was no time to discuss who would fly wingman, and so forth. You just departed. This outlandishly rakish procedure produced some funny episodes. It was not unusual to see some aviator flying bare-ass naked, wearing only a flight helmet. The "gunnies" commented on this being rather chilly. What made the scene more burlesque was that the Huey he was cranking often had the running lights flashing and landing lights ablaze, so he looked like a full strip show.

At one time or another, one of the Mavericks would find he had a passenger in the back seat for his whole mission. "Gunner," a huge yellow mastiff that was a legendary Vinh Long mascot, often climbed into the back of a B-model when the rounds started dropping. He went along for the ride for the safest place to be during the night's attack; dogs are smart like that. He already had his place in history, because he was a direct descendant of General "Vinegar Joe" Stilwell's son's famous dog. Brigadier General Joseph W. Stilwell, Jr., dubbed "Cider Joe," was the commander of the U.S. Army Support Group tasked with the administrative, combat, and logistical support of all Army activities in 1963. He had all the aviation units under his command then, and he decided to become an Army aviator himself by flying "bootleg"—taking flying lessons from his support-group aviation officer. When he got his wings, he flew around in an L-19 Bird-Dog, visiting his aviation troops, often by surprise. He was said to have been a difficult man, profane and arrogant—presumably trying to live up to his namesake and father. However, Cider Joe enthusiastically supported and protected Army Aviation in its formative years in Vietnam. Much of what we were doing tactically and experiencing in the gunships owed its origins to this general who was behind the myth of our big, yellow Vinh Long airfield dog. The story was just accepted like many other ritualized rumors. Those nights on a mission, "Gunner" lived up to his reputation, and we were all puffed up and proud he performed in such a legendary manner. He was huge as well as smart, and definitely the dominant animal of the Vinh Long "wolfpack," as the airfield commander called the canine contingent of the soldier's life. Mark Howell recalls seeing two of these dogs when he first arrived at the compound; perhaps the other dog was Gunner's sire. I wonder how many mortar attacks Gunner experienced in his lifetime. . . .

Meanwhile, back in the bunkers, really ridiculous things were happening. Guys packed these things like sardines, back to belly in the darkness. You would hear murmurings and questions: "Is that you, Joe?" "Yeah," would come the reply. Other men would be recognized by their voices, with responses such as, "You're in here, too?!" A lot of four-letter words would be stifled by some comment, "Hey, there are some ladies in here, you guys!" The ladies would have been the two nurses who would come over to the "Mekong Manor" and hang out with the majors for conversation. The older married men needed some white women to converse with; we nicknamed these Caucasians "round eyes." One was "Ole Red," and I've forgotten what descriptive term we gave to the brunette. The younger aviators were not as enthralled with them. Anyway, the vulgarity from the fearful moment would taper off, and then you'd find some guy behind you feeling up your haunch. "Not me, you asshole! I'm a guy!" The hand would move off to another target of opportunity, I surmised. The petite Vietnamese waitresses would be in there, too, at times, and were just as frightened as the rest of the crowd. They'd be littler, and about up to your elbow. "Yassuh, I am in here, too. I am so very frightened also, sir!" After a while, you figured out the whole inventory of who was sharing this sardine can with you.

Everybody breathed pretty heavily, and the worst thing that could be done was to have some scared-stiff jerk chamber a round. You'd hear, "Ka-chin-n-ng," and everyone would groan and growl, "No chambering of rounds!!" I don't know whom he was going to shoot, but if a firearm had discharged, the bullet would have had a fine old time ricocheting around the interior of the CONEX container and going through several people. Another pleasant idea to think about while inside. After a few months' experience with these monthly mortar attacks, I was glad to be the last one inside the container. I figured that worse things maybe could happen to you inside that bunker than outside.

Once the incoming fire had lifted, the men would pour out of the containers and stand around just outside the bunkers. Then the conversation would shift: "Were you scared?" "Naw, I wasn't scared. Were you?" "Naw, me neither." Yeah, right, after what I had just experienced? I often slept in the raw in that tropical heat, so I would be standing there with a towel wrapped around me, as would many others. But at least I had the good sense to stay away from the perimeter fence, where quite a few of the guys would go and look out toward the ramp area to see how many ships had been damaged. They'd be standing there wearing white T-shirts or white shorts, or a towel wrapped around their hips like me, and then lighting up a cigarette! At this point, I would have to remind them that if a ground attack ever occurred, it would be precisely at this point. Artillery or mortar fires shift to let the opposing ground troops come across the terrain just impacted—then you get it! So this was not the moment to relax, but instead to get some clothes on and grab whatever weaponry you felt would defend you rather completely. For some reason, it was always like back-to-basics to discuss this factor at this moment. This was a bunch of aviators, not infantrymen.

What became apparent to me over time was how smart the VC were just to take out a few aircraft, instead of blowing us up in our beds. They only wanted to interrupt our mission scheduling. Losing one or two ships really set us back from satisfying all those in MACV who needed our ships, and this was a good way to harass our delivery capability. Creating just a little trouble instead of a lot of havoc upset us, but it didn't increase our security measures. If they had killed Americans, we would have put in more ARVN forces, pumped up our guard posts, tightened up the perimeter beyond where it was, killed a lot more of them than we were now doing, and so on. This would have stopped all attacks. The VC were very clever not to bother us any more than they did; otherwise, they could not have bothered us at all. Defensive stratagems by us would have prevented them from attacking at all, and would have stopped them completely from conducting these monthly assaults. During my tour, they never did place a round inside the compound where we lived—they only blew up the helicopters out there on the ramp and along the runway, as they intended. Just enough incoming rounds to ruin our peace of mind and burn up a few Hueys so that we would be inconveniencing those we served. Typical Vietnam War reality and VC guerrilla strategy. Getting used to these events and their patterns is what shaped your development as the months progressed over that year.

I'll always remember my first mortar attack. As much as I'd heard about these ferocious episodes, I was unprepared for my first experience. The second platoon at that period of time was up at the other end of the compound, in newly constructed Quonset-style huts. It would be a while before anyone realized we were a long way from the runway and our ships, but that would be taken care of after Christmas. It mostly meant a long walk for preflight by the copilots, who had to investigate the ship for any defects before takeoff every morning. That meant at least an extra 20 minutes or so for the copilot to precede the aircraft commander, who trusted everything the crew chief was doing for the ship, anyway. I saw the routine as just part of the learning curve for the peter pilots to continue their expanding knowledge of the Huey after flight school. In my naiveté, I thought we would be living here in these hooches forever. They were home and here we'd stay. I mean, they were new, and they'd just been constructed for us, right?

Then rounds fell one night; the entire mood changed as if we were all experiencing the outbreak of an earthquake, and I ran out the front door like all the rest. Except Rheihofer, who was drunk and holding onto a bottle of wine; he was refusing to move out of the vinyl chaise longue chair belonging to someone in the Outlaws' second platoon hooch. I could not detect if all this was bravado, laced with some secret knowledge, or maybe he was too intoxicated to do anything intelligent. I ran out, respecting his demeanor but worried he might not have caught on that we were under fire. The rounds were landing down by the runway, and I really didn't feel any immediate danger, but I still moved out with proper haste. "Come, come, dear boy," I said in a mock English accent, "we can't have you being blown up now, can we?" Rheifhofer just nodded and smirked, and still didn't move. I left him and headed for the bunker. Brave, I thought.

Coming out the front door, and heading left to the bunker immediately outside the hooch, I saw a different sort of soul—a nearly naked man wearing only a webbed belt, steel pot, and boots. He was brandishing a rifle of some make and striding back and forth on the concrete sidewalk in front of the Quonset hut. I took note but still headed into the bunker. Most of the second platoon was gratefully there, and we all counted noses and were doing what we thought best. I mentioned that the Snake was delightfully drunk and immovable; what should we do? "Leave him," was the response. I felt I could come up with something better than that, so I went back into the hooch, sensing great danger. Now I knew Mike was being cool, because he'd been awaiting my return for further encouragement. I said, "Mike, I know you're sufficiently drunk, but not so drunk you can't hear me or come with me to the bunker. What'll it be?" "I'll come with you," my macho friend said. "Oh, good. Let's do that." We walked back outside and joined the rest in the container. At this point, everything was nearly over anyway. The naked guy was still walking around as if some enemy force was going to materialize out of the sky and rain down upon our position. I decided he was more fearful than anything else so far, including Rheihofer's reputation. Again, my overall impression of myself and of those around me told me that I was going to do all right in this tour called Vietnam. I was beginning to believe that in the final tally, I'd probably come out OK. Some of this was actually fun, as well as funny.

12

"FNGs"; Ski and the Rigging Crew

In the mornings, when the flights formed up, we often had to carry various personnel to the staging area of the operation. At first these were the Pathfinders, a 10-man group led by a young black lieutenant and a white one, both of whom had been at Fort Benning Officer Candidate School (OCS). While they were very crisp at first, as young lieutenants often are after OCS, it wasn't long before we all realized we did not need Pathfinders with the ARVN soldiers. The South Vietnamese troops knew well enough when they were coming home at the end of the day, after looting their countrymen of their ducks, chickens, and puppies; they could form up easily enough on the rice paddy dikes. The black-baseball-hatted Pathfinder officers were both enjoyable young men, however, and the EM squad members they collected for the task of assembling troops for pickup moved on to help Delta 9, our aviation coordinator with the Ninth ARVN Division, and other similar assignments. The two lieutenants, Mike and Benny, disappeared, and I never encountered them again. I felt bad about their loss of morale; it can happen quickly if you are in the infantry branch. Jobs dry up. I was glad to be flying for a living.

So, it wasn't surprising to have someone hurdle into the D-model at the last moment, saying he was en route for the day's activities and had been told to climb on board this ship. We didn't pay much attention to them or their reasons for being with us. After hitching a ride, they would be disembarking on the airstrip when we got there.

At the end of the day, however, it was a pain to be delayed in going home yourself by being assigned to transport some of these various personnel. The flight Lead would assign these "ashy-trashy" missions to individual slicks as required, and it could make your day longer when you were already bushed. One late afternoon in the southern Delta, a single aircraft made an inadvertent transmission that reflected all of our moods that day as things wound up. The floor-mike switch would transmit out of the aircraft involuntarily if the intercom panel was on that radio choice, and if it was on "2," your feelings would go out over the company net on UHF. While the pilot thought he was on the intercom setting, in fact he was broadcasting to the world what should have been a conversation only among that particular crew. This mistake was known as a "hot mike." The irate AC sounded something like this:

"We're always getting *fucked!* Do you know *why* we're always getting fucked? I'll tell you why we're always getting fucked! We always have to carry those *fucking* Pathfinders; that's *why* we're always getting fucked!"

The usual response to such a broadcast was to inform the pilot about his mistake, that he was on "hot mike," by repeating the last few words of his transmission. Then he would realize he had transmitted something he had no intention of sending out over the airwaves. The other aircraft commanders couldn't wait to get on this one!

"Always-getting-fucked; check 'hot mike'!" came the jeers.

This was gleefully repeated a few times to convince the party in question that he had depressed his floor-mike switch while being on UHF. And, I will tell you that *it was NOT I* who made that inadvertent goof that flying day, even if it did sound like my voice and everyone in the unit agreed with the expressed opinion . . . .

As the ships cranked in the early morning hours, they would call in to Lead, and report as I did, "23 is up!" on the Outlaw's FM frequency. Others called in quite rapidly as their radios warmed up. All the rest of the starting procedure occurred prior to clicking on the various radios; that was the last thing you did. Finally, when Lead had logged in all the first and second platoon aircraft with whom he was flying, he'd call the tower on its UHF frequency:

"Vinh Long tower, Outlaw Lead."

"Outlaw Lead, Vinh Long tower."

"Vinh Long, Flight of 10 Outlaws requesting departure."

"Roger, Outlaw Lead. Winds are zero-eight-zero at five knots. Altimeter setting is two-niner-point-eight-two. Cleared for takeoff from the Outlaw ramp."

"Outlaw Lead, Roger."

We would take off in the order in which we would be forming up as a "V." This had already been discussed and agreed upon. One ship at a time would take off, with the rest following suit in the appropriate departure frequency. Outlaw operations at the base of the tower knew who was flying which aircraft and handled all the paperwork on our flight time and connections with the airfield. The tower operator already would have known all the tail numbers of the aircraft leaving that day.

As I was heading out with the formation, and tending to the small details of getting the flight underway, which was already going well, a voice screamed into my earphones:

"Jap Zeros! Twelve o'clock!"

My head swirled around as I looked into the blue-and-white firmament. My brain raced, telling me, "Wrong war! Wrong war!" I turned around to see who was warning me of imminent attack, and there was this bantam rooster of a guy wearing a flight helmet, holding the mike switch in his hand, and squatting there with the rest of his people, who were *not* wearing any flight gear.

"Who the hell are *YOU*?" I bellowed.

"I'm Don Seliski. I was with your flight school class at Rucker."

"Well, then, what are you doing wearing just a flight helmet?" I asked, rather dumbfounded at this whole train of events.

"I don't have a ship. They're getting me one. I'm with the 611th Transportation Company. We're the rigging crew," Ski said.

"You mean *you got over here* and they don't have a helicopter for you?"

"Yeah, and until I get one, I have to hitch rides with you guys."

What a crock, I thought. I hadn't run into this before. Up to now, they all had been champing at the bit to get new pilots into these aircraft. Usually there had been more helicopters to go around than pilots; here was the reverse. I just shook my head and felt glad it wasn't my situation. Don Seliski went on to tell me that this group of EM with him were personnel who rigged downed ships, either fixed-wing or helicopters, for sling-loading and transport by the Hillclimbers or Pachyderms, some of the heavy-lift Chinook outfits. These huge two-rotor-system helicopters could lift 10,000 pounds without a strain; our Hueys often were pulled out by them after being shot down or unable to fly due to a maintenance problem. This was to be Ski's job for the year, and eventually he would be known by all the units throughout the Delta. He was a real hot ticket, from Montana, and a small, cocksure kid who made friends with everyone. This was the beginning of a lifelong friendship. Of course, I was also glad there were no Zeros around to shoot me out of the sky.

As the early months rolled by, we were joined for the first time by guys even newer to the game than we were. These were the "Brown Hats," the first flight-school classes (66-15, -16) to produce pilots other than the standard one-graduation-group-per-month that we all had experienced up to this point. These neophyte aviators were the first of many classes to be produced every two weeks throughout the Vietnam War. This would also continue while we were back in the States as flight instructors, where we would turn out as many as 750 new pilots per month to fly helicopters in the Vietnam conflict. Three times as many helicopter jocks and machines would be plying the skies of this third-rate country in 1968 and 1969 as I was experiencing in 1966. Knowing by now the caliber of aviator required to handle this equatorial flying task—combined with the absurd mission of tolerating Vietnam—we began to wonder about these people who would be sharing our cockpits and flying endeavors henceforth. Already after only a brief period in-country, we realized we had become far different from the people we had been not very long ago. It wasn't so much that this place made a man of you, which it did, but it did something constantly to your psyche so that you knew there was a development going on within. One look at these new guys' faces and you sensed this phenomenon internally, if reluctantly.

For the officers, Tommy Mitchell and wiry Jim Huey were the newest lieutenants. Pat Tominey and Mike Stansbury were the latest warrants and were good pilots. Stansbury was especially so, as were two much later arrivals, Carson Snow and Ray Novotney, who appeared in March and were amazingly collected and high performers right from the start. I once hard-assed Novotney about finding a town on the map, somewhere in the Mekong Delta, and he found it. Trouble was, the advisor in the backseat had made up a fictitious name from *two* villages he had in mind, and in Vietnam, you could find that name on the map if you looked hard enough. Ray got me to some teensy place in the area south of Can Tho, and upon landing beside some village huts, I stormed at him that he had erroneously placed me somewhere in nowheresville. But he said, "No, no. Look at the map!" There was the town as named, and there we were on the ground, totally unprotected in a spot in the rice paddy culture that probably had never seen a helicopter up close, much less the MACV advisors and VN cadre who were on board as passengers. I got out of there fast! It was probably the most unsecured landing of my life, but I had to respect Ray for navigating me to exactly that place on the map, even if we had been given a faulty name. It made me ease up a bit on my copilots after that, if only for a while.

Pat Tominey was a black-haired Mormon, and I'll talk more about that later. Mike Stansbury was a redhead from Kansas or Nebraska, and a really all-right kid. He was cool under fire and always a dedicated, no-nonsense aviator—oops, pilot. (The Army used the title of aviator for commissioned officers, and pilot for the warrant officers. There was no end to discussions about whether this was a term of derision or acclamation. At least this left it up to each person which moniker he preferred. It is true that many of these warrant officers were well under the age of 21; that's how they got the name of boy-pilots.)

Tommy Mitchell was an armor branch lieutenant with the strongest imaginable southern accent out of Arkansas. He immediately went through a lot of harassment as "Goober," like a Gomer Pyle candidate. He was slow and thoughtful, and would drawl, "Y'all don't bother me none." And I don't think we did, despite some red spots high in his cheeks when he made this statement. He had already ridden Brahma bulls in rodeos, and I had to respect that. I've never figured what would possess a person to do that trick. Bronco riding, maybe, but bull-riding? No way.

Jim Huey was actually named that; when people would question his name, he'd say, "Just call me 540!" The name given to the Bell "Iroquois" helicopter had originally arisen from describing it in Army lingo as HU-1A. Later they adjusted this to UH-1B, or UH-1C, or UH-1D. The "U" stood for utility, and the "H," of course, for helicopter. The early name stuck as slang for this magnificent product from Bell, and what Jim Huey was referring to was the "540" rotor system installed on the Charlie-model gunships. It was a wider rotor blade that was supposed to give more lift and thus assist with flying these heavily loaded helicopters. Jim Huey had arrived at one of those illogical coincidences of war, where such things as your name and your aircraft are one and the same. Truth can be stranger than fiction; who would have written that? He was a small, red-haired artillery OCS graduate from Fort Sill, and he never let us forget it. However, we ROTC graduates had the highest disdain for all those who had entered the Army via any route other than ours. We valued our college educations and extracurricular experiences as growth; we hadn't seen anything in the Army yet that qualified as competitive with that. West Pointers were OK as long as they didn't let their pinheaded ways interfere with our progress. Yes, we harassed the poor OCS types in the same highbrow, college-boy fashion we had used to survive our campus life. It didn't matter; they didn't get it anyway. It was fun to pick on them at any rate, when opportunities presented themselves. They were so-o-o serious . . . . Amazingly, they thought we were dirtbags in comparison to them.

We referred to all of these guys when they had just arrived as "FNGs," which of course meant "frigging new guys" (in the polite form). The correct vernacular was the other F-word, but we won't spell that out here. We used this term to designate the guys everyone knew needed a lot of work to make them effective in the cockpit.

Captain Lou Paulin came in from Germany, where he had been a fixed-wing pilot, flying U-8s, as I recall. He had transitioned into helicopters with 50 hours in a "Q" course (which means "Qualification"). That's all he had behind him before he went directly to Vietnam. He was a smooth pilot, and it didn't take much flying with him to realize that he was also very experienced. As thoroughly skilled Huey drivers with at least 300 hours of in-country flight time, we had to restrain our arrogance around anyone else who wasn't as expert as we were. One day, not long after Lou arrived, I flew with him up by the Seven Mountains area, and I was impressed with his thoughtful questions about what the Huey did and his comparison of the Huey to the U-8 Beech Baron. He was a senior captain, and this was his last tour before getting out of the service and chasing the airlines; Pan American was his first choice. Like so many of the college boys now flying, he had been an athlete, playing lacrosse as a midfielder at Penn State.

Lou not only made AC fairly quickly, he also was elevated to platoon leader, when Major O'Kane moved up to Outlaw Operations—becoming Outlaw 3 and flying with Outlaw 6 in the Command and Control aircraft. Lou would become Outlaw Lead in 21 and alternate with Ray Leuty every other day in that job. He enjoyed leading us Outlaws in very smooth formation landings, but I don't think he relished the platoon leader job. It was stressful to be an administrator on the ground *and* fly the Lead formation slot every other day, trying to outwit the enemy who looked forward to shooting us up at any opportunity we gave them by not performing tactically. The Lead aircraft had to think as an aircraft that was five helicopters wide—a little cumbersome and not very flexible once committed. Prior planning was essential for the touchdown and exiting of the landing zones. Not everyone could do it well, and you would hear feedback quickly from the guys if your performance was not up to par. The concentration required all day was also very intense, with plenty of radio traffic and instructions from the gunships and Outlaw 6 on what to do next. Lou did all right.

He stayed with the second platoon for many months until late in his tour, when he received a fixed-wing assignment with a Signal Corps outfit above Saigon. Just before leaving Vietnam, he flew over our formation at a higher altitude and called down to us, "As a former Outlaw, how is it going down there?" We replied up to his height from 2,500 feet, "Hey, Lou, how's it going?" "Nice to hear from you!" "When are you going to talk to the airlines?" and all that sort of thing. He replied he'd be talking to Pan Am the next week. I still miss him; he's one of the guys we have never caught up with again.

"Card game in the fourth ship back!" was his familiar sign-off on the platoon FM as we shut down after a lift.

13

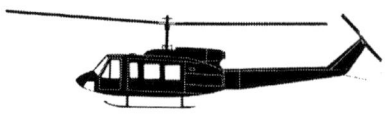

JOHNSON

Not only did we experience new pilots being assigned to the unit, but we also had new enlisted personnel moving in from time to time as crew replacements. I had gone to the villa we rented in Vung Tau for a few days of in-country R&R (the less said about any experiences there, the better), and when I returned, I heard nothing but bad news about my new crew chief, whom I had yet even to see. Replacing MacDougal, he was completely green and just in from the States. Even when they were "school-trained," we didn't expect much from anyone until they had gotten through the hangar portion of their training here and were deemed ready to be a Huey crew chief at Vinh Long. Outlaw Maintenance was superb under Major Bob Millward, literally a legend in himself. All the kids on the flight line took great pride in their mechanical abilities in crewing the individual ships. There was no need to motivate them; they were intensely competitive among themselves, and they passed the word along when any one of them was not up to snuff. When I returned from Vung Tau, the message I received was that my new crew chief was just not good enough. There were complaints all around. I already had the weakest ship in the platoon, and now I had the greenest crew chief; everyone was very underimpressed with him. The news that every AC dreads hearing from other enlisted men and fellow aviators hit me hard. I had a problem.

The following morning, I walked out to the Outlaw ramp and saw the new man fussing about the radio compartment under the nose cowling. He was busy but seemed scattered and not really concentrating. I kept my eyes on his motions as I strolled up to Outlaw 23 with my flight helmet in its bag, weapon over my shoulder, clipboard and map in hand. Johnson suddenly looked up and saw his new first lieutenant aircraft commander approaching and reacted badly; he freaked. I had an immediate revulsion and a bad read on this man. He snapped to a salute, saying, "Good morning, sir!" My gut response even surprised me.

"Don't you even *dare* to salute me!" I screamed in rage. "All I've heard since I've come back from Vung Tau is how *lousy* this ship has been since you took over crewing it. You don't *deserve* to have me return your salute. I want to see this ship's maintenance entirely improved starting right away! Is that clear enough for you?"

"Yessir!" Ron Johnson stammered. He looked terrified.

"Good!" I put my flight-helmet bag inside the left seat and asked the copilot what he had found wrong during his preflight. He had noted a few things during this inspection, and we addressed them. What I was trying to determine was whether my new crew chief was completely ignorant of the UH-1D's needs or whether he was just too incompetent on an attitude level? This had to be considered immediately before this aircraft fell out of the sky, or worse. Relating to aviation maintenance crews was different from some other branch of the Army where discipline has to be carried out, but the negligence of the EM in question there, in most cases, isn't going to make you inevitably crash and burn. No matter how Johnson reacted to my harsh appraisal of him at first sight, I had to ascertain some things right away. He seemed nervous and unsure of himself, but he was not dumb, just undereducated in an unprepared way, despite his obvious intelligence. I decided he might come up to speed if we all kept on him. I knew I could depend on the other EM to give me the straight skinny if he couldn't cut the mustard. Maybe there was hope. We went flying.

I found out later he hated me at that first moment of contact. That was OK in the Army; we weren't supposed to love each other, just obey what rank imposed upon our individual lives. I was sure going to miss MacDougal, and I knew there was nothing I could do about getting him back, since he'd left the Army. Whatever was going to develop here would run its course; I knew this was the essence of being an officer. You had to work with what was given to you.

O'Kane was still platoon leader during this time, and he had yet another "deal" for me. He had made me scheduling officer for the missions in the platoon, and this was quite a load. By now, I was well used to his leaning on me for my own development as a young officer, and with all the responsibility I'd handled during college, I knew I could handle it—eventually. One day, he came up to me on the airstrip and complained that I was not keeping the ACs with their particular ships every flying day, and he wanted it done that way. I asserted that I was having some trouble assigning missions and rotating aircraft in for their 100-hour maintenance shifts, but I'd get better at it. He snapped, "Don't get better at it; do it!" "Yessir," I replied. This rank thing worked two ways. After that, he had yet another situation for me to handle.

"I'm handing you Mike Farr as your door gunner. He's trained as a crew chief but is not very good at maintaining a ship. I've taken him off crew chief orders and demoted him to door gunner. He's yours. See what you can do with him, and let me know if he screws up at *all!* And I mean *at all!*"

Good God, I thought, as I watched him walk away. Talk about the pressures of command. Lucky me to be able to relieve him of so much of it! I looked at poor Mike Farr, who had climbed into the right-hand seat in the rear of the Huey, where door gunners always sat. He looked like a beautiful blond orphan boy dumped off somewhere not to his liking. Utter dejection was all over his baby-faced countenance. I had a hard time believing anybody so young and wholesome looking could be *that bad* a crew chief. I pondered, and then I asked him, "Are you *really* that bad?"

"I guess so, sir. I tried my best and I guess they don't like me much."

"Well, now, I can't afford to have *two* bad crew chiefs. We have to do something here. Either I can face that, which I can't, or I can start perceiving that I'm very lucky to have one-and-a-half crew chiefs, and no other AC that I've noticed has that privilege! Can we work from there? Can you learn from Johnson, and can you teach him something he doesn't know about yet? Can we do this?"

I remained stunned and imperturbed at the same time. Something had to give here. Mike Farr looked over at Johnson on the other side of the ship, and Johnson glanced back at this waif through the Huey's cabin area. Their eyes read each other for a serious moment, and Johnson looked away. Mike kept looking at Johnson, and then replied, "Yessir, we can do it." Johnson looked up only a moment, then back down, but he nodded, "Yes, we'll do that. We'll work together."

"OK," I said. "Let's try to get this ship up to where it's supposed to be and at least improve it to where it's not the "dog" of the second platoon."

They both nodded and said they definitely could do that part, it was pretty basic.

"You *CAN?* That would be great! Let's start from there; let's show somebody what we can do!" I was actually full of spirit, or relief or something. Whew! Maybe this leadership thing wasn't so bad after all.

The hard aspect of being a pilot is that you are not also a mechanic. Some pilots are, but it is rare. This is rather like being a sailor or a boatbuilder. Not many people can do both, which is to build the thing *and* sail it around the world. Nice dreaming, but it usually doesn't cut it. The other part of this dilemma is that it is cruel to take an experienced maintenance person and make *him* a pilot. In our flight-school class were some old warrant officers who had waited throughout their careers to enter flight school after crewing everything in the Army and Air Force inventory. While they were initially happy to be pursuing their lifetime dream, it quickly became obvious that *they knew too much* about what could go wrong with the aircraft. In our dumb, innocent naiveté, we just saw a speck of grease on the cockpit's bubble; in their minds, they saw the whole rotor system coming apart. One very experienced warrant at my table in Primary Helicopter School actually crash-landed his Hiller OH-23 just because his Plexiglas door came open on the right side. He even called in an emergency to the tower. (Their reply to his call was, "Well, why don't you just land and close the thing?") In his earnestness (or perhaps fear), he put it down in a plowed field so hard that he broke the rear crosstube joining the skids. The hard landing created more damage to the small training helicopter than the loose door ever could have, but he imagined that flimsy thing coming completely off and going back through the tail rotor. He was very proud of how he'd handled the affair for quite a few weeks—until he came to a full understanding of his foolishness. After that, he never really recovered from his shame. When these guys got to Vietnam, they were best kept in the hangar as maintenance test pilots. The rest of us could be daring young men in our flying machines.

Learning all you could while preflighting an aircraft was good, but it took me almost a whole year to have the fingertip skill our EM had in checking out the hub. There were bearings up there that had ten-thousandths of an inch of play, or even twenty-thousandths of an inch. Try figuring out that much motion by squeezing something the thickness of a piece of paper. You could feel proud you were beginning to duplicate the manual dexterity of your maintenance people, but you were still only approximating it. When you had the best crew chief in the platoon, you could walk proud. It was also very good life insurance; they were irreplaceable. This was what made a crew tight: the best AC, the best crew chief, and the best door gunner who never let the M-60s jam when you needed them to be firing. The only new element introduced everyday was the peter pilot getting his copilot experience while rotating from ship to ship during his apprenticeship. When the whole platoon was cookin', that copilot was receiving some very good, informative development indeed. Trust was the word here; mutual admiration was the next emotional experience. A topnotch crew was envied and respected, and its reputation was known all over the compound. The affection we could have for each other on a Huey was palpable.

The point is that the AC might hard-ass his crew chief into becoming a better mechanic, but it was up to the other enlisted men in the unit to clue in this novice about what he should be doing. Only they could share with him the knowledge of what he must do to keep the ship flyable. In the Army, the crews had to fly on the very ships they maintained, so there was some strong motivation. No sense dying as a result of your own incompetence.

As the crew chief developed skills and confidence, both the AC and the crew could commit to caring about the aircraft and bringing it up to the highest standard. Everyone could look forward to PE, the periodic 100-hour maintenance working-over of the ship, and requisitioning new components and various equipment or materiel. It became fun to make our ship the envy of the platoon and a joy to fly, and to register the feeling of tightness in our crew that made other air crews wonder how we had achieved that. We became cocky in our success.

This is what Mike Farr and Ron Johnson undertook after that conversation we had. Each day, we would all work hard toward the goal of being a whole lot better than where we started. I was such a green pilot that it took all my skill to take off with loads in this weak ship. All the other D-models could make it off the runway with 10 ARVN; I could only do it with nine when fully fueled. The engine ran hot, even up to the red line. No one in Outlaw Maintenance ever figured out why Outlaw 23 always ran this way. Perhaps it was a short-shaft problem; we'll never know. Even with a new engine that was installed at a much later date, the ship was always weaker than its sister ships. We fixed up everything else, but that despicable matter remained. This helicopter flew beautifully, though, and always did everything you intended to do with it. It was just gutless.

Many times, Johnson painted the floor its proper gray color. Every chance he had, he installed new seats—nylon and very light, exquisite in their collapsible design. They were taken out on troop lifts and reinstalled when we were ferrying passengers on single-ship missions to the towns and outposts. I think everything was replaced sooner or later. At times, I felt we were completely rebuilding the aircraft. We got better, and so did Outlaw 23. It became clean and shiny.

Johnson was funny. He had a head of black hair and grew a mustache to go with it, of course. He often wore sunglasses and thought he had a way with the Vietnamese. We all wished we could communicate with the peasants who flocked aboard our ship as the safest and cheapest transportation around, but this was mostly wishful thinking. Here we were, living in a strange land, and none of us spoke the language! We could not believe the Army had never given us *any* language training in preparation for our tour of duty, supposedly assisting these people in their time of need. Bar-girl talk sufficed, and I don't pretend to this day that we had any real command of that, either. Probably the natives thought we were absolute fools even to try talking to them, because the Vietnamese language was full of idioms and regional dialects that emphasized certain accented word sounds. Even if the Army had tried to teach us, we would have had a very difficult time attempting to learn this language. So we just got through one day at a time, assuming we knew what the peasants were saying or talking about all around us. Since the crew members spent so much of their leisure moments downtown, they felt they knew something about communicating with the local people. We officers were pretty suspicious of that, but we let them have their illusions. There were plenty of other things to be concerned about besides their reports about the whores.

The crews did funny things that surprised us officers from time to time, especially when we were new pilots. An experienced crew member might say one day, "Sir, can you turn on the radio?" You'd look down on the radio console and wonder what the hell he was taking about, as all the aircraft's radios were certainly turned on.

"They *are* all on. What do you mean?"

"Turn on the one with the rock-and-roll, sir."

You'd stare blankly at the AC and shrug inquisitively. Then the experienced pilot would come back to you: "They want the nav switch on their intercom panels up so they can listen to the automatic direction finder tuned into the Saigon Armed Forces radio station." He would lean over and roll in the AM frequency. It was rather like in the old days, when flying the U.S. mail in Gypsy Moths was done by homing into one commercial broadcast station after another, and flying to that tower in the next town. The ADF had a small handle for tuning in the station, in the "null," and there you were. Into the headsets of the crew came the Rolling Stones just as fine as could be—good ol' rock-'n'-roll from the States being piped into the flight helmets in the backseat. The ADF's needle pointed north to Saigon.

"Thank you, sir."

Flying troop lifts was the hardest part of working with Outlaw 23. As the ARVNs filed on board, Johnson and the door gunner had to grab them however they could, usually by the backs of their collars, and pull them against the helicopter's transmission. The next five troops were inserted into the crotches of the first ones seated on the floor, and as rapidly as possible. This was done rather roughly, in the most expedient manner possible. Up front, I didn't care how this was accomplished; we had to take off fully loaded pretty quickly with the lift. It didn't make much sense to these passengers that they were crammed toward the rear of the aircraft, when there was half again as much floor space in front of them. There was no time to explain that this was all a matter of CG. The center of gravity was under the mast of the helicopter; if the load was any farther forward toward the nose of the machine, it meant a more difficult takeoff. I doubt the average Vietnamese soldier would have able to comprehend such an explanation, nor did we give it to them. So they were rudely manhandled into place by the American crews as quickly and adroitly as possible. Each of the crew chiefs and door gunners had his own techniques of accomplishing this. I saw one crew member just take his hand like a basketball player and mash the steel-pot helmet over an ARVN's face and maneuver him around blindly until he sat him down appropriately. At this point, it was a good idea to intervene, because this callous treatment could get your crew shot if that lean, little

Vietnamese soldier was having a bad day.

Usually, however, they were quite placid and had an aura as if it were no big deal to go to war every day. They liked being photographed in the backseat for authentic pictures to send to the folks back home. The smile of Buddha adorned their boyish faces for these poses; I think they thought they were going to make the front page of a major newspaper. If they moved around for comfort after takeoff, they often sat five abreast at each side of the cargo space of the Huey. Nothing to hold onto, just swinging their feet in the breeze at 2,500 feet as if they were aboard the best amusement park ride in the Delta. They seemed fearless about the possibility of falling out. Looking about the flight, there were scores of D-models from the four companies of the Delta Aviation Battalion, wearing their various insignias from their units on their fuselages, loaded with nonchalant Vietnamese soldiers sitting in the doors. This scene seemed totally incongruous at first, but we got used to seeing it.

Sometimes they were so relaxed, they'd fall asleep. They would nod off, still holding onto their carbines and the old surplus M-1s we had emptied out of our military warehouses. (I had to learn that their slight bodies were as strong as ours were, and capable of carrying these nine-pound rifles.) Johnson developed a technique of waking them up just prior to the final approach to the LZ. He took an aluminum seat support that looked like the baton you use in track meets; it was about the same heft as well as length. He then rapped it on the helmets of the sleeping Vietnamese. You could hear him going, "Dong, dong, ding, dong," like he was playing "The Bells of Saint Mary's." He lightly tapped each helmet in turn, and the little ARVNs would wake up, shaking their heads sheepishly, and ready themselves to go into battle. The technique seemed to work, so I left him alone.

One time, during short approach, I could hear Johnson laughing loudly over the flight sounds of the Huey. I asked him what was going on back there, and over the intercom came: "Nothing, I'll tell you later." He hardly could get that out, he was guffawing so hard. I turned around and looked at him sitting in his crew chief's seat on the left side of the ship; he was doubled up in giggles, holding his mouth. There was a carbine dangling from his mounted M-60, swaying by its sling in the slipstream. It was upside down, just hanging there off the machine gun. "What the hell is that?" I inquired. "I said I'll tell ya later!" he replied again. "OK," was all I said.

When he regained his composure and we were well out of the LZ and regaining altitude, I asked if he could tell me what the carbine was about. He described what had happened:

"You know how I tap these guys on the helmet just before landing?" he asked.

"Yeah, I know you do that, what's that got to do with the swinging carbine?"

"Well, this one guy just woke up and went *right out the door!*" Johnson told me, breaking up again. The guy's carbine got hooked on the machine gun.

"Hey, weren't we up about 1,000 feet when he did that?" I asked.

"Yeah, yeah. Yeah!" and he cracked up again.

I just shook my head and directed my attention forward again. The EM could see humor in these incidents beyond which we could fathom as officers. Stranger things than this would occur during our year of flying these Vietnamese around. Brother. One time, on another ship, a crew member started screaming over the intercom, "There's a *hand* walking around back here!" As grisly as this war was, the AC at least had the presence of mind to know that a severed hand cannot walk around by itself, so he replied, "Well, see if the hand is attached to something!"

The crew chief looked out over the side of the ship and, peering down at the undercarriage, saw a scrawny Vietnamese hanging there on a flange of the left skid. His pack strap had hooked on the small piece of metal upon takeoff, and he had been picked up while on departure. For quite some time, he had been at altitude, with a lot of air between him and the ground, swaying by the shoulder strap of his own knapsack. After a while, apparently he had tried to signal his presence to the enlisted crew inside. He had extended his hand just far enough to reach above the floor, and his fingers were tapping right inside the open door to try to alert someone to his predicament. I don't know what the outcome of this story was. He might have fallen off soon afterward, or remained in that state until the aircraft touched down and released him from the skid. I have always had a mental picture of that guy dangling there in the breeze and have wondered what prayers were being formed in his mind.

We certainly never would have treated American troops with such disregard. That was very apparent to us. There was prejudice and racial disdain by our EM toward the small Vietnamese soldiers. The EM quickly registered early on that there was no basis in reality for the notion that the United States was here to assist the Saigon government. They formed their opinions in the first few weeks in Vietnam, totally abandoning the John Wayne version of our purpose of being in this Indochina predicament. As officers, we had some hazy historical knowledge of the French occupation of this country, but we realized we were going to learn a lot more before this year was over. The average enlisted man had no such intellectual hunger for learning about this recent past; he just saw things as they were and had no regard whatsoever for the South Vietnamese or the Saigon government. Any vestiges of patriotism and allegiance to America's foreign policy disappeared fairly quickly among these young men, who represented a broad cross section of the U.S. populace. And their negative attitude was constantly exhibited with animosity toward the ARVN soldiers.

On takeoff with Outlaw 23, we often had to lighten the load in order to get airborne. Unlike the other Hueys with a standard complement of troops, we could not make it with 10 ARVNs in the backseat and a full fuel load of 1,400 pounds. As we lumbered along at our allotted point of departure, the RPM would bleed off from 6,600 to a low of 6,200 with the overload on the turbine. This meant that the aircraft was dragging down the rotor RPM as well, thus resulting in only half the lift that the blades needed for flying. Halfway down the instrument panel, the red square of the low-

RPM light would come on, flashing "Emergency!" and the low-RPM audio siren would sound in our headphones. That alarm's sound was worse than the flying problem we were having, and the guys would attempt to turn off that toggle switch when they heard this ludicrous screaming sound in the headset. But since the RPM would still be below normal, the alarm would just reset and continue beeping insanely in our ears, "Beep-beep-beep-beepn!!" "Gawd! I hate that," the guys would exclaim, and wishfully keep switching the thing off, which would come right back on anyway. It was more worthwhile for the other pilot to call off the RPM as it came back up than it was to keep flicking that switch. Scared us, it did, that metallic sound.

The EM in the back were all too familiar with that flashing red light on the panel, and they would already have grabbed an ARVN by the shirt collar with one hand and webbed belt at the waist with the other—ready to heave. At the next bounce, they'd toss the soldier onto the runway, eliminating a hundred pounds or so. If the aircraft still could not fly then, the AC would yell, "Throw another one out!" Usually at this point, however, the ship would become airborne after screeching sparks down the airstrip, attempting to take off. This was a common occurrence in the D-model. We didn't know if these Vietnamese soldiers received any damage or not from this practice; no one ever commented later. After burning off some fuel in flight, we could take off a whole lot better for the rest of the lift, but that initial departure, fully fueled, was a tickler. It was nice to have a strong ship; Outlaw 23 wasn't, and I'll always retain an image of Johnson with his sunglasses, as dark as his mustache and hair, totally concentrating on that red light, with his hands on the ARVN in mind, and ready.

14

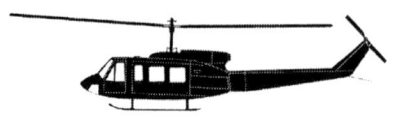

VI THANH

EPITAPH
On 14 January 1967, 1st Lt. Arthur Russell LeGrow, Jr., crashed and burned in a small clearing in the jungle somewhere near Bien Hoa. While flying with the 173rd Assault Helicopter Company, his 90-degree tail-rotor gearbox separated from the aircraft while in formation flight. He died in a UH-1D with the tail number 65-09595. He was the first person from our flight-school class to be killed. Apparently his intuition was very accurate, indeed. . . .

EVER SINCE I FIRST ARRIVED at Vinh Long and was assigned to the second platoon of the 175th Aviation Company, Airmobile Light, I had heard about Vi Thanh. It wasn't just the name of the airstrip out of which we staged in the southern end of the Delta; it was about a battle that surprised the second lift one day landing in an LZ that turned out to be very bad news. I never learned exactly what happened in this event, which occurred prior to my arrival, but it was always discussed in a tone that sounded very sinister and macabre. The VC had had the upper hand that day and inflicted very great losses upon the ARVN and the American helicopter crews that ferried them in. If you had been there that day, you were a combat veteran; everyone who had weathered the experience agreed completely with that assessment.

Harvey Persyn and Major O'Kane had arrived very late that fatal day at the Vi Thanh airstrip. They had been flying elsewhere and were designated to show up toward the end of their mission and report directly to Vi Thanh. When they got there, Harvey explained, a flight of about 12 Hueys was coming in to land in straight trail. Corpses filled the cargo areas of all the Hueys; at least 10 dead ARVN were in each aircraft. These bodies were offloaded and placed into the huge interior of a C-119, the famous "Flying Boxcar" of World War II vintage. O'Kane was newly arrived in-country, and he and Harvey observed the carnage from the day's battle. Harvey never got over the sight and scale of so many dead Vietnamese soldiers from that one attack upon the landing formation. None of the pilots who received that fire ever forgot that onslaught, either. Vi Thanh remained the worst thing that had happened to anyone on his tour in the Delta.

As many times as we had flown out of the small airstrip halfway between Can Tho and the U-Minh Forest, we had not experienced anything as bad as these guys had seen many months earlier at Vi Thanh. It seemed like a bad rumor to overhear, and probably struck us as something that would never happen again, especially to us. But it did, on 15 February 1967—the "Second Vi Thanh." This episode taught me for the first time what combat was actually about. I never thought I would live through the length of that day.

Mike Stansbury was my copilot. While flying together in the early morning, I had been explaining to him our tactics if and when we took fire. We were to be the second lift into the landing zone. The first group into the LZ had experienced some small-arms fire, so I told Mike that since we had established contact with the enemy, we would shift over 500 yards or more, and drop the troops we had on board a safe distance away. They would engage the dug-in enemy as they moved in on foot. Mike listened attentively as he understood that this was a good idea. He was on the controls as the gunship platoon leader radioed us instructions for landing the second wave we were carrying. Suddenly I realized that these were the same directions he had given for the first lift! We were going to land in the hot LZ! "Holy cow!" I said. "We're not supposed to be doing this! We're going to get our ass shot off." Since we were at the tail end of the formation, which had gone to staggered trail, I told Johnson to shoot *any bush* that looked like VC. I was afraid they would target the ships that were last into the LZ; they had a way of waiting until you were all in, then opening up on the stragglers in the rear, where we were. Johnson agreed with the suggestion and was ready on the gun. The hazy, early morning light was beautiful on the straw-colored grass, and also on the long columns of Hueys from several companies as they settled in for a landing. As we touched down, the formation of the dual columns looked competent and perfectly arranged for an aviation photo.

Instead of our being hit from the rear, the front of the flight got it, and suddenly, too. I looked up and saw Captain Stewart's lead aircraft, of the 336th "Warriors," flip over onto its right side. Thirty- and fifty-caliber fire had raked his ship, and he died with a bullet between the eyes. As he was hit, he clutched the cyclic to his chest, and that turned over the aircraft before the copilot could react to this reflex. The ship's rotor blade was sticking straight up into the air. I'd never seen a bird in that condition; it was shocking and unreal. ARVN squads getting out of the Hueys were being mowed down in the deep, blond rice paddy grass as if a giant piano wire were sweeping through the LZ, cutting them off at the knees. Whole squads of ARVNs were losing their lives due to the grazing fire. The radio was full of guys screaming, "I'm hit. I'm hit! I'm HIT!" Rounds were coming into most of the ships up front. Jack Payne said the ARVNs never made it out of his aircraft; the Knight pilot saw the men buckle as they exited his ship. The same bullets hitting them laced his right front door and bounced off his armor-plated seat. I looked all across the landing zone and saw similar scenes repeated. Total mayhem.

Mike Stansbury never faltered on the controls, and he called out to the crew as he swung the tail boom around: "Turning left, clear my tail right." The EM in the backseat did so, but still had not fired at anything in our area of the formation. We had lucked out. All the action was up in front of us, and the VC had sprung up out of fortified positions, firing out of trenches on three sides of the landing zone directly into our lift. They had shown superb discipline, waiting until we were at a hover, attacking us while we were in our most vulnerable condition. Then they had let us have it. I was petrified, and amazed at how cool Stansbury was under fire. He was performing exquisitely for a new guy. He needed no help from me, and I did not know if I could give him any if he asked. He calmly continued to turn the Huey around.

We climbed out as aircraft continued to fall out of the sky around us. There really wasn't a formation, and I was hoping desperately that somebody would come up with one. We formed up on one ship that happened to be in last place on the way in, figuring he might be the guy to follow out, because we were departing in the exact opposite direction from where we had flown in. Mike said, "What do I do?" I replied that he should keep on flying on this ship; everybody else who was still in the air was beginning to do that. The UHF was still full of pilots screaming. The visual effect of watching the ships get shot down was rather like watching trailer trucks on the George Washington Bridge go right down through the asphalt lanes of the bridge and fall into the water far below. I wasn't used to seeing aircraft cease flying because of gunfire. It was unnerving, to put it mildly. They weren't supposed to be doing the bad things they were doing all around me. The guy we were forming on was only going 60 knots or so, and he was worrying me, too. Finally, someone said, "Uh, aircraft in the lead, can you pick up the airspeed a little bit?" As I said, "Yay!" to myself, back came a cracker accent, the voice of a lifer: "I ain't in charge of this show." Oh, my God, not even now, not even at this moment of being under fire will one of these son-of-a-bitching lifers ever take command of a situation! At that, a captain from Soc Trang moved forward, passed in front of the lifer's aircraft, and took the lead. Whew! Thank you! We were going to live!

I looked over at Stansbury and told him, "Buddy, you've got ice water in your veins. You were cool as a cucumber back there! My hat's off to you!" He replied, "Gee whiz, thanks." I nodded, impressed.

"How about that helicopter tipped over back there! Wasn't that something?" I said.

"What helicopter tipped over?" says Mike, staring over at me, then back.

"The one that was flying Lead. The one that got shot. Didn't you see that?"

"See what? Who got shot?" inquired Mike, still focusing on the lead aircraft.

"You mean you didn't see any of that back there? All the ARVN and everything?" I was getting incredulous.

"No," said Mike, as he started to get the picture. Meanwhile, the medevac was getting shot down as it made the required rescuing approach to the downed crews. We could hear that Mayday over the air. Mike stayed fixed on the aircraft which he was flying a 45 on, but he was beginning to lose it.

"Hey," I said, "don't you get the shakes! I can't fly over here. I'll stop talking."

He had not seen a thing. When a new pilot joins a unit, he can't do anything except fly the aircraft and listen for landing and departure instructions on the platoon FM frequency. He can't even monitor yet what's going on over the company UHF channel. His vision is so concentrated on the gauges and what he is doing in the immediate vicinity of the aircraft that it takes months before he can entertain other information beyond this periphery. Mike had missed the whole terror show.

My whole body was jumpy, and I couldn't stop shaking and quivering in my seat. I was glad that Mike was still able to fly, even though I thought it mildly humorous that even with all his natural aviator skills, he had not noticed the catastrophe happening all around him. When we shut down at Vi Thanh, I got out and desperately needed to walk the strip. Quite agitated, I paced up one side of the runway and then back down it again. I had never been so conscious of living one minute—no, one second—of my life at a time. I couldn't cope with the next instant, much less comprehend that I still had to get through the rest of the day. I couldn't see how that could happen. I knew there would be many more missions into that LZ during that day, and I just couldn't perceive how I was going to do that flying. Others were also walking about, keeping their thoughts to themselves. We certainly didn't converse. I had never felt emotions like what I was experiencing; they were completely new to me and very overwhelming. I kept striding, eventually realizing that nothing was going to miraculously fix my situation. I went back to the ship.

Missions were being readied. We would be assigned to go back out there in groups of three to five ships at a time. The more experienced ACs would lead these little flights. We had requests to go to particular squads in the LZ for medevacs or pickups of materiel they thought important for intelligence matters. I was too rattled to pay much attention to these instructions. Just going took all my effort. We cranked and took off, heading southerly back to that river-bend LZ.

We broke out of the sky and descended rapidly in a low-level, high-speed approach. The Delta was so flat that you had to maneuver quickly and fly as flat-out, close to the ground as possible on the way in. Gunships averted collisions with us as we passed under them. Once into the LZ, I saw an advisor stand up, his upraised arms in the position that meant to land right at him. I did so. He was a sergeant and not in a good mood. His men started loading old French machine guns into the cabin behind me. I started shrieking out the window at him that I wasn't here for rusty old French machine guns, give me something else! I could see his mouth moving with words, like, "You goddamn fugging lieutenant!" I was yelling back equally intelligent statements like, "You goddamn fugging sergeant!" We were having a fine old time as the mortar rounds began dropping in on our position. Meanwhile, my crew had dumped the old relics of the French and Japanese occupation out the far door and had loaded the ship with Vietnamese wounded, whom I thought far more deserving of my valor. We pulled pitch and turned right just as the incoming mortar rounds found their range and landed where we had just been. I looked out to the front, and a similar thing was happening to Dickie Hyde in Outlaw 25. Beneath him, the concussions of the exploding mortar rounds were forcing the helicopter into an extreme position, angled way up on its nose. I thought, "Now, that looks interesting." I followed him out myself, realizing that all this rice paddy mud was absorbing a lot of shrapnel that otherwise would have been penetrating the thin skins of our aircraft. Lucky me to be flying in this war instead of somewhere else.

We got back to the airstrip OK and then waited for the others to return and check their condition. After I shut down and looked things over, we were still all right. At that point, another flight of Hueys was coming down the runway from their time in hell, and Stets was with that bunch. I realized he was in trouble. Smoke was pouring from his aircraft, and I hoped he'd get to the ground in time. "Oh God, Oh God," I thought. "Not him. Not HIM!" I couldn't imagine what was causing all that smoke. As he touched down, we excitedly ran up and inspected the ship all over. Opening up the right side engine-compartment doors to check the damage, we saw a bullet hole about an inch from the bottom of his engine oil cooler. The remainder left in the tank was the only thing that had kept the turbine from freezing up. All the rest of the liquid lubricant had sprayed out over the fuselage, and it was smoking where it had hit the hot exhaust stack of the Huey. It was a wonder the ship had not caught fire, but maybe engine oil doesn't burn up that way. It didn't that day, in any case. I ran around and said, "You were just about out of oil. You're luckier than hell!"

"Oh, yeah? Look at this!" he said, pointing to a huge blotch torn out of the sliding panel on his armor-plated seat. A round had hit right where his head would have been if the shield hadn't been there. Another bullet had come up through the floor of the aircraft and bumped into the bottom of his armor-plated seat. He was safe, and also grounded until the ship was repaired. Mike Hershey, another classmate in that platoon, came up and said under his breath to Stets, "You lucky sonofabitch"—Fred's being at risk that flying day was over. My concern for my good friend was also relieved, but this was the first time I had to consider the idea of great harm coming to my buddy. Not pleasant to think about. It was another emotion I experienced for the first time completely and deeply.

We would go in for quite a few more missions that day. The

more we did, the better I felt; it was good to find you could live through it. The VC stayed in contact throughout the remainder of the day's fighting, then slipped away across the river in the darkness. With it at their backs, they'd been trapped all day. We would have to go in at night and extract the South Vietnamese troops without revealing ourselves. By this time, it wouldn't be a great challenge to do anything I would have thought impossible that morning; I just wanted to stay alive. Mike Hershey led a flight of us in there, and to this day, I'm still amazed about it. We went in completely blacked out, not even running lights, in staggered trail, low-level. Without the benefit of landing lights, we dodged bushes and small trees at 80 knots almost by sheer intuition alone. I could sense one coming and lift up just enough as the vegetation went by in the darkness. I was pretty proud of us by the time we reached the touchdown point. Then we circled around in the dark like square-dancers; we didn't hit each other or chicken out and turn on a landing light. We then set down, picked up the remaining ARVN forces, and departed. When the next flight came in to pick up the very last of these troops, they used their landing lights and immediately received mortar fire. Ray Leuty's ship took a direct hit in his fuel cell, and his crew chief was hurt. Upon hearing this transmission out of that LZ, we were very glad we had not taken a chance with any lights. But we weren't home yet, we realized. Eventually the day's work was over and we headed back to Vinh Long to sleep.

This was the first time some of us received decorations, so we learned what earned you a medal. Some of the EM got the Soldier's Medal for getting out of the aircraft in the LZ mud and assisting the wounded into the helicopter. All the pilots received an Air Medal with "V" device for flying into the fire, including myself. Depending on their actions, some people received more, such as Distinguished Flying Crosses. We were now combat veterans, and we discussed what constant exposure to this type of action might do our psyches. Most agreed we'd go nuts.

I think the funniest story about anyone getting medals that day came from Dickie Black; I heard the tale a short time later at the officers' club bar in Vinh Long. He told me he had gotten the Purple Heart, and I was impressed, but I didn't see where any bullets had come and gone through him. He replied that they hadn't.

It seems that Don Seliski was looking for flight time, as usual, and for some reason replaced Dickie's copilot in a D-model on the Vi Thanh airstrip. Maybe Dickie's other seat had been hurt, I don't know. Ski soon would have plenty of work rigging the downed ships in the LZ and on the Vi Thanh airstrip; they did that a day or two later when the action ceased. Ten ships were nonflyable from that day's shoot-'em-up, but Ski would recover them all, to be fixed up by the maintenance crews in the various aviation companies. It seemed as though Hueys could be patched up indefinitely; they were great warhorses. The media never quite understood that truism; 10 ships lost that day did not mean they were lost forever. No glory there (sigh . . .).

Dickie Black later flew in either the Cobras or the Lancers of the 114th, a gunship heavy aviation company, but that day he was still flying slicks in the Knights. Apparently a round came through the Plexiglas window of the right door and hit Dickie in the head. Stunned, he turned to Ski and said, "Where did this bullet hole in my window come from?" Ski busted up laughing, and said, "You just got *shot!*" He was laughing because Dickie's flight helmet had twisted around on his head so that only one eye was showing, and the earphone on the side of the helmet where the round had smacked him was dangling ridiculously alongside his face. Anyone who knew these two personalities would have realized they should not have been flying in the same gunship together! Both realized what had been said, grabbed the controls, and got out of there through their joint efforts.

Dickie received the Purple Heart not because of the round that had tunneled around inside his flight helmet between his scalp and its material—he never did shed any blood from the bullet—but because a sliver of Plexiglas from the shot-up window had scratched his wrist and given him a half-inch cut. That's what his Purple Heart was for—not for getting hit in the head by an enemy projectile! Nah! You need to bleed for a Purple Heart! I began to get used to these bizarre stories.

I learned several lessons from that day's events. One, the VC were mobile at night and settled down in previously fortified circumstances during the day. They weren't just wandering about, which I guess is what we thought. If we found them en masse, it was because we had foolishly landed right on top of their entrenched positions, so they had to fight when discovered. They were tremendously disciplined and dedicated fighters and knew how to grease us once we had disturbed them. An appropriate analogy might be that it was like landing into a hornets' nest. Two, if there was a river behind the LZ at their backs, which they couldn't cross safely until nightfall, that meant we would have a pitched battle until day's end. Over time, we realized a couple of points about getting into a heavy firefight. They occurred for two reasons: either the Vietnamese brass *knew* the VC were in their entrenched positions or they *didn't know* they were there and the guerrillas surprised us. Either situation was devastating to the vulnerable helicopters. We sure found Charlie.

Extraordinarily, the ARVN brass always left a means for the VC to get away; we referred to it as leaving the back door open. They did it almost tactfully, even diplomatically—almost as though the VC could save face by escaping instead of being annihilated. The Americans could never understand why the Saigon troops did this when we were over there for one big manhunt of a war. We were supposed to kill Communists; didn't everyone else want to do that, too? To the South Vietnamese, letting the VC get away at the final hour was just good military planning. So they left, and the ARVN did, too, at the end of the day's fight. All our battles were in the LZs where we had inserted the troops that morning; they didn't go anywhere beyond this point. The fighting was always at point-blank range, and the gunships were our air strikes, artillery, and everything else. Their suppressive fire kept enemy heads down while we performed our valiant resupply, medevac, and rescue missions for the rest of the day. Often the enemy was within 150 yards (or less) during the firefights. We flew right up to positions in contact with VC forces well in sight. We had to get things done quickly or become casualties ourselves. "Fly fast!" we would jokingly say. We began to understand why the frustrated American command wanted to lead American troops into battle with this elusive enemy. They felt deeply that they could do much better than what they had experienced for several years with the ARVN. And that is how the war expanded so much beyond the level with which we were dealing in the early part of the war up to 1966 and 1967.

One last note. On that fatal day at Vi Thanh, all the cameras that we had purchased in the PXs before this lift were stolen from our helmet bags by the Vietnamese soldiers we were flying into and out of that hot LZ. Our guys had a habit of keeping their Pentaxes and Canons hidden under their seats, zipped up in their empty helmet bags while flying. This was a handy location for instant retrieval from between your legs if you wanted to snap a picture. These were valuable SLRs and proud possessions. Every single one on board that day was pilfered by the ARVN troops we transported out of the Vi Thanh airstrip during that operation. They just reached under the seats from behind and sneaked them out when we weren't looking. This affected our attitude and damaged our morale almost as much as being shot up.

15

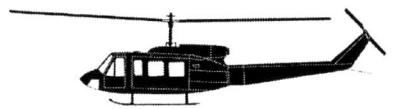

A CLOSE CALL UPON MY LIFE

MIKE FARR AND RON JOHNSON had taken the ship's condition pretty far in the time we had been together on Outlaw 23. They did some very good work on the ship one down day, and they told me about it on the company street at Vinh Long, just outside the 175th Company headquarters. Both saluted me there and reported that they had devoted the entire day to working hard on the ship's appearance and maintenance. They felt particularly good about their progress. Maj. Don Casper overheard the conversation from behind my shoulder and was smiling at the building camaraderie among us, as crew and AC. I ribbed them a bit but was proud of their devotion and the skill level they were attaining. I felt sure we were going to make it, and that made me feel better than I could adequately express.

Determined to increase my working knowledge of the Huey's innards myself, I asked Johnson if I might help out some day and gain a bit of appreciation of the maintenance required to keep the bird flying. I didn't think it was anything I could retain, but I supposed it would build morale if I assisted my crew chief with his routine tasks. He said, sure, he'd be glad to have me around sometime on the Outlaw ramp when he was working alone. Although it was highly irregular for an officer to help out this way, I thought some mechanical experience might increase my ability to fly the ship. It was sort of a reverse move on our teaching the crews to fly the Huey when we could. I was a little leery of proposing this, because some of the officers senior to me thought Johnson and I were getting a bit too close with each other, and it is always deemed improper for an officer to get overly familiar with his EM. I went forward with this idea anyway, taking the risk.

Come the day this was agreed on, I was in a T-shirt and fatigue pants, looking on dumbly while he had the Huey's turbine open in a way I had never seen. I didn't have a clue what he was telling me or anything. He said we were changing O-rings—thin, doughnut-shaped rubber rings that looked like they'd be rubber bands when they grew up. I could rapidly see this was going to be a waste of time—his and mine. Our preflight inspection had always been just a matter of checking to see if the nozzles he had removed were put back on correctly. I wasn't mechanically inclined enough to comprehend what he was telling me—which of course made him feel superior and start lording it over me. I felt reduced to a "gopher," not an aviator assisting his crew chief in getting the aircraft ready for flight. As I continued to feel stupid, he escalated quickly to being *my boss*. This was rapidly becoming unworkable, and I was glad no other members of my platoon were there to watch this situation develop.

Then he said he didn't have the proper-size O-rings and would have to take a trip to the hangar to get the right ones. "You stay here and watch the ship," he said. "Johnson!" I bellowed. He giggled and drove away in the platoon's three-quarter-ton truck. I settled down and waited. Then I waited some more. Time passed. "He's just having a good time with his buddies in the hangar, having a good laugh on me," I was thinking. Gawd, was I beginning to rue this. Dumb!

In the heat, I was sitting in the aircraft as if I'd been spending a lazy July afternoon on a farm porch in the Midwest. To complete the scene, all I needed was a pitcher of lemonade and buzzing flies. Johnson still did not return and this was really getting boring. I kept trying to doze, shifting from one position to another; my mood was *not* improving. During one adjustment, I looked out the door of the Huey and saw a Vietnamese peasant very near the aircraft, bending over and picking up discarded M-60 machine-gun ammo bags. It was no major crime to pilfer these tiny bags with their cloth shoulder straps; we threw them away. I knew he was collecting them for his people to carry rice, but what was he doing here on our ramp? This was supposed to be a secured area. He would have had to come across mined areas, through a barbed-wire perimeter, and past sentries in sandbagged bunker positions. How could a Vietnamese civilian have such ready access to our parking area? This was spooky and unreal, like something out of the *Twilight Zone*. Obviously, he had not expected to find someone out here either, and his surprise was as great as mine.

Still clad only in a white T-shirt and olive-drab pants, I got up and said, "Hey!" He took off, looking like Santa Claus with a bundle of M-60 bags bobbing over his back. I took off after him; whatever was going on here could not be allowed. He ran down a rice paddy dike at a good clip, as I realized that he had been here many times before. He knew what he was doing. I was becoming incensed and increasingly dutiful. We always worried about the VC accessing the ramp and placing satchel charges in the aircraft at night. If any civilian peasant could walk up to our ships in broad daylight, this was a matter that needed rather complete investigation. He kept running. I settled into a miler's pace, not knowing how long I would be following this man on the earthen dike. It was quite an established footpath, I noticed. I was prepared to follow him out to the perimeter, with its tanks in sandbagged emplacements. The outer edge, with its barbed wire, was in sight. We were halfway there when he ducked into a bunker that we had been approaching. He came back out right away.

He was an ARVN! No uniform, but apparently he was one of us, our perimeter guard! Well, that was a bit of a relief—except that now he had an M-1 carbine in his hands and was pointing it right at me. He had had enough, I guess. I screeched to a halt like in a Western movie, saying, "Whoa! Easy with that thing!"—not exactly an appropriate line. He wasn't kidding around, either. He made a gesture with his head, and a roaring noise emerged from his mouth, sounding something like "Unh-h-h!" in Vietnamese. Then he chambered a round: "Ka-chin-ng!" Wow, I had never before experienced a gun being held on me, and it is the most intimidating thing in the whole world. I was looking right down the barrel, half expecting the bullet to come out and say hello to me like a ballpoint pen refill does when you click it. Sort of a preview show, like when the man who gets shot out of the cannon at the circus comes up and waves at the crowd before they blow him out of his contraption and across the arena.

There was great danger here. I had placed myself in the same circumstances our EM did when they got too rough with these leathery guys. The man muttered something guttural again and motioned with his head to scram. I said, "OK, OK!" and moved back. I turned and took the path back to the Outlaw parking ramp, hoping not to hear the crack of that small rifle behind me. I was in a sweat.

Gaining the ramp, I got into the right seat of Outlaw 23 and donned a flight helmet after hitting the battery switch overhead. I waited for the FM radio to warm up and called Outlaw Operations on 37.5, our frequency. "This is the aircraft commander of Outlaw 23. I've just had a weapon pulled on me by an unidentified Victor November on the Outlaw ramp and I want an immediate response, over."

Outlaw Operations rogered my call and said they'd have some MPs out there in a minute. I was impressed, and I had my manhood a bit reassured. There is nothing worse than being held up at the point of a gun, and then someone doubts your story. I needed to regain my moxie. There was a weak feeling throughout me; my entire body felt clammy and about as strong as a pipe cleaner. I can't say I recommend having a gun pointed at your abdomen from a few feet away; it will immediately ruin your ego—and your day.

Within a very short time, a Jeep carrying a big black MP, a small red-haired MP, and a Vietnamese QC (their military police) pulled up in front of my D-model. I told them what had occurred and proceeded to button up my first lieutenant's blouse and join them. This was the top part of the jungle fatigues, and I was beginning to realize that this guy had not known I was an officer when he pulled the carbine on me. Not only had I been out of line by assisting Johnson, but the Vietnamese sentry probably had never encountered a commissioned aviator asleep in his Huey on the flight line in the middle of the day. It was not, of course, what we normally did. I pulled down the visor of my officer's baseball cap tightly over my forehead and was fourth in the single-file pilgrimage to the ARVN's bunker.

When we all got there, out he came, smiling like a Cheshire cat, thinking he was going to be inspected. I waited until we all had stopped just in front of his sentry post, then I slowly raised the visor of my cap and gazed steadily into his eyes. All hell broke loose. He dived back into the bunker, going for that carbine. Right in behind him went the three MPs, like some vaudeville show. It was comical, but there was danger right away. I followed them into the bunker, where people were barreling around like a bingo machine loaded with Ping-Pong balls. I was wondering who would get "I-19!" This slender guy was fighting with the strength of 10 men. He knew what was going to happen to him for pulling a loaded weapon on an American officer; his life was over. The three MPs were managing OK, but this was a behemoth donnybrook. The black MP shouted, "Grab the carbine! Grab the carbine!" I said, "OK, I've got the weapon! I've got the weapon!" "You've got the weapon? You're sure?" said the red-head. "I'm sure. I'm sure!" I replied. I felt so valuable, as they continued to bounce off the walls, floor, and everything. When the three finally were close to subduing him, he held onto the barbed wire of the enclosure where he had spent so much time, and as they tried to drag him away, he insistently maintained his grip all the way to one end, raking his hands before he let go. His palms' flesh was hanging on the wire in small chunks. This fellow was one tough character; I'm glad I hadn't taken him on alone. As they handcuffed him outside the bunker's entrance, he was exhausted from his strenuous defense and resigned to his fate. Deep sobs emerged from his chest, and his face showed total dejection. He marched away with us, head down, gazing at the ground just in front of him, four or five feet or so.

Back at the helicopter, they asked me a few more questions and then drove off with their quarry in the MP Jeep. The Vietnamese man never looked up at me again. I was distraught, thinking about how such a serendipitous, unplanned incident had nearly cost me my life and was certainly going to mar his. At the end of this remarkable episode, Johnson drove up and asked what had happened. I told him that *I* nearly had gotten shot, and that *he* now had a helicopter to fix *all by himself.* He looked puzzled, but I had had enough for one day, and I strode away toward the strip.

Months later, an American officer from downtown with the ARVN compound approached me in the Vinh Long officers' club. He said that the man who had drawn the weapon on me was now coming up for trial. Did I still want to press charges? I said, "I'll bet he's been treated pretty roughly up to now, hasn't he?" The man bringing me the news only nodded up and down quietly. "Well, let's let it go then. That man probably has suffered more than enough. Anything I would testify to would cost him his life, right?" The American officer nodded again. "Then let it be over with. I can't have that man's life on my conscience." The advisor nodded once more and left.

16

PLATOON HOOCH LIFE

On down (nonflying) days, we drank beer. We also read a lot while getting a tropical tan, lazing around in our vinyl-covered chaise longues. Vinh Long had an excellent library, supremely air-conditioned, where I used to borrow many a book on Texas history and other subjects. I planned to return to Fort Wolters, Texas, as an instructor pilot. The choice, as said, was either there or Fort Rucker, and I knew I didn't want to go back to Alabama for my last year in the Army. The Palo Pinto area of Texas, where many of the stage fields were built, was the scene of many Comanche raids on the early white settlers, and for some reason there were quite a few books in the library on that era. When we were flight students there at Mineral Wells, we learned that the remains of Comanche chiefs had been found buried in the rock crevices of the cliffs when Possum Kingdom dam had been built by the WPA in the 1930s. This history fascinated me, and I endeavored to learn all I could about the mid-Texas area to which I would be returning in a year's time. The locals around Mineral Wells (which had been a health spa at one time), Jacksboro (where they had hung the last Comanche chiefs), Ranger (the town that still carried six-guns), and other outlying towns in that region had developed a hobby derived from finding arrowheads in the plowed soil of the farmlands. They would find so many that they would make decorative arrangements of their collections in various designs, showing Clovis points among the newer Comanche arrowheads. All our flying in the advanced phase of primary helicopter training would be over these cliffs and mesas around the Brazos River, and I wanted to know more than I had learned during my first time there. This historical information was a lot more interesting than just the cheap cowboy boots we had bought on our first pass in that locale. Some flight school students even bought authentic cowboy hats while attending rodeos during this portion of their aviator lives. Yee-hah!

Reading in the hot sun on these days off produced a very deep tan on one side of the body—the front. We would still be white on the backside. As our tour went on in Vinh Long, people would laugh at me when I'd get up from the chaise longue. But I was too busy reading and drinking beer in the heat to worry about it. I mean, I would have made a point to get a tan on both sides if there were girls around, but there were no girls around.

The other thing we did, besides drink beer and get a tan, was to record music on our newly purchased tape recorders. We were in Vietnam at the time when the Japanese were just starting to market their marvelous TEAC, Sony, and Akai tape decks, along with their speakers from Kenwood, Pioneer, Sansui, and others. I bought a tube amp, possibly the last of its kind, as most were fast turning to solid-state construction. Turntables were not of much use, although we bought the Garrard Lab 80 model for future enjoyment. The Vietnam PXs didn't sell any records; we had to wait for somebody's wife to send a stereo tape of some Motown group. Then everyone would copy it. By the time an "album" we desired had made the rounds of the compound for copying, the tenth or twelfth recording was pretty low in fidelity. The game was to record the master copy, if you could determine that it was such, and then always monitor the VU needles on the face of the tape deck while doing so, as though you were a professional recording engineer in the studio. This was very serious business, and you needed to coordinate with a buddy to wire together the white and red jacks of the two tape decks appropriately, so this often took some prior planning. He might be flying when you had an off day and wanted to do recording. We had fairly good electricity in Vinh Long, like everything else that was superior about the place, so we didn't have to worry about wrecking this outstanding stereo equipment. Some guys did pack up their well-researched and cherished stereo possessions and send them directly home after purchase, especially if they bought the Fisher line. Mostly, we just blared out our beloved rock-'n'-roll on our down days and steadily built a collection of the music we were missing. The Beatles saved our morale more than can be stated. The Vietnamese knew it downtown, too, and they would put green or red plastic 33 1/3 RPM pirated albums (from Hong Kong) on their turntables to make us buy more drinks, or Saigon tea for the bar girls when we weren't watching.

It was one of the incongruous things about this Vietnam tour that every single hooch room of these near-bamboo-hut-level BOQs was loaded with high quality Japanese stereo equipment. Beside the Army cot covered with mosquito netting, a small electric fan for air movement at night, and the French closet with a light bulb inside, there would be nearly $1,000 worth of high grade recording equipment in each aviator's room. This gear was of utmost concern and a prideful attainment, because we had come from postwar families of the 1950s and 1960s, where only classical music and Broadway musicals were ever played on the living room hi-fi systems. We kids only had 45 RPM portable record-players paid for with our hard-earned lawn-mowing money. Rock-'n'-roll was held in such complete disdain by our parents that it of course did not deserve to be played on high quality sound systems—ever!

So, we thought we had really made it when we bought these Japanese stereo components. As we became knowledgeable consumers, we traded off information; we all knew the price ranges, models, and, of course, the actual quality of any of this gear. I don't know of any aviator in that era who didn't load up on this equipment; we were set for life! What was cool was that with the helicopters, we could hear of PXs out in the middle of nowhere that had just received a load of Sansui or Pioneer amps or speakers, and we'd fly there. We would work into the next mission how to land directly in back of this small PX with $140 of military scrip in our pockets, buy what we wanted from that supply of receivers or whatever, and transport the precious goods back to the waiting helicopter. Our stick buddy would still be at the controls, with the ship running and holding onto everything until we got back there with our prizes. We networked constantly on where this stuff was located.

We could get pretty blitzed drinking that flat beer and overseeing all this wonderful recording, but we did take breaks to go to the officers' club for lunch. We had a very nice mess there, with the bar attached to the dining area in the Mekong Manor, as it was called. Delicately built Vietnamese women were recruited to be the waitstaff. This could get pretty funny at times, because they didn't understand much English, but we all managed.

Jon Myhre and Bob Lakey used to do a lot of recording on their tape decks in the first platoon. With their acoustic guitars, they made a pretty good folk duo. The rest of us often joined in on these recordings, doing our best to sound like Peter, Paul, and Mary or the Kingston Trio. Sometimes this impromptu folk group would serenade the Vietnamese women working at the club, just across the graveled driveway. With what these guys were delivering to them in lust-filled love songs, it's probably a very good thing these young things didn't understand English too well.

Just behind the club was a tennis court; to the north of that was a basketball court. Here and there around unit hooches were some pull-up bars and sit-up ramps. I remember the latter being used, but I never saw anyone on those pipes doing chin-ups, even though muscles do atrophy on aviators. Other activities on a down day, which occurred after about every seven to 10 days of flying, were to go swimming in the pool over at the Irish missionary nuns' convent or to go downtown itself. Some of the guys frequented "Madame Nhum's" quite a bit; I never went, so someone else can tell you those stories. If I even went into a bar, I incited all the bar girls to very bad behavior in record time, so it was bad medicine to include me in any lust-filled jaunts. "You cheap Charlie! You number 10!" these sweethearts would screech. They caught my attitude about them, I guess.

One down day, when we were still in the green Quonset huts at the far end of the compound and I had about 10 beers in me, Capt. Lou Paulin showed up, screaming in my overheated, thoroughly plastered face one afternoon: "Get down to the flight line and get out on the river! They've got a whole VC battalion crossing and it's an emergency scramble!" he yelled. "Everybody else has been flying his ass off today, and you can too!! We're damn tired!"

"Lou! Lookit," I informed him. "I've got about 10 beers in me and I've been drinking all day. It's my day off; you can't put me up there!"

"Oh, yeah? Put on a flight suit over that bathing suit and get your ass to the flight line—right now!"

Hmmmmm. Guess I gotta. I put the old Air Force flight suit they issued us in flight school onto my suntan-oiled, sweaty body and headed for the strip. There I was able to inform Tommy Mitchell, who had had only about a month in-country then, that I was indeed very drunk and he'd better fly well, because I didn't think I was in any great shape. In his usual drawl, Goober said, "Don't bother me none. I can always fly OK." My reaction: Oh boy, an attitude, too.

We took off and flew with the scrambled flight up the river, and I tried to fly in our formation slot, but it was weird. "We" went up, down, and all around. This was worse than drunk driving. There wasn't any firm pavement under the wheels here, and nothing to keep us from weaving in that third dimension, either. After a while, I just gave up and turned my life over to Tom: "It's up to you. I can't save us, so don't screw up." He said, "Y'all don't bother me," and proceeded to fly only about half as badly as I had been doing while flying drunk. It was an amazing feeling to be in a cockpit as an AC and have no confidence whatsoever that I could save us, or the ship. It was absolutely up to my new guy, peter pilot. As a further disappointment, there weren't even any VC crossing the river. After a while, we were allowed to return home to Vinh Long. Neat time flying drunk . . . .

By the end of February, the airfield commander (or somebody at that level) moved us down by the first platoon's living quarters, which were older but right alongside the officers' club. The idea was that we would be closer to the flight line if they needed us in a hurry. Oh, . . . I see. I bitched like crazy about having to pack up all the stereo equipment and our life's possessions, such as they were, but I got over these feelings as we became used to our new digs. As a Navy Junior, I'd always hated moving and wanted a home! However, it was a better arrangement in the long run, and centrally located. The showers were about 20 yards away on one sidewalk, the club was literally the same distance across the grass. The Vietnamese laborers cut this lawn with hedge clippers, sitting there in a squat while doing so. Jon Myhre would look at them and quote, "Jo-Jo, the bum!" They would reply back, "Ya-a-ah!" to our amused faces. They even took their smoking breaks while in the same position. There were sidewalks beyond leading to the Knight hooches, with trees painted white up to about three and a half feet, as the French were prone to do in the past in prominent Vietnamese cities. Some of the guys obtained real banana trees from somewhere while on missions and planted them around the second platoon hooch for some landscaped greenery. I thought we looked like the Brooklyn Botanical Gardens after this effort. Whoopie-doo. Miniature fence railings were added as an afterthought, with some pride.

We had Vietnamese hooch maids and boys for each building. They did a superb job of polishing our boots, sweeping the rooms, and changing the sheets. Outlaw 29's AC, Tommy McCarthy, was in charge of collecting the funds to pay our hooch maids. Somehow, he consistently ensured that the refrigerators were always stocked with beer—Pabst, Schlitz, or otherwise. Tommy also took care of Outlaw, the black cur that was the mascot of the second platoon; Outlaw's original masters had long since departed. Except for Mac, he bit everyone, especially Hershey from the first platoon, who would never notice Outlaw in the darkness, lying in a certain puddle as Mike headed for the showers. The mongrel would bite Hershey in the ankle nearly every time he walked by en route to the showers and the latrine. With a white towel wrapped around his waist, Mike would curse and kick the dog; this seemed to be a ritual between the two of them. I never knew until returning to Mineral Wells that Hershey always had had a pair of matched Belgian shepherds as his constant companions, and that he knew dogs very well. You never would have guessed that from the drama at Vinh Long.

Some of the hooch maids were very pretty but not amorous, to our great disappointment. We sure tried, though. They'd just get the giggles and brush off our advances. Mine would say, "Yoo goe to Madame Nhum's! You go to Madame Nhum's!" Other hired help was just plain nuts or deficient in some manner, like Sanh in the first platoon. I don't know who hired these Vietnamese for the compound. Nonetheless, overall, they were pretty loyal to us. Often the VC would attempt to entice them to steal from us in petty ways. If they resisted such pressure, sometimes the VC would execute them, their children, or worse. Once, later in my tour, my crew got on board one morning and reported that the VC had cut off the hands of their hooch maid's children. She had come in to report that she no longer could work for the EM's lodgings. That was shocking. We never got used to the VC atrocities that surrounded and invaded the lives of the local people.

Our houseboy, Lais, said he was going to quit because of VC pressure and go to Saigon to become a QC. He was so slightly built that I couldn't see this as a good career choice, but that's where he went. Before he left, he asked me for my Argus C-3 camera as a parting gift. I replied, "No, I need that, and my uncle gave it to me as a wedding gift. I really shouldn't give it away." He took it anyway when he left, and even though this disappointed me, I had to feel that he thought our friendship was worth a gift of that esteem. He left me his photo where the camera had been kept, and it said: "Lais, Vietnamese, and you American. Number 1!" That's about as well as he could say it, I think.

17

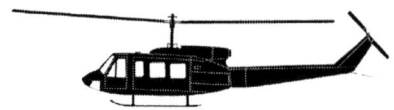

OUTLAW 6'S LUAU

MAJ. ROGER LACOURSE was stepping down and going home. His esteemed gunship platoon leader, Maj. Jerry Hileman, had preceded him. Together, these two men had teamed up to be the perfect combo of company commander of the 175th and Maverick Lead. Enough can never be said about the genius of Jerry Hileman; ask any Maverick who flew for him in 1966. He had the battlefield scope few men ever attain, and the kind of unspoken loyalty from his airmen that any commanding officer can only dream about. These two would be truly missed and never forgotten. The change of command would be honored by a party, of course; these zestful institutions created their own legends in themselves. A Hawaiian luau theme was agreed upon, and the officers' mess sergeant of that ethnic background would be in charge of all the arrangements. Roast pig was certainly to be the main course, but where to get such an animal?

Terry Holley is said to have found the pig. Up by Sa Dec, he saw the hog tethered to a tree. I have yet to learn the rest of the story about how this large animal got to Vinh Long, but it probably went like this. Terry would have been in a light fire team of the Mavericks, operating in the nearby area. When he saw the pig tied to the tree, he would have had to get some slick in the area to land and steal the pig, and quickly. The gunships would have circled in a daisy chain to provide cover while the slick went in on this clandestine mission of securing the pig. How the crew got the huge hog into the D-model Huey is certainly a matter of conjecture. It had to be a scene to be remembered.

Back at Vinh Long, the first platoon was in charge of preparing the pig for slaughter and putting on the cookout. Ron Petty from Georgia or Tennessee was to be the designated pig-sticker due to his self-proclaimed proficiency at the task. He wielded a huge knife to prove his point. Others would join him. One morning, on a down day, I came out of the officers' club to hear some horrible squealing coming from the direction of the first platoon's hooch. Curious to know who was dying, or why, I strode out in front of the porch of the Mekong Manor and looked at the cluster of men by the first platoon's door. There, with knives flashing in the morning sun, were about 10 men assassinating the prone pig, which was out of sight and below the kneeling killer-butchers. Apparently they were doing a poor job. The pig would not die, and whatever Ron Petty knew about "sticking a pig" was maybe erroneous. It looked like a serial killing. Arms rose and plunged, over and over again. The pig squealed like hell. I was glad I'd been in Vietnam a spell; I don't think I could have handled this murderous deed without the combat experiences I had acquired up to this point. This was ludicrous. The pig squealed. Arms stabbed. I was reminded of epic biblical movies that had been popular just a few years back. All we needed at this point was the Spanish Army to finish killing the pig. Maybe we needed them pretty quickly.

Finally, after about 20 minutes of ax-murder mayhem, the pig was done for. This revolting episode was pretty embarrassing for the members of the pig-dispatching team, and I was glad that we probably would have a different theme for the next change-of-command party. One pig slaughter was enough to experience.

Come the night of the party, the battalion let us have a down day the following morning-after, except for one mission. As operations officer for the platoon, I felt I should volunteer for it. Now, whom should I select as my copilot? Why Pat Tominey, my non-drinking Mormon warrant officer, of course. He agreed, saying he didn't drink much. "Then it's done!" I said, and pledged to remain sober myself. We actually intended to do so, no fooling.

The party was held on the tennis court, which had been decorated with a lavish Hawaiian theme of palm leaves, banana stalks, and the whole works. Very spectacular and very impressive. Somebody had done a lot of work. The Hawaiian steward was completely happy with the outcome and said everyone had participated well in pulling off the plans. A band had been hired. A stripper showed up at the appropriate time. Just then, overhead, the Seawolves howled by in one of the dilapidated B-models the Army had given them, showing us the "round eyes" Rocky Rowell had fetched from Saigon. These American women would be the highlight of the evening's orgy and the stuff of talk for many a year to come. "Those Navy pilots sure knew how to get some tail!" about summed it up.

Tominey and I would see each other occasionally throughout the evening and kept checking in with each other about our joint sobriety, but after a while, it was a lost cause. We got as snockered as everyone else was, completely out of control. The first platoon hooch was utilized by the women in servicing the troops. They just took on everybody! I didn't partake, but I *did* hear that those imported Saigon office workers had incredible sexual endurance. They just lay there and awaited the next lusty young American pilot who would grace their naked forms with his needy self. This was not the only place of debauchery. One of the Outlaws told me that one couple was doing it on the rotor blade diving board down at the "Cobra Pond," close by the runway. He said the board was springing up and down with their actions. Someone else and his friends were having drag races up and down the airstrip in deuce-and-a-half's. This debacle continued all night. In the morning, Tominey and I stumbled into the club for breakfast after passing inert sleeping forms under bushes and up against buildings. Major LaCourse was there with squinty pig eyes that had pinpoints for pupils. He didn't look any better than we did. Those men still alive and vertical were in sad shape, but eating. The majority seemed to be asleep outside, wherever their revelry had ended the night before. You couldn't recognize who they were; all that could be seen were the butt ends of Bermuda shorts sticking out of bushes, where they had assumed a somewhat fetal position. Very drunko here.

At that moment, in walked the six or seven American women, in dresses and makeup and looking none the worse for wear. They weren't even staggering or listing. They proceeded straight up to Major LaCourse, who was as awestruck as the rest of us at seeing them, knowing what these ladies had been up to all night. Then they addressed him. I could tell he certainly didn't pretend to know what they might say. "Major LaCourse," said the apparent leader of the group, a black-haired woman in a red dress, "we had a wonderful time at your retirement party. And we want to say that all your men were perfect gentlemen, and we wanted to tell you so!" With that, her female entourage turned on their heels and marched back out the door of the officers' club. LaCourse's mouth hung open like a barn door. You could have put a lot of stuff in there before he closed it. Wordlessly, he looked awestruck at me, and I did the same back at him. At that instant, I knew for sure that we were the weaker sex, and would be forever so.

Tominey and I made it to the Outlaw ramp. We climbed into the seats, groaning as we did. We cranked. I said, "Take her up."

"I've never taken a bird up from between the barrels," he stated.

"I don't care. Fly, fly!" I commanded. I was too hungover to do anything but pull rank on him.

Pat carefully nudged the D-model back on the heels of its skids and lifted up. The tail didn't waggle too much and we proceeded to a higher hover of three feet and then moved out of the yellow-painted 50-gallon drums the airfield used to protect the ships from mortar attack shrapnel. We all thought the narrow lane of water-filled barrels was more of a hazard for us than any actual mortar attack, but what the heck. Pat moved off into flight and I groaned. Then we got up to altitude to proceed toward Ben Tre and I groaned again. Pat groaned, too. The EM in the backseat asked if we were sick. "Nope," I said, "just drunk."

Soon we landed at the Ben Tre airstrip and joined Soc Trang aircraft assembled there. We told them we were the lone Outlaw ship they had requested. They thanked us for showing up and said that if all went well, we might be released by noon. "Oh, swell," I said, and I truly meant it.

The flights took off, and we had to land in fairly slender LZs eastward of Ben Tre. These irregularly shaped landing sites were problematic as to which formation might be most efficient for getting the ships in. Colonel Dempsey, Delta 6, was overhead of the operation's altitude and started suggesting the formation we should be using to land in these banana-shaped LZs. "What you need down there is a *right oblique!*" Dempsey squawked over the radio. "A right oblique, that's the formation you need for that LZ!" I could imagine everyone in the flight listening to this, searching their minds, and saying within their ships, "What's a right oblique?" My sodden head was saying, "Oh, boy, not today, not today, God, please. Why now?"

Then the Soc Trang guys gamely tried whatever they remembered from flight school about this formation. We all lined up on a 45 way out to the right, all five ships, and went in. The rotor wash was terrific, and we all staggered up above the ships below us, trying tricks to beep off the RPM as it oversped, screwing the cyclic round and round in small circles to shake off the lift on the blades. Nothing quite worked enough. There were helicopters above us, helicopters below us; every window of the bird had a Huey trying to make our acquaintance. You could look down through the chin bubble and see one. You could look up through the greenhouse window and see one. They were out in front of the windshield; lots of helicopters out of position, trying to come down out of the sky. Dempsey was caterwauling in the headset, "That's the formation, that's a right oblique. That's what you need for that LZ!"

Pat and I were in great pain and trying to fly the thing together while surrounded by helicopters. These Soc Trang Tigers and Warriors *were really flying terribly* today, and we didn't need this idea of a cruel joke imposed upon us in our condition. This was too much. We couldn't even emote adequately, much less fly the aircraft. When would this terrifying endeavor end? We longed to be on the ground, and sooner rather than later.

When we finally did land back at Ben Tre, I slithered down out of the left seat and collapsed on the ground. Pat did something similar on the other side. The crew looked at us lying there and said, "What did they do to you guys last night, anyway?" I only moaned unintelligibly and smushed my face into the cool grass of the shade created by the Huey beside me.

At this point, up came a Jeep, and in it, of course, was Maj. Robert LaTour. Again. He turned off the engine and said, "Hey, is there a First Lieutenant Eastman here, by any chance?" The crew said "Yeah," and pointed to me down on the ground.

"Hi, sir. Can't get up," or something that sounded like that.

He tried to make conversation and I just waved him off, feebly.

"Hey, they might release you guys pretty soon. Do you want me to look into that?" LaTour queried.

"That would be fine, really nice," I mumbled. I couldn't even look up.

A short while later, somebody from the Soc Trang lift rumbled up in a Jeep and said we could go: "It sure was nice for you guys to come down and help us out. Looks like we don't need you as much as we thought we might. Thanks for showing up." With that, I staggered up and attempted to stand straight, my eyes rotating in their sockets, trying to focus. "Pat, are you there? Did you hear what they just said?" I could just barely detect his low-octane reply, but yes, he did comprehend.

We cranked and got the thing in the air again, feeling at least assured that out of all those drunken forms we had seen in the morning at Vinh Long, that we alone had been able to get to an aircraft and get it airborne. We felt some smug satisfaction in that. We left the ship to the EM and staggered down the ramp in the sweltering heat, knowing they were still shaking their heads behind us as we made for our hooches and rest.

18

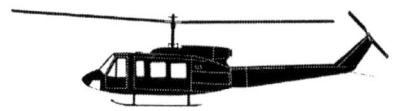

Major Juri Poometuu

WALKING INTO THE CLUB ONE MORNING, I saw a new man sitting with several of the higher ranking officers, and my initial impression was that he looked distinctly different from others I had seen around the Delta so far. With his shaved head, curiously intent eyes, combat infantrymen's badge, and First Air Cav patch to go with his aviator wings and senior parachutist jump wings, he looked like a real professional killer. I wondered what he was doing with us, as I went over and sat down at his table. He scarcely looked at me while the senior majors present informed me who he was and what they were discussing with him. He appeared completely absorbed in their accounts of Delta actions. I hadn't seen any of his type since Fort Benning, and I said something to that effect. He then turned to me with that Teutonic stare and said his brother was an instructor at the Infantry School. I ran that through my brain and then recalled that I had encountered a Capt. Tonu Poometuu there in the Infantry Officer's Basic Course. He had been friendly enough at explaining the nationality of that funny-sounding name on his uniform, when several of us second lieutenants had inquired about it one Georgia afternoon. The name was so unusual that it had stuck in my mind. These men were Estonians, escapees in their youth from behind the Iron Curtain. They were a bit of a story, perhaps even a legend in some circles.

After informing Maj. Juri Poometuu that I had indeed met his brother, I asked what he was doing here with us at Vinh Long. He said he was actually already a rich man, having made his wealth in construction in New York. He'd left a penthouse apartment in that city to join us fighting communism as an Army reservist. He'd started his stint with the Cav, and they had sent him down here after a few months. I nearly choked on my food; I was thinking this was a little too much comic opera first thing at breakfast. I tried to be tactful, saying, "Oh, I see, sir." After about a third of a year in-country, I wasn't able to process such Stateside patriotic histrionics. It really remained to be seen what this dude was all about. As much as I wanted to believe that some expertise had been released for our benefit from the Cav, I knew there had to be more to the story than what was expressed, so I kept quiet and kept a straight face. I knew that the Cav got rid of its losers.

"Lieutenant Eastman, since Major Poometuu is new to the unit, we thought he might fly with you today and go along on your missions. Is that all right with you?" said one of the majors present at the table. After four months in-country, it seemed I was gaining some respect for my competence. It was a comfortable feeling.

"Sure. I'm just going over to My Tho and then Saigon after that. Should be a good day to break in the major to the Delta's flying. It'll be an easy day and enjoyable." At least I had the privilege of finding out first what made this guy tick and what his real story was. I'd clue in the other pilots quickly.

I flew into the My Tho helipad, finished my business there, and then took off over the electric and telephone wires at the south end, climbing up and turning over the brown Mekong River before handing the controls to the new major. I was getting smarter as an aircraft commander, learning when to let a new man start in on the stick for the ship's safety, so I only gave it to him when I had gained 2,500 feet of altitude and the power was at the cruise setting. This was also tactful for handling a newly arrived officer of his rank, so that if he was rusty, there would be no sweat flying the ship as comfortably as I could make it for him. It was the decent thing to do as a young AC, when giving the controls to a more senior officer. No matter what, the man could just sit still and hold 80 knots, flying straight and level, even if he just acted like a vegetable. The Huey was that kind to people. I told him what heading to hold as we proceeded northerly toward Saigon. This would be a piece of cake.

Poometuu took the cyclic and the collective in his hands and commenced to perspire profusely while beating that aircraft all over the sky. I'd never seen such a battle to fly straight and level. His strenuous effort was so intense that I almost thought I was going to see him sweat blood. The perspiration on his grimacing face was more like globules of sweat. This was incredible. I knew we had a problem.

"Sir, if you'll just relax, the thing will fly itself!" I told him.

"It has been a while since I last flew the Huey," he responded in his thick, guttural accent. I felt like I had met Doctor Strangelove; I certainly felt like I had just gotten a part in that movie. Oh, boy.

At the end of the day, I let other members of the second platoon know that we had a strange one on our hands. At first, we thought we had lucked out, because they detailed him to the first platoon, which broke Ray Leuty's heart—they replaced him as platoon leader with this Poometuu clown. The senior captain could hardly conceal his disgust at this fluke of a man having descended upon his unit and replacing him as its commander. It was like a cancer or a boil wrongfully inserted into a healthy body. Nowadays, it would be like getting AIDS from a filthy hypodermic needle. The word spread about Poometuu's flying, and I hoped they wouldn't cut AC orders on him, which was possible just because of his rank. They did.

Then the worst of all possible disasters occurred—they gave him to us! Maybe Lou Paulin was junior in rank to Ray Leuty's captaincy, I don't know. Poometuu was now our problem; he had become our platoon leader. I had absolutely no respect for him, despite his rank, and I treated him as some foul-acting animal we had to constrain and restrict so that we could all do our business of flying while staying alive. We couldn't imagine how such a cartoon character had been kept around in the reserve ranks, and what strings he had pulled to wind up overseas in this position. It was an unreal reality far beyond anything we had yet experienced in the Army. We simply saw ourselves as all-American boys headed up by a kook out of a *Little Orphan Annie* comic strip. I was still missions officer, and that gave me a lot of power to run things as I felt they should be done. Poometuu caught my drift, and stated, "Loo-ten-annt Easzman hass a very beetchy personali-tee . . . ! Do not bother him when he is scheduling the missions."

In the aircraft he was crazy. Flying Outlaw Lead, he would hold the cyclic stick with one hand and dial in the new frequency on the UHF with the other. And those were the wrong hands—he was flying left seat. To paint a clearer picture, this means he would be holding the cyclic in his left hand and peering down at the radio's face on the console to click in the new frequency's numbers with his right, with his attention completely within the aircraft. You may be able to get away with this as a single ship all alone in the sky while navigating, but not as Lead. After a while, the formation knew when we probably would be changing frequencies, and all the ships would then give a wide berth to Lead as he flopped around in the air like a dolphin until the new frequency was up. No verbal command ever came from any of us; all the guys would just move way over sideways and out at the appropriate moment, then resume their tight position once the radio was changed. It looked funny in the air. "Out-lawz are up theees frequency, now," Poometuu would broadcast to the world.

What wasn't funny was assigning people to fly with him. On alternating days, I would assign Pat Tominey and Tommy Mitchell to fly in the Lead aircraft with this madman, because they were my most senior copilots and maybe could handle him. He'd have killed somebody else. "Don't let him touch the controls, don't let him touch the controls! Think of the guys; think of the guys!" I'd implore them. They got no sleep the night before flying a mission with this fop, and their faces were gray-green.

"I can't take it anymore, Dave. You've got to let somebody else fly with him. You've just got to!" Pat Tominey would say to me. "Please!"

"What am I going to do? I've only got you two. I have to do it this way!"

"He's a major! I'm just a warrant officer; he's also an AC. What can I do?"

"Do whatever you have to do! Just keep him off the controls all you can, at all times, if possible," I'd reply back.

Some men left. Dickie Hyde went over with Major O'Kane in Operations. Tommy Mitchell eventually would transfer out of the platoon to the Mavericks, where he found a home. All the men I had come to know in the 175th rotated around this strange character, avoiding contact. Poometuu walked alone in the compound, always cloaked in his austere way, never perceiving any harassment. I never saw him make any friends. He was considered strange by everyone—whether above him in rank or well below him. Apparently oblivious to all the stares, he didn't take personally any of our reproaches. He lived in his own private world of fighting communistic aggressors wherever they might surface in the free world. Any time I approached the senior officers with appeals to do something about this perverse man in our midst, they told me just to ride it out. It was as though they had been handed a dossier from Command and General Staff College on how to handle an odd character like this. He was certainly a new experience for us, or maybe he wasn't—perhaps something out of our collective nightmares about crazy parental monsters. Here was someone who could cost us our lives with his macabre strangeness, an alien adult invading our esteemed combat-aviator reality. We felt like we were being violated in our role as Jack Armstrong, All-American boy. Here was a new kind of character that the writers should have included in the script, and they'd completely forgotten to mention his existence. Our lives to this point hadn't prepared us for this complete jerk; somebody should have told us such people existed.

Let me explain what it was like to have this man leading a flight. When Poometuu reported over an RP (Reporting Point) to the gunship platoon leader running the operation, things would go like this. Normally at that moment, and usually with this point of radio contact, the flight Lead would receive instructions on how to proceed to the drop-off point for the troops in the LZ from this geographical point recognizable on the ground from the air. RPs were located around the periphery of the operational area. This dialogue was so organized in the Delta that it was like listening to air traffic controllers' directions Stateside for the airlines. You were given direct information on letting down from your flight altitude, changes to headings for landing, and so forth. Poometuu didn't let down. He cruised the flight over the LZ at 2,500 feet *until* he had the smoke pots in sight, then he'd say to the gunship Lead, "Outlaw Lead has the LZ in sight!" Uh-huh, well this was because they were throwing every smoke grenade they had on board to alert the nerd to the location of the thing directly below. Not only did we stink up the show, but the real problem we were facing was what came next. Poometuu now transmitted over the platoon FM, "Outlaws, this weel bee a steep one!" and commenced to dive straight down at the smoke grenades streaming their colors below. We would screw the helicopters down out of the sky, because we could not adequately follow him in formation; the rotor wash was severe, and the bottomed-out controls would not allow us to descend in any regimented manner. It was barbaric, even life-threatening. This clown then would hit the ground in a sort of controlled crash, because he apparently could not bring the thing to a low hover and then touch down. The Huey would slide across the LZ, kicking up dust like a roostertail for about 70 yards or so. He made it look like he was in a hydroplane race, but the ground was far less forgiving than water would have been. When the ship finally would lurch to a stop, with all the heads and bodies of the crew jerking around like so many crash-test dummies, he actually would have the nerve to say over the UHF, "Outlawz are down in the LZee!" Yeah, like no kidding. I thought the aircraft would jerk itself off the skids, but fortunately Bell Helicopter really knew how to make them. They must have seen this guy coming. It was terrifying to the crew on board, and a laugh and a half to the gunship crews escorting us into the LZ. Nobody had ever seen anything like this. You could hear the chortle in the gunship pilots' voices as they rogered Poometuu's embarrassing landings. He was dangerous.

Other times, in single-ship missions, he would want to hover up to the treelines closer than the gunships would allow us. "We musst assist our leetle allies every way wee can!" he'd signal. The assertive gun platoon fire team Lead would say, "You put those troops down right there, Outlaw 21!" The general feeling was that this guy was right out of the war comic books we had long since outgrown. He didn't really reflect who we were as a unit; he lived in his own head, and we just put as much distance as possible between our own image and him. It was pretty obvious to everyone that he was a loose cannon.

When Poometuu was assigned to redecorate the officers' club, he would send his peter pilot and a crew chief in the other seat to the operational area because he was too busy choosing the new wallpaper. Of course, both probably could fly better than he could. He would discover old ammo belts in the water alongside the runway and have the EM crews pull them up and "save them from being used by the enemy." Everyone knew how long ammo lasted in a usable condition in this tropical, humid climate; not Poometuu. He had the true revolutionary spirit. He became a plague to any realistic functions in our unit for two months or more while he was with us and out in front of us. One afternoon at a company gathering, he actually marched the platoon over to the hangar as a parade unit, calling out cadence and exhorting rhymes right out of *Battle Cry*—all to our great amusement.

Poometuu's most ridiculous moment came when he spent a weekend at the villa we rented in Vung Tau. One day in the second-platoon day room, he asked us in a comradely way, "You boyz musst tell how to get the gurls at Vung Tau. Soon I go there and you musst help mee out!" We didn't say much, and I wondered what would become of this disgusting jaunt. Harvey Persyn was up at the villa at the same time, and he recounted just what did occur with Poometuu's appearance in that seaside town. The first day of his visit, Poometuu went around to all the bars and nightspots of Vung Tau and approached every whore he met. He paid them the going rate of 10,000 piastres and then some, which was something over 10 bucks in our currency. He scheduled them to show up two hours apart for the two or three days he would be in town, and they agreed to the schedule. He had one at 1 P.M., another at 3 P.M., 5 P.M., and so on. To remedy any complications he might incur from these Vietnamese prostitutes, he had a mayonnaise jar filled with anti-VD medication capsules that he called "no-sweat pills," which he placed on the nightstand by his bed. After every sexual encounter, he would throw a handful of these pills down the back of his throat like they were jelly beans. He strongly recommended them, and offered them freely, to the other two or three guys who were at the villa at the same time. There were no takers.

Major Meehan (this was when he became the new CO) got wind that Poometuu was at the villa and decided to take action to bring him back. It apparently had been decreed that no officer of field-grade rank could partake in the prurient pleasures that Vung Tau had to offer; it would appear too unseemly to officers of our rank and station. Therefore, Meehan and the XO, Maj. Lem Magoon, along with Hershey from Operations, went to pick up Poometuu before things got any further out of hand. I'm so glad they were looking out for our morale. Now, it's important to note that Bill Meehan was very Catholic, Magoon was a right-wing, fundamentalist Christian, and, well, Mike Hershey was appropriately aloof and very prepared to be astonished by whatever it was that was about to transpire. They trooped up to the second floor of the French villa, a setting that looked like something out of the Humphrey Bogart movie *Casablanca*, and found Harvey Persyn sitting against the wall outside Poometuu's bedroom, sipping some George Dickel from the bottle, as he was prone to do in his Texas way. They asked Harve where the major was. "In there," Harvey said, without too much thinking. They then opened the door, which Harvey hadn't figured they'd do, and in they marched. The three of them caught Poometuu in the act with a 13-year-old

Vietnamese whore. He was in the saddle, and never missed a beat. He just kept on humping. They said, "Get your clothes on, we've come to take you back!" Ole Poometuu kept right on stroking, and said, "I'll be with yoo in a meen-ute!"

When I heard the story, I absolutely cracked up. I hilariously told Harvey, "I'd have given my right leg to have been there! What did the girl do?" Harve replied, "Ah, she just rolled her head over like that," indicating her posture, laughing as he did so with the gesture. I asked Hershey for his impression of the event, and he said, "It was *disgusting!*" Poometuu actually seemed slightly mollified by this comeuppance.

I find it quite difficult to describe this obscene interruption in our platoon's life. The problem probably is that we junior officers were not allowed *ever* to complain in personal terms about a higher ranking military individual. It being 1967, this was well before such buzzwords as "personality conflict." You could not say your boss was a dork. There was neither conflict resolution nor counseling. These procedures developed after the 1960s—perhaps even *because* of them. Back then, it was as though we were frozen in time, our behavior rather like that of midshipmen in the Horatio Hornblower sagas or of officers in the Napoleonic era. Military customs forbade this type of dialogue. Orally, and among ourselves, we could chew the fat and communicate our disgust of an insane authority figure for whom we were making adjustments. The Army had no mechanism for dealing with their having placed an inept, crazy man in command of us. It didn't matter who he was or who we were; there was just no remedy for this situation. Save one. Promote him up and out to a safer position for all concerned; decorate him, too, while you're at it. And this happened over and over again in Vietnam. The result was that a completely hideous personality with no leadership characteristics or everyday graces could wind up very high in the chain of command. We got used to encountering "crazy colonels," especially at the lieutenant colonel rank. As senior majors, they had been elevated in order to remove them from the ranks below, where contact with troops typically was much more on a one-to-one basis. This was the only solution for a thoroughly contemptible person whom everyone regarded as a son-of-a-bitch for his entire military life. Our situation was compounded by the fact that the career-minded West Pointers had already passed through the Delta on earlier assignments (in 1964 and 1965); during their second tour, they would be commanding American troops farther north. We were getting the less-than-desirable hangers-on who were being sent to Vietnam to get their tickets punched. At the time, I had no idea why we had 10 different platoon leaders within a year. It made being a first lieutenant very difficult. The warrant officers below us needed our capable interfacing with these senior captains and majors to make their days livable at times. We got used to having outlandish and outrageous figures commanding us, and had to be extremely tactful and courteous in a military way with these men planted in our midst, guiding them as best we could. Gradually, we began to under stand that we were in a corrupted system that could not police itself with men that were one step away from the loony bin. Those senior officers we respected let us know this was the case, and told us to deal with it as best as we possibly could.

19

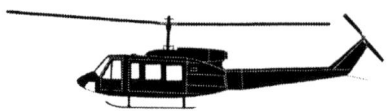

Tay Ninh Again

SEVERAL NEW PILOTS had come into the unit as a group—Gary Wesselman, Andy Keeney, John Niemier, and Larry Reeves were the latest new guys. We now certainly had a full complement of pilots, and they seemed younger all the time. It became obvious what flight school was becoming: the place to train college boys and former enlisted men to fly helicopters in the Vietnam War. Reeves was on his second tour, having been an MP on the first visit. He was a very marginal pilot, although obviously sophisticated in the ways of the Army. He found a way to talk to his wife several times over the "Mars line," which was designated for emergencies only concerning family business. It didn't bother him any to utilize it once he had discovered this handy long-distance service to the States. He bore watching in the aircraft, however, because he would not come out of a dive once he instigated it. We came out of the air very fast in Vietnam—initially a vertical descent rate of at least 2,700 to 2,900 feet per minute, trying to minimize our exposure to ground fire and limiting the VC to as little target practice on us as possible. Reeves would just keep the aircraft screaming toward the ground in an uncontrolled dive, as if the bottom were never going to be coming up at us at the end of the maneuver. I would say to him, "You know, you've got to start backing off the airspeed on this thing pretty soon if you want to slow the descent in time." He would stay numb, seemingly almost unable to listen to guidance. In these rapid diving approaches, we would glide to a landing at the very end and pull in the power to arrive at a low hover, using all the performance that the turbine had to give at just the last minute. It was a power-on autorotation, really—that's what a Vietnam high-overhead, circling approach technically was about. Reeves just didn't seem to be too aware of the potential outcome, or what to do about it.

The other three from this flight school class seemed rather naive overall. Their ages were not much different from those of other pilots who had joined the war, but this group needed mentoring for any progress toward maturity and toughness. All others I had experienced over here had grown up fast. This whole flight school class seemed tender and more vulnerable than any others I had seen—there was no toughness in the lot. They were just friendly young men needing to grow up; a lot was going to be beyond them.

Beaulieu was another case entirely. For some reason unbeknownst to us, he had been sent down from the Cav as a replacement, but he acted very macho and experienced. He seemed to believe in his own legend; he was ex-EM, and a Cajun from Louisiana. With his background, he seemed an older warrant than others, so he was respected from the start. We knew the Cav had it tough, and did a lot with very little, so we accepted his stories as gospel. At Vinh Long, we knew we had it better than anyone else in the whole country, so we weren't going to question or contest anybody else's hardship tales. We openly regarded this new addition to our platoon as a weathered man; we figured he'd learn our tricks fairly quickly and well, and the rest was whatever he was about to become friends with.

However, there was more. Beaulieu flew drunk. When he became an AC all too soon, he would fly up to another aircraft in the platoon and do rolls around the surprised ship. He would laugh shrilly over the radio—as if his stunt flying was not already enough to put him in deep trouble. He wasn't too swift, either, at learning the tricks of the trade for flying to Delta outposts, and we realized that he wasn't that combat savvy for a man with his many months in-country. His drunkenness was covering up some great fear and blocking his own self-knowledge. Now we had another problem besides Poometuu. Both these men seemed oblivious to their faults, and they could not be approached to correct their flaws—professionally or personally. The platoon was starting to acquire a lot of scar tissue. We experienced ACs had to watch more and more whom we were flying with and what they did, and we had to keep communicating closely (and confidentially) with the other ACs concerning these new pilots. You couldn't take anything for granted anymore. Flying with these new personnel was akin to being a classroom teacher and having to be all eyes and ears in order to maintain discipline and teach at the same time. Acclimating ourselves to these realities made us grimmer as people; we became harder.

While I was at Vung Tau for the second time, and avoiding trouble far better on this visit, the outfit moved up to Tay Ninh again in late February for Operation Junction City. I hitched a ride and rejoined the unit after a few days, when everyone had already been well situated in the tents. But a couple of things had occurred in that short a time while I was away getting some rest and a beach tan at Vung Tau. Upon my arrival in Tay Ninh, John Savelli read me his "Dear John" letter from his so-called fiancee back in New Jersey, who apparently was going to marry someone else. This was my first experience of seeing a guy let down by his girl back home, and here we were, jointly sharing the emotions of receiving such an epistle. It was interesting but fortunately, John came to his senses and got over the dumperoo fairly quickly. I noticed that I must have become one of the senior ACs, since he extended this familiarity so spontaneously. I took heed of that; it's always nice to be finally welcomed and included.

The other news with which I was greeted, and carrying the same weight, was that Major O'Kane had used my ship to get two downed Mavericks and their EM crew out of the bush. He had ruined the rotor blades while doing so, and my main rotors and tail rotors had been completely replaced by the Outlaw Maintenance crew working in the field at Tay Ninh. I was immediately gratified at having brand-new blades to fly with, but the most impacting news of all was that Rheihofer said that after installing them, they tracked better than any set he had ever put on! This was amazing, considering the conditions under which the hangar personnel had to work. Major O'Kane told me that my crew had behaved superbly and he could not have done the rescue without their outstanding performance. This pleased me tremendously; I guess Mike Farr was out of the doghouse.

I learned that O'Kane had hovered down through the treetops, cutting branches out of the way as he did so, like a giant chain saw. Johnson and Farr had guided him with slight twitches left and right of the tail boom, so he could put the ship down through the foliage without ruining the blades to the extent it would not fly, and therefore kill them. I guess it made one hell of a sound cutting through those limbs as it came down in the B-52 bomb crater that had created an opening in the bombed-out teak forest called "Hobo Woods." The Huey could nearly fit in, but not quite.

What had happened was that the Maverick fire team, led by newly promoted Second Lt. Terry McDowell, was escorting a huge lift of 70 ships (not our own) on the first day of Operation Junction City, in which our presence only lasted two weeks or so after this date. Terry had rank on veteran gunship pilot Jim Hardbeck, a CW2 on his second tour in-country; Hardbeck had been back about only six weeks. McDowell's superiority was not only because he had recently received a direct commission to second lieutenant in the Transportation Corps. (He had applied for the gold bars; it could be done in Vietnam if you wanted to become a commissioned officer, but this would have been called a battlefield commission in earlier wars.) The ex-WO1 also had been flying fire team Lead for several months, and he had been assigned to that again the night before by 1st Lt. Bob Lakey or 1st Lt. Don Shipp. McDowell was leading the two-ship fire team when Hardbeck, his wingman, called that he was having a "high-side governor failure." After this emergency call, Terry immediately turned around and became Hardbeck's wingman. Then he watched Hardbeck's ship flame out as his engine quit, plunging the experienced Huey driver into the teak forest. Hardbeck and his copilot, "Goose"

Gerwe, dropped down through the triple-layer jungle canopy, ceasing their 150-foot fall just before the helicopter hit the ground, supported by the remaining branches that had yet to break. They suffered back injuries in the crash and went into shock, thirsting badly. It was noted where they went in, and a rescue was set up among the Outlaw slicks, helped by the Maverick gunnies.

John Savelli left copilot Andy Keeney in a savanna-like clearing filled with high elephant grass, with an unfamiliar M-60 in his hands for protecting the aircraft on the ground just behind him. Savelli took the crew with him, and since Andy was totally unfamiliar with the machine gun and his circumstances, he later elected to stay within the ship after he shut it down, instead of out there in the grass. He, too, had only been in-country for a few weeks; he really didn't know what else to do. Capt. Rob Bridle of the first platoon had landed a second Huey near the same spot, but out of sight of that first ship, and he and John proceeded into the jungle with their enlisted crew members on a compass heading to see if they could locate the Maverick gunship containing Hardbeck, Gerwe, and the two gunners. WO1 Ron Cone was left behind in Bridle's ship. Occasionally the Mavericks flew overhead to guide these two aviators on foot to the crash site, and to recheck their compass directions by throwing smoke grenades to lead them along. Gradually, they made it to the site and lifted the injured pilots out of the wrecked ship. Then where to take them? It was decided to move them (with their broken backs) to an Air Force bomb crater about 800 meters from the crashed helicopter, so they could be airlifted out. They couldn't be carried far in their condition, and it was hot, humid, tiring work for the rescuers. The forest had been blasted and splintered by the bomb strikes, probably 500-pounders. The sooner they could be removed, the better, but it was rough going for these resourceful fellows.

Jim Hardbeck remembered later that when the rescue personnel first found the gunship, they immediately ignited a red smoke grenade to show they'd been found. This frightened him considerably, because the two pilots were hanging helplessly in their straps, completely soaked with fuel. He also had a bleeding jaw—

the loose chicken plate in his lap had come up and smacked him there when they impacted. This steel plate was not the ceramic device enclosed in an olive-drab vest that we had later, but was an unsecured, body-armor item that hurt Jim when he crashed.

Major O'Kane elected to widen the bomb crater's destruction of the canopy to accommodate the breadth needed by the Huey's rotor system. He slowly hovered down to the men below, feeling his way, gauging carefully how much the ship could take in this self-destructive process. My Outlaw 23 crew hung out, judging the branches' diameters and toughness, using their handheld mike switches to communicate with O'Kane up front. What trust! There is no way a pilot can look over his shoulder during such an operation; while he is keeping his attention riveted up front, he cannot be looking toward the back of the cabin to see if his enlisted men are doing their job. He can only depend upon them utterly to do the right thing, and very well indeed. For the party on the ground, the racket was intense as the helicopter made its way down through the foliage like a huge chipping machine. The first two or three feet of the two main rotor blades became frayed from the experience, but evenly. At the end, the tail rotor was located between two substantial trees. At first, the helicopter landed right on top of the casualties! Hardbeck remembers feeling the front of the skid starting to put down on his head when it first settled on the ground. Then he watched some guy frantically wave O'Kane back up to a four-foot hover. When the landing to a hover was completed, the hurting Mavericks were transferred carefully inside the ship's cabin area, and O'Kane repeated the process back up through his hole in the treetops. The next morning, he ws awarded the Distinguished Flying Cross for his noble efforts by General Seneff.

A very curious thing happened to Savelli and Bridle on their way back to their parked ships. The rescuers were tuckered out by now; they and their men had to stop and rest in the intense tropical heat, leaning their backs against the trees they suddenly found themselves needing. Now, Rob Bridle had already spent nearly three years in Vietnam, because he had a Vietnamese wife, and a

Catholic at that. Why he had not returned to the States with her was a matter of conjecture, but let it be said he was far more of her world than he was with the first platoon's. With all of its new people introduced to the scene of this Third World conflict, an man of his experiences simply has lost comraderie with his existing unit. So though he was commonly seen flying with the first platoon, he wasn't close to anyone there. He was friendly enough to us, but distant, and at times curiously hostile to his situation. We didn't know how he would handle his marital predicament, but that was his business. Needless to say, he understood and spoke excellent Vietnamese.

As he and Savelli took a well-deserved break and caught their wind, their group was surrounded by quietly speaking NLF passing through the jungle all around them. These were the Viet Cong of the 9th regiment of the National Liberation Front—guerrilla soldiers the whole operation was interested in finding and killing in War Zone C. Bridle could translate what they were saying. As he and Savelli kept very still and let these small Asiatic men pass by in the jungle, he listened. What he revealed from overhearing them, was that these NLF had been very well aware of the Maverick helicopter crash. When he had a chance to talk, he said they had even observed the whole rescue operation. Bridle said they were saying that it was not worth their while to expose themselves to the whole American command by doing something to the downed crew or the rescuers on the first day of Junction City. They had decided against that and were just moving on with great discipline, making their concealment a priority. When Bridle reported this story back at base camp, it made everyone's skin crawl. Obviously, the Vietnamese were the ones who decided when and where we would have contact with them in this war. All our efforts at "finding Charlie" were a joke; it was literally a mistake on their part when we stumbled upon them.

I learned from this mishap that the most important piece of equipment on the helicopter during a crash and while awaiting rescue was the Igloo water container we commonly carried for refreshment. Loaded with ice water, it could keep a crew alive once they had gone into shock in that awful tropical heat after sustaining bodily injuries. I always kept my crew fully aware that this was what would save us if we ever had the misfortune of being shot down and marooned for a while. Hitched to the transmission area with bungee cords, the water container meant so much more than just a source of a refreshing drink on a hot afternoon. For instance, it was always amusing to see American advisors we knew go rapidly supine once they got into the helicopter during extractions. It's awesome what thirst can do to an exhausted man. They'd slither to the Igloo and literally claw off the top of the cooler to get at the contents inside. They weren't human again until they had slaked their thirst.

During this second visit to Tay Ninh, I had several unusual flying experiences for the first time. One of them was landing on the huge, isolated mountain adjacent to the province's town of the same name. Black Virgin Mountain was quite a landmark. It was Nui Ba Dinh in Vietnamese, and it stuck up like a large volcanic cone, which I suppose it was. And it was there for all to see, even from a considerable distance. One clear day at altitude in the Delta, when everything was socked in to the deck below us, Dickie Hyde and I saw Tay Ninh Mountain sticking up through the clouds like Japan's Mount Fuji. What had made that sight even more spectacular was that we were the only ones on the air at that moment in the Fourth Corps, or beyond for that matter. When we called in on flight following, Paddy Radar had screamed, "Didn't you get the message on not flying until all Hueys got their batteries moved forward out of the tail's fuselage?" We rogered that we had indeed received that maintenance order, and that we were the first ship out of the Outlaws to be flying that morning with our battery now safely inside the cargo area, well away from the rivets the battery acid had eaten, undetected, inside the tail boom. There was a quiet, "Ah," out of Paddy, which just confirmed that Outlaw Maintenance was far superior to maintenance crews in all the other aviation units in Vietnam. It was a while before other birds came up on the air, but by noon, everything was jammed up on the frequency, as it normally was. Apparently, some tail booms had come off and killed some Huey drivers because of that leaking battery acid. I always thought the D-model's tail boom was a pretty weak place to put that heavy aviation battery anyway.

The crazy thing about Nui Ba Dinh was that the Special Forces camp on the peak was completely surrounded by VC. The mountain was honeycombed with caves and owned by them, in plain sight of the American troops at the Tay Ninh compound. This fact is mentioned in many accounts of combat efforts in the area over time. Later in the war, the mountain was circled with B-52 strikes, and almost completely stripped of any vegetation by this bombing. I don't know if it did any good.

So, I had to land on top of this summit with a USO troupe to entertain the Special Forces guys stuck up there with all their communication equipment and towering antennas. When I raised them, they told me to come in high and fast, and not to trust the place's apparent innocence. I didn't, and I made a fairly decent pinnacle landing on a very small helicopter pad. Pleased with myself, I was ready to leave when they warned me to take off very steeply. Some guy in the radio shack informed me, "Don't take off level, and fly straight away. You'll get shot at!" What the hell, I decided to believe him. I pulled maximum pitch, climbed into the sky, and departed the dumpy place. What a weird place to live.

On another evening's mission, I had one of the most pleasurable flying experiences of my entire aviation career. Lou Paulin, Dickie Hyde, and I were in our separate ships going into an LZ that was like lush, mown grass in the fading sunlight, the beginning of a beautiful evening. This landing zone was out of a Midsummer Night's Dream, with massive overhanging trees. But those majestic trees were the troublesome part of the landing. They were reaching up and out like ancient New England elms, and they crowded the approach into the area where we would be assisting troops. There was a verdant quality below this park-like canopy. The opening in the crowns was not adequate for the Huey's rotor disc; it was just a mite short of our diameter's size.

Lou Paulin gauged it and found it so, but he had an idea. He said he'd go first, describing the dimensions as he passed through, and then he would give his suggestions for our approach.

What Lou did, and recommended for our two ships, was to start down in a left bank and hold that while we passed through the tree canopy's restrictions. Maybe only a fixed-wing pilot would think this up, I don't know, but he made it. And then Dickie Hyde—a more experienced pilot than yours truly—tried it. He signaled me to come through, just as he did. I commenced the bank from altitude and held my breath—as well as my angle of bank in the turn—as I moved through the shady green snare. When we had passed under the tree branches reaching out for us, we could level out, and there was room to spare for the rotor disc as we set down. After the troops loaded on, we would need to reverse the process to get out, but this time we'd have a demanding load. Now we had to commit, know our aircraft, and hold onto that bank as we lifted off with the power available. Lou passed through and whooped! Dickie scurried across the verdant LZ and climbed adroitly through the hole, too. Then they urged me on like a parent bird fledging its offspring out of the nest, telling me it was a snap. "Hurry up and try it!" they said. The early twilight's gloaming surrounded me as I heaved the aircraft into the sky and twisted through in a right-hand turn, almost caressing the branch tips as I went by, but with no contact, and up into clear air that held vastly more light than the forest glade we had just left behind. What a beautifully sensual moment of flying we had all just experienced! As we three flew back for the night, we laughed and exulted over the radios.

Not all risky flying in Vietnam provided such bliss. Just before I had arrived at the Tay Ninh encampment, Ray Leuty had tensely led the entire Outlaw flight back to the airstrip when they were almost all out of fuel. The 20-minute low-fuel warning lights were on in many of the ships; this wasn't fun at all. Not one ship fell out of the sky, but it was close, and something no one wanted to experience again. Nobody believes the manufacturer knows exactly how much fuel is left anyway; the light is only guessing at a differing amount remaining in each aircraft. The light on the "Christmas tree" board could indicate twenty minutes for one ship, but it could mean only ten for another ship.

The other experience I completely missed was the time when Poometuu failed to brief the flight on the only combat air drop the 173rd Airborne Brigade conducted in the entire Vietnam War, on 22 February. The very LZ in which the Outlaws landed was the same Drop Zone designated for the cargo parachutes! The 780 173rd Airborne paratroopers dropped in somewhere else, jumping from the C-130s overhead, but where the sitting helicopters were waiting out the operation in the grass, the cargo drop descended down and among the Hueys. Everyone rolled back to flight idle, which was 70 percent of the turbine's RPM, and prayed. The beautifully camouflaged green chutes drifted down into the trees surrounding the lift and miraculously avoided all the spinning rotor systems of the ships on the ground. One after another, the parachutes plunked onto the turf with their loads—without mishap. The Outlaws waited out this fiasco with considerable nervousness, to say the least. As usual, everybody forgave Poometuu; what else could you do with that knothead?

For years I had thought that Warrant Officer Fred Miller in Outlaw 18 had gotten out of his ship that day and cut the shrouds of one of the chutes, hauling it back into his aircraft. We would later use a parachute with the same leafy-looking fabric as a huge parasol for the patio area between the first and second platoon hooches in Vinh Long. However, it turns out that Jon Myhre got that one down at Can Tho, where the Special Forces packed their chutes. It made a nice sunscreen.

20

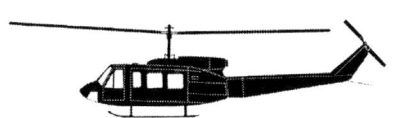

THE MAVERICKS GET A NEW LEAD

WHEN THE OUTLAWS RETURNED TO VINH LONG once again, yet another new gunship platoon leader had arrived to take over the Mavericks. Capt. Joe Moffett had been serving as Maverick Lead for all of a few short weeks; now that was suddenly over. A new man replaced him. Not much was known about Maj. Farley Jordan except that he was a second-timer. There would have to be a lot of ability in this gentleman to fill the shoes of the phenomenal Maj. Jerry Hileman. All the Mavericks of the third platoon awaited the new Maverick Lead's demonstration of his own personal style of leadership and tactical know-how. They were ready for their next demigod. The Mavericks were a proud bunch, and very possibly the best gun platoon in the Delta. Each one wore a red kerchief tied around his neck—the unit's personal insignia. It was the same bandanna people often wear on fall hayrides, or during bonfire parties sipping cider and doughnuts. It's available in a blue or red print at retail clothing stores featuring rural garb. You know it as a farmer's handkerchief.

    The Mavericks' prideful scarves actually had a functional origin. When the door gunners in the back were firing their free guns, the expended brass cartridges often wound up flying down the necks of the pilots up front. They were mighty hot going down the backs of their shirts! A few years back, somebody in this outfit had thoughtfully tied a red kerchief around his neck to prevent this hot brass from slipping down his officer's blouse and searing the gunship pilot's skin. The technique stuck, and the famous red farmer's handkerchief, with the square knot tied in front, became the official uniform signature of the third platoon of the 175th. Their painted insignia on the B-model gunships was a yellow bull's head blowing smoke out of both nostrils in a steady puff, with the word "Maverick" over this symbol. When you took a hit, you received a metal "beer-can" art pin of this symbol, and you couldn't wear this Vietnamese sidewalk production piece until you did. Believe me, these cherished bits of insignia were a very big deal in-country, and highly significant.

The door gunners of these gunships were a breed unto themselves. One of these fellows could disassemble an M-60 machine gun in his lap anytime it jammed. Not only would he know instantly what had gone wrong with the weapon, but he could replace the malfunctioning part and have the gun firing on the next pass. The M-60 often was slung by a bungee cord from the ceiling of the Huey, but it was the responsibility of these young door gunners never to let their free gun go nuts in the aircraft and shoot the aviators flying up front. This could happen with a hot gun, or if the crew member was shot, as often was the case. With the Huey moving along at 80 knots or more, VC commonly hit the crew just from a lead-and-lag physics situation. Rounds hit the tail boom even more, due to this airspeed phenomenon.

The crews of the guns had to rearm the ship as well as maintain the armament systems of the flex kits. Try to comprehend this task when the miniguns fired 7.62mm rounds at the rate of 5,000 per minute. That's a lot of links to snap together when reloading ammo. The rocket pods on both sides of the ship had to be refilled after every mission, too. Each of these held seven rockets; "the Hog" held 24 rockets on each side of the platoon leader's ship. Maverick 39 not only held a total of 48 rockets, but it also had a grenade launcher sticking out of its nose for some maximum firepower. This thing dumped the same 40mm projectiles that looked like giant .45-caliber bullets the infantry's M-79 grenade launcher fired. Major Hileman once caught an entire VC platoon running down various paths into a copse of trees and emptied everything "the Hog" had on board that day into the small treeline, decimating that band of unlucky guerrillas.

The Maverick EM were very, very good and did not get into this prestigious unit until they had proven themselves elsewhere, crewing first in the second and first platoons' helicopters. They wanted to be in the Mavericks more than anything else in the world, and they worked hard to earn the esteem of the other EM in this third platoon. There was no room for anything but excellence in the guns. Too much depended on these young kids and their marksmanship. They reminded me of Indian scouts in the Old West. While the helicopter was twisting in a steep bank and moving rapidly itself, these door gunners could hit a moving target with just a burst. They had to be that good. When the gunship was turning away from its hostile target, they provided the flanking cover and often leaned out on their "monkey straps" in the slipstream as they fired, commonly holding the gun upside down and shooting with their little finger, to avoid the air rushing by at 80 knots jamming their guns because of expended ammo cartridges. On a gun run heading directly on the target, they leaned out and fired the M-60 right by your flight helmet, just outside the front window—so close that it could blister the olive-drab paint on the APH-5 you were wearing. Is it any wonder I have hearing loss? The kids would play with you, too, if you were a new pilot, by holding the gun just so when firing; they'd splatter the expended brass all over your flight helmet like you were in ding-dong school. This wasn't really harassment, just initiation. Fun, fun fun.

The EM in these gun platoons often had exceptional abilities, like those of an expert animal tracker or a cop chasing public enemy number one. Just seeing a naked foot sticking out of some rice paddy grass could cause them to call up front: "Sir, I just saw some VC action back here, and I think there are 26 VC hiding back there in the deep grass of the rice paddy we just flew over!" When the fire team would wheel in and start shooting their rockets and miniguns in the designated area, that door gunner's perception often was rewarded—there *were* that many enemy in that field! It seemed at times that such personnel had a sixth sense, and this is what made them irreplaceable. In later years, the fast-moving Cobra gunship helicopters did not have these crews on board, resulting in a notable difference in their vulnerability. The protection of the flanking fire put out by these kids during the aircraft's high-speed turn was sorely missed.

Maj. Farley Jordan decided to lead a Vietnamese/English language class, and we were all for it. At last, someone had taken the initiative to teach us the speech of the native people we were constantly encountering during this tour; thank God somebody in the Army thought we should learn Vietnamese. About 20 of us showed up after one supper to attend the first class being put on by Jordan and two of the airfield commander's secretaries. They were well accustomed to our incompetent use of the language. Their primary job at Vinh Long was to ensure we were communicating accurately with the Korean construction firm that used various Vietnamese personnel to do all the manual labor on our airfield. The secretaries had to oversee that the local workers fully understood what we wanted. It looked like a really possible scenario to finally learn this language we were confronted with everyday.

With his prim little mustache and paunchy belly, Jordan sat down. He looked more like the piano player in some South Pacific rummy joint that you've seen in too many summer-stock performances, but nonetheless, he remained silent while the slim Vietnamese girls took charge of our language class. It quickly became apparent to us that there were 20 different ways to say "Ko," for instance, depending on the inflections of your palate, tongue, and other parts of your mouth. The pronunciation indicated which part of the country you were from, your economic and ethnic status, and so forth and so on. And there were many different meanings for the same word, too. It was baffling. We had already suspected this much, but we soon felt we were making no headway at all. It was beginning to get tedious and frustrating, for the girls as well as for us.

Major Jordan suddenly stood up. "That's enough for our language class for tonight!" he said abruptly. We were stunned but relieved. Maybe he had an excellent sense of timing as an instructor. But we were totally unprepared for what happened next.

"Men, I know you think I assembled you here tonight to learn the language of Vietnam, and you are partially right. But that is not the real reason I wanted to make your acquaintance as a newly arrived man at the Vinh Long airfield. Some of you know that soon I will be taking over as Maverick Lead, but that still is not my message for you people sitting before me this evening in this class. Gentlemen, I have the solution for the Vietnam War, and I want you to know that I have been sent here to finally bring about the resolution of this hostile conflict, and this is what I wanted to share with you this evening."

With that, he turned to the shocked Vietnamese women and told them they were dismissed but that they had done a very good job. Perhaps there would be more language classes, and soon. Then he turned back to us. Boy, were we curious. We had never heard of *anyone* who had the solution to the Vietnam War! We were all ears to this eccentric gentleman. Maybe he knew something we didn't. The girls left, confused and embarrassed. It seemed to me that they had been "had."

"Men, I awoke one night at home in my bed and *knew* I had envisioned the plan for the termination of this war. I woke up my wife, who was lying asleep alongside me, and told her of my vision." She said, "My God! You've got to tell somebody!" "So I did," he told us. He called his commanding officer at that moment in the middle of the night. The CO rolled over and picked up the phone, and after listening to Major Jordan's speech, said, "You're right, I'll get the base commander right on the phone. Hold on." This man listened sleepily but quickly got the essence of Jordan's scheme. He woke up fully and said, "Hold on, I'll get the general I know who should be informed of this!" And so the story went on and on. The only thing that totally registered with me was that Jordan had a thorough knowledge of the chain-of-command like you have to memorize when you are on guard duty at ROTC summer camp, if you unfortunately got that assignment for the night. His story was perfect, without blemish in that regard.

Finally, the keynote. By 4:30 A.M., with his brave wife still listening beside him, Jordan had contact with the Secretary of the

Army, then the Secretary of Defense, and then—you guessed it—the President of the United States. Ole LBJ himself, Lyndon Baines Johnson, was astonished at Jordan's brilliant idea, and said over the phone lines, "This is it! You've got to go back over there and win that war! I'll get orders cut on you immediately!" Jordan turned over to his wife, and said, "It's done. I'll be going over there again." Wifey-poo of course said, "God bless you!"

We listened numbly. Not a man spoke—until one young EM begged the question. The only question. There's one in every crowd. "Uh, sir, can you tell us what your solution for the Vietnam War is?" Oh, Gawd. Major Jordan immediately responded with his crispest, gravelly command voice, "I'm sorry! That is classified information and I'm not at liberty to share that with you right now!" Oh, boy. We rolled our eyes as we made silent contact with each other in the room; eyebrows went up. All I could think was that we had another live one in our midst. The men glumly stood up and put away their chairs. We had a feeling that there would no more Vietnamese language classes, and that we had seen the real show. Oh, my, I felt, if only my friends in the Mavericks knew what they were in for. Imagine. Someone selectively sent back to win the war.

When Jordan got into a gunship, he often forgot to push in the circuit breakers so the armament systems would be active. These buttons were overhead in the Huey's cockpit, at the rear of that console, and they needed to be pushed in all the way for the electronics of the guns and rockets to kick in and make the things fire. This was a safety device, and these circuit breakers were always pulled out when the gun crews were on the ground. Nobody needed to be shot by his own weapons system while rearming it. Jordan didn't know a thing about this stuff.

Jordan would often roll in on target, with nothing activated, and try to shoot. Of course, nothing worked—just inert red buttons on the cyclic's handle were the result. He would pull off and call the CO overhead in the Outlaw 6 Command and Control aircraft that his armament systems were "down." Often, the young warrant officer flying with him would reach up and surreptitiously push in those forgotten circuit breakers, then say to Jordan, "Sir, why don't you try it now? Maybe the armament systems will work this time." Jordan would roll in on the target again, and this time, things would fire! "Maverick Lead, back on station, weapons systems fully operational!" he'd call out in an officious, gravelly voice that sounded so on top of things. This short little man was spooky and bore watching; he was quite an act to catch.

It would be a long time before we learned that he had run a Hollywood talent agency that had failed and gone bankrupt. He was a retread and had gone back *into* the Army to fly again for a second tour in Vietnam. We had no idea how he had pulled down a slot in the Mavericks, much less become their platoon leader. He learned literally nothing from his expert gunnies.

The right seat fired the rockets through a sight that lowered down in front of the pilot's eyes. This was rigid and had a tiny lighted dot, called a "pipper," in the center of the round glass frame. The flight path of the Huey determined where the rockets would go, and the aviator had to set up a long glide that could not speed up beyond 80 knots, or the rockets would go everywhere except where intended. They then would swoop past the target, usually a hooch that was suspect; this would be frustrating to the pilot flying until he got the hang of it. The one-to-one vertical vibrations inherent to the helicopter's flight didn't help matters, either. The pipper danced along while the pilot raced in with his load of mayhem.

On the left side, another device lowered down and was handheld for the shooter on that side of the aircraft. He fired the miniguns, which had replaced the flex kits using the four M-60 machine guns originally implemented. With a flick of the wrist, one could mow a whole field, firing 5,000 rounds a minute. Obviously, new aviators coming into the unit sat on this side first, getting the feel of the gunship's firepower. This articulated targeting and firing apparatus, given to us by the Navy, also had a pipper on its glass screen, and you could put it right on the forehead of the man you were going to shoot. Seeing all that ammo going out from both miniguns and the two door gunners, along with the rockets being fired in continuous salvos on one sorry VC suspect running like hell in a rice paddy, could be very impacting on the brain. The lone Vietnamese in the wrong place on the wrong day looked like he was standing in a cloud of smoke with a squinched look on his face before chunks of his body started spinning off into the air around him, looking like selections of roast beef offered to you by your butcher. Whole pieces of his human trunk and other components would erupt out of that dazzling display of tracers, dust, smoke, explosions—all happening where that man stood before he eventually went down. Sometimes they didn't go down right away and ran, but they took an unbelievable amount of punishment before succumbing finally to the violence being inflicted upon their bodies. It was not a pretty sight, and something to witness.

Many of the door gunners lived for these moments. They wanted to see how many ways a body could flip as they expended their ordnance upon these VC suspects. To them, this gunship life was an experience unto its own. Many of the other personnel on the compound looked at these crews with awe, since they desired no part in such killing. It was a macho attitude that not all shared, nor wanted to. Somebody had to do the shooting, and it was essential, important work to suppress the enemy when they surely wanted to kill us in all seriousness. We needed these gunship crews, but they were a breed apart from the majority of people flying helicopters in that war. Most pilots inwardly felt they didn't need to know what the gunship crews experienced.

21

MEEHAN BECOMES OUTLAW 6

BILL MEEHAN HAD COME INTO THE UNIT TO SUCCEED the outgoing Maj. Roger LaCourse. Senior majors about to become lieutenant colonels filled the position of aviation company commander in these airmobile light unit configurations; this was a prestigious event in a man's military career. If he loused up here, he probably wouldn't go much further career-wise, but there was usually little danger in that. Therefore, we often felt the new officer coming in probably had his stuff together and was a serious personality intent both on his career and on leading us well.

William J. Meehan was an affable guy, obviously an ex-basketball player by his size, style, and demeanor. Those guys always looked like they were going to shake your hand just before a jump ball between two college teams starting up a game. It seemed like an unconditional reflex, one they used all the time. Every move was going to be a handshake, pat on the butt or back, and then, "Hey! How's it going there?" I've always had a jump-back reaction to one of these ballplayers, like, "Hey, we already did that!" I was at the ready, and I knew their response would be, "Oh, yeah! We did!" I guess that's what the game does to you.

Meehan had been in flight school class 55 and had already been in Vietnam in 1962 through 1963 with the 93rd Transportation Company. Returning to the 13th Aviation Battalion for his second tour, he seemed eager to retrace his steps and relive his experiences. On one of his first few days in-country before he was assigned to be our commander, I flew with him in Outlaw 29. I often tried to grab hold of senior officers their first few days in Vietnam when they were champing at the bit to get some flight time and sand in their shoes. Putting one of them in the cockpit as copilot allowed one of my guys to be down for a precious day of rest. Besides, flying with potential senior brass was good politics for me and my unit for use at a later date, when I might need to bend their ear to our side of an argument or have them see our view of a predicament. As scheduling officer for the second platoon, I jumped right on these guys as soon as I heard they wanted to fly with someone. All too quickly, they would be too tired to request any such deal, but before they had received their orders, they were eager.

After supper early one evening, I found Meehan staring at the tennis game in progress directly behind the officers' club. He seemed intent on the progress of the match, observing the level of play very seriously as he leaned against the chicken-wire fence surrounding the court. I approached him from behind and went into my "good first lieutenant act," which I presented to all senior officers when initially needing to address them. They always reacted well to meeting outstanding first lieutenants at the top of their game and serious about their responsibilities.

"Major Meehan, I hear that you wish to fly with the second platoon of the 175th," I said, standing behind him.

"Yeah, I do. I was just watching the tennis game here. Boy, do I want to get in some of that, too. Do you play?" the friendly face inquired, as he turned around.

"No, I don't, but there are plenty of people here on the compound who love to put time in on this court," I said.

"I hope to do a lot of things like this on this tour," Meehan stated. "Boy, the first time you're just too darn busy to do all the fun things this place has to offer. I'm glad I'm back!"

I knew these feelings wouldn't last too long. We all got pretty fatigued in our busy-ness and even forgot we'd had initial impressions like this, but it was always interesting to hear these inspirations all over again, keeping one refreshed.

"Another thing I'm going to do is to take a lot more pictures of the kids," Meehan continued as he strolled away with me. "Gosh, they're so goldarned cute. When you get home the first time, you realize what you didn't take enough pictures of. I'm not going to let that happen this time! Might even adopt one of them," he continued. I was becoming astonished.

"Well, sir, I think the mission we will have tomorrow will bring you in contact with many enjoyable elements of the village peasantry in the region in which we'll be flying. We will be up around the Seven Mountains area, and there is a lot of very nostalgic village life to be seen up there if things go right."

Flying Outlaw 29 that day, which wasn't my ship, taught me that it sailed during approaches. As we went into outposts, I was demonstrating our high overhead circling descents to the new senior major, and I was lousing up because this UH-1D really floated at the end of the spiraling dive. I was getting frustrated at the aircraft, and he thought I was blowing it because I was "rank-conscious," too aware of his presence. I told him that wasn't the case, but I appreciated his sensitivity and overall nice-guy approach to dealing with a subordinate officer. Outlaw 29 was Tommy McCarthy's ship. For the first time, I was glad it wasn't mine, but because its tendency to float was very detrimental to coming down out of the sky when you urgently needed to do so. This was the aircraft I had asked for when O'Kane assigned me Outlaw 23, and at that moment I realized that the gods-of-war had smiled kindly on me and left me alone. Other than that, the day went fine, and I continued to think we had a new CO who would be very decent to know. He did get the job.

Another individual I flew with for a very short time had been a presidential helicopter pilot with the White House, flying those big Sikorskys. He was a senior captain, assigned briefly to the second platoon. It was obvious he was pulling every string he had collected in his distinguished career to get the hell out of the slicks and get back to some stirring job that had no risks. I flew with him one night down on the Bassac River, watching some outpost get it from the VC. He was curious and treating me with considerable respect while I worked with the gunship light fire team, as I knew my job and definitely liked it. That was all right on your first tour, it seemed, but you outgrew it with 20-20 hindsight; I was getting that from these second-tour guys. He was filling me in with the details of flying the old H-21s in the early days of the war. Apparently you were very lucky if you even got 200 hours on those things before they fell out of the air. He said they used to chop those old Piaseckis in half when they wouldn't fly anymore, then sling-load them out over the South China Sea and drop them in the drink. One H-21 had carried half of another; two completed the job. That's how they had eliminated most of them from the Army inventory. He was very impressed with the fact that we could get as much as 1,200 hours on many of the Huey's components; he'd never heard of such a thing. We were proud of our birds and of Outlaw Maintenance's high performance.

As we watched the interactions between the gunships and the outpost defenders, he answered my questions about being the White House pilot for the president, going over to Camp David or Andrews Air Force Base from the lawn, and so forth. But what was going on below us on the ground seemed to be far more interesting for him than recounting his White House experiences.

The outposts had what was called a "fire arrow," to indicate which direction the most intense VC fire was coming from. This was nothing more than a bunch of smudge pots loaded up with kerosene or some other petroleum derivative. The number 10 cans were loaded up with rags and sand, then set ablaze on top of a plywood arrow. From the air, this looked like the oil pots that used to line a highway during roadside construction. Before all those blinking signboards were invented we have now, they would blaze in the dark to warn motorists. The burning arrow would be rotated by the outpost's garrison, pointing at the enemy, so the gunships could determine where their firepower needed to be laid down. "Gosh, they sure got those guys," the captain said. "That thing really works!" It was a treat watching all that tracer fire lace the attackers, and eventually we were released to go home, after watching the show.

This was the night Ron Johnson asked me to let him know when I was about to discard my cigarette out the left front window, because without considerately alerting him ahead of time, it looked like a tracer coming right by him as he sat back there in the crew chief's seat.

A nice thing happened to Johnson and me in early March. The Inspector General's office had Vinh Long on its list, and this was interesting to watch. We in the Outlaws had an outstanding maintenance record, and when you hit 90 percent availability month after month, for six months in a row, the Army got nervous. We even had a month when we hit 99 percent! Other times, we saw 96 percent and 93 percent. When things were going that well, they wanted to investigate you and find how come you were so darn good. They put real pricks into this business, I guess they'd be good insurance-fraud detectives in the civilian world. For every awful job, there are always some bad people who crave it.

Maj. Bob Millward's hangar crew was outstanding, driven by this short, tubby man with the heart of a bull terrier. He flew "Road Runner," a UH-1D totally equipped to take care of any problems we might have in the field; it would have put any AAA tow truck to shame. He never let us forget what it had been like to fly single-pilot missions in the OH-13E and -G models in the post–Korean War era, and we got the picture when the movie *MASH* came out later in the 1960s. He always felt we should occasionally be flying single-pilot in our Hueys, too, to stretch out meager resources, but we let that go. Nobody would take that seriously at higher command levels, so we just let it be his opinion and tolerated his suggestions. However, that's the way he was in all things, and he was a character. There was no slovenly work done in Outlaw Maintenance; he pushed his troops hard, and it was probably a relief for some of them to get out of the hangar and be assigned to an individual ship out on the flight line.

The other side of supplying us aviators with what we needed was Mike Mikuchonis, the supply warrant officer for the 175th. He was really a character! Mike insulted every major and commissioned flyboy in sight. "You goddamn *Ahv*-iators!" he'd mumble drunkenly in your face at the bar. Major O'Kane and a few others had to rein him in at times, but we all loved him. Mike could have outfitted Napoleon's army on its retreat from Moscow. He had procurement tricks that most of the Army probably had never heard of, and never wanted to. I always felt he was borderline prison-time for his feats, but he always retorted to such a threat with "They haven't caught me yet!" through his proud, beery breath. He had a real cohort in his sergeant, whom we called, "Rice Paddy Daddy." Together, these guys could have robbed a country blind. To me, Mike will always be the stereotypical example of an old warrant that no flies will ever settle on. He swapped half of Vietnam by enticing his "victims" with a blued Smith & Wesson .38, and I don't think he ever gave it away in trade. It sure titillated the supply sergeants. As much stuff as he gained for us by using that weapon as bait, I think he left it with one of his friends in Outlaw Maintenance when he departed. With its legendary past, it ought to be in the Aviation Museum at the Smithsonian.

One day, Mark Howell and I were assigned to fly Mike and his rotund sergeant up to the First Infantry Division, north of Saigon. The supply dump was pronounced "Zee-ann," and I believe it was spelled Di An. Located halfway to Bien Hoa, it was the center of the massive buildup of American supplies for the GIs in the bush. Mike had made some kind of a deal with an E-6 there, and he obviously had him over a barrel for that desired .38 pistol. Outlaw 22 was assigned the mission; Mike got together with Mark and me, when I was still flying copilot, and told us he wanted no crew but his sergeant and him on board.

"And take out all the soundproofing, too. I want *all* the weight we can get out of that bird taken out! So we can really load it up!" Mike said.

We rolled our eyes. We had heard what it was like flying for Mike when he had a big deal in mind. Even more surprises were in store.

First, we landed inside the fence of the supply compound. Mike had looked down from the air and told us specifically where to land. The sergeant soon appeared. Mike looked at him, and asked, "Whaddya got?" The sergeant mumbled something in a noncommittal manner, and Mike said, "OK, let's load it up!"

The first load of cargo was reasonable enough; it even looked like we needed it. Mike stayed on the ground and yelled, "Go on, get outta here!" We hadn't planned on flying back alone, without any crew on the machine guns or helping us out, but Mike knew how to stuff the copter to the max; it didn't include his being with us. Mark bitched at him; I knew he was already mad at Mike's tactics as he growled under his breath in his froggy voice, "The Army system works. The supply system works! You don't have to do it this way; not this shit!" I knew then for sure that Mark was serious about staying in the Army for a career; he was going to be a lifer.

I was rather surprised to watch this theater. The supply sergeant thought he had made himself a nice deal to get that blued Smith & Wesson, but Mike wasn't through with him yet. "We'll just sorta mosey around here and see what else they got while you are flying that stuff home," Mike said. I could tell the woes were just beginning for that supply sergeant.

After a few hours' flight time, we returned to find a Jeep-load of more stuff. As Mike was cramming his pillage into the helicopter, I had to ask him finally what all of it was good for. We looked like a moving van.

"Hey, Mike! Why do we need an easy chair and a water cooler? And that floor lamp—who is that for?"

"We'll swap it—all of it—for something else, someplace else!" he replied.

There were even several AR-16s in there, and those are issued by serial numbers. Could we get in court-martial trouble for doing this deal?

"Mike, there is no way you can take these rifles! They're in the inventory *somewhere!*" Mark and I announced—good first lieutenants that we were.

"Don't worry about it! We've got that covered!" said Mike.

Good gawd. There seemed to be nothing this man couldn't do to get around the Army. By the third trip, the anxious sergeant now was becoming ashen-faced. He knew he'd been taken. His face was almost as green as his old fatigues. Just as we landed, he hurried out again from the piles in his overloaded Jeep, slamming on the brakes at the end of the tail boom, and skidding to a halt just at the cabin door. This man was now worried about being discovered. Hurriedly, he heaved his items aboard; he had Mark's whole sympathy. The saddened EM knew his stripes could be on the line if he were caught; Mike had him on the ropes. There was no going back. He stood there, shoulders slumped, in front of Mikuchonis.

"We'll be back next week if you got more stuff," Mike said.

The poor sergeant was whining by now. He was also making feeble attempts to snatch at the pistol, which Mike was holding just out of reach in front of him. The supply warrant held it flat in his hand, at a 90-degree angle, and every time the sergeant plucked at it, he moved it away, like a pet owner playing with a cat. This was a very rehearsed gesture, I could tell. The sergeant's goose was cooked; he couldn't say no at this point, and he was not going to get what he wanted just yet, either. He nodded up and down, numbly.

"Good. We'll see you *then*. Nice doing business with you," Mike smiled at him. He climbed in the back and we departed. Mark was still unhappy about doing supply work like this; he was still muttering about the system working if given a chance.

"Rice Paddy Daddy" and Mikuchonis tokenly held onto the machine guns on the way out. Gosh, didn't we feel well protected.

Together, these men had amassed a huge load of material that wasn't supposed to be on our books, according to the Army's way of doing business. In this war, there was always some incredible swapping or "scrounging" going on for the items you really needed to operate with, and the guys who were good at this task were given the honor of doing so for their units. Outlaw Maintenance therefore had seven Lycoming turbine engines it wasn't supposed to have; during the IG inspection, they hid these down at the Navy Yard near the other end of the town of Vinh Long. About nine deuce-and-a-half trucks filled with supplies Mike wasn't supposed to have were parked over at the Irish missionary nuns' convent. On the day of the inspection, they flew every aircraft that wasn't being used on a mission out to airstrips around the Delta and parked them; none were bunched up at the same place. Gee, I was impressed with my senior officers!

Only one Huey was left at the Vinh Long airfield for the Inspector General's team to go over. That was our ship, Outlaw 23; good ole 800 itself. By this time, we had rebuilt it, repainted it, brought it up to peak condition, and lordy-lordy, they thought we had done just fine without anyone ever mentioning it to Johnson or me. It sat there alone on the Outlaw ramp and awaited its vultures. We walked away smugly and flew another aircraft that day; we pent up our anxieties until the fateful inspection period would be over.

When we returned, we went over the green logbook and quickly scanned what they had found wrong with our bird. Surprisingly, not much. We looked and looked again. On Outlaw 23's -13 logbook report was the comment, "There is an inch-and-a-half scratch in the grey paint of the cabin floor." We got down on our hands and knees and eventually found it. Barely discernible. To pick it out, you needed to see it from an angle that caught the light. Good work, good eyes, we thought. Way to go, IG inspection!

Another senior major with whom I happened to fly during March was Maj. Lem Magoon. I could tell he was a saber-rattling, straight-leg Infantry type who somehow had gotten aviator wings, but he was a ground-pounder at heart. These types scare flyboys, because they never really take us seriously and think the only legitimate command is with troops on the ground. Most helicopter pilots I knew in this war felt they wanted to die with a clean shirt on; we prized our job, and you could very well have the rest of it. And how come we couldn't make our own occupational choices in this man's Army without always having to pose as a career officer, "in for 20?" We were in for our three-year obligation and a little more; wasn't that enough? How come they didn't appreciate us giving our time?

I flew with Major Magoon one day for the same reasons I had flown with Major Meehan, and apparently I impressed him enough with my demeanor throughout that flying day that he asked me to join him later at the bar. I did so, once again for political reasons, and he beamed at me as I sat down. I could detect that as a young officer I had made a good impression that might be valuable down the line.

"Lieutenant Eastman, I would think a fine lieutenant like yourself would give his right arm to be with an infantry unit up north!" was his opening line.

"Are you shitting me?" I said, putting my big foot in my mouth. "That's exactly what *would* happen to me! It's already happened to a few classmates of mine from Benning. No, sir, that is not what I want at all!"

Looking up at his face immediately told me that I had blown it, and possibly for all time. This is how you make enemies with these Regular Army pricks. One has to be astutely political at all times, being what young officers are supposed to be. The warrant officer pilots had no such criteria to dress up to. They could be military slobs as long as they flew well. Back in Texas, my flight commander would call them, "Flight-line-hippies." With their gunfighter mustaches, they fit the bill. Now here was Major Magoon, who would soon be Outlaw 5 and one more nonflying XO who did not take a shine to pilots. Totally competent around the company area, hard-assing the troops while the CO flies, but to me, a Regular Army boor who would be taking his tour in Vietnam as an aviator but posing always as an Infantry officer—all the way to full-bird (colonel). With my crossed rifles on my collar, I was always in conflict with these types, and they put me off. They were always condescending toward aviators, as the Marine Corps habitually has been, even with all we were doing with the Hueys in this remarkable helicopter war. These types literally kept me from "staying in" this man's Army. Well, the deed was done; there was nothing I could do to keep this man from taking off my head any time he would have the opportunity to do so from this moment on.

Seven Mountains area near the Cambodian border, just south of Tinh Bien. All photographs by the author unless credited otherwise.

Sunrise at Vinh Long, showing the Mavericks' parking area at the east end of the runway. The water seen in the foreground will soon be the Cobra Pond.

Soc Trang and Vinh Long ships in a joint formation. That's a "V" of five ahead, with a straggler aircraft to the right. Gary Wesselman photo.

Major Don Casper, Outlaw 3, and acting airfield commander; later Delta 3. Don Casper photo.

Major Roger LaCourse, Outlaw 6, with some VC suspects in the background. Don Casper photo.

Major Gerry Hileman, Maverick Lead, standing on the left, with his beloved Mavericks--all sporting "goatees" in late 1966. Young Terry McDowell is getting some help growing his, by one of the third platoon of the 175th. Terry McDowell photo.

Major Bob Millward, 150th Maintenance, standing in front of "Roadrunner." He is sporting the chest protector we all wore, and that Dempsey and Casper should have been wearing on Easter Sunday. Bob Millward photo.

Crew chief MacDougal and door gunner Coleman cooking up some C-rations over the "white-bread-and-JP4 stove."

WO1 Mike Rheihofer overlapping rotor blades on the way back from Saigon.

The Outlaws "parked" in deep grass while awaiting a lift outside of Camau.

Captain "Willy" Stout's Outlaw 19 with a number of patches covering bullet holes in its tail boom; "Negative Suppression!" Gary Wesselman photo.

First Lieutenants Troy Tison and Fred Stetson share a moment in front of a 114th Red Knight aircraft, just after landing at Tay Ninh.

An Outlaw ship flying in front of Nui Ba Dinh (Black Virgin mountain), over strips of defoliated triple-layer jungle below. This was the infamous "Agent Orange" sprayed by the C-123 Providers.

American troops disembarked and tactically deployed in a typical savanna-like LZ in Tay Ninh province.

Outlaw 23 on short-final on a resupply mission for the American troops in the big November operation. Gary Wesselman photo.

We're back home! Smoke trails from grenades wired to Outlaw 21's skids as we return to Vinh Long.

First Lt. Dave Eastman becomes the AC of Outlaw 23.

Duke Cone and Roger Kalinger are having a tough time bartering with this fruit vendor at Moc Hoa. The EM door gunner is saying the kid is charging too much.

The tower celebrates Christmas at Vinh Long, 1966.

The compound's "company street," just in front of the 175th orderly room.

The first and second platoon living quarters of the 175th aviators. Note the freshly planted banana trees!

Our two hooch maids; old Sanh the house-boy about to swig a beer.

Stets taking it easy on a down day by the Outlaw hooches; a book of Robert Frost close by.

Spec. 4 Ron Johnson, crew chief of Outlaw 23, and door gunner Coleman.

The Outlaws landing in straight trail down the Vinh Long runway.

The awards ceremony following the Battle of Easter Sunday. General Seneff pins the award of the Silver Star on First Lt. David L. Eastman. John Niemier photo.

The new Maverick C-models were quickly painted up by Oscar the artist. Spec. 4 Daugherty does the windshield wiping service.

The "Hog" with its 24 rockets on each side. Maverick Lead's aircraft.

Captain Joe Moffett briefs a fire team before they relieve other gunships in the OA.

Crew members Farr and Von Schwedler alongside WO1 Terry Holley's "Ba Moui Ba."

Looking inside at the minigun's targeting sight and trigger apparatus; the rocket firing scope is on the far side of this Maverick cockpit.

Outlaw 23 parked on the Outlaw Ramp.

Looking over the river at Chau Doc, headquarters of a Special Forces "B" team.

Vietnamese soldiers playing their traditional two-string instrument while taking a break

A village group somewhere deep in the Mekong Delta. It is possible that these people, by their dark features, are of Cambodian descent.

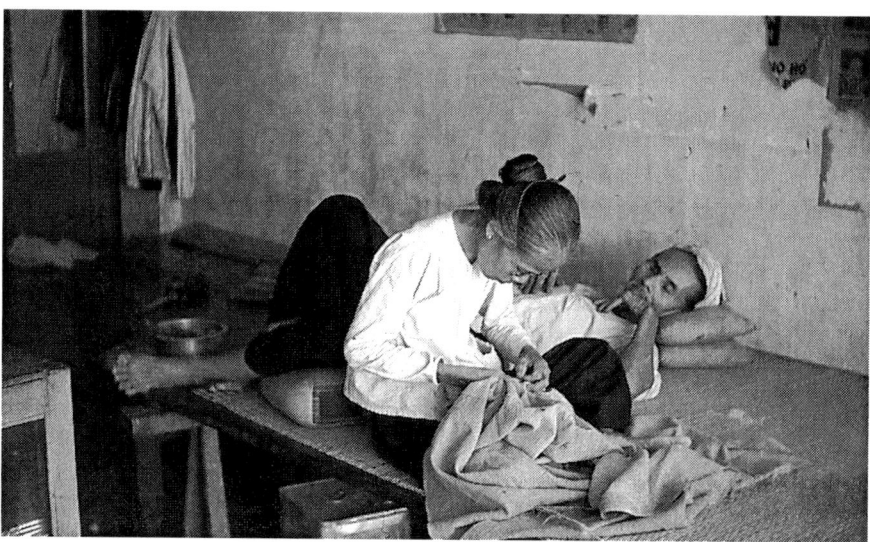

These two old people have most likely spent their entire lives together, just like this.

Typical over-the-water hooches and places-of-businesses near Rach Gia. Gary Wesselman photo.

Extended "left base" over the Mekong River for the Vinh Long airstrip.

Jim Martinson returns to flying status at Vinh Long, as he recovers from being wounded twice on Easter Sunday. Jim Martinson photo.

Another extraction is nearly over! ARVN soldiers depart from a 20-to-30 ship lift of Soc Trang and Vinh Long "slicks" on the Vinh Long airstrip. Jim Martinson photo.

The Outlaws picking up the troops at the beginning of a long day. The landing formation is straight trail.

Gunships patrol overhead as the slicks land the MACV advisors and Vietnamese soldiers in a rice paddy LZ.

The author as Outlaw 24's aircraft commander at the tenth-eleventh month level of his Vietnam tour.

Stets and Nguyet pose together as we depart Vinh Long on our last day; Hershey joins in for the picture.

22

THE BATTLE OF EASTER SUNDAY

MIKE HERSHEY HAD LANDED A NEW JOB. His aircraft, Outlaw 19, had been retrofitted to be the 175th's smoke ship. Mike, always looking for a position that would make him quite singular, would be flying "Smokey," a near suicidal aviation idea that provided an obscuring smoke screen alongside the landing zone for the incoming flight. This supposedly provided visual protection for the lift coming just behind his aircraft, but it also made him an absolutely easy target for the VC to fire upon at the head of this smoke. The smoke ship would make a very fast pass at the treeward side of the LZ for the flight, and thus hide the crews from the VC in their positions. This would be done initially at considerable speed, with the pilot in command pushing down the "Chinese hat" atop the cyclic stick's handle to create the amount of smoke needed, slowing back to 60 knots as he did so. Bullets, however, would still come through the smoke at the formation, but the VC were firing at something they could only hear, not see. Seeing the tracers coming through like bronze darning needles was eerie, even surrealistic, and very discomforting.

This smoke ship was used extensively throughout the month of March. Mike would zoom down the treeline on one side of the flight with theatrical effect. Sometimes the smoke would drift over the incoming formation, causing some confusion, and other times it would also disperse too quickly. I had my doubts about the effectiveness of this new concept, and I thought any aviator performing this valorous feat quite brave. "Smokey" took a few hits during his working day.

The "smoke" was engine oil sprayed into the hot exhaust of the Huey's turbine. A generator pumped this oil into the ring surrounding the exhaust stack; the thin ring had small holes in it for squirting the oil into the hot flame. Electrical controls leading from the pilot's cyclic stick activated the generator's pulsing of the oil outside to the ring. The smoke came out with a big "whoosh" and created a white roostertail plume behind the speeding Huey as it raced alongside the LZ. Very showy and vivid, and an exceptionally easy target.

Mike soon was shot down in the vicinity of My Tho. Although the Mavericks closed in on him quickly, and protected him from any further onslaught by the VC until Meehan in Outlaw 6 rescued him, it was quite apparent that this was a dangerous mission assignment. The smoke ship obviously was destined to take a lot of hits.

The earliest Easter Sunday I have ever encountered was 26 March 1967. As the years go by, I await an Easter of the same date, but none has ever arrived as early as this historic date engraved in my mind. We were supposed to have a down day for this important holiday, so no flights were scheduled for the Vinh Long aviation companies. Therefore, it was with some surprise, and considerable irritation to hear the alarm siren go off in the second platoon hooch right over my bunk while we were bent on sleeping in.

"All Outlaws report to the flight line. This is a scramble! All flight crews move directly to the flight line! Move to your aircraft immediately!" said some strange, authoritative voice over the loudspeaker.

I didn't even know they could talk over this alert system. The siren signal was different than what I had heard before, too. Usually when this speaker sounded off, it was remarkably like the "low-RPM audio" beeping in the Huey when the liftoff had sucked the RPM down into a dangerous area. It was not fun to wake up thinking you were crashing inside the Huey, instead of just experiencing a mortar attack. I hurriedly dressed and headed out of the hooch toward Outlaw Operations beneath the tower. I was the first one there.

Having never been first in anything in my life before, I was slightly astonished at myself. The sergeant there, with other EM I always saw in our operations told me I was to proceed to Sa Dec and pick up the command group there. I said, "OK," and picked up Andy Keeney, who had just shown up at that moment, as my copilot. We would together ferry the Senior Advisor and his contingent to wherever they had to be put on the ground at the CP for whatever was unfolding.

The Sa Dec helipad was up over a river, and when you took off from the riverbank to the east, you were immediately immersed in your own rotor wash's spray droplets, splattered all over the windshield. A tricky moment, with the ground effect of the hover also being dispersed by the over-water takeoff. This 9th Division helipad was downtown, in an urban area, so during landing, we had to be on the watch for kids flying kites over the buildings. Not only could these kites get caught up in the rotor system as a hazard, but, even worse, the kite string could demobilize the aircraft, wrapping itself around the push-pull tubes around the mast and ceasing all control measures to the rotor blades. Definitely dangerous—and the kind of quirky thing to which helicopter pilots have to be attentive in their lives.

We loaded up the tall bird colonel, his top sergeant, and the rest of this senior advisor staff, and pulled pitch. Just as we cleared the embankment, with the water spraying up from the surface below, this crazy colonel handed me a note, hanging it right in front of my face, and I couldn't see a thing for the takeoff! I screamed, "Andy, take the controls! Finish the takeoff!" He did, and avoided losing too much RPM and crashing into the drink. For a brand new pilot, he did a very good job under the circumstances. Irritated, I turned to the large colonel standing over my seat, with his wrinkled note in his hand.

"Sir, if you wish to speak to me, you may hand your note to my crew chief!"

"Hush! Just hush!" said the tall, hawk-nosed colonel. "Just shush and take me to this place on this note! *Here!*"

I then looked at the small piece of paper he had given to me, and it was scribbled, "Tra On." I told Andy I knew where that was, and we proceeded to this little outpost on the north side of the Bassac River, just across from Can Tho. I couldn't help but remain upset about his moving forward on takeoff and nearly putting us down into the river.

Upon landing, the irate colonel started yelling red-faced, "This isn't the place! This isn't the place!" I quickly showed him the map, and he then informed me he wanted to go to Tra Vinh. He had mistakenly taken two towns' names and invented a third with the combination, and we had surely found it for him, showing once again it could be done. So we proceeded over to the Tra Vinh airfield. Then he wanted to be transported to Vung Liem and land in the marketplace there. We did that, and on short final, all hell broke loose in the rear of the ship. A tremendous thumping occurred as we settled into the marketplace area; I thought we were losing our transmission or something of that nature. As we made it to the ground, amid all the Vietnamese vendors and their stalls, I turned around to inspect what we had just survived. I couldn't detect anything right away and inquired what had happened to the ship. The first sergeant was looking back at me with a pained expression on his face: "It's nothing, sir, he does things like this *all the time!* Please forgive us." It turns out the bird colonel had been throwing a tantrum on short final, actually stomping his feet on the cabin floor of the Huey with all his leg strength. It had sounded like we were seriously coming apart. I was becoming increasingly appalled with the old gentleman's strangeness. The staff got out of the ship, looking very perplexed. This was my first contact with Colonel Robert Bringham, Senior Advisor to the 9th ARVN Division, who had a considerable reputation as a nut-case. He was indeed very frightening. I learned later than many senior pilots had filed complaint reports about flying with the old man.

We still did not know what had transpired to affect the emergency scramble, but were beginning to overhear that a town's outpost had been hit hard during the night by an entire VC battalion anxious to secure the weaponry inside the mud fort. Whether or not this was the true story, it was typical of the VC to hit with overwhelming force, and to calculate that our having a down-day holiday meant our helicopters would not be able to react in time. It also was not unusual for us as a flight crew to let the day proceed onward and see if there was any truth to this unfolding rumor. After all, the senior advisor staff didn't know much more at this point, either. This was the way most of our life went in Vietnam anyway.

We were to be sent over to the temporary command post being set up at the Caumoy Bridge, where highway 7A from Vinh Long crossed the Mang Thit Canal. As I headed there, I heard over UHF that a helicopter was down with maintenance troubles somewhere alongside this road on the Vinh Long side of this waterway. I asked Paddy Radar for coordinates, and plotted them out on my plastic-covered map. Looking over the site from my cruising altitude, I saw nothing, and asked for the coordinates again, just to check out their correctness. At that point, the entire Outlaw lift passed underneath me at a lower altitude. I could recognize our ships by the two broad white stripes we displayed on our cabin tops, which thoroughly set us apart for identification purposes. I had never before been separated from the flight in formation, and we certainly looked pretty from this higher position. They were swinging around like a huge school of fish, apparently headed for Vinh Long, about sevens miles away to the northwest. This was immediately after their second lift into the LZ area; I would learn later they had just moved troops from Tra Vinh. I decided to get off Paddy Radar and switch the radio to the Outlaw's UHF frequency to learn what was going on. I was curious.

I listened for a while, and heard that a *number* of ships were down—two to be exact. Since I was flying empty at that time, I volunteered my services. I was told to stand by. Then I heard gunfire in the back of the radio transmissions and realized there was a war going on. This wasn't a maintenance situation at all. The two ships had been shot down in the LZ from which the Outlaw flight had earlier escaped. Now, the radio traffic seemed to indicate that Colonel Dempsey in his Delta 6 ship was planning to go into LZ Alpha as a single aircraft, and others were warning him against this rescue. This was not an uncommon situation for the old Oklahoma cowboy, who I'd heard had served with General George Patton in WWII. He often took a lot of hits doing these stunts, and ruined a lot of ships, besides getting his crew shot up occasionally. Pursuing these heroics, he could be a young gunship pilot's worst nightmare. Just recently, the 82nd Medical Evacuation unit had told Major Casper, now the Delta Aviation Battalions' operations officer, to let the "Dustoff" pilots do the aeromedical rescues and not risk losing the battalion commander.

He wasn't going to make it this time with his impulsiveness. Dwayne Williams, flying with Major Farley Jordan in Maverick Lead, saw Dempsey going one way as they flew down the edge of the treeline in the opposite direction. There was no way they could have covered him, even though the major gave out with the customary: "the Mavericks are on you." For some reason, Jordan leaned over and switched off all the little toggle switches on this young pilot's intercom panel so "Willie" could not hear what else Maverick Lead had further to say at this moment. I heard Delta 6 broadcast, "I'm going in after my men!" despite the fact that Meehan in Outlaw 6 was advising him against it. It was rather like listening to Custer's Last Stand, if that had been broadcast over aviation radios. The guns recommended stridently that he not go in, but he replied he was on final. The Mavericks tried to close in on him as he descended, firing rockets into the tree line to the south of the LZ, but it was all for naught. As Delta 6 landed, smoke was already pouring out of his tail.

"This is Delta 6. We're hit. We're down in the LZ!"

No further replies came to the Mavericks' desperate pleas, and I was beginning to feel glad that nobody had let me go in and help out those downed ships. It was obvious that something serious was going on here, beyond my previous presumption of a maintenance problem, so I decided to fly over and take a look-see. Several plumes of ghastly black smoke climbed into the misty sky over the LZ east of the Mang Thit Canal. They looked out of place, like oilfield fires polluting the air, coming straight up with their awful smoke. Delta 6 was now down in the LZ, along with the medevac ship that had tried to rescue the downed crew of Outlaw 17, Jon Myhre's ship. Something had gone terribly wrong on the initial lift; I felt lucky to have missed out on it. I returned back to the CP at the Caumoy Bridge and landed, quite shaken.

The MACV advisors there, peering over maps and charts that every command post keeps on hand to oversee the battlefield's progress, asked me if I had seen what was going on. Did it look bad as it sounded? I replied that indeed it was, possibly even the worst I had seen in my tour so far. The white-haired lieutenant colonel addressing me looked at me intently, and said, "Really?" I didn't mean to sound like a leading authority on warfare, but nodded numbly. He pondered this response and went back to his maps. "We will have you go back up there and fly C & C for us, as soon as we get some people together here to do that with your ship." I indicated I understood, immediately figuring I was going to miss out on the war that day, being safely up at altitude watching this big show, while my buddies were going to get shot at and had already been shot at. I wondered in my mind what their story was.

When we were airborne again, I informed Outlaw 6 that I was a regimental Command and Control aircraft in the area, and I was told what altitude to maintain in order to avoid a mid-air collision with any of the other aircraft on station. O'Kane and Meehan were flying together, and I knew O'Kane would be immensely helpful to the new CO this day. Once these communications were done, this status gave me almost an amusement-park ride on the northerly side of the operation, as we watched incredible airstrikes go in below, courtesy of the U.S. Air Force. They pulverized the thick treeline from east to west with antipersonnel cluster bombs that made the ground look like huge, exploding Fourth of July sparklers. It didn't look as though anything or anyone could survive these bombings, but that was what was happening. As soon as the air strikes would pass, the VC would be somehow firing again at the gun platoons. They seemed indestructible to the tonnage being dumped on them. We listened to all the astonished cries from the gunships as they continued to receive withering fire during their passes. While we orbited elliptically, the advisory team in the back seat looked outward and down to the ground. It was if we were looking at the war from the top of some grandstands. I couldn't help continuously thinking that I was having the easiest time of it for a very terrifying day for everyone else concerned. I felt left out and slightly guilty; it doesn't get this soft, I figured.

This was Andy Keeney's first shoot-em-up, and the young warrant officer was showing his boyishness. As he watched the devastating show out his right front window, he started turning to me and quoted, "War is hell! You know what I mean? They say it is, and it really is. I didn't know it before. War *is hell!*"

I replied, "Yes, Andy, I guess you're right. War is hell, I get it." This exchange went on all day as the young man registered his first trauma at seeing combat from a helicopter. The first time is always the worst, and you don't know how you're going to take it. The movies haven't quite got it right yet; I could help them a lot with the special effects. . . .

Skyraiders from Binh Thuy airbase down near Can Tho pummeled the treeline, and then aircraft began showing up from the Tactical Air Control Center in Saigon, as requested. We watched F-4C Phantoms rake the treeline with their bombs, and F-l00's, too. It was a real show, looking like some combat aircraft module hanging in a young boy's room on thin, nearly invisible strings. All their attacks were directed at this 600-yard-long treeline of tropical forest, which was at the most 300 yards thick fronting LZ Alpha, where the downed crews huddled amongst the ARVN. Gunships passing over their forms radioed that all the downed pilots and crew members looked OK; they had observed them hiding behind the rice paddy dikes crisscrossing the very muddy LZ. We could only hope they weren't hurt, just stoically waiting for rescue after their ships had gone up in flames.

After a while, the backseat let me know we could return to the CP, which I was glad to hear, because I had done all this so far on two hours of fuel and didn't have too much left. They nodded affirmatively to this information and we went and set down. There wasn't much to do there in the hot sun but wait, and that's what we did. It was weird to know that a war was going on only a few miles away. Looking up at that smoke still billowing skyward was eerie. We felt disconnected, knowing what those downed crews were going through. They were having a hard time of it, and watching a Skyraider suddenly climb up at that distance produced even more of a disenchanting feeling. It was like watching someone else's town burn up a safe several miles away, while you are hearing the news of it over the radio in your kitchen. The slight columns of smoke rising at such a distance belied the terrible things happening beneath it all.

Suddenly a Major Palenchar strode out of the CP, carrying a carbine and all dressed out in combat gear. We put away our C-rations that we had been eating for lunch and stood up. He said, "The advisors that originally were put into the LZ with the first lift are all shot up; some even dead. We're going in to replace those men!" I motioned for Johnson and Coleman, my door gunner, to untie the rotor blades from the tail boom and get ready to crank. Oh boy, I thought, we *would* see some action today after all. The Huey came to life and we lifted out with Palenchar's five or six men who would be replacements in that hot landing zone. After notifying Outlaw 6 of my mission while enroute, I descended from altitude to the LZ and came rapidly over the treelines in conflict, diving down in a speedy approach and rushing past scattered palms and banana trees from the east. I low-leveled the best I knew how, but I nearly hit one gunship coming from my right; it reared back and passed over me. I soared into the LZ and then right through the damn thing because the easterly wind was at my back with this approach angle! Standing the aircraft on its tail, I ridiculously sailed through the smoke being laid down and out into clear air again, well beyond my touchdown point. Still going at high speed, I wound up in the open area beyond the LZ and just on the other side of the western treeline bordering the conflict. I couldn't let this foolishness happen any further on this downwind approach, so kicked left tail-rotor pedal while I flared the aircraft's nose up high and to the left. I had nearly killed us doing the same thing a few weeks earlier, and Johnson knew it. He didn't like seeing me try this maneuver again; I could feel that from the back seat. It was a dangerous way to kill lift; you could sink through and crash. However, this time it worked, and the aircraft ceased its high speed glide through the rice paddy area, and stopped. Palenchar had to get out in the clear, but he did have a safe treeline in between him and the LZ, so I hadn't totally put him in deadly peril. Maybe this placement even kept him alive. As we set down, his small squad of rescuers dispersed, and I took off again. I climbed back up to sweet altitude, and thought my job was over.

Little did I know that while I had been on the ground at the CP, Major Farley Jordan, with Meehan's permission, had planned a huge rescue operation for the downed crews. Old Flash himself had designed a daring plan that no self-respecting gunship platoon leader ever would have devised, but it worked this day. Jets could strafe their targets and zoom back into the sky after overflying the enemy, dropping their bomb loads or napalm directly on them, but this was *verboten* for helicopter gunships. They were constantly warned *never* to overfly their VC targets, no matter how much target fixation caught them up in their task. It was just too easy for ground troops to kill the slow-moving Hueys then, no matter how fast at 80 knots their pilots thought they were performing their gun runs. "You can't outfly a bullet," I was always telling my copilots.

Lt. Rex Latham, a little red-haired infantry advisor, had crawled up to the downed crews hiding behind the rice paddy dikes and assembled the wounded for rescue. He also got on the radio to the CP, informing his superior officer, Major Palenchar, that his immediate commanding officer in the LZ was dead and things were not looking good. The VC were very close to the helicopter crews, some in bunkers out in the open only 50 yards away, or even closer. During the air strikes, the VC had turned their attention skyward and shot at the Air Force, then resumed their firing at the pinned-down ARVN in the LZ, who were not returning much fire themselves. Many were seriously wounded. Not much progress was being made in this dangerous onslaught, and there was a real fear that the downed crews might be captured themselves. Without the air cover, the VC might have overwhelmed the troops in the LZ at any moment. The South Vietnamese certainly were outnumbered, and probably short of ammo by this time. We would learn later that the VC actually left their bunkers and laid down in the mud, almost among the ARVN forces, while the jet strikes occurred. When over, they went back into their camouflaged bunkers and resumed their heavy automatic-weapons fire. It is tough for a helicopter gunship to put rockets *into* the door of mud-walled bunker, so the Viet Cong battalion had been able to continue their fight all day. They were doing well, and were very coordinated.

Major Meehan had no more time to waste. This was the only moment to rescue the downed crews. The rearming and refueling of the armed helicopters at Vinh Long airfield had gone so well, that the turnaround time had shortened from 20 minutes to around eight minutes before each ship could get back in the air again. Jordan thought up a plan of having all available guns link together in a long daisy chain and put suppressive fire *straight down* on the entrenched enemy for a rescue attempt. The entire team of gunships would be led by Chief Warrant Officer Jerry Daly, in "Viking Surprise"—their version of the smoke ship in Soc Trang. Daly had a .50-caliber in the backseat, sitting on a mattress for further armament in this converted D-model. Jerry Daly was already famous, and the most decorated helicopter pilot in the Delta, having received the Silver Star, three Distinguished Flying Crosses, two Bronze Stars, and the Purple Heart twice over. This incredibly brave man would lead the gallant daisy chain of 11 ships and lay down smoke to hide us as we rescuing helicopter pilots went into that vicious LZ. Daly figured how many passes he might be able to make, wagering his supply of oil for the smoke generator. It took him approximately 32 seconds per leg, flying directly over the fortified enemy. He had the emotional reserve to discipline himself for measuring out this necessary oil for the repeated passes covering us on the ground as we made our medevac attempts. He also had an adverse wind, which would keep blowing away the smoke he had laid down over the treeline.

I only learned of all this preparation while I was climbing back up into the sky after dropping off Major Palenchar. There never had been a briefing on the ground to collect the rescue helicopter crews. Other than the Medevac ship, this was all spur-of-the-moment stuff—absolutely spontaneous. I let Outlaw 6 know that I was empty and very available to go back into that LZ again. Meehan replied, I'm sure without thinking, "Sure, sure. Go ahead, Outlaw 23!" He probably didn't even know where I had come from. Mike Hershey was now with Major Millward in "Road Runner," because he had been the first ship shot down that day with the initial Outlaws lift. He had limped back to the runway with Outlaw 19 and parked his smoke ship at the west end of the strip, where it said "08" on the pavement, because it could go no further. Walking down the runway along with his copilot, Ron Petty, he had bumped into Major Millward and decided to fly with him the rest of the day. The 150th maintenance ship was always orbiting nearby in the operational area, which was his job. That's why "Road Runner" was available for the rescue. (Mike has since told me that the first round he took in Outlaw 19 that day severed the electrical connection to the oil generator, so he couldn't even lay down smoke as he made the first pass down that dangerous treeline.)

The third ship was a real Dustoff from the 82nd Medevac, and the final ship is Major Juri Poometuu himself, flying with John Niemier—or more likely, *being flown* by the young warrant officer from Malibu, California. This Outlaw ship had just dropped off some troops in the nearby area, so he was also readily available for the mission. The four ships were assembled for this rescue mission on this very impromptu basis.

At 2,500 feet after making the decision, I turned around to my crew and grimly said, "Everybody get a personal weapon on them. We may not come back up out of this one!" I figured this was a decent thing to do at the time; many people never thought of this necessity on the way in and then wound up on the ground defenseless. And, having been in there once already, this time I was not going to blow the approach! We were going to get this one done right if we were going in at all. Everybody said OK, and I commenced the dive.

We came in down through the same gap in the trees I had found the first time, and approached the burning ships in the LZ. I thought of something I had learned of previously, and that was to go up behind the blackened helicopters, and utilize them as a shield. "Let them take the fire!" my head was saying. Their burning smoke would hide my bird, and their damaged fuselages would absorb a lot of bullets intended for my ship. We came to a stop behind a derelict ship, maybe Delta 6's, and I looked out across the LZ. My eyes were searching for the downed crews and I was seeing none. What I was observing were the flattest human beings I have ever seen in my life. The remaining ARVN soldiers were hugging the mud with such agonized expressions on their terrified faces that their eyes were mere slits in their grimaces. They had pressed their bodies so deeply into the rice paddy mud that I immediately thought of the flatness of "Sail Cats." Those are the run-over animal bodies one sees on asphalted highways after too many vehicles have run over the same form. Here, you couldn't tell which Vietnamese were dead and which ones weren't—until they turned and faced your ship with that traumatized look.

Jerry Daly went by again and again in the D-model smoke ship accompanied by his copilot McDonald. All the available gunships in the Delta dutifully followed him around, pouring down all the munitions they had on board with point-blank desperation. It was incredible firepower, suppressing the VC a scant 150 feet away from us. Thus, 350 members of the VC's 306th regional main force "Tato Battalion" were not able to adequately prevent our rescue effort, even with their close presence. (We dubbed this outfit the "Potato Battalion," as a nickname that sounded like their

Vietnamese word "Tato.") Trembling with fear in my ship, I still was not seeing any Americans, however. Looking over my shoulder out the right door of the Huey, I saw the other three helicopters drift into the LZ, settling in for their landings. Suddenly, my aircraft started being loaded with Vietnamese wounded. The surviving soldiers were frantically heaving their corpses and critically injured soldiers on board, and I truly thought they would overload me before I could accomplish what I had come in to do. I could just visualize for a moment, 20 or more corpses sliding out one door, while they continued to load them feverishly from the other side of the Huey. I petulantly screamed over the intercom at my crew, "We're in here for Americans! We're in here for Americans; don't let them put any more wounded on board!"

At this moment, I saw Major Don Casper. He stood up just in front of Delta 6's smoldering helicopter to my left, and then casually started strolling through the mud toward my ship. I thought it incongruous that he was taking things so well when all around him were showing the greatest display of human fright and panic that I had ever seen. Then he stumbled. I quickly realized he was very hurt, and said to Johnson, "Goddamnit, Johnson, go get him!" This was more from an adrenaline response than anything thought out, but Johnson, God bless him, went out. He ran through the gunfire like a heroically motivated nurse, with his flight helmet mike cord snapping about behind him as he sprinted. My very next thought was that I had just given an order that could cost this man, now my friend, his life. I suppose as an officer you *think* that might possibly happen some day, but it is a heavy realization when you realize you just did that act.

Johnson got to Casper, stopped his high-speed pursuit, and embraced his wounded charge with all the dispatch of a medical orderly. They slowly moved towards my ship as if they were in some hospital rose garden, taking an invalid's walk. Casper later recalled his legs felt like they weighed several hundred pounds each, and the mud kept pulling at his boots. The gunships circled and laid down intense fire. Daly selflessly came down again and again with his repeated passes, constantly taking hits, while these two looked like they were out of a old age rest home, with all the time in the world for a nice stroll. It was high contrast.

When Johnson got Casper to the ship, the young crew chief also plugged in his helmet cord, which I always instructed my crew to do so that we again had immediate commo with each other. I knew that Casper was now down at Battalion as Delta 3, so quickly inquired through Johnson where Delta 6 was. He must have been flying with Colonel Dempsey to be in the LZ at all. Casper snarled loudly back with his response over the sound of the gunfire: "He's dead, and you're gonna be dead, too, if you don't get outa here!" He obviously did not want me to be the fourth burning ship in the LZ, but I was even more taken aback with the news of Dempsey's death than my own present situation. Wow, did that information ever stun me and I really needed to tell somebody about this shocking development! Until now, we had thought *everybody* was OK—not even wounded, much less dead So there I was in the LZ feeling like Lowell Thomas, and I had to broadcast this like a newscaster to the known world:

"THIS IS OUTLAW 23 IN THE LZ. I HAVE DELTA 6's COPILOT ON BOARD. HE SAYS DELTA 6 IS DEAD. I SAY AGAIN DELTA 6 IS DEAD!"

Meehan's voice came back: "Roger, 23. Get the hell out of there, 23!"

We started to pick up, and I didn't know how many wounded and dead ARVN's we had back there, along with Casper. This was going to be a downwind takeoff severely overloaded, and I didn't know yet whether this weak old ship is going to make it. Airspeed would have to suffice over power because we sure didn't have any in this ship. I started nudging it along, and we were looking pretty good at an ever-faster, increasingly speedy two-foot hover. Then we started bleeding off RPM, and I screamed over at Andy, "Beep me up! Beep me up!!" He said, "I have, I have; you've got all you've got!" He had been helpfully pushing the governor button all along. I said, "Oh. . . ," and put the pitch down a bit. We made it out, and I flared the aircraft up into the sky, taking advantage of every bit of that 120 knots of airspeed I had just built up. I took it right to the redline of "Velocity to Never Exceed" before I pulled that stick back. I'd never been there before. We are climbing up to 2,500 feet when I heard Johnson yell over the intercom.

"He can't breathe! He can't breathe! Level off!!"

I did so at 1,500 feet and gave the controls to Andy. I turned around to look at Don Casper. He looked like a volunteer at a Boy Scout first aid demonstration during some Thursday night troop meeting. Coleman and Johnson had taken down all the first-aid packets that had been adorning the inside of the Huey's cabin up to that time, and they were putting them on Casper's body and right arm, and properly. The major had a hole in his sternum, a web-belt tourniquet around his right arm (two rounds have ripped through his bicep), a bullet under the skin behind his neck, and a few other wounds, too. Apparently Casper had a very high pain threshold, indeed. He sat there while all these bandages were being so amply applied to him, and looked up and said, "They got me, the bastards." And, I'm thinking to myself, "What are we, in some Hollywood movie set, here?" These quotes are too good! What a script!

Behind me and still down there below, the Dustoff ship picks up his downed medevac crew of Hook and Jordan, as well as ARVN and other helicopter crew members like Kidd, Rhodes, and Ross. The MACV seargent carried the wounded Outlaw 17 door gunner, Joe Watson, to this ship and desired to leave himself. He was that scared. Poometuu actually stepped out of his Outlaw aircraft into the mud to help his EM pick up the wounded Americans, including Watson and the half-buried Major Eberwine from the first Dustoff ship. Jim Martinson, Jon Myhre's copilot, also got on board this second platoon ship—his fourth helicopter of the day. Poometuu and the crew all worked together to get the wounded men free of the sucking mud which so held them. John Niemer held onto the controls while our wild anti-communist freedom-fighter acted so heroically. Hershey and Millward got the rest in "Road Runner." As the ships reached capacity, they all edged forward with their loaded takeoffs and finally cleared the rice paddy dikes and dangerous mud, fighting to ascend skyward. They would all make it; we had pulled it off.

One last note. When Jerry Daly set down the "Viking Surprise" smoke ship at Vinh Long, after somehow stubbornly making it there, Major Millward immediately pronounced it "nonflyable" as it had one main rotor blade split by an enemy round, and the rest of the ship had approximately 73 bullet holes in it. I heard he had made 18 passes over the enemy positions, each time taking multiple hits that actually made the aircraft shudder with their impacts. The only crew member injured in this incredible bravery was the copilot, McDonald, who received the Purple Heart along with his Silver Star for taking a shrapnel fragment from his armor-plated seat into his cheek. Amazingly, the uncountable rounds delivered at "Viking Surprise" missed everyone else.

A few weeks later, the after-action report would show that slightly over 100,000 pounds of bombs were dropped on that nefarious tree line, including 28,000 pounds of napalm. (This latter item was wrong, however, because both Meehan and the folks stuck on the ground knew that things would have been resolved very quickly if that treeline had been stroked with napalm. The VC would have been fried in their positions, and the day would have gone much differently. Somehow, these distortions result in any skirmish of war and become factual matter over time.) Over 100 aircraft took part, flying nearly 1,200 sorties. They fired 360,000 rounds of 7.62 mm ammunition. Besides the three helicopters destroyed in the landing zone, Hershey's ship and 12 others suffered reparable damage. Scattered among the bomb craters and grotesquely battered trees were 142 Viet Cong bodies. Twelve Americans were wounded in the battle; four more were killed. ARVN losses were 42 killed and 69 wounded.

23

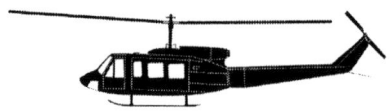

ALL ARE SAVED SAVE ONE

Heading to Vinh Long to refuel, I called up Paddy Radar and asked if they knew what was going on in LZ Alpha. "Yeah, we've heard about that today," the Delta's flight following service said back to me. "Well, I have a WIA in the backseat and am wondering if you could do me a favor," I requested.

"Sure, what is it?" Paddy said.

"I need to refuel in Vinh Long, but I must get this man to the hospital at Long Binh. I only know it is there up by Bien Hoa, but don't know how to navigate there to the medevac pad. Can you give me a radar vector there through Paris Radar? And second, can you do this over the land line and let the hospital also know I'm coming as fast as I can. It's kind of important." I waited for his response.

There was a pause, and then he came back over the UHF. "They got ya, Outlaw 800. When you get there, we'll put you right over the tents of the hospital, then you can land at the pad."

Whew, I said to myself. That's the best phone call I'd ever made in my life.

I only intended to quickly refuel at Vinh Long and hurry forward with the one-hour flight to Long Binh. When I came down on my final approach over the west end of the runway, I could see the sight that had greeted the gunships that Easter. Captain Dale Sherrod stood out in his white tennis clothes, which he had worn all day long while directing the rearming and refueling effort. He was resplendent in these togs, and you could see him all the way down the runway during short final. Everyone volunteering was also in civvies, and close to a hundred people were milling around on the metal surface down where the Mavericks usually parked and took off. That eastern area of the Vinh Long runway had an old PSP surface covering it then; the rest of the strip was crushed rock. The compound's personnel had been linking ammo for many hours and capping rockets for the fray over at that LZ. All those pilots who were still down that day were working on the ground, taking care of their buddies who had been flying that battle on Easter Sunday. Jack Payne and Terry McDowell had been among these, and so was Ray Novotney, newly in-country with the second platoon. They'd had a busy day of it on their end of things, and they had made the difference,

I parked at the confluence of the runway and the maintenance wash ramp, where Outlaw 6 usually sat. Many of the wounded ARVN were being taken off Outlaw 23 by their Vietnamese personnel; in the chaos, Major Casper casually walked off the ship. John Savelli was pounding my chin bubble with congratulations, but I was motioning desperately towards Casper, indicating that he needed help. Savelli looked at me first with those wide-open Italian cow-eyes, then at Casper, then back at me for confirmation. I shook my head emphatically, "Yes, he's hurt. He's HURT!" gesturing with my gloved hand. Savelli hurriedly left my side of the ship and moved over. Major Casper was totally covered with grayish mud, and the bandages were covering up his bullet holes somewhat. Then he said, "Hiya, Doc," as his slim, six-foot-four frame teetered above young Dr. Hillegas. "I'm having a little trouble breathing." When they finally got him to sit down on the stretcher, they lugged him off like he was a mahout on an elephant safari; he never did lie down. His left lung had collapsed, and he was in such shock, he remembered none of my rescue until weeks later. The reason he was remaining upright was that was the only way he could breathe; he couldn't do so lying down. Somehow, he was simultaneously very aware and in great trauma. All of us remarked how strong his constitution had to be.

Doctor Jon Hillegas, our flight surgeon, took it upon himself to set up an emergency room in his medical quarters for the incoming wounded from LZ Alpha. Normally, medical people at the Vinh Long dispensary didn't do much except check us out for VD when we came back from Vung Tau, and treat the enlisted personnel for the same when they contacted these diseases in downtown Vinh Long. Ear funguses were another potent problem, contracted while showering in nonpotable water. That was about it for typical medical problems with the aviation units here.

On this day, lives would be saved due to Doc Hillegas' quick treatment as the rescued men with their serious wounds emerged onto the runway. At the doctor's office, the downed crew members had to be hosed off to get rid of all the gray, clinging rice paddy mud covering them. Hillegas had Casper sit down in the dispensary's room, and he inserted a hypodermic needle between the ribs in his back. He said he didn't get much air; his thoughts were perhaps now the tall major should have less difficulty breathing with the damaged lung. The young doctor asked him if he had been bandaged in the LZ! Casper replied my crew had done the work in the helicopter.

Once the wounded were patched up, they were sent via official medevac helicopters to Long Binh, so I was relieved of my task of getting Casper all the way up there. He was placed on the same Dustoff with that medevac unit's own Major Eberwine, who filled in Casper enroute with what had happened to him. Without Doc Hillegas, Don Casper *might* have died on the way, despite my efforts to get him to adequate medical attention. Until the Ninth Infantry Division moved in at Dong Tam the following year, we Americans had no actual medical facilities in the Delta to take care of us after a catastrophe like this. Only three of the Americans shot down in LZ Alpha had not been wounded—Jerry Ross, Bill Rhodes, and Mike Kidd.

After watching Casper being taken care of on the strip, I picked up the bird to a high hover and moved over to the Outlaw ramp for refueling; my first chance that day. At the moment, I never realized I had completed the heavy takeoff with all those wounded aboard precisely because I *was* nearly out of fuel. About 1400 pounds worth—that's what the difference was, fully fueled versus empty. After shutting down Outlaw 23, I wanted to talk to the guys waiting around the ramp for their version of what happened that morning in LZ Alpha. The two slick platoons of the Outlaws had stayed on the alert out there on the ramp south of the runway throughout the day, tensely awaiting further lift orders. Harvey Persyn talked to me first: "I saw what you did out there. You're lucky to be still alive." He had a queer look in his eyes as he gazed upon me.

"What do you mean, Harve? I haven't seen you all day." I was puzzled.

"I was right behind you when you went into that LZ to pick up those crews. I thought you were a goner for sure. The fire was so intense that I turned back!"

I pondered that for a minute. I had a standing order within myself never to return the exact way I had just come in; I saw no reason to get shot at by the same people twice. Harvey apparently had followed in on my tail and received that fire.

"How come you were there? I didn't hear you call anybody," I said.

"I was out there resupplying with Poometuu. I thought I might try this rescue thing, too. Maybe help out with an extra ship, you know. But when I heard you volunteer on the radio, I said to myself, 'What a ham! That's the last we see of ole Eastman!'"

He was serious. He had pulled off with all good judgment, taking a lot of fire as he did so, confirming his decision. Then he watched the rescue effort by us from on high. Flying into the LZ, I had felt darn near part of a suicide mission; I hadn't seen at all how I was going to survive this recovery attempt. In fact, there seemed to be no way to live through it; I thought I was going to die trying. I was prepared to wind up on the ground a wreck, too. But, it was just unimaginable for me to let those guys shot down in the LZ suffer any longer, nor have us fail to rescue them. I would certainly want it done for me! Throughout this terrifying event, I just worked things out as I went along; my mind didn't have a plan.

My constant feeling all the way through the fast-moving approach in was that my death was always about two minutes behind me; in fact, I should already have been dead. I had no rational explanation for why I was still alive; it didn't make sense. All during the approach, my mind was intensely speeded up, and I was making decisions faster than I could even think. Time had slowed down where five seconds had felt like five minutes. For the first time in my life, I had intensely experienced a lot of high speed psychic phenomena. Most of the time in the LZ, I had been so scared that I was only conscious of "If I could think right now, that was a good decision!" It was over, but I still had not quite come down from it.

After we refueled, I headed back to the CP site, where I loaded up some people for Sa Dec. It was early evening when we were headed back to Vinh Long again. Andy Keeney kept right on saying, "What a heck of a way to spend Easter!" along with his continuous mantras of "War *is* hell! Just like they said!" and "You know what I mean, Dave? War is hell! Did I say that yet? War IS HELL!" Finally the day was done, we were released for home plate, and we shut down the bird on the Outlaw ramp.

One thing I overlooked definitely shows that truth is stranger than fiction. Once we had returned from Vinh Long to the CP after refueling, Johnson was up on the cabin roof checking out the hub. Slipping on some oil that was always leaking from a particular seal, he fell off the cab of the Huey and onto the left-side machine gun that Coleman was working on. The gun went up to Coleman's armpit and discharged a single round there. It burned a hole in his shirt with the muzzle flash, but the bullet exited well beyond his back and into a crowd of Vietnamese villagers mingling around the bridge. Johnson fell to the ground alongside the standing Coleman, shaken up but otherwise unhurt. I had watched the whole thing and nearly had a cow.

"Jesus H. Christ! Will you take it easy!" I shrieked. "You just did a magnificent thing out there; now don't louse it up by killing each other!"

"Hey, I'm still a little nervous, OK? My legs are pretty rubbery after going out there after Casper like that, you know?" Johnson implored.

I looked at him. "Really?" I asked.

"Yeah!" he said.

"OK, well just take it easy and rest up a while then. Stay off the rooftop of that Huey until you can walk straight again." I smiled at him.

That's all I needed, my two crew killing off one another after the VC had failed to do so. The most amazing part of this was that when I returned my gaze to the villagers at the bridge, none of them were writhing on the ground with an M-60 round in their guts. Lucky all around. I couldn't imagine why that bullet fired at armpit level into that crowd didn't hit someone. It was definitely time to take a breather.

Hanging around the platoon hooch that night was different. We didn't know how to dump the extreme emotions we had felt all day. It was a certain kind of nervous feeling, even though we knew the day was over and we had every right to relax. There was, however, a new feeling that we'd never had before to cope with—one of us had failed to come back. Jon Myhre was still in that LZ and presumed dead. When we finally got around to counting noses, he had not been picked up by any of us. His rescued fellow crew members of Outlaw 17 truly believed he had burned up in the Dustoff ship when it flipped over. His leg was so injured that they knew he could not escape the exploding aircraft in time, and perished in this manner. They also had not seen their AC since the crash, so in their confusion, reported to the CO that he had burned to death. This was a truly bad feeling. He was a favorite with all of us, and I was especially close to him, because we used to do a lot of folk music together. He was good on the guitar and I always liked to join in vocally with someone with musical talent. We had enjoyed there being an "us." I could not comprehend his death, nor could I find the emotions to properly address the situation. When the Armed Forces TV in Saigon signed off at the end of that long day, John Savelli looked at the flag waving on the tube while they played the national anthem, and said, "Jon Myhre died for that flag today."

"Gawd, I guess that's what that statement really means," I said to myself.

Apparently when the first lift went into the LZ, the VC had remained absolutely quiet, despite the Mavericks' initial reconnaissance by fire, until the Outlaws' touchdown in two "V's" of five led by Dave Alexander. The gunships were putting direct hits into straw-covered hooches that weren't disintegrating; that should have been a clue that they were in fact mud-constructed bunkers. As I've described, Hershey was hit first in the fast-moving smoke ship, disabling him on his first pass from west to east.

The Viking gun platoon had earlier prepped an LZ a quarter mile short of where the Outlaws landed, and the slicks saw those results on the way in. Jet strikes had resulted in some fires off to their right side. But at the last moment, Meehan ordered the lift to bypass this original area on short final. "The name of the game is support!" the new Outlaw 6 said; he didn't want the ARVNs walking too far. So, the flight extended itself further east into an LZ that had not seen much gunship ordnance expended into it. Some of the Mavericks felt angry about not being allowed to protect their Outlaws more; they thought they should have had more of the preliminary action. So in fact, the resulting LZ Alpha was actually rather untouched.

Joe Watson, Jon Myhre's door gunner in Outlaw 17, was on the same right side of the aircraft as his AC, listening to the Armed Forces radio station in Saigon over his helmet headphones. He saw nothing until they came to a hover. It seemed like just another day, dropping off troops on another boring lift. Then he saw men abruptly standing up over by the wooded tree line on the southern side; they were also starting to fire at the flight—right at his aircraft, in fact. Suddenly, a lot of heavy fire was coming at the Outlaws. Lou Paulin, leading the second "V" of five, had a B-40 rocket explode just in front of his ship while flying with newly arrived copilot, Carson Snow. The mud flew all over the windshield; they futilely turned on the windshield wipers, vainly trying to clean it off. The door gunner in this ship, Spec. 4 Ralph Cella, had a .50-caliber open up from 10 yards away in the palm fronds of that adjacent treeline. The right side of this flight was now raked by intense, withering fire. As Cella fired the Huey's M-60 on his side at the emplacement, his machine gun jammed. When he opened up the breech to clear it, a frightened ARVN soldier leaned over and vomited into it! That ended that gun's ability to return fire. Cella ducked down behind his "chicken-plate" armor vest as he heard the "pom-pom-pom's" of the fifty's firing as it continued shooting into the rest of the formation. For some reason it couldn't lift its grazing fire high enough to get Paulin's ship on takeoff.

Tommy McCarthy in Outlaw 29 had another new pilot on board, Vance Shearer, who was hit in the helmet with a ricocheting round, and collapsed on his cyclic stick, knocked out cold. Mac, attempting to right the ship, went careening across the LZ directly at Harvey Persyn in Outlaw 27, who felt he surely was going to die this time. Skinny little Tommy finally was able to get Shearer off the cyclic just enough, even though the copilot remained unconscious. The round took a big white gouge out of the back of his flight helmet; the ship took almost as many hits as its call sign. While Outlaw 29 was coming directly at 27, with Tommy battling to get the unconscious Shearer's body off the controls, two VC appeared just in front of Harvey's aircraft. They had branches and leaves attached to them and came up out of spider holes. One man stood up with an AK-47 and pointed it right at the windshield. Then, to Harvey's amazement, he turned the weapon six feet away from the ship's nose and fired a burst into thin air, as if he were leading the aircraft in full flight at 80 knots airspeed, instead of at a hover. The VC were trained to shoot at aircraft that way in flight; apparently this one didn't know what to do differently aiming at a hovering Huey.

"Get out of there, Outlaws!" Bill Meehan yelled over the company UHF.

Various Outlaws experienced automatic-weapons emplacements on their very unorganized departure out, as did J.R. Wright, flying with Ron Cone. All was chaos. Duke Cone had only been AC for a week; his copilot had recently come down from the First Cav. They passed right over a heavy machine gun position on a dike line on the way out; it was shooting right at them and other first platoon aircraft. The whole flight sustained incredibly intense fire from the worst Viet Cong battalion around to engage—the "Potato Battalion." This day, they were reinforced by a heavy-weapons company. About 350 individuals were with this unit at this moment, and they opened fire on the Outlaws at point-blank range when they had come to a hover. ARVN soldiers tumbled dead out of the ships as they landed; some had even been hit while still in the helicopters. Most who got out, ran away to the nine o'clock position; the VC fire was all coming from the right. Jim Parrott was amazed seeing this happen. The combustion chamber of Jon Myhre's ship, Outlaw 17, was hit by a B-40 rocket or a .50-caliber round, and he couldn't get the damaged ship out of the LZ. His engine was slowly running, but couldn't produce any torque. The ARVN's wouldn't even get out of this disabled slick.

"This is 'White Four!' I can't get out of the LZ! I can't get out of the LZ!" called Myhre. His rotor blades turned slower and slower.

Ten feet from touchdown, his hydraulics had gone out, and he had performed a hovering autorotation. His engine stopped next, and as the ship took rounds, he and Jim Martinson, his copilot, were hit. Jon's thigh was smashed by automatic-weapons fire, throwing his leg up over the radio console, and Jim's jaw was hit by a round, slicing his cheek open. Stunned, and looking straight ahead, the young pilot was also shot in the arm; he had only been in-country three weeks. The chin bubble on his side blew out on short final, with the rounds coming into the ship and through the instrument panel. Metal fragments filled his face, along with the round that creased his face, and also made the hole in his cheek, which he found himself breathing through. His left eye swelled up and he could only see out of one eye. Blood covered his whole face. He fought desperately to free himself from his pilot's seat, and asked Joe Watson as he moved out to the back, "What does my face look like?" Watson thought that a ridiculous question at this particular time, but the two wounded aviators were successfully dragged from the ship by their still unhurt crewmembers. But after the door gunner and Kidd, the new crew chief, managed to get the pilots outside, Watson was shot.

After dropping out on the ground, Jon Myhre's former Marine Corps' enlistment experience really took over for him. He was recalling many things from basic training as he returned fire with the VC in the treeline. Firing at the muzzle flashes with his carbine, Myhre emptied two banana-clips of solid tracers into the vegetation; he felt successful. Watson and other crew members were yelling at him to get out of the open area and join them. He was extremely angry at his predicament; thinking he was going to die and would never get to see his new-born daughter, who was only six months old. Tracers were flying everywhere across the LZ.

From altitude, Major James Eberwine in the medevac ship immediately went into a high overhead circling descent to come to the aid of the downed first platoon crew. At first, he had no idea how much contact there was going on with the VC. Upon landing, he found out quickly, and turned his ship's tail towards the enemy for some scant protection. They picked up the wounded under heavy fire, but they had taken a pounding themselves all the way in. The medevac's crew chief, Mike Kelley, was immediately shot dead doing his heroic work getting Myhre into Dustoff; so was Captain Mitchell the MACV advisor, attempting to help. Watson was dragging Myhre to the ship through the mud when he was hit again. They were almost too incapacitated from their wounds to climb aboard the helicopter, which the medevac crew did not realize quickly enough. Jim Eberwine finally understood it fully, while Kelley was lying face down in the rice paddy goop, quite dead. He wanted Watson and Myhre to pick his crew member up and throw him on board, and he was motioning to them to do so. But they were just barely able to get themselves on the Huey, and precious time was wasted corresponding in this confused situation. All the

VC fire became centered on the ship. Both flight crews later said the sounds made while the aircraft fuselage was receiving the intense fire sounded like many aluminum beer cans being crunched, continuously and loudly, with the rounds plinking through all at the same time. Viet Cong machine gun fire continued to rake the ship after it was loaded with the downed Outlaw 17's crew; aircraft soundproofing panel material and other interior parts flew apart all over like a gangland killing scene. On successfully accomplishing a takeoff into translational lift, Eberwine, who was the pilot flying, had a round come through the floor and knock his leg off one of the tail rotor pedals. This .50-caliber round come through Major Eberwine's left calf, shattering his shin bone into a compound fracture. The impact smacked this leg into the other one, which jerked the helicopter ninety degrees from the flight path. Both feet had kicked full right pedal. Jim said, "I'm hit. You have the aircraft!" to his copilot, Charley Jordan, but it was too late. The aircraft's unusual attitude caused the skids to hit first, then the rotor blades hit the ground. The Dustoff ship cartwheeled twice before it burst into a ball of flames, after it had been seen barely inching along for takeoff with the injured men. It crashed.

Eyewitnesses to the burning ships later told us that Jon Myhre had perished in the Dustoff ship because he was so crippled by his leg wounds, that he could not have climbed out. The Huey was lying on its side when it burned. Eberwine went out through the shattered windshield, hopping on his right leg. He left behind his camera, a .45 pistol, and a mint-condition Thompson sub-machine gun still hanging on the seat.s Jordan said to him that the patients and Hook were all safely out of the now-burning aircraft. Joe Watson had been hurled around inside the tipped-over ship with Jon, and had valiantly tried to help him get up and out, but could not. They all moved 20 to 30 feet away from the burning wreck, and then it totally exploded. Jim Martinson was amazed how quickly it had erupted into flames, burning with secondary explosions. Somehow Jon Myhre became separated from the rest of the wounded men after this escape; some did not feel he had gotten out at all. He had crawled away in a different direction.

About an hour passed. The Dustoff crew and the remainder of Outlaw 17's crew were about one hundred yards from the VC held treeline, and 30 yards from their burning medevac ship. Eberwine used the carbine's sling for a tourniquet for his injured left leg. A crack-shot, he endeavored to keep the weapon's muzzle out of the mud in case the VC attacked. He felt confident that he could take six or seven of them with him if they did. The pain began as the trauma set in. Lying in the intense rays of the tropical sun, he thought of death and his wife's last letter to him. She had not been having a good day when she wrote.

"You think combat is tough? I have your three sons! I was getting chocolate milk out of the refrigerator; slipped on the dog poop, and threw chocolate milk all over the kitchen. You should be here to help clean the kitchen!" she had told him.

He looked up. A landing helicopter had smoke pouring out its tail, and was rapidly becoming on fire. It touched down so close to him that he had to pull back his arm to prevent the Huey's skid pinning him underneath it. The aircraft's doors opened up and the fleeing crew ran past Eberwine to escape their burning ship. Col. Dempsey was dead at the controls, slumped over in his own command helicopter.

After initially being dragged to Dempsey's ship by its crew chief, Rhodes, and loaded then unloaded when it was shot up and burned, Martinson had had to get out of three ruined helicopters within an hour's time. They all became nonflyable death traps for him rather quickly. From then on, it was a "bad day at Black Rock" for these downed flyers. For the rest of that hot day, they underwent what the rest of us dared not think about ever happening to us. None of them ever thought they would survive; they all felt they would surely die.

When Delta 6 was landing, rounds penetrated the ship and hit the S-3 and Colonel Dempsey. Casper took rounds on short final in the right arm and side. The force of the bullets impacting his body threw him off the controls and against the armor plate of his seat. Every light and whistle in the aircraft was going off. As he rolled over the armor-plated shield on the left seat and went out the door, the wounded Casper dove for the mud. He was spewing blood like a fountain from his many bullet holes. The Plexiglas had exploded with the burst that killed Dempsey; pieces of it went everywhere. The volley of fire came from the front. When the three other crew members were all outside the aircraft and hurriedly crawling away on the ground, they realized Delta 6 was still on board. Casper had hoped their colonel had gotten out the other side of the ship OK, but such was not so. Keeping low, they returned to the smoking ship after the door gunner and crew chief put a tourniquet on the tall operations officer's arm. Laboring, Major Casper and another crew member, probably Bill Rhodes, tried to get Dempsey out of his right seat, but the Delta Aviation Battalion's commander didn't budge as the ship began to burn up. Later, Casper would realize they had never undone his seat belt; that's why they couldn't move him. The colonel was slumped over in his straps, killed by a burst of automatic-weapons fire from a machine gun nest 50 feet away in a dike line. They finally had to quit pulling on him as the flames increased. The aircraft had started burning even before it had touched the ground; so the flames were getting pretty hot by this time. All the while, the VC poured bullets into the ship as they worked; surprisingly, they only turned on the major when they had thoroughly hosed the engine area of the helicopter.

After abandoning the attempt to retrieve Dempsey's body, the crew all crawled away to the nearest rice paddy dike, including Jim Martinson, who had tried to help the effort after being taken to the ship himself. Delta 6's left skid had nearly landed on top of his prostrate form when the aircraft finished its approach into the LZ; he hadn't been hard to find. Major Eberwine had been close by the right skid.

The situation looked bleak. Casper told the crew chief, "Make peace with your maker. Today is the day of reckoning." Rhodes replied back, "Don't say that, sir!" Casper pondered, then realized maybe that wasn't the smartest thing to prop up the young man's morale. They moved across the paddy dike and rested; they were pooped. The young Martinson and older Casper adjusted the tourniquets on each other's arms.

After receiving so many hits, Casper then spent most of the day remaining face down in the mud, hiding behind the rice paddy dike. There, sometime during the long hot day under that blazing sun, an old, wiry ARVN sergeant crawled up to the senior major and checked over his wounds. Delta 3 gladly let the experienced ARVN NCO check out his condition, but did not like his diagnosis. The diminutive sergeant undid the American's blouse, looked at his wounds, and shook his head, saying "No," as if there was not much hope. The former Outlaw 3 and Vinh Long airfield commander didn't need that appraisal! The long, lean major survived on his resources for the rest of the day, seeing no other crews except his own people, as they were keeping their heads down in the mud. Jerry Ross, the door gunner crawled off a bit.

Jim Martinson remained with Major Casper behind the dike, but he was not able to see much because of the concussion he suffered from the round slicing his face. He had been lying face down in the mud, nearly unconscious, when Delta 6's crew had first discovered him. Casper and Martinson continued all day to help each other with first aid for their bleeding arms. When the Air Force dropped its 500 pound bombs, the concussion from the loud explosions lifted their tired bodies right off the sodden ground, bouncing them painfully. Dirt from the shock waves also fell over them, hurting their wounds. The VNAF dropped their ordnance from an altitude of 1,500 feet or more, and this terrified the downed fliers as they worried the Skyraiders might miss their targets. But the bombs went into the treeline at the last minute.

Having no more energy to move any further away, the wounded major had a front-row seat for watching the air strikes rake the treeline. As the Air Force approached to drop their ordinance, the VC would blow a whistle and a tremendous volume of fire would erupt at the incoming aircraft, swinging up from firing at our troops on the ground. Just as this load was dropped, the VC would blow another whistle and the upward fire would cease. Then they would continue shooting across the rice paddies of LZ Alpha, putting grazing fire on the prostrate airmen and ARVN. For what seemed like hours, Casper watched this disciplined coordination by the Viet Cong leaders and waited out this hell. He would peer over the rice paddy dike until the second whistle blew, then pull his head back down below the dike's level for safety. He wondered when the VC would leave their positions and close in on his crew's. It seemed like the best place for the enemy to be. The air strikes then would be compromised, and the downed crews and shot-up ARVN troops would be able to do little to stop them. There could be no more than half of the original 100 Vietnamese soldiers still left in LZ Alpha, and their ammo had to be low. Uppermost in everyone's minds was the constant fear of being captured by the superior force. The helicopter flight crews were all concealed in the rice plants between "the good guys" and "the bad guys."

However, Casper recalled later that the most significant moment following their doomed landing was watching Dempsey roll off the throttle to flight idle as if he were in a normal shutdown mode for finishing a flight, turning off switches and the like. Absolutely bewildering. What was on his mind for taking this outrageous risk? Besides that, they had left their chest protectors in the cargo hold of the Huey, as Dempsey often did. They hadn't thought to wear them while taking off abruptly from Can Tho, and Vinh Long a while later. These two senior officers paid for that indiscretion. The second chance to don the "chicken-plates" had come when Dempsey landed on the runway to brief Outlaw 6 at Vinh Long after the first Outlaw flight had already left.

We went to bed, mourning Jon and thinking over what a big loss he would be to all of us. I slept fitfully, so I was not surprised to have some crazy dreams that night. In one of them, someone was standing outside the screen windows of my hooch, screaming over and over again, "He's alive! He's alive. He's alive." I was convinced I was truly hallucinating. The next morning, at my breakfast table in the club, I tentatively asked the officers there not to laugh at me too much, but I'd had the strangest dream of Jon

Myhre actually being OK and rescued. The two or three guys at the table looked up at me, and said, "But it's true. They picked him up about 11:30 last night. They brought him here first and he's now up at Bien Hoa, and they've sent a second message to his wife that he's wounded in action, but no longer missing in action. He's going to be all right."

I felt simultaneously relieved, and almost faint, as I stood there holding the back of my chair, waiting for my body to get itself together while all these draining emotions coursed through me. This was getting a bit much.

"How did they get him, when he was supposed to have burned up in the medevac helicopter?" I softly asked.

"He apparently crawled away from the burning ship, busted leg and all, and hid in the mud, at a completely different angle away from everybody else. An ARVN stepped on him late last night, and an American advisor was called over to assist them in finding who it was. It was Jon Myhre. A Cobra or Lancer gunship jettisoned its pods and brought him in. They threw him in the back with all the ammo."

That little red-haired lieutenant, Rex Latham, once again had played a significant role in all this. As he searched LZ Alpha for dead and wounded, he had found Jon and radioed to a medical officer from Binh Thuy circling overhead. The doctor diagnosed Jon's injuries accurately, and they dropped morphine into LZ Alpha for his pain. A while later, he was successfully picked up and brought to Vinh Long.

The yelling I had heard outside my hooch in the middle of the night had been from Ray Leuty. When Jon's mud- and blood-caked body was placed on Doc Hillegas' operating table, he was nearly unrecognizable. The young doctor asked for someone from Jon's unit to come up and positively identify him, because too many of the injured men had reported him dead. When asked for his name, which Jon excitedly gave in his doped-up pain, those present in the medical facilities actually told him that was *not* who he was, because people *had seen* Jon Myhre die, so he had to be somebody else! Ray Leuty was Jon's platoon leader, so he gladly went up to make the formal ID in the treatment room. I hadn't dreamed it—I actually had heard Leuty gleefully screaming outside my windows at something like two in the morning; Jon Myhre had indeed risen from the dead on Easter Sunday.

When Terry McDowell, Jon's close friend, heard the news, he ran up to the dispensary in just his skivvies. He said Jon was very animated on the dose of morphine, and he wanted to describe everything he had been through, despite his terrible pain. He was mad about the ARVN who found him earlier in the afternoon, looting him of his Seiko watch, so Terry gave him the one off his own wrist to make him feel better. About a dozen other Outlaws, including Stets and other members of the first platoon, were jammed into the hallway just outside Hillegas' "treatment room" awaiting word of Jon's outcome.

Jon reported that in the afternoon he had played dead when discovered by the first ARVN soldier, who began to immediately loot his body. He let him take everything until the stealthy Vietnamese thug started to remove his wedding ring. Then Jon figured "to hell with it" and slugged him, even ready to kill him if need be. In the resulting fracas, a shot rang out from the VC in the treeline, and the round found the little ARVN above Jon while the struggle was going on. Jon felt guilty about the man's death, but he used the dead man's arm for a headrest the remainder of the day. He used his helmet, too, and at least now had a weapon.

When ARVN soldiers later discovered that Lieutenant Latham was searching in the darkness for wounded, they directed him over to the site where Jon lay. There was also something about a strobe light being used to catch the attention of the Spooky 51 flare ship orbiting overhead, but Jon denies this device being present. The C-47 dragon ship just happened to have the doctor along for the ride, and this Dr. Witta had radioed down the diagnosis so young Lieutenant Latham could help Jon. They had overheard Latham radioing to Major Palenchar the report that he had found a wounded American in the LZ.

Jon's tale of surviving that long, hot day is pretty grim. After climbing with great effort out of the burning wreck, he slipped down in between the skids and the underbelly of the overturned medevac helicopter. Somehow, even with his shattered leg, he managed to climb up the now-vertical surface that had been the cabin floor. Then he fell down into the mud. He said he might have been on fire himself, because all that was left of his flight glove on one hand was the leather ring around the wrist. He crawled away in a different direction from where the other crewmembers went, but not by choice. He just had to get away from the burning aircraft; then he needed to hide from all the VC that were in that landing zone, possibly even up in the nearby palm trees. First, he buried himself almost completely in the fetid rice paddy muck so that only one eye was exposed. He attempted to cushion his thigh, with its leg bones all in fragments. The automatic-weapons fire was grazing the LZ so intensely that the VC's tracers were going just past his stomach. He said if he'd had any more weight on him, he would have been hit by these bullets. This went on all day. He thought every second of every minute of that day would be his last. The noise was intense from both the enemy fire and the Army and Air Force bombing and strafing. He was not wearing a flight helmet, so the volume was louder than any of us had ever realized.

Many months later, after spending time in Walter Reed Army Hospital, he was able to tell us that the reason the airstrikes had not accomplished much was that the VC had whistles and bugles to alert their troops with. When those withering jet strikes had occurred, the VC had come out of their bunkers and laid down all around Jon in the grass. They were very disciplined, and tenacious; none cracked and refused to go back. Each time they moved out, he feared they'd discover him. He prayed they wouldn't and burrowed down deeper into the mud, still trying to cushion his broken leg with its splayed bone fragments. He was in excruciating pain and complete terror, but used his previous Marine Corps training to remain absolutely still. He never gave up hope of our rescuing him, but it must have been horrible when we all took off and left him behind. Each of us thought someone else had gotten him in their ship; we were crushed to learn that nobody had. It seemed a terrible joke that only one man had not been picked up. It was as bad as picking up no one at all; and far crueler than if only half had been rescued.

Jon later told me that I had nearly flown right over him on my departure out of the LZ, with Casper and all those wounded Vietnamese. In the hospital at Bien Hoa, he asked the major why he had not sighted him as Johnson and he made it to my bird. (They brought Casper in to talk to Jon the day after Easter Sunday; it turned out that the lanky major had never been very close to where Jon lay in the LZ.) Jim Martinson was also in the same ward area with the other two shot-up aviators.

Myhre recognized my ship when I flew nearly over him on takeoff, because I had a yellow-and-black target painted on the bottom of the aircraft where the ADF antenna was supposed to be. Johnson had ordered this automatic direction finder apparatus some time earlier, and it had never come in. In the meantime, he had installed a piece of sheet metal over the space. Once down under there, had taken a can of black spray paint and humorously made concentric circles over the lemon-yellow anti-rust paint. He thought it very funny, and both of us had forgotten the joke on ourselves. Some felt it ballsey that we were flying around the country with a target painted on our belly, but we had just plain forgot about it after it was done. Many of the ground troops frequently told me that they knew which ship was mine because of that target; it was well known by all those who were consistently below Outlaw 23. Oh well, that's what absentmindedness will get you.

Over the years, I have pondered what I would have done if I had recognized Jon kneeling up desperately just as I passed by him, while I was earnestly trying to get that RPM up. Would I have jettisoned many of the Vietnamese wounded to save him? Could I have survived doing so once I left the cover of those burning ships? No one will ever know, and Jon has insisted that I would have been killed if I had tried. He was in an untenable position, scarcely 150 feet from the entrenched VC. He makes me feel like a fool for even considering it in hindsight. Maybe I am taking too much for granted after having survived that day, but, after all the pain and PTSD trauma in his life, right down to today, I sure wish I'd had the chance to try it. Really I do. God, give me back that moment to attempt it!

24

R & R AND THE SILVER STAR

FOLLOWING THE BATTLE IN LZ ALPHA, the various bits and pieces of what all the participants had done gradually came together. In the intense moments of combat, nothing is as organized as it seems when watching all the war movies that have ever been made. In fact, quite the opposite is true, and many of the major players never get any credit—only because somebody simply didn't notice their valorous actions. In this case, General Seneff himself overflew the area because of Colonel Dempsey, the battalion commander, had been shot down. It was an unusual event in itself for a man of this rank to be a casualty. Most bird colonels and officers around this rank were orbiting over operational areas in Vietnam, not performing rescue missions down into them. So Hawkwhip 6 himself took a look during the Battle of Easter Sunday.

General George P. "Phip" Seneff, Jr., was not only commander of the First Aviation Brigade of all the independent aviation companies, he was also responsible for most of the airmobility concept we were carrying out in this war. Since January 1966, he had been responsible for the organization, activation, and command of the aviation brigade, whose patch we wore on our left shoulder. It had a hawk pouncing in front of the sword seen on so many Vietnam command patches. This was emblazoned on a dark blue background, bordered with gold embroidery. General Seneff had also been with the 11th Air Assault Division (Test) at Fort Benning, Georgia, when the airmobility development idea started. This group later became the First Air Cavalry, the first airmobile division, the way paratroopers had been the first airborne divisions in WWII. But these guys were jumping out of helicopters on the ground this time instead of planes in the sky. He had initiated the UH-1 and CH-47 Chinook programs for the Department of the Army, and in 1965, he had succeeded in obtaining the Cobra attack helicopter for the Army, an aircraft we had yet to see by early 1967. So, this was the guy who was our general, in charge of the aviation tactics and techniques used by all of us 23,000 personnel in his brigade, flying 4,000 combat aircraft overall. Not only was he our commander; he had thought it all up. He *was* Army Aviation.

When General Seneff observed the rescue by the four helicopters of the downed crews, he told Bill Meehan that he wanted decorations for the aviators conducting the successful mission. Meehan said, "OK, they'll get Distinguished Flying Crosses." "No," said General Seneff, "I want those men to get Silver Stars." An awards ceremony was scheduled soon afterward, with the brigadier general himself present and decorating us personally.

Pat Tominey was our platoon awards officer, and he told me that I was getting a medal. "Really? What'll I get, a DFC?" "No", said Pat, "Silver Star." A chill went through me, and I actually stopped walking at the moment. Immediately reflecting on all the men in the U.S. Army and other service branches who had earned this medal through all our wars and conflicts, I was stunned. I couldn't believe I was going to enter the company of all those courageous men who had shed so much blood and taken such crazy risks for their fellow men. I felt having something akin to a heavy responsibility for joining this fraternity. My thoughts were that I was going to have to do a lot of living to always grace that medal, and uphold its honor. I began to understand what a burden it is to be highly decorated in a war.

Other people so anointed were alerted they would be decorated. Ron Johnson wasn't on that list of people informed. I told Pat that if he weren't included, I would move from the front ranks of any award ceremony, and pin my medal on his chest in the back row, no matter *whom* I embarrassed. He got it that I was serious, and so he went backstage and did the necessary things to get Johnson recognized. Pat got back to me that Johnson would receive a Bronze Star with a "V" for valor, the recognition being given to many of the EM who had pulled pilots from the burning aircraft. I said OK, and rested easy.

Jerry Daly would get the Distinguished Service Cross, just one step short of the Medal of Honor. Poometuu was also up for a DSC, because of his rank as a major getting out of the aircraft and into the mud and helping his crew pull the injured medevac pilot into the aircraft. It seemed the Army liked superior officers performing what men of lesser rank were supposed to do. His Outlaw aircraft had taken a lot of hits while doing so, because he was the last of the four ships in the LZ to exit. Daly and Poometuu were slated to receive the Silver Star as an interim award while the Army processed the recommendations for the higher decoration.

Come the awards day in early April, Major Lem Magoon formed us all up on the Vinh Long company street, with all the flags flying on the metal flag poles paralleling it. Just beforehand, all of those to be decorated had had a brief gathering, so I had the chance to thank Jerry Daly personally for literally saving my life with his daring, smoke-filled flyby's. He just grinned good-naturedly, as if his bravery had been nothing at all. He was a natural combat aviator and a role model for all who ever crossed paths with him. He will always be the person to point to when anyone wants to discuss the greatest gunship helicopter pilot of them all. I certainly wasn't the only person he saved from great harm that day, but I did want to express my feelings of gratitude for his stupendous deed. And I can always say I met *him*.

As we stood at attention, with every one of us doing our best to be in a "West Point brace," Seneff came into view from my right and pivoted smartly, just in front of the center of the first rank. Behind him, was a velvet-covered cushion-style board, holding all the medals secured behind a red ribbon that looked like a French cancan dancer's thigh garter. Kind of gaudy for the military, I felt. An appropriately high-ranking sergeant held this device and followed Seneff down the line. After Daly and Poometuu came Major

Jordan, then Major Gebhardt of the Lancers gun platoon, Major Bob Millward, and then me. In any pictures remaining of this awards ceremony, it is striking to note that I am the only young aviator up there who wasn't a major. Jordan was the only Maverick to be decorated; none of the other officers or young warrants in this gun platoon received any recognition at all. After me came all those receiving Distinguished Flying Crosses. Many of these pilots wore the black T-shirts under their fatigue shirts that indicated they were with the Viking gun platoon from Soc Trang. In the ranks behind were the enlisted men who had performed so superbly with their personal heroics, trying to get their pilots out of the damaged aircraft. Most of the pilots would not have been alive without their assistance. They had done wonderful things under fire. Mike Kidd, Schmidt, and Johnson were back there.

Finally came the moment when General Seneff stopped in front of me. When he pinned the Silver Star upon my chest, I knew this moment would last a lifetime. It was actually true that this was happening to *me*. After he finished clasping the medal on my pressed and starched, olive-drab jungle fatigue blouse, the congratulatory handshake ensued. The Silver Star is a beautiful ribbon holding a metallic gold star with the miniature silver star in the middle; the red, white, and blue colors of Old Glory are represented in the cloth part, almost in an airmail stamp or envelope fashion. On the back of the medal is the statement, "For Gallantry in Action." The nation's third-highest decoration was now mine! Seneff then moved on to the huge, red-haired major next to me, awarding him the DFC. John Niemier and Mike Hershey snapped pictures of the event, behaving like they were members of the professional press photographers corps, with three cameras hanging off their necks, as we'd commonly seen. Hershey was always so suave, copying moves like this.

We remained at attention until everyone had received his medal, then Magoon dismissed us smartly and we broke ranks. The impressive ceremony was over.

Niemier then took a picture of Ron Johnson and me with our personal decorations. Johnson's Bronze Star with a "V" was a deep red ribbon with white stripes and a blue band in the center. All of the combat decorations have patriotic red, white, and blue themes somewhere. It makes them very striking indeed. Johnson had had to shave off his mustache for the ceremony, and he borrowed somebody's fatigue shirt with a PFC stripe on it, because he apparently didn't have anything decent enough to wear. Looking back, it seems that most of the EM wore clothing pretty close to rags, with not much insignia, either.

"I'll bet your father will be proud of that medal," I said, knowing his old man was an E-8 career sergeant.

"Yeah, and he won't *ever again* be able to give me any shit, either!" Ron Johnson stated. Fathers and sons are funny, I guess.

Actually, at the time of the awards ceremony, my father was close to death in the Chelsea, Massachusetts Naval Hospital, having just barely survived an intestinal operation. I was not informed of his condition by my family, my mother especially. When he received word of my decoration, he literally climbed out of his bed in the sick bay, pulled all the tubes and plugs out of his arm, and went around to all the other dying naval captains and marine colonels there, showing them what his kid had done. I hadn't intended to bring him back from the dead, but I guess this award did that for him, too. Funny what these combat decorations do to career military types.

The reception that followed at the officer's club revealed mixed emotions. Many of the Mavericks were openly hostile at the way events had played out. They couldn't seem to break through their sullen moods and enjoy the festivities. Their bravery had been slighted. I knew that a lot of them were fed up with Major Jordan; he had impacted their morale in a big way. Some congratulated me for legitimately deserving the award I was wearing on my chest, and that felt good. There must be nothing worse in the military than faking an award on your records, however you gain it, and living the lie all your days. These combat decorations seem to have a two-edged sword. Poometuu was in a funk because he had *only* gotten the Silver Star so far, when they had promised him he DSC! My god, what a pain he was. He did get it eventually, though—along with a transfer to Saigon and out of our hair.

Around the Vinh Long compound, the men who had gotten recognized for their bravery were quite notable, and the impact lasted for quite a while. For those who had participated in the Easter Sunday action, it had been not only a noteworthy achievement but also a personally significant event that would remain forever in the minds of those engaged in it that day, on the ground or otherwise.

Major Gebhardt, Lancer Lead, had gotten the Silver Star for making a low pass through the LZ, without the benefit of the smoke ship, while looking for Jon Myhre later in the afternoon. Once we realized the Outlaw 17 AC was still out there, the gunships had hoped to find him or his body. Fred Stetson went in with another second platoon aircraft, *and nearly landed* in a two-ship mission to resupply Major Palenchar late that same afternoon, and he received nothing for an award. Norris Marshall, in the other Outlaw ship, *flying on* Stets, received a DFC. So go figure. Errors in recognition last many years, creating great hurt. They savage the award process, and people don't forget it.

I became so impressed with myself that I elected to go guns. I applied for membership in the Maverick platoon—especially after hearing the news that Major Farley Gordan was going to be reassigned to Can Tho, to the most appropriately entitled position of battalion awards officer! He would be chairborne with all his delicious fantasies. Casper would see him down there after his own return. Like the rest of us, he would be perplexed by this major's fruitcake ideas—such as Jordan's brainstorm of giving all the Vietnamese joyrides so that they would love helicopters so much that even their VC friends would enjoy riding in them incognito and the war would then eventually end. . . !

Stets told me a juicy story of being over at the 175th company headquarters when Jordan was still with the unit. Jordan had just exited Meehan's office, and when the CO emerged to greet Stets and call him in for whatever he needed him for, he was cracking up. "Can you believe that guy just asked me to put him in for the Medal of Honor?! Wow, what a guy!" Yup. I can believe that.

Stets and I had gotten our R & R together, to go to Japan. Being young first lieutenants from New England, we had planned on going to northern Japan and do some skiing on this weeklong rest and recuperation junket. Terry McDowell and Dickie Black had already attempted this idea, but hadn't gotten out of Tokyo once arriving there. Dickie had been a ski instructor at Alta, Utah prior to enlisting in the Army—supposedly to curb his heavy-drinking, partying tendencies. The two guys had so thoroughly enjoyed the benefits of the Ginza that they quickly forgot about skiing. They figured they could go do that any time later in their lives; they were ready to appreciate these decadent moments of leisure. So Stets and I were on our own with this adventuresome thought.

We got to Saigon and looked up our Intelligence friends stationed there. They were dangerous company, because the VC liked to blow up their Jeeps. The motor pool was having a very difficult time assigning them any more Jeeps because they lost them so fast. Most of these Intelligence lieutenants had been at Benning with me, but it had taken the Army a long time to get them to Vietnam—so long that the guys were kept at Fort Holabird, Maryland for about the same amount of time it had taken us to get through flight school. They had told them to pack a toothbrush and wait. And they waited. Finally, about a year after this statement, they had arrived in Vietnam. Most had top-security jobs in Saigon, and we were hoping they could tell us high-level inside stuff about battles like Easter Sunday. But what they had to say sounded like Greek to us. Like something from another planet; nothing we had actually experienced. Oh well, so much for this brilliant idea of an inside, top-secret security clearance trip.

Eric Kronen was a classmate of Stets' from Middlebury, in fact, they had been roommates for a year at this small Vermont college. He had been in my squad in IOBC 4, the basic course for ROTC second lieutenants sorry enough to choose the Infantry branch. They put the Intelligence guys through this misery, too, just in case they might forget what the Army really does. Joe Gorman was the other lieutenant friend from that particularly infamous Infantry Officer's Basic Course class, and anxious to show us downtown Saigon, the fabled haven of press junkies and legendary authors who wrote about the "Paris of the Orient." We wanted to see the Caravelle and other dens of inequity where the Vietnamese heads of state and the CIA head honchos and other grandiose soldiers of fortune had hung out. In the old days, the earliest pilots and advisors used to be on the top floor of the Capital Hotel and watch the war from afar as they toasted their swashbuckling bravado. When these men came back on their second tour, they would now say that the war "was everywhere"! The "Pearl of the Orient" had sandbagged sentry posts on every corner, and the city had become so Americanized that it was oft complained about its "Dodge City" look.

We wanted to taste the cuisine at the sidewalk bistros and get to know the town in this fashion as these lieutenants did, living out their year here. At one point, Kronen leaned across the sidewalk cafe table and nodded at Gorman, "Did you see the lettuce on this guy's chest, eh?" Joe nodded and said, "Yes, I did. Did you get that for this recent battle in the Delta on Easter Sunday, Dave?" I informed him that I had. He said, "We're still going over that. The Delta is my particular piece of turf to analyze," Joe told me. I thought *that* was interesting to hear!

We did the sights, and turned in as Stets and I had to make the flight to Japan in the morning. We stayed with the guys in their old French hotel—emphasis on *old*. The billets even had the same old crap hole in the shower, where you relieved your bowels by squatting over this six-to-eight inch wide aperture several stories up in this aged building. We were sure that Japan would give us better accommodations than this Asiatic experience. I pitied the guys for having to live like this in an urban setting of this backward country. The young lieutenant I roomed with that night in his quarters wanted to know about my flying experiences, and I related a bit to Bob of what we had been through. He told me about Dean Pape, my old IOBC 4 roommate, who was out in the field, torturing VC suspects with 55-gallon drums of water and Jeep batteries. Ugh. Yep, we all agreed about that. Alan Perkins, one of the Benning lieutenants who had missed flight school on a medical, had finally wound up in Vietnam as an infantry platoon leader, and then company commander. He had stepped on a punji stake—a very nasty VC booby trap—and injured himself pretty badly. Somehow, the guys had found him in a hospital. The least "military" of all of us, he had always kept us in stitches with his profound, unfettered disgust of the Army. Even the cadre at Benning found him unbelievable, as he was very vocal and withheld no opinions. Perkins always acted like he hadn't quite gotten it he was actually in the Army. Another Ray Snoddy type, meant for aviation alone. He probably was an excellent pilot candidate but the Army had found something wrong in one eye. This vision problem had gotten worse, not better, and he had never advanced to flight school. We had only chosen the Infantry branch because in ROTC they said the most pilots came from there. It just had not worked out for Perkins, but thankfully he was the only one of us this had happened to. If you couldn't make it through flight school, you got an assignment within your branch.

The next day, we were transported by our friends back to Tan Son Nhut, and boarded the big silver bird for Japan. A lot of the enlisted men waiting to board at Camp Alpha were decorated, and were wearing their proud Combat Infantryman Badges for the first time. The CIB's were worn higher than all else, and the airborne Jump Wings were on their flash patch below all the ribbons, on the breast-pocket flap of the tan Class B uniforms. It was always interesting to scan the chests of all these young fighting men and see their blushing pride at being recognized for their exploits. They too would be getting some well-deserved rest, of all kinds, on this trip.

As we sat in the air-conditioned splendor of the big Pan Am 707, the first thing we delightfully experienced—besides the pert, enthusiastic, and oh-so-wholesome stewardesses—was a container of honest-to-goodness dairy milk. Nectar of the gods! For six months, we had not had anything but reconstituted milk in our messes, and here was the chance to drink chilled whole milk! This was amazing in its pleasure. We troops put this down like puppies just acquired at the pet store. Then we turned over on our headrests and fell asleep like we were at nursery school. Benign bliss.

When we landed in Tokyo, it was dismally wet, with a cold, continuous rain. Stets rapidly found out that this had ruined the skiing conditions up north, so we abandoned that idea right off. He then said that Terry Wolkersdorfer had train trip tickets to the southern part of Japan, and that sounded like a good substitute. Terry was Stets' Intelligence friend from My Tho, with the Seventh ARVN division. A very brainy Notre Dame graduate, Terry was a very sophisticated, cosmopolitan traveler. I knew I would be in good hands with these two comrades in this strange but very developed Asian land. Japan's modernity contrasted dramatically with the backwardness of Vietnam. Here was a country very ready to launch into the twentieth century, and I knew at first glance, we'd better look out. The Honda automobiles that were their taxi cabs struck me as being on the quality level of Mercedes Benz products, even if the Japanese drivers seemed to have suicidal tendencies. For a quarter, you could go anywhere you wished, but if you failed to pay the fare, you would go directly to jail. We were warned that debts were unforgivable to the Japanese. They would accept no crime whatsoever, and this in itself would be a relief after experiencing the Vietnamese corruption for six months. We were in civilization!

First stop was at the PX to purchase my beloved Nikon F with the Photomic "T" device. The price of $209 at the PX was cheaper than $215 or more downtown. Wolkersdorfer was exquisite with his knowledge of the variety of Nikon products. I spent most of my R & R money on accessory lenses; Stets pledged to grubstake me for the rest of the week. Good friend that he was, and is, he never told me at the time how much he always hates being in that particular situation. "Never a debtor nor lender be," could be his motto on money between friends. I would spend the next six months paying him back for this generosity.

Between getting off the military base and heading downtown, we had exchanged money at a post bank. We still had not shed all our military togs, and I was wearing my flight jacket over my civvies for warmth. A gruff, fiery-eyed old master sergeant behind me in the bank line said to me, "Lieutenant, if you really *are* a lieutenant—you may be masquerading as one—if you don't get that jacket off, there are some military policemen around here that will put you in jail for your whole Japan R & R experience!" I apologized for being out of uniform, explaining that it was a matter of having just come from Vietnam, and needing proper apparel to keep warm and dry. He retorted, noting what the consequences could be, and I thought to myself, "Oh, please! Enough of these Army assholes who can't even appreciate you're here all of five minutes after six months of combat!" Gawd. The Navy lets its pilots wear their sheepskin-leather flight jackets with civilian clothes as part of the clout these aviators enjoy, but not the goddamned Army! I returned to the BOQ and told Stets about this weird encounter, and he immediately cut all the rank and insignia off his flight jacket. It was only thing he had for keeping warm in for the week. I had a water buffalo rawhide jacket that I had bought at Vung Tau. It looked like a Range Rider coat out of the Old West, but it would get me through. We decided to get as far from the U.S. military as we could—and far from all white people, too, for that matter. If possible, we were determined to avoid all Caucasians. We wanted *out* of our culture for a while. We were ready to thoroughly experience Japan in all its rich exquisiteness.

We departed Tokyo on the ultramodern, comfortable "bullet train" which was quite speedy indeed. Terry brought along an American first lieutenant from Korea as another traveling companion. I can't recall his name, but he seemed nice enough, and I couldn't think of much worse than seeing a country on your lonesome *after* also being stationed in Korea. With so much of the military's energy being focused on winning the war in Vietnam, other places around the world were given short shrift. I would not have wanted to be stationed in any of these locales at this time.

During this second week of April, with its misty, cold climate, we headed down to Osaka, Kyoto, and Kobe. I was loaded like an American tourist with my prized camera gear, and we took photographs of the Japanese in their kimonos and dark business suits at the train stations as we passed through. Their buildings and vegetable gardens were quaint, neatly kept, and orderly in their fashion. I was conscious of hillsides covered in orange groves or pine plantations. Every bit of space was being preciously utilized to its best advantage. The black-uniformed students we encountered immediately wanted to try their English on us, and they would sit at the dining-car tables with their compact language books, experimenting with accents and words. They were most earnest in this experimentation, and I regarded it as another warning of where this industrious country was going. We would see them soon.

We first visited the famed gardens of Kyoto, then the temples and shrines around that area. As the rain descended in buckets, we reluctantly but wisely joined another group of American tourists who were headed by the busload to see the massive stone Buddha and Japanese timber-frame architecture of the sacred buildings. See-through plastic raincoats abounded. In the drizzle, I snapped away at the incredibly wrought stonework and temples, and the ornamental vistas with the superb Japanese style of landscaped gardens. We were drenched but educated.

The mossy splendor of Kyoto's gardens made me realize we had been doing something very similar in developing the walkways and paths to overlooks and waterfalls along the Kancamagus Highway in my native state of New Hampshire. I yearned to return to the Saco District of the White Mountain National Forest when I completed my time in the Army, and the scenes unfolding along the carp-filled reflecting ponds made me realize the oldtime woodsmen I knew weren't too far off the mark from these Japanese artisans. There were like 20 varieties of moss mingling with each other beneath the cherry trees and twisted conifers. The rocks had been placed just so to derive the highest spiritual benefit while contemplating them and when causing one to move around them. I felt almost home again in these elegant landscapes. The soaking rains, however, hampered me from taking many pictures.

That evening, we spent time in a Turkish bath, with very polite care from our Japanese mistresses, who shampooed us, trimmed our nails, gave us a shave and a massage—but that was all despite our hopes—and sent us on our way, quite refreshed and clean. We dined on Kobe beef, tempura, and other delicacies with names we couldn't ever again pronounce or memorize. This was a very settled country with a great deal of class. We did our best not to be offensive, leery of the "Ugly American" title. A great respite for our jaded sense of the Asian.

We wished we knew more of the grand sights we were seeing, of great temples and the grounds of the Emperor's Palace in Tokyo. Everything was ornate and orderly, with a great sense of forbearance and unity. Even the predominant colors of the country—rusty brown and medieval stone tones—exemplified the deep commitment the Japanese had to their national heritage. Only Tokyo's excessive neon street lighting revealed their urge to move into a highly electronic age. I took pictures out of the hotel window of Tokyo at night with all this carnival-like lighting. It was gaudy.

Finally our R&R time had come to an end, and we had to reassemble for the flight "home" to Vietnam. Many of the enlisted men were quite rowdy and insulting the older officers, mostly Air Force colonels who had no rebuff for them. As much as I felt sympathy for these young men returning to god-knows-what-for-assignments and another six more months or more of jungle hell, it wasn't a good idea to let them get away with their drunken belligerence. No "first john" is going to take any crap from troops, ever. When they tried their stuff on Stets and me, we stared them down, and got them back into some more appropriate behavior. I knew they were not looking forward to returning, and they quickly turned their eyes downward and said, "Sorry, sir," before moving away. It was an unpleasant moment for us, too, but got us in the mood for reentry.

25

A Month with the Mavericks

RETURNING TO VINH LONG, I had to inform Gary Wesselman, a warrant officer in my platoon, that unfortunately I had not been able to cash his personal check in Tokyo, no matter how hard I tried, and therefore I hadn't also purchased a Nikon-F for him. He was crestfallen, and I felt miserable at not having done this for him, as he was a budding photographer and vastly enthused, as I was, about the prospect of owning the finest color SLR camera in the world. Nikkormats were sold at PXs throughout Vietnam, but not the Nikon. You had to go to Japan or Hong Kong to get that. At times, I felt that the whole purpose of my tour in Vietnam was to get that camera.

Gary was the last person I saw that night as I handed him back his check. He also lent me his blue-handled screwdriver, which had a Phillips head as well as the regular slot-type screwdriver point. I was lying in my bunk and he was sitting over by my stereo equipment, which I would have to disassemble the next morning because I was moving over to the Mavericks' hooch. He was lending me this tool so I could unscrew all the wires and jacks leading from the back of the amp to all the other devices hooked up to this receiver. It was a pain packing up all this gear and returning it to its original packing boxes, but we all got used to the process every time we switched units or abodes. Our stereo gear comprised about 60 to 70 percent of our possessions over there. It was always amusing to see young pilots walking from one hooch to another as if they were working for a music store and delivering purchased goods to a consumer.

Stets had to fly the next morning, but I didn't. I got up in a leisurely way and went over to the officers' latrine about 7:30. I was sleepily brushing my teeth—humming through my toothpaste and generally happy with myself and the morning—when O'Kane came in and used the urinal. He zipped up his fly and said to me, "What are you so happy about?"

"Well, you know, just got back from R&R and I'm going over to the Mavericks this morning," I replied.

"Well, knock it off," he snapped. "Didn't you hear? Wesselman and Reeves just bought it off the end of the runway this morning! Can the gleeful chatter." And he left.

I stood there stunned, my mouth full of toothpaste foam and my arm stuck in midair. I just couldn't believe that the last person I had spoken to before sleep was dead before I woke up on that morning of 19 April 1967. Vietnam had plenty of shocks for you, but this was the strangest one yet. I finished dressing, went over to the club, and found out what had happened as I breakfasted.

The end of the dry season was still producing the early morning ground fog that could be continuous from the ground up to 500 feet. As the morning progressed, this fog would lift slowly to a cloud base of 1,500 feet or so, but it took some time before there was any space to fly under this. Only a few hundred feet or less meant dangerous exposure to VC gunfire, so the guys would take chances going through holes to the blue sky on the other side of this cloud bank. The consequences of doing this have been well documented throughout aviation history. "Flight of five all crashed due to heavy ground fog" appears in many file folders of crash investigations. You just don't do this if you have any aviation smarts at all. Wait it out. Don't try to make it down through a hole just barely the size of the aircraft. The holes can close up, and then you're blind. During the time I was in Vietnam, the Army loss of Huey helicopters was 269 to combat, 14 to attacks on the airfields, and 335 to accidents—with the majority of these due to inadvertent IFR. If these fellows in the latter category had flown more safely, 50 percent of those casualties could have gone home alive. I was a bear on this subject.

John Savelli had led a flight of four Hueys to Sa Dec early in the morning. Some of the EM were late to the flight line, so they had missed Wesselman's Outlaw 22 takeoff with the rest. He and Larry Reeves had flown without their crew. Ray Novotney was third behind Gary, who had only been an AC for a few weeks, and Stets was in the fourth aircraft with Jim Parrott. On their return from Sa Dec, Savelli in Outlaw 26 had gone down through a hole to make the Vinh Long airstrip. It was a mistake. When he came down the runway, the people on the ground said you could reach up and touch his skids with your hand, but you still couldn't see the aircraft above them. The hole closed up on the others. Stets, with his experience, saw the fog close in around the windows of his aircraft and said, "No way," lifting back into the clear air above. Novotney had followed the leading two aircraft down and broke out on the deck, scooting over the rice paddies well short of the canal at the west end of the runway. As he did, he saw something that looked like a burning rubbish pile. As he passed, he momentarily thought, "That's a helicopter!"

Gary Wesselman never had a chance. Larry Reeves may have been on the controls instead of him, but that remains speculation. In the second platoon, we always religiously swapped off flying legs, no matter how dangerous the mission, so that everyone had a chance to fly. That's why Reeves could have been flying instead of Gary on the return leg from Sa Dec. Gary would have been playing fair, as he'd been taught to do by us. Otherwise, the AC would unconsciously hog the flying time, and you would have a very bored, inexperienced peter pilot on your hands. We wanted to develop people in the second platoon, and that's why pilots such as Gary had waited a good three months to make AC instead of moving on to another unit or assignment. We liked each other, and our pilots rarely left--because they didn't have a better place to go. I was leaving this caring unit for the Mavericks only because I thought I could, and should, make a contribution to the gun platoon. We were so close in the second platoon that the brass sometimes became angry with us when they were unable to pull any of our experienced pilots away to other needed positions.

As it gradually dawned on those who survived the descent through the ground fog that Gary's ship hadn't made it, those on the ramp awaiting the four ships felt real remorse. John Savelli was overcome with the tragic outcome of his decision, and he fell forward in his seat on the stick, crying hysterically with grief, as the aircraft shut down.

A lot of our Vinh Long superiors and other compound personnel went out to the ghastly crash site. Gary's ship had hit the ground inverted and going approximately 120 knots. I'll spare you the rest of the descriptive observations from those who saw the scene. It shook us up; we prided ourselves on our safe flying as O'Kane had inspired me earlier in the game. We all immediately wondered *what* we could have told Gary that would have made a difference. You figure by the time you've exhausted all the things a guy could learn from you in three months that there is nothing more to say, but there is this: "Watch out for your buddies who haven't made AC yet; they will try to kill you in the aircraft. They haven't learned all that you have; wait and see this. There is a reason you're an AC and they are still not." Nobody ever said that to him. Half of us feel he wasn't on the controls at his death, others say it's unfair to fantasize the outcome.

A few days after I moved into the Mavericks hooch, Father Logue held a memorial ceremony in the Vinh Long chapel. Everyone came, including Maj. Don Casper, looking stiff from his wounds; he had returned to Vinh Long to heal. Two large black-and-white wreaths with Gary's and Larry's names were just in front of the altar area. We all filed into the pews, and I sat with the second platoon that day. The mood was somber, reflecting the great loss of such a fine comrade as Gary Wesselman. He was a blond, Germanic kid who looked surprisingly like my college friend Bob Walther. They could have been brothers, and I did a double-take when I first saw Gary. I thought they'd shipped my old UNH forestry buddy to my Army unit—when I *knew* he was flying KC-135s as a navigator in the Air Force! Gary also had all of Bob's facial grimaces and his sheepish grin. I marveled constantly at their similarities.

Erasing Gary's and Reeves's names from the scheduling board seemed just too trivial a way of vacating their presence in the platoon. There had to be more to this exit from our group than wiping off a grease-penciled last name on the clear plastic-covered mission board. There *had* to be adequate grieving yet to go through. We were all stuck in our thoughts, and nobody felt that we were completely addressing this awful business of losing one of our own. It was hitting us hard that this could in fact occur to the unit and our lives; hadn't Jon Myhre been enough? We knew then that this was something we'd better start getting used to. Andy Keeney had been Gary's roommate, and he and Mike Stansbury, along with Ray Novotney, packaged up the young warrant's belongings to be sent home. We all felt this was a process we didn't want to learn any more about. Stets and I got off to the side and mumbled what each of us needed to know if disaster struck either of us. We went through the necessary conversation about our personal effects very quickly; Gary's death made us confront our own.

Gary's ship, D-model 66-16088, was itself a replacement ship for Outlaw 22. We never seemed to be able to keep a ship around with that particular call sign in the platoon.

My work acclimating to the Mavericks began in earnest. I felt like an FNG all over again. Just when you're convinced you're getting very good at something, you have to go try something else and see how dumb you are. At least you can begin to see what you have been putting your poor peter pilots through. My friend Terry McDowell was with the Mavericks, as was Jack Smith. I looked over at Smitty in the cockpit of one of the brand-new Charlie models that had just been delivered to the Mavericks, and said, "Well, Smitty, here we go again." He just acknowledged me with that level-headed smile of his. He had been a stabilizing force with the Mavericks, too, all during the time that crazy Farley Jordan was pulling his stunts. I would be flying left seat with various aircraft commanders while I learned the tricks of the trade. I didn't know how much of a hired killer I would become, but I was ready to throw back some lead after all the rounds that had been fired at me. What was particularly different about the gunships was that their day just began when they were shot at, whereas a slick would turn tail and run when the enemy opened up. These guys wanted to engage. I thought I had earned my spurs and wanted to contribute myself to this esteemed unit, as any good self-respecting first lieutenant should want to do.

General Seneff had a hand in getting the Mavericks their brand-new Charlie models with 540 rotor systems. The old, stressed-out B-models they'd been flying were all traded in for these spanking new aircraft. The Maverick gun crews couldn't be prouder of these new steeds, and I was lucky enough to join the unit just as they arrived. Oscar the artist was brought up from downtown Vinh Long and hired to paint the nose art and other Maverick insignia on the new birds for the ACs. Terry Holley had the third ship in the platoon, with the call sign "33," so he named it "Ba Moui Ba," after the Vietnamese beer that was half formaldehyde, and he had its red label, "33 Biere Export," painted on the pilot's door. That looked sharp. Some of the other names inscribed were "Satan's Playmate," which looked like motorcycle-club art, and the "Morning After," which was an apparition of a grisly hangover cartoon face. The ships looked smart with this artwork. Oscar outdid himself, and now all the ships of the 175th indeed looked like "circus ships," as the guys at Soc Trang liked to call our aircraft.

Some of the other personalities in the Mavericks at that time were 1st Lt. Don "Titi" Shipp, who of course was anything but small. He looked very much like the former Texas university tackle that he was. Joe Gammon was a kick and a half; he reminded me of what I had missed by not going to school in the tidewater South. He always seemed to be halfway out of a college fraternity party that wasn't quite over yet. There was a small, quiet warrant officer named Bryant; no one got to know him too well. He was just always there. Dark-haired Jim Mondeaux was from New Jersey. Joe Moffett was now the platoon leader, a senior captain who had returned from Benning too soon, because after Vietnam everything had become boring. He loved the Mavericks, and I don't think he had anything else.

The other guys had all come over from the first platoon. The Mavericks never took any inexperienced people; you had to serve time elsewhere before being accepted by them. Jack Smith, Terry Holley, Tommy Mitchell, and I were the only guys who had ever come over from the second platoon; we just didn't produce gunship people there. Both Mavericks named Terry (Holley and McDowell) would rotate soon; their time in-country was "short." Bob Lakey was a brainy engineer first lieutenant who liked to play his music soft on his stereo and then tell you about its sound engineering, all of which was completely over our heads. Ron "Duke" Cone, from Alaska, was about as handsome and dashing as a flying young man can be, almost like Errol Flynn. His buddy, Jack Mankin, looked like a high-school football guard who would never have the weight to make a college football team, but he had the mashed-in face that earned him the nickname "Bulldog." He was proud of that, and was an avid gunship pilot from the start. He loved his job and would teach me a lot. Dwayne Williams, very dedicated to the unit, was a somewhat new pilot with the Mavericks at this point. He and Phil Reichard ("Baby San") had been there for a while after initially spending three months in the first platoon. Those were all the Mavericks, except for Jim Hardbeck and "Goose" Gerwe, who were still in the hospital recovering from their aircraft crash up at Tay Ninh in February. They would return to the unit within a month or so.

Flying in the Mavericks gave me less flight time than in the slicks. Where we commonly averaged 120 hours a month with the second platoon, I was only getting 70 hours or so in the guns. There was a lot of waiting around to be scrambled, which could happen anytime, 24 hours a day. When that happened, we often wound up shooting a lot of "VC grass." The enemy was not so obvious, or anxious to engage us. We'd fly around the rice paddies at a hundred feet or so, but the Viet Cong were clever at hiding from the gunships while they were intent on shooting someone else. We could be in an operational area all day without drawing fire, but when that slick on a resupply mission came over that treeline, *he'd* be shot at quickly. This would perturb the gunship drivers to no end.

Sometimes while the ARVN ground troops would be moving through an area toward their objectives for the day, the Mavericks would intentionally try to draw fire just in front of the advancing troops. This could be done by exposing the belly and then the side of the helicopter while making a rapid pass at low level, trying to give the VC a tempting target in a way you normally would not fly. Scary, but often unproductive. I would be holding onto the articulated firing handle for the flex kit's miniguns, but not much was happening that made me feel we were in a war. Apparently there were many days like this, and I was already beginning to miss the multifaceted mission days of the transports. Hmmmm. I certainly hadn't expected to be bored, and I was.

Terry McDowell had told me that I would not like this job, and apparently his intuition had been right. The hardest part of the job was snapping the ammo together after we had expended everything on board; sometimes fired in as little time as five minutes. Then you would laboriously click all the galvanized links together on the runway with the troops, sometimes for as long as half an hour. Very tedious, and hard on the fingertips. For morale purposes, the pilots often helped the gunship crews in this rearming; glad this wasn't my MOS (Military Occupational Specialty), and I was an officer/aviator. After a couple of stints with this rearming gig, I wondered why any kid wanted to sign on with the Mavericks as a door gunner. Cella, Johnson, Farr, and Von Schwedler had come over from my second platoon, though, for this esteemed air crew work.

The other part I didn't like was flying wingman. You were not supposed to fly over the same ground track as your fire team Lead, nor were you supposed to let him out of a 10-degree range of being in the center of your windshield while he wandered back and forth, eluding the VC with his flight path. The visual effect of two gunships careening about the sky, 250 feet off the deck, was like watching two drunken aviators having a great time at a dance. More tedium. Red-lining the instruments in these banks while flying the heavy ship was not fun for my aviator blood. And then we constantly flew with the force-trim on, which ruined the control touch I had so carefully cultivated. This electric device manually locked the controls in a mode where they would stay if you let go of the stick. This could allow the other pilot to grab hold of the cyclic if you were shot, and give him time to right the aircraft. The feeling was like shoving against something heavy and metallic, instead of enjoying the nice hydraulic control sensation of flying a Huey. Your brain would be saying, "Ummph!" instead of, "Ahhhh . . . ." Flying this bird became muscular work instead of a gracefully moving through the sky. This was not my cup of tea.

Time dragged on, and then finally, out on a mission one day, a call came from the ground-pounders that they had a VC suspect running. We quickly reassembled our light fire team from what we were doing on one side of the operation and hopped over to where they needed us. They gave us permission to fire, and we wheeled in on the man. Coming from a few hundred yards out, we could not detect much until we moved in closer, firing all the way. Rockets were whooshing out on both sides of the aircraft, I was laying down 5,000 rounds a minute with the miniguns, and the two door gunners were blazing steadily alongside both pilots' front windows. As we got ever closer, we finally could get a better sense of what the man looked like.

Jesus Christ! He was an *old man!* He looked like Ho Chi Minh himself, with a long, wispy, white beard hanging from his chin, straw conical hat over his withered face, and black pajama top. Oh lordy, he was praying! His peaceful hands kept moving up and down in that Buddhist manner, while his body was half concealed by all the dust and smoke the rockets and bullets were throwing up around him. I'll never forget the appeal I saw in his eyes as all our armed fury effectively destroyed him. Mankin looked over at me as we wheeled off the target, resuming our flight outbound. "You'll get over that, Dave, you'll get over it. You'll have to!" he said as he looked at my face. I hadn't experienced nausea at killing my first human being, but this was nothing to write home about. I had thought my first kill would be something valorous, if not courageous and prideful. I never had considered that it might be some old codger at the wrong place in the wrong rice paddy. This was ridiculous, and I hoped I'd see no more of it.

I stopped by Stets's hooch that night and talked to him in the dark. I could tell the other aviators were listening in on the conversation as I told him I had killed someone for the first time. You could almost hear them holding their collective breath as they monitored my intense feelings recalling the event. Stets compassionately listened as he always did, and said I had a lot to think about. "Yeah," I said, as I moved out of his room and passed down the first platoon hooch hallway into the night's stillness.

After six months of the dry season, the monsoon season started again. While one fire team went out on station, the other waited on the ground, rearmed and refueled to relieve them on call. In a B-model or a 540 Charlie-model gunship, there wasn't much room for the whole crew to get out of the rain and catch up on some sleep—especially with all the galvanized sheet-metal boxes of belted 7.62mm machine gun ammo taking up the space. Another disadvantage to flying guns. The D-model could become a nice, cozy little home during cloudbursts; all the crew could stretch out and catch some Zs while waiting out the rainstorm. No such luck with the famous Mavericks.

At night, we did lightning-bug missions, looking to shoot up sampans transporting VC loot and supplies. (More about these later.) During the day, we flew with operations looking for VC suspects caught out in the open. Sometimes we were just assigned a free-fire zone, where we would maneuver through and fire on anything suspicious. The friendly locals were told to stay in their open-topped family bunkers to get through the day. I killed a few more people and was not enjoying it, despite the fact that I was doing a good job overall. I was being groomed as a fire team Lead due to my rank, and I knew it. I also had taken over the position of scheduling officer to rotate the aircraft and crews for general, all-around fairness and maintenance orderliness. This was obviously what my last six months in-country were going to be about, and I was not liking anything to the extent that I had enjoyed the first half of my tour.

We were often alone out on some lonely road between rice paddies, with just ourselves for company. This was nothing like the multiple-ship lifts of the slicks, nor did it involve crowds of comrades and the other folderol that went on between Outlaw flights. It was just the two fire teams of the Mavericks, with or without the platoon leader's "Hog." Sometimes, when someone was shot, as Jim Mondeaux was one day, taking an armor-piercing round through the ship's bottom that rolled around on the floor after bouncing off his chest protector, there would be no one but us to witness it. This was glamour? I thought not, and I wondered who had created the legends surrounding the gunships as if they involved some swashbuckling, romantic duty.

Finally came Terry McDowell's last day of combat flying in Vietnam. He was returning to Vinh Long from some nondescript airstrip below Can Tho where we were parked. He was taking his fire team with him, because it wasn't needed in this particular mission. All the Maverick gunships had been out there together that morning in two fire teams, following a night mission on which we'd been scrambled. Shaking my friend's hand and congratulating him for making it through the tour unscathed, I bid him adios for his last Vietnam helicopter flight. He smiled as he welcomed the good-natured, harassing farewells. Then he took off, with just a few hundred pounds of fuel. Goose Gerwe was flying again, after just getting out of the hospital, and was with AC Joe Gammon in the other ship. Terry then did the only dumb thing he had ever done during his whole year in-country, and he did it because he was so low on fuel. He decided to spit in the eye of the devil for his last moment in combat, although Gammon concurred with the idea. Flying on a nearly straight line from Binh Thuy airbase to Vinh Long, he low-leveled his two-ship fire team through the "Y," a VC stronghold halfway between the two rivers north of Can Tho. The area was so thoroughly controlled by the VC that it served as their headquarters at the confluence of these two distinct treelines. It was universally understood that you *never* went near there. They once hit a Chinook at 5,000 feet with a .50-caliber for overflying the place. Very impressive. When people take chances like Terry did on this last flight, they've been in-country too long and are exhibiting "combat fatigue." Believe me, we all wanted to do (and did) wacky things our last few days in-country; you shudder to think about it later.

The second ship was hit by a burst of machine gun fire while flying on the deck. A wild shot through the chin bubble opened up Goose Gerwe's thigh, and blood was splattering all over the cockpit. Joe Gammon went into a screaming climb—as straight up as possible to as much altitude as he could get. The wingman (Terry and Dwayne Williams in their ship) immediately came back around to cover him. They dumped everything they could, suppressing the suspected treeline while covering the ascending retreat of the shot-up Maverick, and both aircraft "di-di'ed" hurriedly to Vinh Long. Despite his leg artery spewing its contents all over them (and muscle tissue on the overhead console), Goose seemed to have been the calmest of all those involved. He pushed the pitch back down to regain RPM while Gammon climbed toward the sky. When they landed at Vinh Long, Jack Payne of the 114th "White" Knights was on the runway and helped unload the wounded Gerwe from the ship. He was a close friend of both Gerwe and Gammon; apparently he'd heard they had radioed in to the tower as they approached. Jack was on his way to the showers and breakfast when Doc Hillegas sprinted by him, heading for the flight line. Hurriedly putting on some boots instead of the shower clogs he'd been wearing, Jack joined the flight surgeon on his way to the strip. He said the bullet came through the calf of Goose's leg and exited through the upper thigh muscles. It had entered at the ankle area.

Gerwe was sent right back to the hospital at Bien Hoa. Terry was so upset with himself that Doc Hillegas had to administer a sedative to calm him down later that day. Drinking the bar dry had not helped. It was a hell of a way to end a great tour of duty, and no one could bring him any comfort in his out-of-control grief. Terry would be leaving Vietnam in a few weeks, after he put his administrative affairs together, as we all were allowed to do during our last days in-country. Most of the units provided a guy with some down time at the end of his tour to accomplish these things, giving him a break from combat flying to keep him out of harm's way.

Goose eventually would be sent to Japan, then on to Walter Reed Army Hospital for extended convalescence. It would take several operations to get particles of his flight-suit material out of the site where the deflected bullet had entered his leg. He and Joe Gammon would wind up together again as flight instructors at Hunter-Stewart, sharing a house there. They remain close friends in South Carolina to this day. From time to time, they enjoy bird hunting, and they reunite annually to watch the Super Bowl.

One day, late in the afternoon, I stopped by Joe Moffett's hooch room, briefly noted the tiny TV he had up on a shelf that we didn't, and said I was going to be a lot more careful when I made AC and fire team Lead than I probably should be. After killing four people up to that point, I was beginning to feel a lot more responsible than other men seemed to be about this firing on VC suspects. I had recently rolled in on a man standing all alone in a rice paddy in his civilian clothes. When I had him exactly in the pipper, the thought struck me that this man was no strategic threat at all to my country. If he died, it did not matter; if he lived, my country was not in jeopardy. He was of no consequence to the future of my nation-state whatsoever. When this electric insight jump-started through my body, I next had the thought, "Then what are we doing any of this for, anyway?" If that was the case, I was going to be a lot more goddamned careful about exterminating life over here. We passed up killing the man, but the conclusions I had drawn lingered with me. I wasn't thinking about quitting the Mavericks, but I thought it time to discuss these feelings with my commander before any more responsibility landed on me. Too many people are dependent on any one person's performance in the guns, and I had to act responsibly about my feelings.

I explained these thoughts to Captain Moffett, and he quickly said, "Dave, you're out of a job!" I was utterly stunned at his enlightened appraisal of my analysis, but I knew he was right. The position we were in would not allow my proposed level of discretion. In fact, the whole reason I was going to my platoon leader with my problem was that I was afraid I might be costing someone else his life for my desired degree of precision. It could not happen; the theoretical threshold was below that. Some other aircraft following me could catch the fire intended for my ship just because I was being overly conscientious in this war. The rules of engagement simply would not permit my level of care; my days as a gunship pilot were over. I had to respect Joe Moffett for his perception and compassion. He showed remarkable comprehension in this discerning, judicious leadership position he had to live in, and he deeply impressed me. It wasn't what I had expected to hear or have happen when I walked into his room.

26

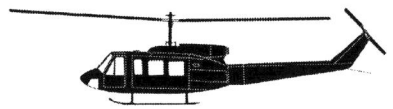

BACK WITH THE SLICKS AGAIN

MAJOR MEEHAN DIDN'T LIKE THE IDEA of my transferring back to the second platoon. "We can't have people just jumping around from unit to unit around here," he said, as he sat with me in a meeting at the club. I said I wasn't, that Joe Moffett and I had a legitimate understanding, which we had reached quite profoundly, that I just was not cut out for the job the Mavericks did. I respected that and so did Joe. I was already known as the bravest "slicky" pilot around, so this was no slight to my morale or my reputation. Some even thought my decision was courageous; I took no macho behavioral stance. However, Meehan got up with a "Humph!" and I was beginning to wonder what this was all about, beyond my personal conscience. I always did things that were my very own business; I couldn't understand why anyone else should have an opinionated reaction.

Many did. They walked up to me in various places, at almost any time of day, and posed the question, "Don't you *like* to kill?" My response was that I had not specifically given that a great deal of thought. I had taken myself out of that line of duty because I had a dangerously lukewarm attitude about it. Essentially, this was a technical matter. I was a bit astonished about my not having extreme feelings one way or another about it; I was mostly ambivalent—not a wise position in this job of flying gunships. Some people took me aside and had much more revealing conversations with me. One was old Jim Hardbeck himself. He had just returned from the hospital, so this great gunship pilot and I had not had the joy of flying together. He was on his second tour after spending only six or seven months Stateside. He had not liked what he was doing while there, and he returned voluntarily to Vietnam to the Outlaws with whom he had served in 1965.

He obviously wanted to reach me. As we spoke at the bar, he said he'd had troubles with killing on his first tour, and had to spend some time in discussions with the chaplain. I was a little astonished at his singling me out with his compassion, but I gladly gave my attention to him as he recounted his troubles at that time. I let him know that I wasn't feeling especially guilty; I just thought I wasn't going to be very good at this killing business and wanted to find something else to do instead. The whole thing had been a surprise to me, too. Jim Hardbeck seemed to be the only person who completely understood what I was saying and feeling, and we formed a bond at that moment. He has always been one of my proudest acquaintances in life, and I feel lucky to have known him then and now. Among all the aviators who have ever encountered him, he was one of the Delta's esteemed gunship pilots of that period. Many more young warrant officers flew with Jim than he'll ever remember, but they all remember their day in the cockpit with him.

When I returned to the second platoon, Lou Paulin shook my hand and said, "Welcome back. I knew you wouldn't be gone long." I smiled but said I had no idea that it wouldn't work out. "You can have your old ship back," Lou said. "Beaulieu has it now, but we'll cut AC orders on you and you can fly it again." This was swell, although probably not administratively or politically the way to get things back in order. However, that was Lou's way of arranging things for the sake of our valued friendship more than for any official procedure. I worried about how Beaulieu would take it.

The next morning, we were to form up on the west end of the runway to pick up the troops. As we cranked up the Huey's turbine, Beaulieu was sullen in the right seat and wasn't saying much, but I knew *I* had a problem when I picked up the D-model to a hover without the force trim on—as I'd been accustomed to flying with for a month. The cyclic stick felt like a wet noodle, almost as if the handle were flying around in the air, loose. I lifted up and followed the four other Outlaws from my platoon in a big circle from the ramp to the runway, a few hundred feet up. The ship felt funny, and we were circling down through the air like a dance of falling leaves. This was astonishingly new to me, and I wondered how I could have lost so much of my "touch" so fast. It was too different after those overloaded gunships. We landed on the strip and the troops jumped in. On takeoff, I started bleeding off RPM, then settled down off the ground cushion and began scraping along the runway. Nothing new there . . . .

Beaulieu came on the controls and howled through the headset, "This ain't no goddamned 540, Dave!" I relaxed on the stick and he let go. Then he grabbed again and let go. Instead of getting airborne, the ship was screeching along the ground, throwing sparks from the titanium skid shoes attached to the aluminum skid tubes. Major O'Neill, who had been standing alongside the runway, serving as Delta 9, the aviation liaison officer, dropped his radio and was running *away* for some reason. With this giving and letting go by Beaulieu, the blade was pivoting dangerously close to the runway surface; I was just trying to smoothen out the takeoff. This was becoming a classic example of "who's in charge here?" I had worried that this might happen, but not so quickly and catastrophically. Finally, I told him to "take it," if that was what he wanted to do. I didn't want some ego conflict to end my life. O'Neill would tell me later that he feared "blade strike" and ran for his safety; "I knew something was going to happen!" From his vantage point, he could see that the tip of the Huey's blade had been about 10 inches from making contact with the runway; we were that close to disaster. As Beaulieu got the thing airborne, I knew I had to reconsider going directly back into the air as an aircraft commander.

After this disastrous flight, I went to Lou and said I had better fly as copilot for a while until I got my control touch back. I also suggested that he let Beaulieu continue as AC for Outlaw 23; there was not much sense in having a turf war, no matter how little respect he had from the others. I would just await the availability of another aircraft. All the guys thought it a huge joke that I had lost my control touch while flying the guns, but it was no joke to me. Harvey Persyn laughed, "They've ruined a perfectly good slicky pilot!" So, for a couple of weeks I rotated as copilot with the ACs who were my friends. I needed to.

Harvey had a crew chief named Benny Blalock on Outlaw 27. Amazingly, he kept that aircraft in an absolutely disheveled condition. In was in such disarray, looking at its dirty appearance made you think it was as badly maintained. When you found things wrong on the preflight inspection, Blalock would stand off to the side and mumble, "I know about *that!*" This would made you feel puzzled, and when Harvey finally strode up to the ship after the preflight, naturally you'd go up to him and say, "Harve! There are a lot of things *wrong* with this bird! And Blalock seems to know what they are. How come he doesn't fix them?" Harvey would then retort, "This is a combat aircraft, not a static display on a parade ground. Blalock knows everything he needs to know to keep this aircraft flyable. Isn't that right, Blalock?" I'd look over at this grungy crewchief, and he'd be nodding his head maliciously, a grimy smile plastered on his face. Unbelievable. These two were quite a matchup. Harvey nicknamed Blalock "Nasty McNarr," and he deserved it.

Blalock was in fact a natural mechanic and could afford to keep the ship in near-nonflyable condition, because he knew it so well. All the other crew chiefs had to do everything and learn all they could to keep their ships flying; not Blalock. He was completely in tune with his own near self-destruction. Hailing from southern Appalachia, Blalock originally had come to Vietnam as a combat infantryman. Upon seeing what was involved in that role when he arrived in-country, he trashed his orders in the nearest 55-gallon drum. He informed people he was a school-trained Huey crew chief, but had lost his orders. Nobody ever questioned his story, so they put his young ass to work in a hangar somewhere in

Saigon. There, he had learned all he needed to know about a Huey's maintenance. He then found out the Delta was *the* place to be assigned, so he got there. Having Harvey as his aircraft commander must have been an additional windfall. He had found his protector for all his evil ways.

When Blalock went to the States on leave after extending, not only did he sleep with his brother's wife on the visit, he also brought back black-and-white photos of her porcine shape. Her poses definitely lacked a certain je-ne-sais-quoi, but he didn't mind showing the photos around, along with appropriately lewd comments about her sexuality. Blalock also brought back a load of BB handguns for shooting at Vietnamese kids. He felt this was a good business proposition, and the ultimate solution for keeping the kids away from the ships while they were shut down on the airstrips. He was nothing short of amazing in his dereliction. He actually did sell all of these handguns, but we had to put a stop to the shooting at the diminutive Vietnamese kids by his EM clientele who had made the purchases for this bizarre activity.

During one midmorning lift operating out of the Cao Lanh airstrip just off the Mekong River beyond Sa Dec, Harvey was complaining about how sick he was. He had a respiratory bug that I would pick up at the end of my 12 months and carry with me for years. It produced a raging fever and incredible chills, no matter what the outside temperature was. It was also very contagious. When this bug was its height, it was impossible to think straight; no doctor ever was able to diagnose it while I had it. Eventually, my system just built up the antibodies to handle it. This was what was wracking Harvey that morning, with violent coughing spells. When this viral disease hit him, he would become outraged, and say, "The Army can't make me fly when I'm this *sick!* This is wrong!" He'd start acting like Douglas MacArthur being personally wronged and out-competed by the brass in the World War II Pentagon. This display never failed to strike us as funny, so it didn't gain him much sympathy.

On this particular morning, I was in the other seat and watching his misery as we awaited orders to crank once more. He then blurted out, "Blalock, find something wrong with this aircraft! We're going home!" I watched, astounded, as Benny Blalock bolted out of the backseat and climbed up on the cabin roof, moving like a giggling monkey on the Huey's footsteps to get there. "I've been saving this for *two weeks!*" he gloated, as he flew by me, sitting in the right front seat, perplexed. I wanted to call his bluff, so I went right up behind him.

"Show me," I insisted.

"Put your fingers right there, Lieutenant," he instructed, "and put your other fingers *right there!*" I did so.

"That's twenty-thousandths of an inch play, and only ten-thousandths is allowed for that bearing!" Blalock stood proudly atop the cab as he delivered this info.

"Wait a minute! I want a second opinion. Get a TI over here!" I said.

We climbed down and got the attention of the "Road Runner" maintenance ship. A tall, black technical inspector rambled over, followed by a small entourage. He was not very excited, but I was. I was spotting fraud here. The lanky TI climbed onto the Huey's roof and checked out the rotor-system bearing, just as Blalock showed me how to do.

"Holy Toledo!" he cried animatedly. "That bearing has twenty-thousandths of an inch play and it's only supposed to have ten-thousandths! You've got to fly this thing home right now. I'll sign the book as a one-time-only 'Circle Red X' flight! Wow! That thing has twenty-thousandths of an inch play!" Blalock smiled.

Harvey cranked the ship and said, "Good job, Blalock!" between sniffles and coughs. I put on a clown act, pretending to get on the radios to warn somebody about what was being contrived here. Worried, Harvey blurted, "Don't let him touch those radios, Blalock!" Benny seemed to be wondering about physically restraining me and risking a court-martial for manhandling a commissioned officer. I really had Harvey going, but he was too sick to see the humor.

I eventually took over the controls and flew back, to give Harvey a break from the sickness that was devouring him. When I put Outlaw 27 down on its pad, I slid the skids all over the place with my lousy control touch before ultimately getting it secured in place. Over the intercom, Blalock laconically said, "Well, we're finally down!"

Then he told me he also had something he ought to see the doctor about, so I said, "Fine. Get Harvey here to the dispensary and then check back with me. I doubt we'll be flying again today with somebody else, but you never know." The two departed for Doc Hillegas's examining room.

I was still waiting around the second platoon's day room when a call came from Blalock. He told me he probably couldn't fly any more either that day, for medical reasons. I said, "Oh, well, we probably won't anyway, but what's wrong?"

"I've got syphilis," Benny said.

"Oh, jeez, Blalock! I can't think of a *nicer* person to have that happen to!"

Vietnam had such a nice way of taking care of personnel problems that way. You just had to wait for things to catch up to somebody you didn't like because of their incompetence, misdeeds, or out-and-out ignorance. The odds were too great. Posturing didn't keep you alive in Vietnam, which came as a surprise to old-line lifer sergeants and commissioned career or dead-wood officers who had been shams up to that moment. It was interesting to watch—the greatest personnel management program I've ever enjoyed watching. Someone suddenly would be gone after a while due to their own damn fault; but you had to have the patience to wait it out.

When Meehan went to Bangkok for R&R, Major Magoon had to serve in his place as Outlaw 5 in the Command and Control ship. Major O'Kane was still head of Operations, but he flew with Magoon and showed him the ropes. I wondered how the exec was handling our extensive flying days after been chairborne for most of his time with this command. At one point during that week, while we both were handing over our meal chit-tickets one evening, he looked at me with a baleful, but hopeful, look in his pale blue eyes: "I've never been so tired in my life!" He watched my face for a fraternal reaction. "Yes, sir," I said, and moved on. It must be quite something finally to join the crowd, I thought to myself, and be one of the boys. By this time, Moffett and Meehan thought Magoon had turned into a pretty good guy. He was a very competent officer on the ground with problems in the compound's area. Personally, I still had my reservations, and I was not ready to extend him any consolation or friendship.

Two days later, this C & C aircraft decided to go down and pick up a wounded man, even with all the Vietnamese brass and their command radios still in the back seat. While on the ground, a single round came in through the Huey's left rear sliding door, missed the radio console and all the legs of the ARVN officers, and found the back of Lem Magoon's knee as he sat in the right front seat. It entered there and exited out the front, blasting his patella all to hell with it. Totally took off his knee cap. After he was medevaced out, we never saw him again in the unit. It would take a great deal of time before he was reunited with the guys at Rucker.

Then there were the people you didn't want to hear about losing. One night when I was still with the Mavericks, Troy Tison came over to their hooch and found me in my new quarters. He had a strange look on his face; he was bare-chested and was wearing shorts of some type. He sat down.

"Hey, Eastman, I heard old Ruehle died, I just heard it today that he got a bullet up in the Cav, and he's gone. I can't really believe that; me and him were close friends, you know?"

I actually stood there with an inappropriate foolish grin all over my face. It just couldn't be right. Guys like easygoing, good-natured Med Ruehle from Ohio just *don't* get killed in wars. They go home and raise hogs, cattle, wheat, or whatever that's on the farm report, make lots of babies, and enjoy their big-bosomed wife for the rest of their years. They don't *die,* for chrissake; it's not in the script for these kinds of good guys. They're too *good* to get killed in a dumb, smelly war like this one.

Troy stood up: "It just don't make sense, old Ruehle going just like that. I thought I'd come over here and tell you about it. Gotta go." I still could not wipe the embarrassed grin off my face, full of disbelief. I wasn't functioning well with Troy's grief, which was being expressed a whole lot more legitimately than mine.

I don't know how Troy found out. Med, Troy, Joe Mirabella, Mike Lovett, and I, and some other lieutenants, had been together all the way from Fort Benning, transienting through all the things that had brought us here. There were about 10 of us Infantry types from that same class who had known each other intimately during the various trainings we had undergone in the Army. Med was a classic farmboy through and through; he exposed that reality to me. As we went through the Airborne and Rotary Wing schools after our IOBC class, it had been interesting and eye-opening, to encounter and get to know the many regional types America had to present to us. We had shared all the weeks of our early marriages, and the births of babies, too. Med would leave behind a widow and a child; he was a completely married man.

Bob Vandel, another member of that Benning class, would later tell me that a single round from a sniper had gotten Med right between the eyes, the only casualty of that landing. The Cav had intended to bed down for the night, and of course, their pilots slept right there with the Hueys. As Med had stood just outside his left door that evening, on the step of the skid, a shot from a sniper had rung out from the jungle surrounding that LZ. Vandel said he had known that LZ was not secure, and he was mad no one higher up had paid any attention to his information. He, too, was a serious gunship pilot. We all were saddened at the loss of Medard Ruehle. To this day, it doesn't make sense; he should never have been lost at all.

27

OUTLAW 24

I FINALLY BECAME AIRCRAFT COMMANDER of the strongest ship in the platoon. This was cream-puff duty after Outlaw 23. The two EM crewing this particular bird had even requisitioned me to be the AC. They thought I would be worthy of them, I suppose, because of our respective roles in the Easter Sunday battle. All of us who had distinguished ourselves among the downed crews and rescuers that terrible day were a bit set apart from everyone else on the compound at this point; it wouldn't last too long, but it did exist. Before Poometuu left for Saigon, he invited me and two of the EM who had been so helpful on the ground that day over to his quarters. There, bare-legged and clad in his fine silk bathrobe, he was diligently trying to squeeze out of Schmidt and another crew member their remembrances of his actions. This apparently was supposed to help him gain his Distinguished Service Cross. I'm afraid I wasn't being much help, because I was openly smirking the whole time, observing his tail-rotor blade hanging on the wall. We could pick up these things on the maintenance trash pile after expended rounds had dented the leading edges of the blades and made them nonflyable. If you got one that wasn't too old, and the paint job was still there, it made a nice decoration, much as wooden propeller blades did in World War II. What had me giggling was that Poometuu obviously had taken this one out in a field and shot it up with his .45-caliber sidearm, putting *real* bullet holes in his war trophy! Then he had taken the tail-rotor blade downtown to Oscar the artist, who emblazoned on it the major's name and the

Outlaws' unit numeration, along with "Vinh Long, Vietnam. In the heart of the Viet Cong infested Mekong Delta!" I gave him some gas about that.

When Spec. 4 Jerry Ross called me at the second platoon officers' hooch and literally recruited me to be part of Outlaw 24 as their new AC, I almost had to laugh. I restrained myself, trying to be polite as I could. "This isn't the way this is done," I had to tell the door gunner over the phone. "Other powers-to-be select who is going to be with whom, but you are nice to call." Ross previously had been detailed to Can Tho to be with Colonel Dempsey in Delta 6, and he had acted very responsibly in trying to remove Dempsey from the burning ship that Easter Sunday,

"Uh, yes, sir, but we sure would like to have you with us if all of that can be arranged, sir." I felt Ross might try to sell me a vacuum cleaner next.

This was out of line, and I suspected I'd get this ship anyway, but I knew these kids shouldn't be proselytizing their needs and desires. It was a stroke, but it's not the way the military operates, and I needed to instill that firmly in their heads. Enlisted men constantly seemed to want to adjust the system according to their immediate demands or dreams, and this meddling kept an officer on his toes. It made one feel constantly like a teenage parent to teenage boys.

The orders finally came down, and the EM in the ship's crew who requested me got their wishes, but their happiness was short-lived when they found what a sonofabitch I was. Too much had been skewed around because of all the decorations stemming from Easter Sunday.

It was good to be flying at 2,500 feet again. The best part about gaining this altitude in the skies over Vietnam was the temperature up there. The outside air temperature gauge on the windshield often registered 12 to 15 degrees Celsius during the whole year I was there. It didn't have a Fahrenheit outer circle, or an inner one, to translate this, but it meant I was flying in 60- degree Fahrenheit weather at that distance above the ground. After the constant, 100-

degree heat of Vietnam, it was a welcome relief. Not only were we safe from the VC moving about in the tropical foliage of the treelines below, but we also felt as though we were *out of the country* when we were cruising up there. Over the radio came friendly chatter among all those flying with the various forces stationed over there, and there was a strong feeling of camaraderie, a sense that we were lucky to have such great flying jobs. We had a good feeling every time we escaped the danger of the ground and once again became airborne at our safe flying altitudes.

The Air Force had the airspace from 3,000 feet up, and if you flew there or higher, you soon would find a major-size fixed-wing looking straight at you, approaching at your twelve o'clock. In that case, you had to move rapidly over to one side or the other, so he could commit to missing you, too. No one wanted a midair collision with a C-123 or a C-130; it could ruin your whole day. They had no interest in greeting you at that altitude either, so you could count on some raunchy words coming at you pretty fast if you had one of these close encounters. The message in effect was that Army guys weren't supposed to fly this high—so amscray. Their cruising speed, too, was considerably more than ours.

Single-ship missions in the Delta produced the greatest joy in our year's assignment to this area. The various ways of utilizing helicopters in the IV Corps seemed endless and extremely interesting to all of us. We knew we had a more diversified life than any of our flight school classmates flying with the American units to the north in the other three corps areas. They only played Army, Army, Army, while we almost played a Third World Peace Corps–type role with our missions. Opportunities abounded to experience the native countryside in all its primitiveness, and we never knew what a day's mission would bring us as an adventure. It was exciting to return home to the Outlaw hooches and regale each other with some of the things we had experienced throughout the flying day. Guys honestly looked forward to each day as a new and remarkable venture.

I tried to be extremely efficient in getting all the flight time we could for the outposts when we were resupplying on these single-ship missions. Some of these MACV mud forts had to wait for a helicopter for a month or more, and when you showed up, they had a long list of what had to be done during that special day when they had your help. Slicky pilots were seen as a valued opportunity. We would have six to eight hours of flying time, with refueling and lunch stops, between our early morning arrival and our departure at the end of the day. There was no time to waste, and it was important for an AC to stay on top of this aircraft utilization. You had to show *them* how to accomplish this, and not to let any time be wasted because of any officious posturing on their part. Some of the MACV advisors in the backseat couldn't even navigate with a flight chart to identify their own outposts from overhead; if you knew what you were doing, you made sure you had the right instructions while you were on the ground, before ever pulling pitch. The way to do it was to invite them to your side of the cabin deck before you cranked; then you would grease-pencil their destination on the clear plastic covering your map. It was also very important to establish with these captains and majors that you were the pilot in command of the aircraft, and no superior-ranking person would have anything to say about what that ship *did*. Some of these guys tended to regard your Huey as some sort of a Jeep. Others were of the opinion that you had escaped a real officer's job by becoming an aviator. You had to watch these tendencies and be thoroughly in command, especially if you had field-grade or higher-ranking officers on board; they could be quite infatuated with their military knowledge.

What they didn't comprehend was the weight factor we had to consider in all our takeoffs and landings; we had to load the aircraft so we could maximize our deliveries for them. If you could get them on your wavelength, then the cooperation could begin. You had to watch their arrogance, though, which could translate quickly into ignorance and get in the way very fast. What constituted a safe takeoff weight for one place might not be safe for another outpost town down the line. I'll never forget the time we had to land in one little market square down below Tra Vinh in that province.

The town might have been Tieu Can, but the name escapes me at this point. We actually landed the Huey in such a small space that it permitted almost no room for a running takeoff. I remember that there were terra-cotta tiles on the roofs around the minuscule square, and it was such a demanding departure that it could make your hair stand up. Here's the way one particular day went.

Landing at another remote outpost named Long Toan, in a dangerous area near the coastal mangroves, one of the senior colonels in back had implored me to take an athletically built black soldier from there with me because he needed to go on R&R. If he couldn't catch a flight this very day with a helicopter like mine, he was going to lose his slot. I explained, "No, I can't because the next few places we are going to won't permit a takeoff with that much more weight." He looked a good 200 pounds to me. I thought I had explained myself rather well, but I noted when we departed from there, over the barbed-wire minefield, that the ship hadn't performed strongly. In fact, it had nearly mushed through. I thought this surprisingly curious, and I mentioned it to my pilot, but then I thought no more of it.

When we landed next at Tra Cu, I noticed the young black soldier stepping off the ship. I asked my crew, "Where did *he* come from?" One of my kids said the colonel had let him slip on board at the last outpost after I had forbidden him to climb on board. I was livid. I asked my copilot to take over the controls and continue to shut the thing down; I had something to say to my passengers, immediately. My crew chief moved the sliding plate back from my armored seat and he opened the left pilot's door, as he always had to do for my exit. I flew out in a rage.

"Sir! Who is responsible for this man being here? What is he doing riding in my ship after I said he couldn't come along?"

"Well, I did, Lieutenant. I couldn't see how it would really matter, and I suppose I felt badly about this young man possibly not making his R&R flight," said the very puzzled senior bird colonel, already engrossed in conversation at this destination. He thought he had done the guy a favor with his high rank.

"Well, sir, he may spend his R&R *right here,* because the next place we're going to, I might not be able to get out with just the load we're already carrying! This is as far as he's going on my ship!" I was emphatic and totally sincere in my anger.

The colonel still was not getting anything informative about aviation from this exchange, and now he was in the predicament of having to tell the young soldier that he wasn't going anywhere, maybe not even back to his own outpost. I was fuming as I turned on my heels and strode back to the ship. I asked my crew what had happened to allow this passenger on board after they heard my instructions. They just admitted the sly colonel had pulled a fast one and let the guy board at the last minute just before liftoff. I told them firmly that if anything of this nature ever happened again, they were to get on the mike and talk to me over the intercom. They had been bamboozled by the rank. They said OK and acknowledged my instructions.

The senior officers returning to the backseat after the stopover probably still didn't totally believe me and thought I was just being sticky. When we landed in the little town square of Tieu Can, famous among all of us transport pilots for its tightness, it was roughly 2 PM. Two story buildings surrounded this ridiculous place for a helipad. Density Altitude for the day was at its peak, and the helicopter definitely would feel the thinned out air when we attempted takeoff. The Vinh Binh Province chief's team completed its business and signaled we were ready to go. I always planned my circuit of this province from Tra Vinh clockwise, so this stop would be the last landing with the least fuel remaining. You got smart about these things.

We lifted up to a low hover, got the turbine's power stabilized, pulling off all of it we could, and began rapidly moving forward. We climbed up over the first roof we had to get over, and that's as far as it went. The ship nearly set down on the tiled roof as it sunk through. We had too little to get out of there. There was a vast "Aaahh!" out of the backseat, as we settled down again into the courtyard square. My copilot of the day looked over at me and said, "Whaddya gonna do?" I replied I'd think of something.

What I did was back the tail boom down an alley off the

square—an alley that was just a skosh wider than the nine feet of the horizontal stabilizer on the D-model Huey. I backed down the small street, following the directions of my two crew members, and totally trusting their commands as I did so. I couldn't see or even take the chance of looking back. Most of their statements were, "Don't come any farther over here!" And on the other side, "Don't come any closer over here!" We had to be dead center as we moved backward. When I was finally as far back as I could possibly get, I put the nose down and came racing out of the alley, where I had nearly inserted the entire tail boom up to the wider part of the cabin and engine area of the Huey. The rotor disc area was above the buildings' heights. We went zooming across the tight, crowded, little square with all its Vietnamese peasant and merchants watching enthralled, soared up and *over* the red-tiled roofs this time, and climbed out. The sounds coming out of the backseat were like the noises on an amusement-park roller coaster ride. I guess I made believers out of those fat colonels that day. They didn't question me any further.

There was a lot to learn about the conditions around each outpost we serviced with these missions. For instance, the map showed an airstrip *and* a helipad down in the mangroves around the Long Toan outpost. It made sense for a novice pilot to head for the airstrip shown on the chart, and secondarily opt for the helipad shown. The only problem with this logic was that the VC now owned the former strip. "Don't go there" would be the radioed transmission from the MACV team when you made contact. If you were over there orbiting around while you tuned them in, you might already have been shot out of the sky. It was only a distance of a mile or so, but it made all the difference in the world. In the other direction was a helipad with the name "Long Khanh" on the map. It, too, was no longer in use. Once safely inside the grassy little landing space at the "real" Long Toan outpost, the crew would have to keep the Vietnamese kids from crawling all over the birds. They would set up a perimeter to keep these tots from getting too invasive with their curiosity. Taking pictures of these scenes for the folks back home made you feel as if you were with Lowell Thomas on his last visit to Shangri-la.

As our business finished up in each of these village forts, one of the MACV majors often would ask if we could possibly carry one or two of the Vietnamese peasants standing around with us. Now, you could never just shake your head affirmatively at this moment. If you knew what you were in for, you didn't react too soon to this vigorous request. Simply nodding your head took all control away from you and your crew, because the major would then turn around to the chaotic crowd and hold up two fingers. That wasn't sensible, as what happened next was to instantly turn the crowd into a trampling mob hurrying to your helicopter with baskets of chickens and other foodstuffs, kids in hand, feeble old people tripping and falling, people clawing, screaming and fighting to get on board. They literally ran over each other when the signal was given. Expecting your two crew members to handle this swarming, desperate flight from hell itself was like being the last person on the *Titanic* and fresh out of life jackets.

The smartest tactic was to inform the major that *he* could choose *two* of the people, and that would be it. This worked, and nobody panicked and ran over each other's bodies trying to make it to the Huey. The rest of the Vietnamese would stay back where they were supposed to be, and would remain surprisingly docile. The contrast between these two solutions was absolutely amazing. You just had to figure out how to make it work. Many of these situations took some getting used to.

If the whole advisor team cooperated with us, we often refueled "running" back at the beautiful Tra Vinh landing strip to maximize flight time. My crew chiefs fidgeted over this after four hours of continuous running, as they wanted to check over the bearings in the rotor system at every shutdown they could. It was reassuring to hear your crew chief's concern, because you knew he had the ship's operational safety well in mind. Back at the fuel pumps at Tra Vinh, a Sergeant Beaver always made my day there go splendidly; he was emphatically efficient and loaded with hustle. He possessed a lot of charisma as he enthusiastically went about his job. Any aviator getting that much cooperation out of any ground crew always is impressed when it happens—even though the flying side of the business is continually demanding such service. It makes for a good working day; everyone goes home satisfied with a job well done. It wasn't unusual to get nearly nine hours working the Vinh Binh province out of Tra Vinh city. I have a lot of good memories of flying that mission day, and I'm sure a lot of other slicky pilots do, too.

We weren't always nice to the people for whom we flew. If, in fact, they infuriated us, well, we could give them a ride. For instance, a certain major with a squeaky radio voice in Go Cong Province always wanted to go for a ride over a certain treeline southeast of his encampment. He apparently had yet to fathom that there were *no* VC in Go Cong Province. He was stationed at Tang Hoa, a rather small outpost mud fort southwest of Go Cong itself. Once aboard the helicopter, he would ask you to go take a look at this little canal line running toward one of the northerly branches of the Mekong. I don't know what he thought was festering there, but he was always adamant about asking every helicopter pilot working the province's outposts to take him up and over that treeline. It was his fetish, and most of us would always humor him, but after several orbits to peer at that canal, it got boring. We would then tell him that time was up and that we had better things to do; other people were waiting. He would peevishly climb back over to his seat and await landing. Every pilot became well versed with this routine while on a mission here.

One morning, when we took him up for his customary fix, he wandered forward and wanted to talk to me directly, in my face. I started my usual spiel of how he needed to talk first to my crew chief, who would convey his desires to me, without his walking around the aircraft. He was having none of that, and I firmly repeated my message to him.

"Sir, if you want to talk to me, please talk instead to my crew chief, and he will relay to me anything you need said. I really want you to *sit down*, SIR!"

He was having none of it, and his beetle brows and dark complexion were hanging over my shoulder as he intently persevered with whatever he was trying to tell me. Little did he know that I was slowly, almost infinitesimally, lowering the collective pitch to almost zero power on the turbine and the blades. My copilot knew, and he had a slight smile on his face as he witnessed this deceleration. I had also brought the airspeed back, imperceptibly. The major kept persisting with his intentions, until I said for the last time, "Sit *down*,, sir!"

At this point, I dumped the nose straight down from where I had rotated it back to the airspeed attitude of 60 knots, which not only caused a tremendous rate of descent but also plastered the major's face all over the instrument panel. I fondly remember his nose being bent all across the big attitude indicator, splayed to one side of his face. He flew forward with great force. Next he started scrambling back between the two pilots' seats, heading for the jump seat of the Huey. When he got there, I dumped it over on its side so that he was looking not only straight *out* the cabin door of the Huey, but also *straight down!* He didn't know it, but I did, that the centrifugal force would keep him in the aircraft during the tight bank. But what the hell. During this extreme descent to his outpost, I asked my crew, "What's he doing *now?*" They replied over the intercom, chortling all the while, "He's trying to buckle his seat belt!"

When we landed, the major walked away without a word. Did he learn anything from this event? Naw. The next time up that day, he did it again, and we did it again—except that this time, he only had to catch the look in my eyes as he came forward before he started racing back for his seat. And this time, with the aircraft in a tight, descending spiral, he had his legs braced on the ceiling of the Huey while futilely trying to snap his seat belt together.

All in all, I considered flying with the Outlaws the best assignment in-country for any branch of the services. And there were moments when this was emphatically confirmed, even without my testing it. One time, I was sitting at the bar of the Pacific Hotel in Vung Tau, the billeting for American officers, during one of my in-country R&Rs at the villa we rented in that seaside town. An Air Force major suddenly started talking to me. On each collar of his fatigues was the small gold leaf of his rank. Then he just opened up on my right side like "True Confessions." He was an F-4 pilot, he said, and began with, "I wish I was in a better flying service like you are. Mine really loses, and I'm ashamed to be a part of it!" I thought he was talking about maintenance or something, so I replied that I was very satisfied with my unit, and considered myself proud of Army Aviation, and so forth. I always felt I had my right choice of the military branches.

"No! That's not what I'm talking about," said the mustached, wavy-haired major. "I mean about leaving someone behind while you're engaged with the enemy!" I sensed he was deeply disturbed.

"We would never do that," I replied. "Our contact with the ground troops and each other goes right on whatever, every day. The helicopter is really useful for extracting the wounded, be it the grunts or our own air crews," I continued, still searching for his message.

"Well, I hope I never have to meet the guy we left behind. If he's alive! He's either waiting for me on the other side, or maybe still walking around this earth if he survived the day we abandoned him. If he's still alive; I'll bet he's dead, though. Either way, I hope I never have to meet him!"

The story was getting interesting as the major genuinely warmed up. I had never had an Air Force jet jock approach me at all, and now this guy wanted a shoulder to lean on with his tale of shame. He went on to describe how he had taken off later than his flight of jets, which were already strafing an area that was under attack. Apparently an infantry rifle company was surrounded by the VC and in great danger of being overrun. The company commander on the ground was desperate, in a really bad way, and screaming on the radio for air cover's assistance. When this major joined up with his unit, he was fully armed and had plenty of fuel remaining compared to the F-4s who had been working over the terrain, keeping the enemy pinned down. They finally had to pull off station and regroup to return to base. The Air Force had all kinds of regulations of allowing 15 minutes for this and 15 minutes for that, plus needing an alternative base for landing if the weather changed, etc. Listening to him was like hearing instrument flying regulations for Stateside flying.

"We have run into our 20-minute low-fuel warning lights on a number of occasions," I said. "It's pretty common for a flight of Hueys to get overextended to the point of falling out of the sky during some operations."

"Well, buddy, you are in a better military aviation branch than I am, because I can still hear that guy screaming as we pulled off, leaving him in contact with an overwhelming enemy force. I pleaded with my squadron leader to let me remain on station and dump what I had on my wings. He gave me a direct order to return with the flight. I had plenty of fuel and time remaining, but he wanted the whole unit to stay intact so he wouldn't get his bureaucratic ass in trouble. I've never been so disgusted with the Air Force way of doing things in my whole life! Just to comply with a bunch of flying regs!" He was indeed remorseful.

It was hard to believe what I was hearing, and I was dumbfounded that such an incident could occur. Vietnam was many different things for many people, and I was beyond the dread of being in any circumstance other than the life at Vinh Long, but I guess I needed to be jolted a bit to understand the good deal we had. The major finished up his tale of woe, thanked me for listening, and was ready to depart. I jokingly commended him for talking to a lowly helicopter pilot, and I mentioned that I had plenty of respect for his flying skills. Then he flashed a look in his eyes that indicated it didn't count for much if you were in the situation in which he had found himself.

At that moment, I was distracted by something else happening over on the left side of my vision. Down the marble-tiled corridor of the Pacific Hotel came Jack Koslow—but he acted funny. He was approaching the bar slowly, doing something like the "squaw dance" I had last seen in the Order of the Arrow Indian dancing in the Boy Scouts. He placed his left foot in a circling motion, then his right one for a few steps. It was a pretty good rendition of the old Plains Indians woman's dance we used to perform as part of our repertoire. I hadn't seen him since flight school, and he had been with me at Benning in our IOBC class.

"Hey, Koz! Hey, Jack Koslow! What are you doing? It's Dave Eastman, come on over here and see me!" I called out. He was getting embarrassing.

"Oh, hi, East. Yeah, I saw you over here. I was coming over . . . ." He looked fuzzy and out of touch. I was wondering what had happened to *him* in the First Cav.

"What were you just doing over there coming down that hallway?" I asked.

"*That* is the first solid flooring I have stepped on in the last six months," he replied. "I had forgotten the feeling. I have had nothing but dirt floors and tents for some time now." He still had a vacant look in his eyes. He had not ordered yet.

"You're with the Cav, like most of the guys from our flight school class, right?"

"Yeah. I see everybody all the time," said Koz. "We're all in the same boat. The maintenance is terrible and I've had a lot of close calls flying in the crud. We do a lot of instrument work without the instruments to do it. I've gotten used to having holes in the instrument panel where there is supposed to be an attitude indicator or something else. And we do instrument takeoffs all the time. One of those times we did, we were in the clouds and I had another ship go right in front of my windshield, completely out of place from where he should have been. Scared the shit out of me. I've had a lot of crazy things like that happen. It's no fun, let me tell you."

This was the first time he had escaped this Cav existence, getting an in-country R&R to Vung Tau. I informed him that we did this all the time, renting a villa just down the street. (Mike Hershey, for some reason, was in charge of this and collected rent from all of us for its use.) We rotated visiting it, usually for about three days at a time, flying a Huey over with a couple of guys. The returning party would fly it back to Vinh Long. He was rather amazed at such decadence. I went on to describe our lifestyle and degree of accident-free flying and outstanding maintenance. His face sort of hung out as he listened to the contrast of living in the Delta versus living with the Cav. Our conversation continued for a while as I caught up with his experiences and found out what the guys I knew were doing up north around An Khe. Eventually we finished our reconnecting and I moved on. I then pondered the extremeness of circumstances between the Air Force jet jock who had been on my right, and my poor friend from the First Cav who'd been to my left at this bar. I sure was proud to be part of the 175th at Vinh Long.

28

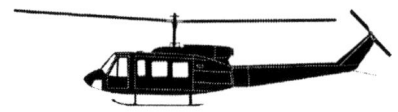

DEFENSE COUNSEL

WHEN JACK PAYNE, TROY TISON, AND I all got secondary jobs as commissioned officers in the two aviation companies that shared the Vinh Long compound, we were surprised suddenly to be appointed as counsels for the defense and prosecution for all upcoming court-martials in the units. We received these assignments around our second month in-country. Only Jack wanted to be a lawyer after finishing his stint with the Army; the rest of us had no such yearning, or any appetite for the legal field. I became Jack's assistant defense counsel, and then later, defense counsel for the whole compound. Maybe I cared too much about representing the rights of the sorry personnel who found themselves in trouble with the UCMJ, the book that details military rights and wrongs, which are handled differently from the way they are done in civilian courts. Everything was spelled out here in the military justice system, and it was very defined and detailed. It was up to me to uncover the true story of how some young soldier had gotten arrested, and thus now needed representation. This went on for eight months of my tour; needless to say, it was very educational.

A great many of the cases concerned racial strife, which was news to us. A lot of our generation who had attended college in the early 1960s had supported the civil rights movement, and some had even been Freedom Riders. Southern boys like Troy and Jack were at the other end of the experience; they had witnessed well-intentioned northern college students invade their communities and become "outside agitators." The members of these two divergent groups had not had earnest dialogues until we were all in the Army together, when we found ourselves playing cards across from one another some Friday evening in our first homes. This was political unrest up close and personal. Troy would say, "Hey, y'awl are talking about US!" We had never seen it that way up to then, and we realized we were being educated *real fast* about our friends, and *by* them. The Army experience had its blessings in this regard.

While we learned about their side of things, for the most part we perceived that something had been accomplished in the area of racial relations, and progress had been made in civil rights. Looking back, this was pretty much a sacred cow for the majority of us college graduates, and we thought it a done deal. Consciousness raising had been very "in." (Anyone want to have a "Hootenanny" at this point? Sing along with me, "This land is your land, this land is my land . . . . ") So, it was with great consternation that we found black soldiers not getting along with white troops, by choice, in the off hours of compound life. Also, the blacks did not want fellow blacks associating with white kids in their leisure time, and they actually segregated some of the bars downtown, designating them as "Black Only." Not only did this seem to be reverse discrimination, it also flew in the face of all that we had battled for, struggling to eliminate "Colored Only" bathrooms and drinking-water fountains in the Deep South. At first, it seemed incomprehensible that these were the facts. It astonished the commissioned officers on the special court-martial board; they came back with various prejudicial stances, depending on where in the United States they had come from. This job was getting interesting.

We talked with our EM on the flight line about this phenomenon, which we officers were almost embarrassed to discover under our noses, and knew nothing about. "Oh, yeah, the blacks are OK to work with during the day on duty, but after hours they keep to themselves, and you are not allowed to hang out with them. Any black kids that do this get in trouble with the black power types, and get hurt, quick." Our mouths were hanging open at this information—everyday smarts to the EM in the platoon, but we had never before noticed it. Of course, we didn't hang out with our crews after hours, so we could not have known. The news smarted; it flew in the face of all the consciousness-raising we had done on our college campuses.

When I approached a young black enlisted man whom I was supposed to represent, I initially would tell him that the U.S. Army would pay for a trained civilian lawyer to represent him if he wished; he didn't have to put up with me. They always said no to this, wanting to stick with my services. I don't know why, but many told me after the trial that they had never had an officer stand up for them. They would go on to say that I had done everything I could for them and that they appreciated it. I never once beat the rap, so I had to respond that I hadn't saved them from punishment, but to a man they all felt I had done a sincere job of representing them. I think some of the officers on the special court-martial board felt the same way too, but perhaps without the same feeling of goodwill toward me.

In beginning conversations with a client, I might find that he had tried to avoid violence, but his adversaries had triumphed. This was almost never a cut-and-dried, black-and-white scenario. One black soldier accused of using a cut-down M-1 carbine in a bar, and charged with second-degree assault, had actually *not* used the weapon while being carved up by several knife-wielding black assailants. He had been told never to show up in that particular bar because he was friendly with white kids. When he did show up, they pinned him against the rear wall of the cafe and slashed at him while he held the carbine at port arms, trying to defy them with its presence. When the MPs finally arrived, they saw him with the small rifle, and the attackers had gone. My defense was that he had never once used the loaded weapon, even with his life in danger. The news of what actually had transpired in the small Vinh Long bar transfixed the members of the court-martial board and moved the brass into looking further into the racial tensions obviously prevalent among our EM. In revealing the entire story, beyond the evidence that had first been presented, my hope was to get the soldier in question a lesser charge and far more realistic punishment than would have seemed appropriate at first. I worked at trying to tear down first impressions by providing a broader picture of what had occurred. The field-grade commissioned officers running the compound had enough evidence to commit the soldier in question; it was up to me to relieve him of some of the dire consequences of his actions.

There were cases where a trooper had fallen asleep on guard duty and the like; there were also other charges that seemed to indicate a deeper, more troubling situation for a young enlisted man with a major psychological problem. One black soldier behaved terribly when drunk; he literally had become a crazed killer. When I picked him up for trial at the Long Binh Jail (LBJ), I determinedly handcuffed him to the Huey's seats so I would have no trouble with him. He wailed, "Ah, man! Not this!" I said, "Cooley, I saw you that night when the MPs had you secured to a steel cot and you were not human. You were frothing at the mouth, and totally out of it. You absolutely needed to be physically restrained. You may not be that man I saw at that moment under the influence, but I am taking no chances!" I let him know I was expecting far better behavior in the courtroom than I had seen that night when he was arrested for being so dangerous. As I got to know him while preparing his defense, I found out he was generally an all-around good guy; but on booze, he became someone else. I sincerely told him I had a father like that, so I was well experienced at knowing the contrasts. If he survived these months in the stockade for the sentence he surely was going to get, then he had to realize that alcohol was poison for his system, that he had a particular problem with it, and that he should never touch it again. He profoundly considered what I had to say to him. After serving his time up at Long Binh, he was transferred down to Soc Trang. (Apparently there was some policy about relocating a troublesome trooper after he had served out his sentence—maybe to give everyone a break.) One of the rare days that we landed down there on that old Japanese airstrip, he came looking for my ship in the Outlaw flight, and joyfully told me he was doing all right and making the necessary improvements in his life. He was all smiles as he said he had me to thank for changing his life around. It was beyond any expectations I ever had for the case, and I was a bit emotionally overwhelmed with his enthusiasm for himself and me. I was impressed that he had made the effort to search me out for his congratulations; evidently it was important to him. I think some of these kids had never had anyone to care for them.

Some of the cases were just too unreal to believe. "CZ" had been Major O'Kane's crew chief on Outlaw 21, and he was always getting in trouble for having "rabbit blood." Spec. 4 Czprina did not seem to know when he was allowed to go downtown and when he was not. He would just find a way to escape the compound when he wanted to go. Apparently he had his own rules about when he deserved time off to make leisurely visits to the downtown bars. The passes necessary for these excursions didn't make sense to him; he just went. Eventually he was barred from going off post, essentially forbidden to leave the compound. This drove him crazy.

When I took CZ's case, he had been arrested for being AWOL; the MPs had picked him up minutes after his arrival downtown. He had gotten there by hiding in the laundry truck's back area, beneath the bags of dirty linen and underwear. The powers-that-be had already surmised *he was downtown,* because he had not shown up for roll call that morning. He explained to me that he had worked two eight-hour shifts, back to back, and thought he deserved some time off. He had done the maintenance shift he was supposed to do, and then he helped a buddy who was new to his ship without having the knowledge needed to do his job. Since he had done this good deed, CZ thought the Army knew all about this and of course would grant his wishes to go downtown for just a little bit. Not that he communicated this to anyone outside his own brain—CZ just didn't possess this relevant amount of socialization; he saw no logical need to deal with the proper authorities. He slept in with a good heart, then got up late in the morning to take his reward in the streets of Vinh Long. The MPs were waiting for him and "cotched him" right up.

When I picked CZ up at the Long Binh Jail for the trial, he had obviously gone through something akin to hell in this terrible military stockade. To my eyes, he looked a lot like someone who had been tortured. The burly sergeants at the military prison were very cruel and sadistic; they even liked their jobs. The barbed wire enclosing the stockade made it resemble a WWII Nazi prison camp, a Stalag 17 lookalike. It was shocking to anyone who ever saw the place. The immediate image that came to mind was that you had walked onto a movie set for the worst possible internment epic ever made. The extreme men imprisoned inside the wire looked like the evilest people the Army had ever made the mistake of recruiting. They were savages, totally corrupt. From behind this fence, they would make catcalls and hoot at the officers moving around to the front gate of the compound. At times, you had to stare them down and directly address them. "Are you happy inside that monkey cage?" I asked a belligerent type one day, feeling no need to tolerate his obscenities. "No, sir," came back the quick reply. I put on my "first john" face and told this young man that when and if he ever got out of this stockade he had better start living a different life than the one he had been doing that got him here. "Do you know how you got there yet?" I yelled. He replied that he had gotten that.

It was a rough experience picking up the very men I would have to defend. When I signed Czprina out, I asked the big sergeant harassing him to go easier on him; I informed the sergeant that he was a very good crew chief. It made no difference. The huge, scary sergeant blasted me, "Look, Lieutenant, you couldn't do anything with him! Now we'll take care of him our way!" He was just short of insubordinate, and I disliked this surly brute on the spot. "Come on, CZ, let's get you out of here," I said.

Even though CZ obviously was ethnically Polish, this funny young lad struck me as rather like an Indian boy just off the reservation for the first time, due to this military enlistment. He always let me know that this suspicion of his ethnicity wasn't so, but that's how he impressed me. He had no clue about military boundaries.

He was like a vital wild animal that could not be constrained.

When the trial was over, and I had to return him to LBJ, I let him fly the aircraft all the way to north of Saigon, where this stockade was located for all of the bad-asses in Vietnam. He even made the approach and pretty much landed the D-model in full sight of the whole compound's inhabitants behind the wire. When we touched down, and settled the weight of the Huey on the skids, I leaned over to him and said, "Now, when you get in there with those bastards, *you* tell them *you* were the person landing that helicopter they just saw out here in the grass!" "Yessir," he grinned back.

My most bizarre story involved the defense of a young crewman who had not returned from R&R on time—like 30 days late. It seems he and the fellows he had associated with had missed their flight on the last day of their week in Japan. After receiving a time and departure for the following day, they elected to go back to downtown Tokyo and resume partying. The next day, they missed that flight, too. This went on daily for weeks, as they ran up tremendous debts for hotel rooms and fantastic meals. They had gotten away with it, and the Army bailed them out, because you cannot be a debtor in Japan; they'll lock you up. Finally, one day someone got wise, held onto them at the airport, and put them on a flight back to Vietnam. The only flaw in this solution was that this particular plane had to stop in Hong Kong for refueling. So the guys got off. After a week spent "eating, drinking, and being merry, for tomorrow we die," the Navy bailed them out of their bills and put them on a flight to Saigon. By now, after having acquired an enormous appetite for this luxurious lifestyle, they kept it going with a binge down on Saigon's Tu Do Street, spending a week living high on the tab there. Eventually they were arrested by the MPs and sent along to their individual units for discipline. For the first time, I didn't think I'd have a chance to present any extenuating and mitigating circumstances to help out this young soldier, despite his marvelous tale of decadence.

Ironically, he wasn't being charged with desertion, because

each day, one at a time, they had made the *attempt* to return. AWOL was the charge, because he had been carried daily on the morning report as being absent without leave. He had no permission to be away that long from his unit. He had just taken advantage of a good situation and luxuriated himself to excess! Spec. 4 Gerald Thompson sat there in my hooch telling me of his enjoyable exploits, and then said, "I want you to know, sir, I'm not making any of this up! I've got all the receipts to tell you what a great time I had. I had the best time of my life!" I groaned and said, "Throw *those away!* That's evidence!"

I wasn't able to save him from "six-and-six"—six months' imprisonment and six months' forfeiture of two-thirds pay. This is the maximum sentence that a special court-martial can impose, and the board did it. Like all the others I had defended, Thompson stood up at the end of the trial and, though glum, said I had done everything I could for him, and he would have to face the music for his extravagant exploits. Once again, I had to fly the prisoner back to LBJ to finish serving out his time.

Unfortunately, there is more to this story. Thompson served out his six months of internment and then was picked up one day in a new Outlaw 22, with the tail number of 66-01099, another replacement D-model for the unit's aircraft.

A new senior major had come into the 175th, and he was scary. For instance, he had a thing about "proper" place settings in the officer's club. He would suddenly and viciously throw knives, forks, and spoons suddenly across the length of the mess hall, infuriated that the little Vietnamese waitresses didn't know how to set the tables properly. This really mattered to him, and it really mattered to us that he was terrorizing these poor, bewildered, little women who were only one step out of the rice paddy. We thought we'd seen them all, but here was yet another kook. He would bellow with rage as he hurled this silverware, and when he pulled this bizarre stunt, the entire group of women would flee the officer's mess, remaining huddled and terrified in the kitchen. It would take a lot of consolation by "ole Charlie," the black cook who had been back there for years, to get them working again. There just was no need for this man to be so berserk over tableware. He never checked in with anybody else about the need for dressing down the help; he just did it on his own accord.

We had no idea how long we would have to put up with this guy; it seemed that his one main attribute was knowing how to fly by instruments. He had been an instrument examiner or instructor—his main occupational calling. When he had to fly one day, he asked for a copilot who was either well versed in instruments or wanted to be. He considered himself pretty special. We watched from afar, knowing that *someone* would take the bait and express a desire to fly with this crazy man. And surely there would be a story to tell afterward.

A new lieutenant who had just come into the second platoon had considerable credentials for a long-term career in aviation. George Sodaitis was full of himself with esteem and ambition. He had completed a five-year degree in aeronautical engineering, which certainly impressed the rest of us. This had given him a boost to first lieutenant's rank while still in school, after having been commissioned a second lieutenant at the end of the four-year ROTC program. This also happened to dentists and doctors, even lawyers; they entered the service with an increased paycheck even though they had not gone through the lower-officer ranks while on active duty. Pretty slick, but I guess the government liked them increasing their education for its potential value in the Army. Sodaitis wanted to fly with Major Latta in the worst way once he heard of his request; he wanted that instrument time. Harvey Persyn, who by now had replaced me as operations officer for the second platoon, could not deter him from this assignment. Sodaitis insisted on having the opportunity to fly with Latta, so Harvey let him have his way, despite legitimate worries. I had an intuitive sense that this green copilot would receive his comeuppance this day.

We watched the day's events unfold. The first chapter was seeing Latta come down the Outlaw ramp carrying an instrument hood in the same hand he was carrying his flight helmet in. (There was no place to fly instruments in Vietnam. After flight following with Paddy Radar and Paris Radar, there were only a few nondirectional beacons here and there in-country. These NDBs were pretty much on the same level as when aviators homed into broadcast radio-station towers in the 1930s.) What was he going to do with that hood? This was not the place to use it; in Vietnam's congested airspace, you had to keep your head on a swivel most of the time. I surmised that this guy didn't know what he was doing. It was open to conjecture where things would go from here.

The next time I witnessed his performance was watching and hearing him enter downwind at Can Tho later that morning. I was on the apron at flight idle while he was breaking into the east downwind leg at the far side of the field from my position on the ground. He was in a panic, with his voice very agitated as he became the fourth aircraft in the pattern, and making his second attempt at it. The first time, he had done a wild 360-degree turnaround, thinking he could not make it in; this was unheard of. Most of the time here, we just called extended base and came right in on a 90-degree angle to the active runway. This guy evidently was incapable of doing what a beginning student pilot could accomplish. I was starting to understand that Major Latta probably couldn't do *anything* without being vectored by an air traffic controller on an FAA radarscope. This aviator needed to be on instruments doing exactly what he was directed to do. He was no seat-of-the-pants flyboy. Sodaitis might have to clean out *his* pants though, by the end of the day . . . .

After this landing in Can Tho, they proceeded up to Saigon. Majors needing flight time for their required five hours a month usually were given easy, ashy-trashy missions, and this was the day that Spec. 4 Thompson was due to be picked up at the Long Binh Jail. Also on board were Spec. 4 Hopper and Kooman, my crew chief with whom I had a personality conflict. Sergeant Newton, the platoon sergeant, and I had not been able to resolve it. We just didn't like one another as people in an aviation crew and couldn't work together as EM and AC. It had resulted in an ongoing problem on Outlaw 24 that none of us particularly welcomed; on this date, however, he was crewing on Outlaw 22 for the flight with Latta.

At the end of our flying this particular August day, Outlaw 22 still had not returned home to the field, and we all wondered what had happened. I couldn't imagine them getting lost. O'Kane was still in charge of Operations, while this jerk had been appointed to be our new XO. (Latta had told Joe Moffett that he would soon be the new CO and he'd relieve Joe *then* as Maverick Lead because he'd found partial ammo belts lying around their parking area. He wasn't making friends.) Major Bob O'Kane and Hershey split to Saigon to find out the reason for the delay. A call had come down on the land line. They found out all right. Latta had hit a jet while it was on final doing a ground-controlled approach (GCA) to Tan Son Nhut. When the event occurred, the helicopter had been flying at 1,800 feet over a tributary to the Saigon River, coming back from Bien Hoa. Highway 1 crosses here; he might have been following it. The jet came down out of the clouds where they were flying on an intersect right up to its descent angle. The fighter was directly on line with the Tan Son Nhut runway, as it was supposed to be.

We never flew that high in that area because of all the air traffic constantly flitting about. It was congested. We stayed down around 500 feet and kept our collective heads in full rotation, peering this way and that, scanning in all directions for aircraft coming at us on collision courses. It was too easy to get killed up there with all the military goings on. "Hotel 3," the Saigon heliport alongside Tan Son Nhut, was the most dangerous place in the country for midair accidents. Sodaitis knew none of this, and neither did Latta. Don Casper, who was now fully recovered and back serving as the Delta Aviation Battalion's operations officer, reported to us that flight following actually had assigned Latta to fly at that altitude. The two Air Force EM governing these two aircraft had not been in communication with each other in their particular jurisdictions at the time. An experienced AC would not have let his aircraft be placed in this precarious situation, no matter who was telling him what to do.

Mike Kidd, who'd been Jon Myhre's crew chief on Outlaw 17 on Easter Sunday, was now down at Can Tho and crewing one of the battalion staff aircraft, Delta 012. This day, he was sitting around at USARV or the First Aviation Brigade headquarters at Bien Hoa when he looked up and saw the midair collision. He said he knew that Latta always liked to climb up to altitude due to his intense fear of ground fire. Kidd watched the Huey fly right into the belly of the descending jet on final. Latta moved directly into the midair fate awaiting him. Kidd watched in horror as pieces of aircraft dropped from the sky. Then he ran in and told his AC, Major Stoverink, what he had witnessed.

The only way O'Kane and Hershey learned the actual facts of the midair was that the jet pilot had communicated, "Just hit a helicopter, ejecting!" on the recording tape of the GCA controller. The accident report filed later said that one of the main rotor blades jammed right into his air-intake scoop, causing the jet to pitch straight down. The pilot had seen the helicopter only at the last moment; he couldn't evade it. The Air Force fighter clipped off the Huey's main rotor system, along with the tail boom. The four crew members and the passenger essentially were in a free-falling box from an altitude of 1,800 feet. Some elected to learn how to fly and jumped out of the decapitated cabin. Their bodies were found a different distance from the wreck on the sandbars of the river. We learned all these gory details when O'Kane and Hershey returned to the Outlaw ramp later that evening. They looked very glum, obviously having witnessed a horrible scene. Kooman and Latta would no longer be personality problems; Sodaitis had come to an all-too-quick end, taking talents that would never be realized. What was in my thoughts, though, was that maybe it had been a good thing that Spec. 4 Gerald Thompson had experienced all that glorious partying for 30 days—with all that Tokyo and Hong Kong had to offer—before his youthful death. Maybe his life's clock knew about this exact exit moment for him.

29

LIGHTNING BUGS

Night missions to find the VC moving themselves and their supplies around were called "bug" or "lightning-bug" missions because we often used some form of illumination to help the gunships locate their targets of opportunity. This raiding from the air deterred the Viet Cong in their movements somewhat, but we had to change techniques and tactics frequently to obtain the element of surprise on these missions. missions. Earlier, big lamps of various sorts were used at the side of the helicopter to illuminate the canals below where the sampans were spotted, but this blinded us completely in the front of the aircraft, even with a screen blanketing us from the glare. This device was eliminated in favor of a cluster of five to seven DC-3 landing lights. These were outside of the Huey but positioned so they didn't blind the pilot. Neither of these solutions was as preferable as just throwing out high-candlepower flares ignited by a lanyard attached to them. The gravity of this falling object pulled its ignition fuse, and the flare floated around the sky on its own parachute at 1,500 to 2,500 feet. The gunships would work close to the ground, seeing their prey lit up by these intense flares that created a backdrop of hot light in the Delta night. If dropped from lower than 1,500 feet due to weather conditions, the flare often was still burning when it hit the ground. Sometimes the hotly burning illumination would land on the thatched roof of some peasant's hut.

The flare ship needed experienced enlisted personnel to throw the gray metal canisters out the back door, because these things were dangerous. They had enough candlepower to melt the Huey in half, especially with all the other flares stacked against the transmission wall, ready to be used next. The EM would heave the things out the door one at a time; if anything got hung up, the crew would not be able to survive the accident. A few months after I'd left Vietnam, a ship did destroy itself when something went wrong on a flare mission, and yes, the Huey did melt in two as predicted.

The gunships would work a particular sector where they thought some VC action was occurring, and the missions would come into the slick platoons to provide a ship and crew for the nightlong work. The guys on lightning-bug missions got to sleep in the next day, but we didn't recuperate much in the hot daytime conditions. It was good enough just to be left alone after a tiring, all-night expenditure of energy. Nights in the IV Corps got down to about 80 degrees Fahrenheit, while daytime highs were often near 100 degrees. Made for some pretty muggy shut-eye if you managed to sleep during the day.

Most bug missions were boringly predictable; others created some memories all their own. You never knew what might happen. It was very obvious after a few of these missions that the VC were extremely active by night. You could see the sampans motionless on the canals, stuck in the glare of the light, while the gunships tried to fire upon them before they moved out of the illuminated area. We worked out of isolated airstrips in the dark, or more developed places such as Can Tho. You never knew what the gunship fire team leader had in mind; you just went along with the idea of the moment that might be effective. The overall impact of the bug missions seemed to be more harassment than effectiveness. The gunship crews strove to give them greater impact; the slicky pilots just wanted to go home as early as possible and get some sleep for the remaining hours of the night.

You couldn't drink the night of your bug mission, and this got in the way for the guys who knew they would be missing something at the club. One evening, a very beautiful blonde German stripper was scheduled to perform at the Mekong Manor, accompanied by her dark-haired, accordion-playing husband. He had a pencil-thin mustache on his upper lip and looked like he was more prepared to be playing with a lithesome monkey on a leash than this beautiful woman. Her skin was alabaster, almost like translucent ivory, and her breasts were pointed and perfectly formed. We couldn't believe she was going to show us this magnificent form, unclad, after supper that night. All were raptly attentive to her presence as she and her husband dined in our midst. Her platinum blonde hair was coiled above her head in tresses, and rhinestone jewelry shone appropriately everywhere. The sparkling gems perfectly complemented her European style. Their accents were intense. The husband seemed used to seeing younger men gawking at his exquisite wife. We waited for the time to pass for this splendidly exotic display to begin.

Jack Payne had bug duty. He was committed to flying the light-ship mission that night, and I knew he could not get out of it. "Oh, yeah? Oh, yeah! I'm gonna get out of it, I can tell you that," said Jack to me at dinner. I told him there was no way, and there was no possibility at all that someone would switch with him when this beautiful blonde was on the entertainment docket. "I will be *here,* and I *will not* miss the show!" said "Smiling Jack" once again. He was so emphatic that it was entertaining in itself to watch the development of this sidelight to the night's main event.

The club was full and the show began. However, Jack was out on the runway with lightning bug. "Aha," I said to myself, as I watched the beautiful blonde temptress begin to swirl and swing her silken veils around, "Jack didn't make it after all." But before too much longer, Jack's sullen face appeared at the door of the officers' club. He came in and took a seat. It was near mine, so I leaned over and asked him how he had pulled it off. "Never mind. I told you I'd be here and I am. I'll tell you later," in his Mississippi accent.

The all-male crowd watched in fascination as the blonde worked her way down to a G-string and rhinestone pasties on her nipples. She was flawless. We all agreed that we had never seen such a physique in all our lives. Her legs, abdomen, arms, and all she possessed were perfection. Her mustachioed husband played away on his accordion, and the lithe, ivory-skinned woman bowed and swirled in her own art form. Finally, she asked for a volunteer from the seated company to come forward. Somebody pushed Major Millward down front. She made him kneel in front of her and then demanded he place his stubby arms behind his back. He did so, and she rapidly swished her breasts across his face, with the rhinestone tassels sweeping across his eyes. She stood up and backed off, looking pleased. He hollered, "They hurt!" The rest of us could have cared less, but we were not offered the same treat. She finished up, and the applauding men showed their appreciation for her classy beauty. We all envied the little organ grinder, too. Given the chance, we'd have been happy to follow her around playing an accordion, too.

She wrapped a dressing gown about her and left. I leaned over to Jack and said, "Now tell me how you got out of bug to get back in here and see her." Jack leaned back and said, "I broke the lights." I said, "What?!" "I got a damn wrench and busted out almost every one of those DC-3 landing lights but one, then I told my crew chief to fix them by the time I got back!" No question, that guy had balls!

In the late evening hours of 21 May 1967, the Vinh Long compound was mortared badly—the worst any of us had experienced during the whole time of our tour. The rounds fell on the Outlaw ramp, and some even went through the roof of the hangar, ruining a ship there. All the explosions were very loud, scaring us plenty. When the incoming fire lifted and we hustled out of our bunkers to see what the damage looked like from afar, the sky was ablaze with the flames of burning ships. They had scored some big hits this particular night, and as we stood outside the second platoon's hooches, the first question that came to mind was, "Is anyone flying bug tonight?"

"Gosh, yeah," said Tommy McCarthy, "Snow and Huey are out there on the ramp right now." We started to get worried.

Most of us were in our civvies as we stood around and watched the burning aircraft light up the Delta sky. We mentally counted faces and realized that the two guys must have been out there with the ships, preflighting them for the mission, when the rounds had first started coming in. We were convinced they were done for, and even if they had not received a direct hit, they undoubtedly would have been hurt by exploding shrapnel from the damaged ships.

Suddenly Jim Huey was in our midst, heaving with gasps. We were more than a little glad to see him and immediately asked about Snow. "He's still out there. I don't think he made it," was Huey's quick, winded reply. "He fell to the ground, and with all the ships burning up, I think it got him." As we turned our attention to the firestorm engulfing the birds on the Outlaw ramp, we were beginning to wonder if *any* of our ships had escaped the enemy's wrath. It looked bad, and it was that much worse to think that Carson Snow's body could be out there getting incinerated as we spoke about him. As we waited out the ghastly situation, we had him pretty much dead and buried.

Feeling mournful, we looked up and suddenly saw Snow right there within touching distance. Except he looked funny, all uniformly gray and even mysterious; we all instantly imagined we were looking at his ghost! It was a weird thought that he had come by to see us one more time before disappearing into the hereafter! What a great guy to remember us in the first few moments following his death! We all clamored around him, touching him, then were astonished to find he was physically there—in the flesh! Abruptly, we started pounding on his back, exclaiming, "Snow! Snow, you're here! You're OK!"

"No, I'm not. Y'all quit pounding me on the back; I hurt something out there." Snow did not look good, making us realize that on top of his totally mud-covered, peculiar appearance, he was in considerable pain. We took him up to the dispensary.

When he returned, we learned he had a slipped disk; for a while, it gave him severe back pain. Huey and Snow filled us in on their escape from the mortar attack that we thought had consumed them. It blew up about five ships in the first platoon section and the hangar but did not damage any of our second platoon aircraft, parked just across the ramp. The VC had targeted the more northerly placed ships pretty well. We had never sustained such damage before; it made us wonder how they had suddenly become so accurate.

Carson Snow and Jim Huey had been standing up on top of the cabin roof and checking out the hub of either Outlaw 27 or 29, parked at the west end of the ramp, when they saw the overhead incoming rounds start to fall. At first, they had suspected some gunship was firing rockets awfully close that night, but when explosions started occurring all around them, they knew they were under enemy fire. It scared them so much that they took off running from the top of the Huey, about eight or nine feet up! Snow fell and hurt his back then. He was lying in pain, watching Huey sprint down the lane of burning helicopters, and trying to decide his next move. For a couple of reasons, he figured he couldn't follow Huey's course of action. First, he didn't think Jim would truly make it, and two, he himself couldn't do anything now but crawl. So he elected to get himself over to a pile of sandbags he could see in the grass alongside the ramp and slide inside the bunker. Except, Carson didn't know it was in a half-finished stage of completion—in fact, he thought it was manned. He crawled through the mud and tall grass, calling out, "American! Don't shoot!" The lack of a response just spooked him more, and he was sure some scared trooper had a bead on him. He crawled closer and closer, imploring the beleaguered defenders all the while to recognize him as a friendly and not kill him. When he got there, he flopped inside the pile of sandbags and found that he was all alone. He huddled there in pain while he watched the mortared Outlaw ships burst into flame and totally consume themselves. Hueys burn really well once they get going. By the following morning, all the mortared ships were reduced to their turbines and rotor blades and light gray ashes. It was a dismal sight.

About a month later, we were all sitting around watching the Armed Forces TV broadcast out of Saigon, eating popcorn that Novotney always made on the hot plate, when Snow leaned forward and moaned, "God, my back hasn't hurt this much since that mortar attack a month ago!" As we all watched him doubling up, suddenly we heard the mortars begin to land on the runway. Everyone bolted out and into the bunker. We were first inside there, of course. Forever afterward, Snow's back would hurt just before the first incoming rounds "car-rumphed" on the strip, and all the second platoon guys in the day room would immediately race out to the bunker. Snow's psychosomatic early warning system never failed us, and the rest of the compound always wondered how we always managed to be in the bunker first during these attacks. Eventually, all Snow had to do was groan, and everybody exited without question. The second platoon aviators were already in the bunker before the first round fell, every time. The only query then was, "Did anyone take the 'Jiffy-pop' off the hot plate?" (Miss you, Snowy Owl.)

Mike Hershey had given the second platoon the mission order for that particular bug assignment that never took off. His ship, Outlaw 19, would have flown the night mission if Mike had kept the assignment himself. But he had something else to do in Operations that evening, so he passed the bug duty to the second platoon. Precisely at the same moment that Snow and Huey were preflighting their bird, Hershey would also have been on top of Outlaw 19, which took the first incoming round of the attack and burned to the ground in a crisp. This was the end of the smoke ship in the 175th. If Hershey or any of their other pilots had been out there that night for that mission, we would have lost some people in the first platoon.

That 21 May mortar attack savaged the first platoon, where most of the rounds landed. One of their ACs, Warrant Officer J.R. Wright, recalled later, from notes written in his journal (a habit some guys followed), that his ship, Outlaw 12, took serious hits from shrapnel. In fact, it looked like Swiss cheese. This was mostly from the piled barrels that formed revetments around the parked ships. When a mortar round hit the old 55-gallon drums, they would explode and their metal surfaces often became projectiles, which then penetrated the skin of the Hueys they were supposed to safeguard. The right-side doors of Wright's ship were all perforated, and the radios and flight instruments on the cockpit's dashboard were severely damaged. The engine and rotor system looked bad, too, but all this could be fixed by Outlaw Maintenance. It was, after a nearly complete rebuild. Other ships did not fare so well; Outlaw 6 was a total loss.

When we walked out on the ramp the next morning, taking pictures of the carnage, it was obvious that some of the Hueys had burned like marshmallows dropped into a campfire. Turbines and transmissions were all that remained. I took several black-and-white shots, but when I had the film developed in downtown Vinh Long, the results weren't so hot. The photos were more like proofs, easily smeared. I used a pencil eraser to make "clouds" above the heads of the people I'd photographed. Then I wrote *Mad* magazine–type cartoon sayings, which were good for a lot of laughs. One had Meehan looking into the tail boom of a destroyed Huey, and saying, "Come on out, Millward, you won't find anything in there!" Capt. Art Hall thought this was funny as hell, but the commanding officer of the 150th Transportation Detachment did not. Ol' "Road Runner" himself squashed the young maintenance captain quickly, saying, "I got some stuff that could make you look pretty silly, too!" Usually, Bob Millward had a better sense of humor than that . . . .

My most memorable lightning-bug episode nearly cost me my life. I was saved by a Vietnamese pilot who flew with us for about 90 days. Le Tran Hung is worth a story in himself. Lieutenant Hung was assigned to us, and we were told by General Westmoreland's command that no matter how it went, we were not allowed to do anything but get along with this man. The Vietnamese Air Force (VNAF) chopper pilots flew H-34s, the old Sikorskys given them by Uncle Sam, and some of them were pretty good aviators, especially if they were former North Vietnamese. It was evident that eventually they'd get Hueys, too. These Vietnamese pilots would be integrated into our units on a trial basis, and we were supposed to live with the situation, however it played out. It didn't matter whether they went AWOL immediately after showing up, or were terrible to fly with, or whatever else. We were charged to grin and bear it, and to survive their presence without any complaints. When the Army talks to you this way, there is no excuse for any foul-up. These kinds of commands make you nervous; it's a no-win situation. You just collectively hold your breath and hope that nothing bad occurs.

I was flying with Lieutenant Hung one day in a lift when we landed directly over a VC position. As we swung around at a high hover over some thatched-roofed hooches, I heard machine gun fire out my left door. I told Duane Liebe, my new crew chief on Outlaw 24, to stop firing. He replied, "I'm not firing." Then, as Hung continued to swing the aircraft around, I heard the same machine gun firing out of my right door. So I told Tommy Greenfield, my new door gunner, to cease firing. He responded the same way: "I'm not doing any shooting either, sir." Then I realized that the automatic-weapons fire I was hearing was directly *underneath* the ship; it was right under our belly and was firing at the flight as we departed. Then big, livid green basketball-size tracers began to carom through the departing Outlaws. I knew these were .50-calibers, with the ammo transported from Cambodia. Beaulieu in Outlaw 27 was hit near the transmission area, it took out a wiring cluster for all his engine instruments. He put the thing down, as all his engine and transmission gauge needles went slack. Hung looked over at me with a grin, and said, "They got Harvey?!" I smirked back, wanting to say some wise-guy thing over the radio, like, "They gotcha, huh, Harve?" but that macho thing really wasn't called for, and I would have just further embarrassed myself, since Harvey wasn't flying his ship that day! I would have had egg on my face with my own thoroughly bad joke. So I didn't, but Hung and I shared the joke anyway. He was so small that he hardly showed up over the armor-plated seat on the right, but he was mighty. I saw him as a brave little pilot, and since he was doing so well, there was no reason to grab the controls away from him. We all got out unscathed and were just lucky that day. I couldn't believe we had landed over hooches with automatic weapons.

A few nights later, when we were gathered in the day room of the second platoon hooch (the first of the two buildings in which we resided), Hung came in the door drunk, really drunk. The guys immediately made light of this and razzed him good-naturedly: "Hey, Hung! Really tying one on tonight, eh?" Things had been going well flying with him, so the guys felt they could get this loose and be comradely. Hung's face was dark and sullen; there was no return smile for the goodwill extended. Instead, we were in deep shit. Hung began going up to each of us, saying, *"You* afraid VC! *Hung* not afraid of VC!" He dressed down each aviator in turn, and we all were thinking we had really blown this, whatever it was we did. He addressed each member of the platoon by name, as he rotated counter-clockwise through the group, and then went through the same retort that *he* was not afraid of the VC. Then came my turn. I winced, ready to take my share of abuse.

"Hung *not afraid* of VC! DAVE not afraid of VC, too!"

I looked at him in amazement: "What the hell did *I* do differently?"

"You not take controls away from me when VC shoot at us!" he said vehemently.

I thought about that, realizing he was right. "And the other guys did?" I asked. "Yes, you are only AC not afraid of VC. All others afraid of VC and take controls away from me. *I* am not afraid of the VC."

"Well, guys, there you have it. Better not take the controls away from this man ever again. OK with you, Hung?" I questioned.

"Yes. Hung good pilot. Hung never afraid of VC."

With that, the incident never went beyond the second platoon hooch, and we started liking and respecting this man. He had set the record straight and was a very interesting person to have around. He became my good friend and told me many things about his country and its problems. Needless to say, things were nowhere near as simple as we Americans projected them. He was incredible company while flying on the single-ship missions because he explained much of what was happening all around us—things about which we didn't have a clue. We were very blind to the Vietnamese people. He was good to the EM and treated them politely, and they returned the favor. Without this war, he would have become a doctor, and would have been fairly affluent by this time in his life, and he knew it. There was no end to the war in his estimation, or the misery all his countrymen had to endure. He had no hope for his nation or faith in the positive outcome projected by the United States for this tiny country. This was a mind-boggling education for me.

Well, back to the bug incident. Hung and I loved to fly together, and we trusted each other's competence very well, especially after his intoxicated dressing-down of the entire officer contingent of the second platoon. Thank God that had not gone any further, to the higher ranks.

After my exit from the third platoon, the Mavericks and I enjoyed working together on these lightning-bug missions; they had real confidence in me and I in them. This particular night, Duke Cone and Jack Mankin were working the area immediately south of Can Tho, and we were doing the flare drops directly over them. Duke and Jack were close buddies and operated easily as a team. We had an exceptionally low ceiling, of about 1,500 feet; the flares were designed to go off at 2,500 feet and burn out by the time they had floated down from that altitude. Released at 1,500 feet, they were still burning when they hit the ground. But we could go no higher, because we were at the base of the clouds, and occasionally right in them. This is dangerous at night, because you know for sure that you are in the clouds only when everything starts to get fuzzy and indistinct; nothing is as discernible as it is in the daytime. You need cues that you've screwed up.

We had some lieutenants on board hoping to get some flight time so they could get an Air Medal—they figured 25 hours of combat operational flying and it would be theirs. They were probably MACV desk jockeys from Can Tho, but they felt sitting on their butts on top of all the flare canisters in the backseat would get them the needed flight time to earn one more ribbon on their chest. At the end of that night of flying, they would need a slip of paper signed by me for certification, and then they'd be on their happy way. The Air Medal was designed for flight crews only, was the way I thought about it. I was a bit arrogant that anyone getting some riding time felt they were qualified to wear our combat air crew ribbon, but it wasn't my system. I just worked in it.

As the mission progressed, the two Mavericks were literally dodging the flare canisters as they hit the ground. There were some real belly laughs, but the job was getting done, and the time was being used up. Hung was in the right seat and I was in the left, as usual with the AC positioning in our platoon. It was felt that for the job we did, the AC needed all the visual contact that was more available in the left seat. In the right seat, a pilot newly arrived from the States was better qualified to fly instruments anyway, with the recency of his flight school experience in tactical instrument flying. The large attitude indicator—what we called the jet pilot attitude indicator—was over there for the right seat. Mine was something like what you might see in a light Cessna or other such small, fixed-wing aircraft. It often didn't work too well. We never paid much attention to the condition of its artificial horizon, because we only used it as a turn-and-bank indicator on the left side of the instrument panel.

Suddenly, I went into the clouds, and the running lights, even on steady-dim, immediately hypnotized me into vertigo. The human mind-and-eyeball connection tries to find level right away, and that is what happened with the rifts in the clouds and the dark sky in between. My mind and eyeballs were not in agreement, and my equilibrium system rioted. I had lowered pitch to get down out of the clouds, and I noted that my airspeed and altitude were at odds with each other. I pulled back on the stick to stop the airspeed increase and taper off the altitude loss, but things were not working out. I felt the air screaming past the fuselage and felt bent over, as if my seat were facing straight down. My sensory world was not true. I was trying to fly needle-ball, because it was obvious my left-seat attitude indicator was not functioning; it showed a slight dive, and something more than that was going on. I pulled back and back on the stick, with absolutely no reduction in airspeed; I was fucked. Nothing was making sense. It was time to let my copilot take over. I started screaming over the intercom for him to "take it." Over the panic in my brain, I surprisingly heard Hung's tinny, accented Vietnamese voice saying, "Leggo, Dave, I have eet."

"You have it? You have it, Hung?"

"Yass, Dave. Leggo. Leggo!"

I released pressure on the stick and felt him push it forward. I thought, "Oh, my God, I have trusted a 'slope' and now he's gonna fuck me at the biggest, most important point of my life!" I screamed again, "No, Hung, don't add airspeed, we are already diving at 110 knots!" The Huey's red line was at 120 and we were approaching that at a rapid clip. I still didn't know what was wrong with this nightmare, but I didn't need him screwing us up even worse.

"Trust me, Dave. Trust me. Leggo," came back his little voice.

Jesus, I had to. I let it play out. The aircraft abruptly came to level about 500 feet above the rice paddies. I still couldn't figure out what had happened. I knew we were safe and later I could find out how. The Mavericks had been calling on the UHF radio for some time. It would be decent to call back and let them know we were still alive, but that's all I could do in my frame of mind. I silently pulled in the mike switch, breathed, and said we were all right; we could go on with the mission. Jack Mankin said no way; we were going in for a cup of coffee at the Can Tho tower's mess hall. It was almost like a cantina; this would be fine for a break. I knew what was going through my fellow pilots' minds—that Hung had nearly killed me. They would want a complete story, but I doubted they would realize that he, as the better pilot, had saved me. We went in and landed in the dark on the wet apron just to the west of the main runway.

When we got inside, I knew Hung was seething with the prejudice the American pilots would automatically have against him. They were keeping their distance, letting things cool down a bit. My old crew chief, Ron Johnson, was the only one to come over to my table. He said, "What happened, man?" I told him that this fellow right here was the only reason I was still alive. Johnson looked down at Hung from his height and knew I spoke the truth. He looked back.

"You're the best, man. How could this happen?" he emoted.

"Anybody can get vertigo; I'm just lucky to have had this excellent pilot with me tonight to make the entire difference in the outcome of the incident," I said.

Johnson moved away and slowly told the story to all the other Mavericks willing to listen. Gradually, Duke Cone and Jack Mankin and others came sidling over and put their hands on Hung's shoulders, willing to make the move.

"So, you're the one who saved Dave, eh?" Duke said with his handsome grin.

Hung just nodded, and sort of loosened up. I was thinking about how rough it had to be to live with so much prejudice always projected at you because of your Asian image. And it wasn't just lack of height. Jack thought we had best just go home; enough for the night. He figured I wasn't as recovered as I thought I might be. I really didn't know. I was willing to trust his judgment, however. We finished up and made ready to leave.

The lieutenants who'd been riding in the backseat got their chits signed. I think several of them gained a vivid impression of what it is to earn an Air Medal. They and the flares must have been bouncing around like Ping-Pong balls. They must have been in a jumble. I'll bet a couple of them would never want to fly a bug mission at night again, or even fly at all.

What had happened up there was a condition called "power settling." We had gone into a tail-low configuration, similar to a jet aircraft going straight up. Instead, we were sinking toward the ground at a rate of 2,900 feet a minute in an airspace that had only 1,500 to give us. The air was moving through the rotor system in a way that was making it nonflyable. The airspeed increase was registering this. It had nothing to do with a diving configuration, as I had suspected. The helicopter was moving to the ground in a rapid descent that was backward, for all proper explanation. It could not fly. Hung had realized this and pushed the stick forward to get it doing so again.

Hung said we were in such an extreme position that he could read the U.S. manufacturer's patent number and place of business on the rear of the attitude indicator. I wonder how many pilots have ever seen that side of the instrument; we were nearly in a never-recover-from moment. If we had gone any farther backward, we might have flipped over and broken the blades off the machine. We had been in a dire predicament, saved by Hung's considerable talent. I couldn't think of any other copilot who could have saved me that night.

Looking back through the years, I still find it remarkable that a true Vietnamese–American friendship that was unique—because it was the *only* one I ever *witnessed*—saved my life. Our relationship was what the United States government had postured would happen among all Vietnamese and American soldiers, as many GIs had experienced in the World War II context. Hung once told me, "If all Americans were like you, Dave, and were friends like you and me, there would be no war very soon." Boy, have I had to learn over time what that piece of communication really meant . . . .

30

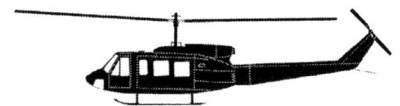

PLATOON PARTIES AND OTHER HIGH JINKS

ALMOST MONTHLY, the units would get together for a platoon party that mostly centered on steaks on the briquettes and a lot of canned beer. This was an opportunity for the crews to mingle with each other, as well as a chance for officers and EM to get down and hang out, displaying all the personality traits of who we were in our off time. The individual crews remained tight, but it was good to have crosscurrents among the various ships, to get loose, and to create a sense of overall unity. The odd thing about an Army Aviation unit was that it was a consensus gaggle of four-man units; the platoon leader and platoon sergeant were almost superfluous, other than during those moments when they were in direct leadership situations. The enlisted men followed their ACs, not their E-6 sergeant. For instance, as we've seen, for Outlaw 27, 1st Lt. Harvey Persyn was aircraft commander, with Benny Blalock as the crew chief and Ralph Cella as the door gunner. These guys were tight with each other, not with their commanding officer or platoon sergeant. There were times when this senior EM was even in the way; he became disregarded by almost all others and became rather battered egotistically as an NCO. He had a rough time trying to direct the enlisted men under his jurisdiction, quite unlike the situation of all other sergeants in the Army. During these beer-and-steak parties, we always tried to console poor Sergeant Newton with his hopeless task of being between the ACs and the men. But he wasn't prepared to be an NCO, either; he had been a TI before taking over the platoon sergeant role. Capt. Dale Sherrod helped him out here, because with all the crews up flying, there was no one to take care of administrative tasks on the ground.

Captain Sherrod, on his second tour with the Outlaws, and was taking things easy this time around. Dale Sherrod had come over with the original Outlaws in 1964, when its deployment name had briefly been the 62nd Aviation Company (AML). It was activated as that unit until it had been redesignated Company A/502nd Aviation Battalion by December 1964. (All these unit changes were for deployment efforts only, transferring assets and equipment.) With a "second-timer's attitude," he remained down on the compound for considerable stretches of time, but overall, this benefited the platoon in the long run. Many matters long neglected were improved with this posture of his; I don't know what they all were since we were all up in the air doing our job, but things had been neglected. Most of us did not fully comprehend what it took for the higher-ranking officers to run the airfield. Somehow, it all was taken care of while we were fully expending our energy on the daily missions. Sergeant Newton had been over his head trying to do everything in the platoon on the compound's surface up to that time, with no help from us officers. Sometimes we had our additional duties, such as mine with defense counsel, but mostly we had nothing to do with running other affairs of the company. We were just up flying or taking it easy on our down days. When the sergeant complained he needed help, we didn't even know how to respond, much less care.

Dale Sherrod had been a halfback at the University of Oklahoma in its glory days, and he looked the part. He was very handsome and very tanned. He also had some very interesting connections with General Seneff, whose wife was living in Bangkok. We believed it was a family relationship of some sort, but Capt. Sherrod's wife was also living in Bangkok and was close to the general's wife. The captain would fly to Thailand with the general, as his guest, every other weekend. This was pretty impressive to pull off, in our view; he never completely told us how it had been done. We suspected he was being groomed to be Seneff's aide. I left him alone and he did the same with me; we had some mutual respect for each other. He thought I was crazy to live so dangerously, and I had no idea how he had achieved such a level of comfort in his military life. Some guys just have the touch. He felt I should have been killed five times over during my tour; he said he had no idea why I was still alive.

The captain could fly very well for the limited time he put into the air. I was only in the cockpit with him a few times, but he impressed me with his skill despite his low hours per month. He was knowledgeable during operations, not slacking off there; he was just intentionally taking it easy until he found another easier job. "See how you'd act if you were over here a second time!" he'd quote to me. I knew we knew each other, but could never be each other. Eventually, he moved north to some cushy desk job at Bien Hoa; I saw him briefly before I returned home on the big silver bird when it departed from there. He was always somewhat self-conscious about his chosen route but never fully embarrassed about it. He possessed the charisma to get away with it.

Sherrod was replaced by another captain, Stanley Arnold, who was also on his second tour but had a completely different attitude. He was anxious to work hard and to fly Lead as well as he could. He had a fretful high voice that some said sounded like he was always crying on the microphone. Coupled with a Nebraska accent, it did sound querulous, even whining, when he transmitted. Stan Arnold had been with the Knights the first tour, and had a good attitude, but he lacked the ability demonstrated by Sherrod to recall all he had learned initially. I helped him out a lot, but he resented it. Flying Lead with the platoon leader as an experienced first lieutenant created a precarious position; you had to tactfully tell your commander what his job was supposed to be, then back out of the way as soon as he could do it. There were times when you literally had to put words in their mouths, "Say yes, sir. Just say yes!" He had to completely trust you, but it put a burr under his saddle to need you that much. I never could figure out the perfect balance; I was just trying to be as helpful as I could and save the day for the guys flying on us.

The platoon parties removed a lot of this tension from the system and allowed us to be human without all our job assignments getting in the way. After playing guitars, telling jokes, confiding in one another, getting drunk, and so forth, usually these evenings ended with many people being thrown into the "Cobra Pond." Particular crews who were most popular tended to be chosen for this wetting down. This former rice paddy along the runway had been reconstructed into a morale-building swimming hole—complete with Vietnamese girls serving cold drinks, hot dogs, and hamburgers in booths right out of *Beach Blanket Bimbo*—but the numerous ear infections *and real cobras* swimming in the water quickly put an end to this idyllic oasis. Out went the California beach-bum lifestyle. The out-of-service, rotor-blade diving board remained installed there, and the surplus Navy eight-man life raft was still floating around, but the pool itself was used only for dunk parties following suitable levels of drunkenness. The Cobra Pond always did impress new arrivals as they disembarked from the big fixed-wing that had delivered them to this new posting called Vinh Long. At first glance, it looked like we were living in the lap of luxury, compared to the likes of the rest of Vietnam. Well, it could have been worse . . . .

The Outlaws had a valuable friend in an ordnance officer stationed at My Tho. His name was Major King, and he adored us helicopter crews. He immediately was christened "Sky King," of course, and he looked for us on every operation. He was especially impressed with our relationships with our crews and often joined us for aviator/crew parties at Vinh Long. I suppose he was a frustrated pilot. My men were polite to him, and he was always welcome. One lunchtime he showed us around the old seminary building that was the Seventh ARVN Division headquarters at My Tho, just down the river from us. He told me that he had inspected a rifle recently and found out the ARVN carrying it on operations had not known he hadn't had a firing pin in it for seven months. There's some action for you.

During one Outlaw party, "Sky King" got happily drunk and proceeded to walk into a huge stand-up fan at the officers' club. When he collided with it in the gloom, his Hawaiian shirt was sucked through the mesh protection of the fan, making a horrible "flap-flap-flap" noise before they rescued him. It was loud and scary. Fortunately, he wasn't hurt from trying that fan dance; he went right to the ground with it.

Another time, he caught me reading a book of Robert Frost's poetry while we were parked between lifts out on some operation. He stopped and said, "Now there's my picture of Dave Eastman. Out here in his helicopter in Vietnam, sitting by a machine gun, reading about Frost and New Hampshire!" He was always nice that way.

The club had some fine incidents from time to time, too. The Navy Seawolves found a female rock band performing somewhere and brought the group back to the Vinh Long compound. They were the "Pretty Kittens," featuring a redhead on the drums, a brunette on the lead guitar, and a big blonde momma on the bass. They had their pick of the men while on tour. Rocky Rowell had already had the buxom blonde lead singer in the sack that afternoon, rather noisily I'd heard, and the other girls were deciding whom they'd pleasure after their show. Somehow or other, someone got the word to me that the drummer, with long, copper-colored tresses, had taken a shine to Pat Tominey. If so, I was determined to run interference for our black-haired young warrant, with his teddy-bear eyes, as he found out this rumor was actually quite true. She had taken notice of his good looks and let it be known he was the chosen one. And she obviously was not interested in anyone else, although no one except us had been so informed. I was quite anxious to make sure my young pilot friend got laid that night; I wanted to be all the help I could!

Before the act went on, the pert redhead was ushered over to our presence, and the obviously shy Pat was introduced to the comely drummer. She knew that plans already had been worked out for this moment of contact, and she wanted desperately for Pat to be all she had projected on him. After a few exchanges of small talk smoothed out the initial awkwardness between the two, she seemed pretty assured she had made the right choice. I felt quite proud of Pat's performance, and the rest of the evening had promise of being productive. I stayed around their periphery to strategically fend off wishful suitors who had not gotten the message yet. And, they were there . . . .

The most annoying guy was a lifer warrant from the Knights whom I had known only in the showers. He had a very polished habit of smoking a cigarette all the while he was lathering up, then switching it around from one side of his mouth to the other while he twisted his head in the shower's rivulets. He was very proud of this habit, and he smoked continually while he talked *and* showered—at the same time. Never, *ever,* throughout all this did he soak the cigarette. In fact, I never even saw him get it slightly wet during the whole year that I watched this clown perform this feat in the officers' latrine! I think he took our gawking as true admiration; I only wanted him to screw up this trick, just once. This guy was all-Army—the kind you never want your sister to date and a personality you would never encounter outside the armed services. Somebody at recruiting offices ought to warn you that you *will* meet people like this in the Army. They thrive there.

The other repulsive characteristic of this warrant officer (ex-EM) was that he had the last "flattop bogie" I've ever seen on somebody's head. This was a straight-up crew cut combined with swept-back hair on both temples, winding up as a "duck tail" (or "DA") at the back of his head. Wow—this look went out with pink Cadillacs in the late 1950s. Here he was, standing alongside Tominey and the cute redhead, leering in her face, asking the fatal question, in a southern drawl, of course. "What's Tominey got that *I* haven't got? Just tell me. Will you tell me *that,* huh?" He was very jocular with this line, repeating it over and over, very self-impressed and putting on his already ugly face his best attempt at an Elvis Presley sneer. I felt like saying, "Let me count the ways . . . . I have a list right *here.*"

After a while, Mr. Obnoxious drifted away, and it looked like

Tominey could take it from there. I left the couple. She looked happy with her catch.

Then the band took the stage, wearing white T-shirts, dark miniskirts, and of course, white plastic go-go boots. We hadn't seen these boots before; that was California stuff going on back in the States at the moment. The big blonde had false eyelashes; her buxom form was well suited for belting out the soul hits popular in 1966, like "The Midnight Hour." She enjoyed her work and we enjoyed her hard-working style, big legs, and obvious musical skill. She was working up a sweat; the other girls looked fairly cool. The redhead banged out her drumbeat and did her rolls OK, the brunette guitarist performed adequately. We were having a good time and they knew it. The club was jammed, and the guys all sat at the tables in front of the band, drinks in hand. It was a good crowd, with all tables packed.

Suddenly the sound of an explosion racked the room. About three-fourths of the men present jumped up instantly and sprinted out the club door. Right over the band. *Right over* the "Pretty Kittens." In their panic, they trampled *the band*, without so much as a momentary consideration of their plight. I sat stock-still and held onto my drink. I wasn't about to share the girls' fate. I also had a funny feeling that this was likely the old trick of throwing a handful of rocks on the galvanized roofing of the Mekong Manor; it made a hell of a noise but sounded different from a mortar round. Others obviously were more duped by it than I.

The girls were spinning around, with instruments and amps knocked over by the stampeding, panicked men of Vinh Long. They were trying to ask, "What's going on?" but the combat-hardened aviators had no time to answer their questions as they stomped out. Nobody thought to suggest to these ladies that they ought to accompany these gentlemen out that door for their safety. No offer to escort here. It was just a wild pack of panic-stricken young men out to save their asses, and frig anybody left behind. I wasn't about to leave my place of safety until this was over. The girls were now really scared, but no one was helping them at all.

Once outside, the pilots who clustered out on the lawn realized the trick had been played once again; "rocks on the roof" was the explanation for the loud noise. With that, everybody relaxed and re-entered the club, filing past the band. They returned to their respective tables and calmly picked up their drinks. With some mirth, I watched all this unfold. Then, these guys had the nerve to ask the girls to pick up their instruments and resume playing! Their facial expressions and composure seemed to indicate that nothing had happened. But the girls were crying somewhat by now, and still questioning, "Did something happen? Is something going on?" The redhead was saying, "Should we know about something? Are we in danger?" The guys just said, "Naw, just 'rocks on the roof.' Go play," as if *that* was an adequate explanation for the loud sound and their ridiculous behavior. None of this was very reassuring to the girls.

There was some doubt now about whether the show was going to go on. After all, we had just scared the hell out of our performers! The guys patiently waited for the girls to collect themselves, and become composed enough to get back to playing. The tearful females still didn't know what had occurred. Somebody finally had the courtesy to inform the band members about the joke, and to tell them they were in no danger at all. Their level of panic was beginning subside. That's when I noticed that the brunette guitar player had a big, black shoeprint on the back of her T-shirt! Somebody had actually run right over her prostrate body in the excited rush to exit the club!

The band members did resume playing after wiping away their tears, apparently understanding they were in Vietnam after all, and that these things do commonly occur. And Pat Tominey happily spent his amorous night with the red-haired drummer. The next day we all treated him with more than considerable respect for being so chosen.

About the time Stanley Arnold arrived, we finally had the new runway finished. After the Air Force had successfully stolen the Caribous from the Army, they couldn't fly them without busting out the tires on this wonderful De Havilland fixed-wing cargo plane. These huge-tailed STOL (short takeoff and landing) aircraft, manufactured in Canada, were beloved by the remaining aviators still assigned to them, but the Air Force considered fixed-wing their baby, so they lifted the Caribous from the rolls of Army Aviation. The difference was obvious immediately: they couldn't land the things in the same places that the Army had been doing so for years. They demanded we resurface our runway with the standard steel planking; it was not perforated this time, as it had been in World War II. While we awaited completion of this job, the Air Force refused to land at Vinh Long. The helicopters had to be used to fly in all the stuff the fixed-wing had been bringing in; we would learn well what all of that entailed.

We had to make an extra trip at the end of the day to Binh Thuy, the airbase down on the Bassac River just west of Can Tho. The cargo always seemed to be mailbags, and a lot of them, so it was motivational to lug these back home. Seeing them in the backseat always reminded me of the time when I had brought Dickie Black back from Saigon, following his and Terry McDowell's R&R in Japan. He had asked for a ride home from Hotel 3. Dickie was still very drunk, passed out on the mailbags I was ferrying south. We were up against the base of the monsoon clouds, being vectored by Paris Radar, when he was awakened by the buffeting gusts of the thunderstorms just above our rotor disc's altitude. I turned around to see Dickie crawling in terror on his hands and knees across the numerous mailbags. He went up to the sliding door of the Huey and wiped off the condensation on the window to look out. Seeing nothing but black storm clouds gave him no comfort. He peered at me, then back out again. I hollered back as if talking to a frightened dog in a thunderstorm: "Dickie, it's all right. Dickie, it's all right! We're on radar!" After nodding up and down in that Huckleberry Hound manner of his, he rolled over on the cushiony mailbags and went soundly back to sleep.

About this time, Harvey Persyn rotated home, as his DROS ("date return over seas"; we pronounced it DEROS) was up, but we would see him again at Fort Wolters as fellow instructors. We got him good, though, with a practical joke for his last mission in-country. Dickie Hyde was still in Operations with Major O'Kane, and they thought up a bogus single-ship mission to "the tip of the Delta" for Harvey. No copilot, no crew chief or gunner; just Harve. It was written up as an official mission and handed down to the platoon with all the others, looking just as legitimate as the rest. He swallowed it hook, line, and sinker.

I watched him standing in front of the operations board, holding onto the suicidal mission assignment to the Nam Can outpost, which existed all by itself down by the U-Minh Forest, and was a very dangerous place to go. Sometimes a two-ship mission was called for in that area, just to provide some semblance of security.

"My God, they're trying to kill me!" said Harvey.

"Whatcha got there, Harve? Let's see what kind of mission you've pulled," said I.

"They're trying to get me on the last flying day I've got in-country! The Army is trying to kill me!" Harvey said with another gasp.

"Well, you know how they treat people," I said. "They'll try to get everything they can out of a man right up to his last minute, even if it means his death."

Harvey wasn't buying any of this. He looked stunned. "I've got to get this changed. I've got to see somebody; this is too dangerous for *anybody!*" He was sounding desperate, ready to bolt out the door for the club.

"Look at it this way, Harve, maybe you'll get a medal."

"Oh, yeah! What good will that do me? I'll be *dead!*"

"Hey," I replied back, "I hear that's the best way to get them, posthumously!"

"Oh, my God! I thought you were my friend! Now I've got to take care of this myself. I've got to see somebody!" With that, he sprinted out the door and went over to petition the majors to get out of the mission. Everyone was in on the deal, so they looked at him blankly, treating him with stonefaced indifference, as they played cards in the officers' club.

"Nope, I can't help you, Harve," Major O'Kane remarked over

his usual good hand of poker. "Those missions are cast in concrete once Battalion cuts them. We just pass them on through. Apparently when they asked for you specifically, they didn't know it was your last flying day in-country."

Harvey tore out of the club, continuing to search for relief. From a distance, we could see him running about, carrying the single piece of paper and approaching everyone who potentially could be helpful. It was a long time before he found out he had been made the butt of a very good joke. In the end, I think he was probably more relieved not to have to fly the mission than worried about having been made the clown. We all had our fun while it lasted. I thought it ingenious for Dickie Hyde to have thought it up.

During his final 10 to 15 days before flying out, Harvey worked harder than anyone at having down days. He'd go out and sit on his helmet on the runway for several hours before coming back through Operations and sighing, "Boy, it was a great day to be flying . . . . Really fine air up there!" The stunned EM in Operations would look at him aghast—mainly because they were above average in intelligence and already knew what aircraft were flying that day and which pilots were assigned to them. Anxiety-wise, Harvey handled his remaining time in-country very badly. He spent more time attempting to look like he was flying than if he had actually gotten up in the sky while awaiting his plane ride home. One day, he was looking particularly pensive, so I asked him why he was so morose.

"They're trying to make me fly, Dave. They want me to fly . . . . Will you fly for me? Will you do that?" he begged me.

"I *already am flying for you*, Harve!"

"Will you fly some more, then?"

Finally he got through all this and rotated Stateside.

Harvey's departure meant that Benny Blalock no longer had a protector; Captain Arnold was dismayed at his exploits on the flight line and out on the airstrips during lifts. I told the good-natured captain that I could inform him a bit about Benny Blalock if he was interested. In one recent episode, Blalock had nearly gotten into a serious fight with a Vietnamese Ranger. The guy meant business, and so did most of his platoon. Only Harvey, fingering his first lieutenant's bar, had saved Blalock from serious injury. It was touch-and-go for many a precarious minute before Harvey convinced the Rangers to leave Benny alone. Harve kept his crew chief behind the closed doors of the Huey while he did the negotiating. Blalock probably had punched one of the Rangers while the aircraft was in flight, and they were going to duke it out with him once on the ground, maybe even shoot him. The Rangers could be a serious bunch, a different breed from the other ARVN soldiers. The outcome of any confrontation depended upon which unit you messed with.

When Harvey went home, Blalock decided he was ready for the hangar, and he started asking to be reassigned there. He was most interested in downtown time. His requests went unheard in the unit, so he wrote his mother. He complained that they would not let him off the flight line after all the many months he had put in there. He also added that there would be less exposure to combat if he could get in with the hangar crew.

Then Blalock decided to embellish his story a bit. He wrote his dear old mom that he also was tired of having mortar rounds land and explode *on both sides of his bunk* every morning, and *then* having to step over the bodies of the "crispy critters" littering the runway on the way to the ship. He added that putting up with this daily carnage made life tedious. He needed some relief, and that's why he needed to go to the hangar. At least he could write about this to dear old Mum; over here, they weren't listening to him.

Blalock's mother got shook; she went into orbit. She *wrote* the President of the United States, enclosing Benny's epistle of plight to him. LBJ handed it over to the Pentagon, to General Harold K. Johnson, the Army Chief of Staff himself. The response came down all the way through channels, demanding a reply from the 175th. O'Kane, now the Executive Officer, had the enjoyable assignment of responding to all the points raised by Benny. Inherent in the directive was to relieve Benny at once from the flight line and put him in the hangar. The message also stated that no disciplinary action would be imposed on the young crew chief, and that all issues raised in the letter would be addressed and sent back up the line for review. Major O'Kane was ordered to address Blalock personally and deal with every point that had been mentioned. Which O'Kane did.

The thing was, Blalock never knew that his mother had done all this for him. He never even considered that she might be so affected by his exaggerations that she would do something this extreme. He was totally in the dark about what he had set in motion. O'Kane had Benny stand at attention in the Outlaw company headquarters while he complied with the presidential request. He watched with considerable glee as Blalock's face registered all the points addressed in the company's response letter. He did not know *how* the major could have even known about these complaints to his mother! O'Kane told me how entertaining it was as he read on and on: "It was worth it, Dave, it was worth it. You should have been there to watch his face. Benny Blalock had *no* idea how I could have gotten hold of the contents of his mother's letter—none whatsoever."

Stets hand-carried the response letter in Outlaw 11 back to Can Tho for forwarding up through channels. O'Kane entrusted him with the dispatch; there was nothing else aboard the Huey on that important short flight.

31

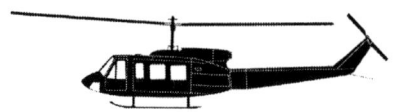

TOMMY MCCARTHY AND I HAVE A MISSION

BEFORE DALE SHERROD LEFT, there were some spooky goings-on. Each night, some AC in the platoon was assigned a top-secret mission that did not go off. We were aware of this and didn't look into it any further. Not only did we not care beyond the periphery of the shit we flew every day, we also weren't willing to add to anyone else's complications. If they had to keep secret about what they were doing day after day, who were we to add to their problems? The only thing particularly intriguing about whatever was going on was that it went on. And on. Beyond a night or two. This in itself made it different, because typically whatever we did usually lost its importance within a day or so. This wasn't like that, so it *did* make us a *bit* curious.

Then one day, Captain Sherrod said I was to be the AC of that night's super-secret mission, and Warrant Officer Thomas McCarthy was to be my copilot. Now, Mr. Mac was a very serious person for 19 years old, and he was already an AC, so this aroused my suspicions. *What* are we doing? was my first question. If they were putting another AC with me, especially Mr. Mac, we had to be undergoing some very serious business by another onlooking party; I wanted to know who that could be. What this was all about then became a very secondary matter. I needed some information. Captain Sherrod said it would be forthcoming, but everything was so top-secret that he couldn't tell me much except "Just show up at Can Tho at such-and-such a time and they will brief you." Oh, goody, this is cool, I thought. Right.

I got in the aircraft and looked around. They had picked the best of the EM, too. I asked Mac if he knew anything more than I did. Nope, he didn't. He had flown with me in the position of AC, so that didn't bother either of us; we had been here before. We could trust each other. We strapped in and cranked up.

But we didn't go directly to Can Tho; we arrived instead at Binh Thuy. There, for the first time, I saw Navy SEALS, a new type of special operations team. They were right out of the comic books—especially those we had been reading recently for references. "Sergeant Rock" was our best guide in this regard. The SEALS had all kinds of camouflage paint on their faces, and more gear hanging off their webbed belts and suspenders than I ever could have imagined. Grenades and knives were evident everywhere. Images of pirates from the childhood classics came to mind. The guys looked stoked and very nervous. I was wondering who was in charge of these hyperventilating dudes; despite my 10 months in-country at this point, I would not have wanted to be their commanding officer. They walked by like zombies intent on their kill-crazy mission, whatever it was. I told my crew to stay by the helicopter as I waited for the briefing that would occur.

There were two Soc Trang ships that I overheard had been practicing with these guys for the previous two weeks. They would fly the SEALS in; I was the backup ship in case somebody blew it. These two Hueys had been flying formation in the dark with just a red-lens flashlight held "on" in the door gunner's armpit to fly on; everything else was blacked out. If they got shot down, I was to drop down immediately and pick up somebody. I got that part. But I still was wondering about the rest of this sideshow we'd been observing.

My answers came quickly from an intelligence captain from Saigon, who did me the favor of appearing at my ship and briefing my crew and me. He was emphatic that we not talk *at all* to the downed American we were about to rescue. "Is he a pilot?" I asked. "No, Lieutenant Eastman, he is a Special Forces lieutenant who has been running around in the jungle on a leash for three to four years. God knows what he has been through or what condition he is in right now. You and your men are *not* to talk to him! Is that perfectly clear?" I wanted to say, "Yeah, sure, asshole, it is perfectly clear. We sort of do stuff like this all the time. What do you do with *your* day?" But I didn't. The crew and I got it this guy was about as uptight as anybody could be; we didn't need to add to his tension.

When he left, one of the kids asked me, "Can you believe that shit? What are we up to, Lieutenant?" I responded that I still didn't know, but I would go over to the briefing and check out what they were doing with each other. I knew that I had my crew's trust, and also that I was the only one expected to be present over there.

What I witnessed was straight out of Fort Benning training, which I thought I had left behind a long time ago. My mind was saying, This couldn't be happening in Vietnam, not at this late date. The SEALS were gathered around and discussing what they would do on the radio for communications. I hadn't seen this foolishness since Ranger school. "One click means NO, two clicks means YES. Three clicks means I don't think so or Don't know yet. Four clicks means . . . ." (You fill in the blanks.) By the time they had gotten up to discussing the meaning of 10 clicks on the PRC-10 mike switch, they all had forgotten what they had thought up before then; this was funny. Then they'd start again. After a while, it degenerated into, "Don't anybody talk! No more talk! Everybody just remember what was said. Just let's go!" Wow, this was where we had been as green second lieutenants; I wanted no more. I was just glad to be the backup ship and nothing else.

The operation was planned for the "Y." Apparently some Vietnamese prisoner had escaped that day and reported the presence of an American in the stick that he was part of. It was determined that this had to be 1st Lt. James Nick Rowe, who had been captured much farther south a few years back. These SEALS had figured out which hooch he was sleeping in, how many VC were guarding him, which ones they would garrote, which ones they would stab with knives, and so on. All of this was so preplanned that it could only go on as planned so long as *not one* of the VC moved. If they were all in the same places where they'd been standing around midday, this scheme could not fail. If, on the other hand, they had moved a few paces or just changed places, this grandly orchestrated attack had more than a few flaws. I had never been part of a charade like this, but it bore watching.

We took off and headed for the rendezvous point. The two Soc Trang birds and I had an understanding, and they went in with confidence that I'd be hanging out waiting for their safe return from this secret mission. "Thank God for Army Aviation," I thought. At least we made sense.

The Soc Trang ships landed and discharged their secret killers, also making their departure OK. Then we were released to stand by at Vinh Long, ready to go at the first sign this mission might be failing or that this Seal team was going to be annihilated. Fine. I needed some sleep.

As we rounded base and turned short final, I zoomed westerly down the Vinh Long runway to where I would park the thing and await further orders. Since it was a hot approach, to be tapered off farther down the strip, I held onto my airspeed. As I did so, I was surprised to see the fire truck race past me, going even faster than my craft. There were also quite a few vehicles assisting the fire truck as it sped down the runway, alongside me. As an aviator, you take note of such things, but you don't always know until later what they mean. They just register on your consciousness.

So, when I swung the thing around, and Tommy McCarthy and I were shutting down the bird, I was surprised to see my left door opened rapidly to a crowd that seemed to rival Lindbergh's landing in Paris. There was the whole officers' club, including many of the Seawolves, and a lot of stars. One stars, two stars, and a whole lot of bird colonels were gaping at me as I rolled off throttle. Obviously, they thought something had happened to me and that I had something to report. I didn't. Up to this point, I thought I was on a top-secret mission, with everything on a "need-to-know" basis; this apparently was not true, based on the garden club membership in front of me.

"What happened, huh? What happened out there?"

"Are you all right? Where are you shot? You must be shot, otherwise why did the fire truck accompany your approach down the runway?"

"Did they get him? Did they pick him up? What's the story on the rescue? Did you see him? Did you pick him up? What did you do?"

Some of these guys were in civvies and holding gin-and-tonics. The brass was more than I had ever seen gathered at any given time in the Delta, and I was beginning to become impressed with whatever this secret mission actually was. Somebody needed us. After I calmed all present with the information that nothing was going on *yet*, I was able to convince them to go away. We got some darkness and peace and quiet around us so we could sleep before something really happened.

Then there's the story behind the fire truck. It seems that a whole battalion of ARVN in reserve was asleep alongside the newly planked steel runway. Some of the soldiers had been sleeping on the warm metal surface for its retained heat when Duke Cone ran over three of them with his alert truck. He was serving as Officer of the Day, and in moving about rapidly, he had crunched three of the men. Not having an ambulance, he had thought of using the fire trucks as such, which is why these were going by me when I was on short final. Everyone had surmised that I was shot up and in need of assistance, perhaps even that I was about to burst into flames. The trucks had speeded up past my setting down, so all the Navy and Army brass interested in me had not gotten the full story. As I remember, Duke unfortunately was unable to save any of the ARVN he drove over.

In the warm night, we slept fitfully. Just as we settled into some restful slumber, Jeep lights came slowly down the runway, so I woke my crew to get ready. The blade was untied and we were standing by when the Jeep pulled alongside. In the vehicle was another Navy lieutenant in his Bermuda shorts, drink in hand. I stood there expectantly, and out came, "Have you guys heard anything yet? Have you heard how it's going out there?" It did not seem to bother him that he was bothering us. When this bogus alert failed us, we tied down the blade after his leaving, and tried to catch some sleep again.

Several times, lieutenants from the Seawolves bothered us with their curious inquiries, which were not official and could have been answered elsewhere. It made for a long time till dawn, which was when we finally got orders to crank and go out there and help out. We didn't know what to expect, but we surmised they had not found Lieutenant Rowe. In fact, he would be a prisoner for a full five years, having been captured on 29 October 1963 and not rescued until 31 December 1968. Many of us would be home a long time by then.

In the meantime, however, the inserted SEALS had become fairly lost and were quite a distance from where they had been left off. They were still playing their games, however, throwing smoke and showing their position to Major Gebhardt, Lancer Lead. What cute playmates, I thought. The SEALS would sneakily transmit which color smoke they would throw, and then the gunships would react. Except they couldn't keep it straight which color signified *them* and which color showed the *enemy* positions. This went on for nearly a full load of fuel. There was a lot of whispering over those radios.

We responded by firing my tommy gun, with which I didn't have much experience shooting. It sort of floated in my hands as I held it out the window and expended a lot of .45-caliber ammo. I thought I was doing my part at keeping the enemy pinned down, even if he wasn't there very much. Nobody could get hurt that way, and the SEALS and the Lancers could keep throwing smoke grenades until they figured out who was who. It was all good practice. Lord knows these guys needed the training. I just needed sleep.

Finally, we were released, and I headed for the club to get some breakfast. I wasn't feeling very heroic, nor could I summon up much respect for the SEALS. Many of the other guys had wanted a part of this action and were anxious to hear about it, but I had to inform them sadly that there really had not been any. These hangers-on kept being in my face while I tried to eat breakfast so I could escape to my hooch and get some shut-eye. I was in a bad mood and quite disappointing company.

Later we heard that when the SEALS reached the onetime prison, not only had the VC guards they were going to kill moved a few steps—they had moved everything else from this temporary camp. There was a casualty, however, when one of the SEALS threw a thermite grenade during the smoke-throwing episode for extraction. He received severe burns and lost his sight.

When Lieutenant Rowe did successfully escape, he was promoted to major almost immediately. Those of us who knew about his ordeal were very glad to hear about that. In *Five Years to Freedom*, Nick Rowe described his nightmare of being captured and held in the Delta for those five years. According to his story, the day of his escape came when he was being transferred with a detail of about six guards. Some of these guards did not trust their leader and were becoming increasingly nervous as the Air Cav was searching their area. This unit was in the Delta well after my time there. Nick managed to convince his guard that they ought to take a path through the reeds that separated them from the group, making them less noticeable. Since Rowe wasn't walking fast enough in the VC guard's estimation, the guard started breaking trail, ordering Nick to follow behind with the guard's camp radio. Other VC in the area were firing at the LOHs (light observation helicopters, the OH-6s or "Loaches"), and these scout helicopters were returning fire. Yet, whenever his guard wasn't looking, Nick Rowe waved and attempted to attract the attention of these helicopters.

The guard had a burp gun, and incredibly, while moving through the dense vegetation, Rowe managed to extract the clip from the weapon. It took the VC a while to discover that this had been done to him, but by that time he was close to exhaustion, dodging the observation helicopters buzzing just above them. The prisoner was able to keep the tired guard moving while the helicopters kept making wider circles around the pair. As they passed a tree, Nick grabbed a two-inch-wide limb and hit the Vietnamese at the base of his skull. After he had struck him two more times, he knew the VC could not continue. Rowe retrieved a mosquito net and the radio.

His next smart move was pushing the burp gun into the mud. He did not want to appear like an armed VC—he was wearing the typical black apparel the Viet Cong wore. Next he enlarged a small clearing in the reedy grass while waving the white mosquito net. He was still quite concerned, however, that the other VC in the area would discover him and recapture him. One of the Cobras passing by overhead spotted him and banked sharply about in a circle. Rowe was almost killed by the American forces at this point. A Major Thompson in the C&C ship instead elected to capture him for interrogation, and he directed the other helicopters to cover him as he went in for the pickup.

One of the door gunners noticed that this man had a fair complexion and a beard, and he yelled that the person was an American! They landed about 15 meters away from Rowe, who ran toward the ship and flung himself on the cool metal floor of the Huey. He yelled, "Go, GO!" and then listened to the first spoken English words he had heard in five years; the pilot asked him his name. He spelled out, "R.O.W.E." The same pilot then asked, "Are you Nick Rowe?" Upon replying, "Yes," the aviator took off his flight helmet and showed him how to talk with someone in their operation who was Rowe's classmate from West Point. The gunner and the crew chief also opened C-rations for him so he could eat some real food for a change. A very relieved Lieutenant Rowe said later that having the American voices within earshot all around him was like hearing music. He had been in the U-Minh Forest for quite a while. His rescue gave the 7/1st Cav a very memorable New Year's Eve in 1968.

While the recovery of James N. Rowe made the news Stateside, where I heard about it, the story didn't end there. Unhappily, Col. Nick Rowe was killed on 21 April 1989 while serving with the Joint U.S. Military Advisory Group, providing anti-insurgency training for the Philippine military. I believe there was something about some grenade training going wrong—very wrong.

32

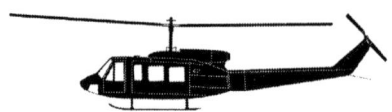

THE COLONEL HAS CHIEU HOIS

JUST BEFORE HARVEY PERSYN LEFT FOR THE STATES, we had an interesting afternoon being detailed down to Rach Gia, on the southwest coast. We had been in the Seven Mountains area with both of our ships when we got the word to fly down to some coordinates well away from where we had been working. This was described as a high-priority mission from the senior advisor for the whole province; we were to stop what we were doing and fly down there ASAP. Outlaw 27 joined up on me in a "45" on my left, as I asked him if he knew what this was about. He replied that he did not, so we let the copilots fly as we did our paperwork for the day's mission, as ACs had to do. Legs such as this were always good practice for the new pilots breaking in with the unit.

Our heading was almost due south to arrive at the coordinates given to us; we were to land to the northwest of Rach Gia. We were getting more curious because this whole area was always dangerous, and it did not make much sense to go somewhere in the middle of nowhere without protection. As we arrived overhead, we saw a cluster of Vietnamese and one heavyset American officer below us in the dark green grass, near a treeline. I was still nervous about the lack of security, but on short final, it appeared this colonel was comfortable with the people to whom he was talking on the ground. We landed the two Hueys, and I was the first to approach the large, stocky bird colonel in his baggy fatigues, armed only with a sidearm. I walked up to him gingerly, still trying to read the situation.

"Is this all I get?" bellowed the white-haired colonel as he turned toward me. He had no other troops with him. He was alone.

"What is that, sir?" I asked. "We were detailed to come down here and see what you wanted." I wasn't exactly nobody.

"Where the hell is *Time* magazine? I want *Look* or *Life* to be here! We're winning the war! Where the *hell* is the press?" This colonel was looking to go Hollywood and I still was not getting what he was driving at.

"Sir, can you explain what this is all about? We were told this is a very important mission; perhaps you can inform me what is going on?" I was bewildered.

"These guys here are the hardest of the hard core. They have just given up! We're winning the war! This is the beginning of our victory! Where the hell is the press?" The colonel was completely serious; he believed himself.

I turned my attention to the Vietnamese men behind him as he described, one by one, what these VC had been doing in the province over the previous year. It was like looking at Geronimo's band or Pancho Villa's bandits. These were swarthy men, real down-and-dirty bad guys.

"*You're* the one who blew up the bridge last June, aren't you?" said the colonel with considerable regard. The VC he was addressing nodded his head sagely. I also noted that he and some of the others were eyeing the M-60 machine guns on our ships with more than mild interest. While all this was going on, they were starting to take their time to become better informed about our armament. I didn't like this at all.

"This guy here is a doctor in civilian life, but up to now he has been one of the top cadre of the local VC unit. This is the toughest bunch in the area; if they're turning themselves in, we're on our way to finally winning this war." The colonel then pointed out a few more celebrity-status VC; I kept wondering how he knew their identities and exploits so well. My mind was racing; these VC were just too curious about scoping out those D-models. I didn't get the feeling the war was over for these guys at all. And *what* were we doing here, anyway? We had seen the colonel's show; now what?

"Sir, why have you called us down here other than to inform us who these individual VC cadre are? Do you want us to do something for you?" I asked.

"Do something for me? Well, let me tell you," he said smugly. "We're taking these guys in under the Chieu Hoi program. Now that they've surrendered, we will feed them and restore them to good health while they undergo an education program to understand what our two governments are doing for them. This is just amazing that a hard-core unit of this caliber wants to participate in our 'open arms' program. This is the greatest success we have had so far; I can't wait to broadcast this to the press."

Now I was getting even more worried. Our two Hueys would be transporting the worst of the worst, without guards, back to the Chieu Hoi ("open arms") reeducation camp at Rach Gia. What if they changed their minds and rioted in the back of the aircraft? They could grab some firearms, grip us in a choke hold, pull a knife, or do something else I hadn't yet thought of to worry about. I moved away from the colonel as the VC company moved adroitly around the Huey for an up-close inspection of something they had only observed from afar. They looked like they had been living a hard life in the jungle. Tough guys. I certainly didn't envy their condition.

I summoned Rhodes, the door gunner, over to me. This was the other EM with the same name as the one who had flown with Dempsey; this man was the bespectacled crew member I had taught to fly when I delivered Harvey to Saigon many months earlier. I told him to be cool and act like we were not having a very important conversation. He caught on. I said to him in a whisper, "Go up to my seat and remove that .45 from its holster when no one is looking. Hide it in your blouse. Conceal it against your stomach and hold it there with your arm. Make sure it doesn't look you have a weapon on you at all." He nodded, smoothly made his way over to the front of the Huey, and passed around in front of the nose cowling. I knew he was going to pull this off well, so I turned my attention away from him. I went over to Harvey.

"What do you think of this shit? Can we do it? Do you think they'll be safe on board the aircraft?"

"I don't know," Harvey grinned. "This is crazy. These people are just going in for a few months of R&R. When they heal up, they'll be right back out here again. That goofy colonel sure thinks this is for real, doesn't he?" Harve thought this was downright funny. He was outwardly laughing in his style.

I was watching him, feeling no humor whatsoever, and I saw that he knew this whole thing was a sham. "What do we do if they pull something funny on us on the trip in? I don't trust these guys," I said.

"Oh, I think they'll be OK that far. If they don't, there's not much we can do to save ourselves. Those guys look like they know how to kill people really good!"

"Oh, thanks, Harve. That's great news, just what I wanted to hear."

I returned to the colonel and told him we were ready. He was preparing to get back in his Jeep and drive back by himself. Maybe this guy was genuinely screwy. He acted as though he had not learned much about Vietnam yet, even though he probably was nearing the end of his tour. I had never seen anyone out here in the countryside without so much as another serviceman along as an escort.

The VC "defectors" marched over to the Huey, ready for their trip. I wondered whether this in fact would be their first helicopter ride. We could often tell when we had real VC when we took off with a suspect, because in the earlier days of the war, the Saigon government's troops had used the flying machine as an instrument of torture. They would take up three prisoners and start questioning them. When the interrogation didn't produce results, they threw out the first suspect. When the next didn't talk either, they threw him out. The third man always talked. The VC living out in the bush did not know we Americans were no longer putting up with that stuff, so any of them picked up nowadays gave themselves away as real VC because they were terrified at being lifted off the ground. Even the captured women and kids of VC families feared it could happen to them. They would be hysterical in the backseat. That's how you knew you had the real ones.

These guys looked like this was a first-time experience; but they also didn't seem too concerned about it. They just kept striking me as extremely observant. I made eye contact with Rhodes, who let me know in an indirect way that he had the pistol. I had also informed him that if he had to shoot some of them, to remember the control systems under the cabin floor. If a bullet severed the push-pull tubes going to the controls up on the rotor system, that would not be very helpful. I had asked him to put the armor-plated seats we were in on the other side of whatever body he might have to shoot. I wanted to live through this. Obviously, he had to follow my line of thought, as he had. These episodes sure built trust.

I let my copilot fly while I smiled a lot at the company in the backseat. I made it look like I was genuinely concerned about how they were enjoying the trip. They smiled back and mostly looked out at the green countryside far below. This was going to be over soon; I was looking forward to that moment of relief.

When we landed at the old strip at Rach Gia, they ambled toward the tents set up for such defectors. Indoctrination would begin right away. We were released and took off with a sigh, releasing tension. The standard treatment for these Viet Cong "defectors" was to give them two new sets of clothes worth 1,000 piastres, a 30 piastre daily allowance for food, and a welcome package containing soap, chewing gum, and other goodies. They would also be handed 200 piastres of pocket money at the end of their time here. Looking back considerably later, I calculated that the few months of rest and reeducation these men would experience was just about the same as the time between then and the Tet Offensive of 1968. Who would have thunk it? At least they knew what they were doing. It felt like we were always playing the fool.

33

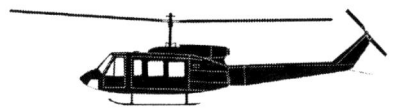

SPECIAL FORCES OPERATIONS

THE SPECIAL FORCES OPERATED up near the Cambodian border, in dangerous areas such as the Plain of Reeds and the Seven Mountains, also called the "Seven Sisters." Despite their macho reputation back in the good ol' USA, the Green Berets were largely educators and medicinal in their touch. They typically were more intelligent than other career Army types we encountered, and in my experience, they were gentle, deep-thinking men. I enjoyed working with these strong men and felt like I made a contribution to them when assigned to do some flying for these guys. They never struck me as blustering or posturing, but I wondered what life in these A-team camps was really like. A lot of mud and loneliness, I suspected, for the 10-man team stuck out here in the middle of nowhere. I often wondered how they could even defend themselves if the VC hovering around the border wanted to attack.

They had a lot of neat stuff to trade, all very clandestine. It gave us thrills to get some of the weaponry they came across, and they knew their enemy gear could get them some fine things back in the rear areas that they could not get through channels. Primitive crossbows, for instance, were very potent trade material. The helicopter pilots and the Green Berets were close friends when it came to this swapping. They were good for burp guns and various camouflaged fatigue uniforms; we were super at delivering mustard and ketchup, and items purchased at retail stores in Vietnamese towns. They could be desperate for just everyday condiments; it was evident on their faces when you made a deal. They *needed* you to come back as promised. It was striking what their lives were about, way out here in the boonies.

Some of the Green Berets, however, were strange men indeed. The most extreme example I ever encountered over there was Maj. George Miracek. He roamed about this area at will and headed up a hand-picked band of nearly 300 men. They were all hired by him and paid well, and they looked to be cutthroats to the last man. He was very effective and loved his job. His wife had divorced him when he would not come home after three years. He moved about at night, sometimes in airboats, as if all this was just a fun-house ride. Nobody else I knew of could cover as much terrain as he did, and as fearlessly. He would show up anywhere and could surprise you with his presence anytime. This Iron Curtain escapee was a fire-in-the-heart patriot. He hated communism and was stoked to fight it here as well as anyplace else. It was his thing. He was the *only* person I ever allowed to walk around while aboard my helicopter; I was always too fearful he or one of his cohorts would knife one of my crewmen for even attempting to get him to sit down.

A few months before I arrived in Vietnam, the Outlaws had participated in a "turkey shoot" during the wettest season the Plain of Reeds had experienced in 20 years. At night, the VC would move across the flat wetlands in their sampans; as the day dawned, they would camouflage their shallow watercraft with cut reeds. With some skill, air crews could discern the path the sampan had made through the marsh grasses, then spot the cut reeds wilting in the Delta's hot sun. Often, the sampan would even be outlined. A few rounds fired around the boat sometimes was all it took for the VC to stand up and surrender. (If they attempted to put up a fight, the aircraft would fire a few volleys into the sampan, and it would soon sink.) The fight would soon be over, especially if a few concussion grenades were dropped on top of the small-arms fire raking the craft. The VC would quickly have had enough. This operation was very successful as long as it lasted.

Many prisoners were taken, on a record level. Eventually the VC wised up and ended this form of vulnerable transportation during this historic wet season.

Hueys with Special Forces people on board would approach floating sampans and check out their gear to see what they were carrying. The VC would stand up as the aircraft hovered close to the sampans. They would soon be loaded on board, and tied up. Then they would be taken back to province headquarters for interrogation. If a situation looked dangerous, sometimes the door gunners had to unload right into the occupants at the side of the ship. The Special Forces guys had the VC right under their noses, but it was frighteningly uncomfortable for the pilots to be hovering there alongside in the water, wondering how this was all going to go. In one incident, Spec. 4 Dougherty had to grease three VC all at once. They turned abruptly dangerous and he fired the M-60 right there on his side of the ship and cut them all in half. He immediately threw up from his crew compartment seat in the Huey. He was a great young kid with a natural sense of humor, and we hated his being affected like that.

Major Miracek that day was enjoying climbing into the sampans and checking out the travelers. He would question them, and if the answers were the wrong ones, he stabbed them in the abdomen. When asked how he felt about killing that way, he replied, "I like to see their eyes turn yellow when they die; that's why I do it." Yikes. He really impressed a lot of people in the Outlaws that day.

One time, late in my tour, I was flying in the Seven Mountains area when I overheard Miracek in contact with the enemy. He was near some mountaintop in that chain of peaks, and a Caribou was trying to resupply him. The long-winged aircraft was having a difficult time of it, because the pilots had to run down a narrow valley toward his position, flying below the summits of the adjacent Seven Sisters. The pilots were getting shot at and complaining rather loudly about it. George Miracek would come on the air from below and pooh-pooh this ground fire, insisting that he had it even worse and that it wasn't bothering him any! You could hear him cackling over the fire of his troops defending his position, and the enemy's too. "Come on down and have a drink with crazy George!" he would broadcast. "Come on down and drink some vodka with me. Drink with the crazy Russian sometime!"

This was showtime, and incredibly brazen. It was also very memorable. The poor Caribou pilots kept trying to complete the run as George goaded them along. I have heard that he has been used as a stereotype for some movies made about that period in Vietnam. He always was OK with me, but I kept my safe distance from him. He struck me as a completely devoted and dedicated mercenary, thoroughly bloodthirsty. One of the Knight pilots saw him open up a VC suspect from navel to sternum with a Bowie knife when the man gave the wrong answers in an interrogation.

Jack Mankin of the Mavericks told me a story about assisting Miracek in a time of need, when he was returning from a long-range patrol in Cambodia. He was in contact with the enemy and they were running him down. He was hurting, and outmanned. The Mavericks were assembled to go up and assist him in his return to the Vietnam side of the border. Jack was fire team Lead and called Miracek, asking him to throw smoke to mark his position for the gunships. The desperate major said he was throwing red smoke to indicate where he and his beleaguered troops were. Jack reminded him that Miracek was to throw smoke, and he, Maverick 1, would call out its color. The experienced gun pilot thought it odd that this combat-enthralled Green Beret was making such an elementary mistake after spending nearly three years in-country. In fact, the ruthless major had a competent plan; the instant he transmitted what he was planning to do, seven or eight red smokes came up in a circle around his location. In the middle of that rough circle came up columns of purple and yellow smoke. That was Miracek.

"Now go ahead and shoot up everything that is red smoke," he radioed.

The Mavericks did just that.

Running a lift operation with the Special Forces could be

unpredictable. A lot of things seemed to occur that didn't happen anywhere else. Beyond Moc Hoa, the Mavericks erroneously once shot up the scouts way out in front of an advancing RF/PF group, after getting permission to do so. As I described previously, they had been reporting two men running well out in front of the Special Forces–led Vietnamese force for some time. Once it was OK'd to fire upon them, the troopers found out this was their own scout contingent, and they had made a mistake. The Vietnamese troops turned on their Green Beret advisors and beat them up. It was very dangerous for a while, and we pilots were very nervous about picking up these guys. Our nervousness increased when, just as they boarded the Hueys, they decided to unload their weapons on the sampans in which they'd just been riding, to sink them. I still remember nearly jumping out of our skins, thinking they were using their guns on us! A lot of racket and gunfire happened right there in the backseat, without their informing us what their intentions were.

One fatal day in an operation out of Moc Hoa, site of the "B"-team HQ, the Special Forces really got in trouble. They often would put in a "blocking force" to anchor the tail end of an operation whose mission was to go up a tree-lined canal, attempting to find VC. However, the Viet Cong forces already understood this tactic, so they went back and tried to annihilate this small contingent at the other end. They attacked in strength before the main unit could return and help out their buddies at this remote end of the line. The VC damned near exterminated them. It was horrible to hear the last man alive in the rear contingent crying on the radio for help. He did not have long to live, as the VC was overwhelming the position with superior strength. We had to get the rest out of there, and we had no cover as we did it. It was an urgent matter of extraction before they were all extinguished.

The first platoon ships were in the first flight of five in a "V" formation. I was leading the second platoon ships in the following "V." As the first group went in, I knew we were in a fix; if this went badly, we could be picking up many downed crews as well as Special Forces–led troops. The worst case would be if all got picked up except for one or two who might be shot down. If this occurred, they could not be helped out by anybody. It had real potential to be a mess. I orbited at 2,000 feet while Stets and the rest of the first platoon went on in. It sounded truly hairy. They got the troops on board.

Ships were overloaded but trying to make it. There could be no second chance, and I sympathized with all those guys down there, realizing what they absolutely had to get done. As I orbited with the second flight, I imagined which formation we should switch to after flying in the "V" shape. As the radio traffic painted the picture, I kept visualizing in my mind what those guys were going through.

All were nearly out except for Willy Stout. He had way too many people on board his ship for a loaded takeoff, and the only way out was downwind. It was also becoming obvious that the VC were coming out of the treeline, firing at the departing ships as they left with the remaining Special Forces men, what was left of them. Captain Stout *had* to make it, and finally he pulled it off. Bouncing along the ground, fighting for lift, he eventually became airborne, to everyone's amazement, and got out of there. They all had made it! There would be no risk at all for the second platoon ships! We had remained up there at altitude, cheering, with completely empty aircraft, while these guys had just cheated death once again! The contrast was amazing between our two conditions at that moment, but that's the way things would go. Ole "Captain Doubt" had flown out with something like 18 men; no one knew how he had managed to do it. It sure saved the rest of us from getting greased.

If you get it that we didn't always take Special Forces operations too seriously, you're right. We liked the Green Berets well enough. It just seemed as though they didn't fight the war so well in an airmobile way. We had to take more precautions about possibly something screwing up than we did about adequately accomplishing the mission of finding VC. That was on the back burner. Maybe they were better at teaching the kids English or giving out medicine; I don't know. When compared with their small-unit tactics, their lift operations always seemed to leave something to be desired.

With them, we would also be operating out of places we normally didn't use much. One beautiful, sunny day, we were to use the airstrip at Chi Lang (which was spelled Chau Lang on the map; see what I mean?). This small runway might have been around since the Japanese era, but ordinarily it wasn't very secure for just a few ships to use. We avoided it. Now, the day of the lift, we had so many ships in the operation that we probably were safe. But we still worried a bit. Everyone kept a weather eye out for something unusual to happen. Those of us who had been in-country for a considerable amount of time were the most jumpy. It just paid off to be so nervous; you just understood that.

While we were standing around, watching the surrounding hills and so forth, we noticed a little metal tag on a waist-high wire running like a fence alongside our parked aircraft. Looking farther, we saw a lot of these tags, spaced every so often along the wire paralleling the runway. The metal tags were fairly rusted and not very informative. Some of the little metal signs were more readable than others, so we tried to decipher their purpose. These had a smaller, darker triangle than the metal around it, pointing to the ground, with very oblique angles on this flat triangle in the center of the little rectangular tag. For the life of us, we could not remember from basic-training days what that military symbol meant. We *knew* it wasn't for nuclear radiation; it couldn't be that! After a while, we collectively gave up, even though there was a sense of unease that we needed to determine what this warning fence was conveying. Nothing came to us, so we walked away.

At that point, across the field, one of the Red Knight aircraft that had landed on the other side of the wire--with the rest of their five-ship formation--blew up. An AC named Whitlow had been shutting down the aircraft while his crew unstrapped; then came the explosion. These guys managed to run away from their crippled ship, now all aflame, yelling, "Mortars!" They scurried across the remaining ground to where we were, then leaped and hurdled over the wire separating our area from theirs. The other Red Knight pilots and enlisted crews also raced away from their ships and joined us on the runway. They all made it across the grassy area and over the wire, and none were hurt. Then someone lifted up one of the curious metal tags and solemnly said, "This means *mines.*"

"Yeah! That's right, that *is* what that damned tag says. It all comes back to me now!" was the enlightened comment from somebody just along the strip near me.

"Them's *mines!*" another authority said in a strong southern accent.

We all cracked up, laughing hysterically. Not only were we shaking our heads at our ignorance, but we also couldn't believe that all those crews were safe after having dashed over *the rest of the landmines* planted somewhere in the ground between us and those parked ships! When we needed to go home, the men belonging to those aircraft had to move around to the other side of the outer wire where their ships had landed and gingerly step aboard from that direction. It was touch-and-go for a moment when these ships cranked, but they all took off without further incident, to our great relief. Apparently, this grassy area behind the wire was an old French mine field, which the brass never owned up to knowing anything about. Other than that, we had a fairly nice day with some strong sunshine; I do remember that. I don't know how the Knights wrote off that burning aircraft as a combat loss. Jack Payne recalled that it took some doing.

34

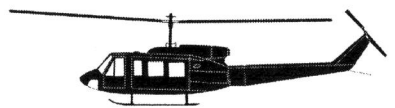

JIM HARDBECK'S LIGHTNING BUG

AFTER I LEFT THE MAVERICKS, I was able to impart much of my training from the gunships into the second platoon slicks. These were little things, but it was very helpful to be able to communicate effectively with the gun platoon when the flight was receiving fire. When the aircraft commanders' ships were being shot up, they did not always reveal the enemy's position or what type of fire they were receiving in any intelligible manner. This was not only completely unhelpful to the guns, but also, of course, dangerous for one's survival.

For example, it did no good to transmit only on your platoon's FM frequency that you were receiving fire. In a sense, this was like talking only to yourself. That was a radio channel only within the flight; it did not alert the accompanying gunships to your predicament at all. You had to talk to them on UHF, the company net. If you panicked and did not get to that point, the accompanying gunships protecting your incoming flight could not adequately do their job. They could not hear you. So I convinced everyone to put the "2" switch on the selector button when flying into an LZ. Then, when they transmitted in an emergency, their voices, however quavering, would go out to where it would do them the most good. The automatic need to tell *someone* you were getting shot at went on *the* frequency that could bring you the crucial response and help. "The Mavericks are on you!" meant a great deal to these guys; they were very proud of being able to cover us.

Since the gunships were monitoring three channels in their aircraft at all times, it was also good to throw out a visual signal that you were receiving ground fire from the VC. You wanted to show you were getting hit, and also to indicate the direction and approximate location of the tracer fire. The Mavericks might be talking to the ground-pounders on the FM at the moment you called (that was "1" on the selector dial). If they were talking on the VHF to themselves on their assigned channel three, of the five possibilities there, that was the "3" switch. I had my kids trained to throw out a smoke grenade and then mark where the suspected enemy position was with their own M-60's tracers firing back. They would call up to me on the intercom what they had observed, and I could get that news out of the aircraft to the gun-platoon guys, who really had something to shoot back with.

My call from the aircraft might go something like this: "Mavericks, Gold Three is receiving fire from that treeline we just passed. Smoke's out. Gunner's rounds mark!" The return acknowledgment would be over UHF, the "2" switch for receiving; the guns could turn immediately on the suspected target and lay down some impressive suppressive fire. They had to be able to *react*. That's what you had to get across to all the other slicky pilots who did not know exactly how to assist the gunships in their job. You had to do something besides just be scared. And there were a lot of guys who didn't get beyond that.

Tommy Greenfield, my door gunner in Outlaw 24, was especially good at firing the gun, pressing the intercom switch, and throwing smoke—all at the same time. I often wondered if he had three arms back there. And it made you feel better for doing the right thing at a very scary time when you could do so. It always makes an aviation person uncomfortable to watch those bronze tracers working their way up to you like angry darning needles that want to pierce all the body parts you possess. Doing something to hinder that threatening process is a very pleasurable act, whatever it is you can do. Informing the gunship fire teams which position of the flight was under attack was everything they needed to know to start doing their job. If you could further assist them in ways I described above, they could deliver rockets immediately. And that was life insurance if you wanted some of it.

There was one day when the whole right side of the flight was allowed to suppress while we were landing from a hover to collect the troops in a pickup zone (PZ). The door gunners on the right side of the ships all pulled the trigger while the troops loaded on the left sides of the Hueys. The formation was staggered trail, and the C&C ship up above said it was an impressive sight seeing all those tracers coming out at once from approximately 15 ships. Watching from up there, Maj. Jim O'Neill, our XO at that time, said you could have walked across the machine gun fire coming from those slicks that day. Made the kids feel good to fire that effectively for once, too. Usually they were frustrated at not being able to fire enough when we got fired upon. Their reaction time was commonly a bit too late.

The real payoff to my short time with the gunship platoon of the Outlaws was the trust we built up for flying "lightning-bug" missions. Having a dependable person upstairs while you were risking your life on the deck at night helped the mission along. My favorite fire team to fly with in my remaining time in-country was Jim Hardbeck's. He was almost a genius at understanding what gunship work meant in the Delta at that time, and many gunnies outright revered him. I think any green pilot could have flown with him and it would not have made any difference in that man's performance. There are many former warrant officers out there who have approached Jim in the years since then and asked him if he remembered the moment they climbed in the ship with him. He almost always doesn't; there were just too many over his three tours in Vietnam. You can see the facial muscles droop in disappointment when the questioner is not remembered, but the feeling I get is this is a lot like asking Joe DiMaggio if he recalled the name or face of every youngster he ever autographed a baseball for. It just can't be done, despite the significance of the moment.

As a CW2, Hardbeck often was given the work of a major. His voice would come on the horn as Maverick Lead, and you could tell he knew his job and loved it. He was a professional, a career Army aviator, and one of the few well-known Delta gunship pilots of that era who were living legends every time they keyed the mike. They were a joy to watch and listen to as they did their jobs. It was a keen experience to encounter and work with them in utter confidence. You felt amazement that someone could do this skillful assignment so completely *and* bravely. The rest of us just tried; they lived it. They gave us something to measure up to. Robin Miller was renowned, and I've already spoken of Jerry Daly. They all had their own unique ways of working, and it was remarkable watching those slight differences in professionalism.

Jim and I had a special relationship from the time I spent my month with the Mavericks. The nights we worked together, I loved hearing him come up on the radio as our three ships cranked for a bug mission. I would be over on the Outlaw ramp as Hardbeck's fire team warmed up over on the east end of the runway. As we checked in, there was always a good feeling in the exchange between us. He'd then call the Vinh Long tower, and the evening flight would depart. Sometimes the free-fire zone was a good distance away; other times it was closer in. Weather always played a role, and sometimes we had to cancel, such as when I was in between cloud layers or inadvertently went IFR. After my incident with Hung, I was never anxious to stay up there too long in lousy conditions. Too many of Vinh Long's young aviators had died while operating out of the envelope in bad weather. Pilot error was the leading cause of death on the accident reports.

One night, Hardbeck told me he had a new way of flying "bug." "Oh," I said, "what could that be?" I was getting pretty experienced, and a new wrinkle now and then would amaze me if it could still be found. Jim just winked and said, "You'll see."

What he was doing may sound complicated, but it was just plain balls-out dangerous and extremely good flying. The light fire team would fly low-level down the canals, with the first ship lit up with its nav lights and flashing its landing light from side to side—basically looking stupid and available to be shot at. The second Maverick would be flying just behind the decoy, completely blacked out. When the first ship began drawing fire, the gunship in the rear would immediately react and hose the firing position. Having served its purpose, the first ship would have rapidly switched off all its lights and turned away from the incoming fire. Now completely dark, this ship would leave the firefight area, and both ships would regroup after fatally suckering the VC ground troops. It worked every time, and both gunships survived their trickster techniques while I was overhead flying cover. The idea for having me along was that my ship would drop down immediately and medevac the gun crews if something went very wrong. They didn't trust just anyone for this task, so my self-esteem rose whenever I went along and we played this deadly game.

To get a feeling of what this low-level nighttime flying was like, try cutting out the headlights while driving down a country road some summer night. Never mind the location of the centerline, just try staying on the asphalt surface at all. Keep an eye on the trees bordering both sides of the roadway; you don't want to hit them, either. Helicopter pilots had to be conscious of their rotor blades' radius at all times; nothing could hit those blade tips. Now imagine getting shot at by a burst of tracer fire from the brush on one side of the road. Bank hard to get away from this automatic weapon firing at you, still with no lights on, and you'll begin to sense the skill level of the men flying these machines after so many months on the job.

Years later, always curious about the exact flying techniques necessary to do this amazing low-level flight in the darkness, I asked Jim Hardbeck one evening how he had managed to avoid flying into the canal or the deck while operating that way. He came back quickly, but in his slow drawl, "Never let the altimeter get below 50 feet!" Geez.

I have to relate one more story of how joyous it was to fly guns in the Delta. My friend Tommy Mitchell had elected to stay with the Mavericks when I returned to the second platoon Outlaws. The big, blond, ex–bull rider told me he liked flying with the guns and was going to stay with them. "Fine," I stated. "It may be your thing, but it is not mine." He nodded and went on to remain firmly with the Mavericks.

I always stayed in contact with any second platoon members when they moved on to Maintenance or any other assignment; we were just that close. One sunny day at Tra Vinh during an operation, I had moved across the runway, waiting out another lift departure, and was spending time talking with Tommy. Knee-high grass surrounded us. We were just shooting the bull when he said, "Well, I guess I've got to go flying." So I proceeded to walk across the runway back to where my ship was parked. It took a short while to get there.

When I turned around, Tommy was right back in the location where I had left him. I walked back across the strip and said, "I thought you said you were going flying." He was wet from the lower rib cage on down. He was also puffing.

"I did. I got shaw-down," he mumbled in that heavy southern accent.

"What did you say?" I asked, not able to understand his speech.

"I did go flying. I got shaw-down." Tommy was gazing off as he spoke.

"Are you saying you got shot down?" I inquired. His eyes looked funny.

Tommy nodded in the affirmative. I thought it best to leave him alone at this moment, so I walked back across the runway, leaving him to collect his thoughts. Here's what happened. He was flying "the Hog," which, when fully armed and refueled, had 48 rockets on board as well as all those nose-firing grenade projectiles in the belt-fed system it brandished. He had taken off from Tra Vinh probably at an altitude of 250 feet, which was usual for a gunship platoon in the Delta flying to its station, when he had encountered *beaucoup* ground fire from a VC unit in close proximity to the airfield. All of a sudden, he was completely on fire. He had only enough time to set the thing on the ground, descending as rapidly as he could through a few hundred feet on down. He said by the time he could park the burning gunship on the wet terrain immediately below him, the rotor blades were on fire, and he could see them drooping in their incinerating heat as they slowed their RPM's. The flames were encircling the aircraft and leaping in the door, licking all around the four dozen rockets in their pods. The four-man crew got out as soon as they hit the ground; the VC with weapons ablaze were coming out of the treeline adjacent to their position. They were firing from the hip, directly at the burning ship, which was all too quickly in ruins.

Troy Tison was flying 2,500 feet above, in a Knight aircraft on a single-ship mission in the area, with nothing whatsoever to do with the operation we were conducting. Seeing the fireball that Tommy's Maverick ship had become as it landed far below, he put his ship into a screaming dive down to the beleaguered gun crew. He red-lined everything. As he completed his approach, Tommy Mitchell's crew had just disembarked the burning gunship. Troy landed his D-model right alongside the burning Hog in a hot flare, picked up the crew in the most expeditious manner possible, and took off. The Maverick C-model exploded, sending all its ammo and fuel sky high. The VC were thwarted and the crew was saved; the ship was a total loss. Troy brought his Knight aircraft around in a turn to land at the Tra Vinh airstrip, put Tommy and the rest of the crew on the ground, and then continued on with his mission. It was at this point that I looked up and saw Mitchell right back in the same place where I had left him. He had just been dumped there by Troy.

I have always told people that this story takes more time to tell than the minutes it took to happen. Troy received the Silver Star for this rescue mission. What I found to be totally coincidental is that they were the only two graduates I ever knew from Henderson College in Alabama. Troy was a halfback for the "Henderson Reddies." These two were classmates, and now serving in two totally separate aviation companies at Vinh Long. They happened to interact very helpfully that fateful day in South Vietnam. Great story for an alumni magazine, eh? I wonder what the odds would be of such a thing happening? Par for the course during a tour in Vietnam.

35

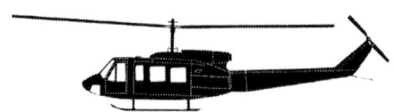

KNIGHT 6 GETS FOOLED

FLYING LIFTS GOT OLD. Often the guys would be flying nine to 14 days at a stretch, with eight hours of flight time per day, and the fatigue factor would build right in, no matter how much you knew you had to maintain attentiveness. After months of formation flying, some things became very automatic, but it was obvious there was a lot of contrast between the experienced ACs and the new pilots fresh from flight school. The latter had to be watched over constantly when on the controls—which could be nerve-wracking for both pilots. There was a hell of a learning curve. The new guy would not even know a move that could be anticipated by a pilot with higher hours, and it would be months before the new guy had put the necessary precautionary thoughts under his belt. Being slow and not too bright could get one in trouble in a situation that was a matter of course to the more experienced, high-time man in-country. Most of the routine in the cockpit for the slicky pilots was in flying lifts in one formation or another.

Switching from one style of formation to another had to be polished and rehearsed, as I have noted. Occasionally, overreaction was just as bad as some other deficiency in the maneuver. I began to fly Trail in the second platoon while the first platoon leader, Capt. Bill Stout, was flying Lead. The duty for this position was to give the Lead eyes in the back of his head, and report forward when the flight was down, loaded, formed, or whatever. "Trail's down, Lead," signified that all others had landed in the LZ, too. "Your flight is formed, Lead," meant the formation could stop holding back at 60 knots and proceed up to cruise speed of 80 knots; all the aircraft had caught up after takeoff. If Trail said, "The flight is still going 60 knots," it meant that the whole lift was frustrated at Lead's not picking up the pace after the flight was formed. Sometimes the flight commander was seemingly asleep at the switch, perhaps thinking about something else coming up, and had forgotten to move along at cruise speed. These tedious moments resulted in a longer day, wearing on the nerves, and tried experienced pilots' patience. It was important for morale to execute the procedures in the flying formations as adroitly as permissible. Lacking that finesse weakened unit esteem; it also made every young warrant think he was as smart as the guy flying Lead up front.

At 2,500 feet in the southern part of the Delta, too many days in the air nearly brought death to two members of the Outlaws late in the year. We had just gone from "Vs of five" to straight trail. I was flying Trail that day and watched the flight efficiently execute the command. I had a very clear picture of all 10 ships ahead of me, counting my own. As the first platoon ships moved quickly into the column that straight trail creates, Stets found he could not join up in his proper place; he was being crowded out as the fifth aircraft. He veered quickly to the right, skittering away. What happened next was downright frightful. The second platoon formation had gone straight trail also, and having completed that, was now swinging back to the left as a column of five to complete the 10 ships in a row. The second platoon's lead was feeling randy and moving just a little too fast to create this new formation. In Outlaw 11, Stets still looking to the left at whatever he had avoided, moved *under* the incoming lead ship of the second flight. What I saw next was overlapping rotor blades; a mid-air seemed imminent!

"Look out, One-one!" I screamed over the mike, surprised that I did.

Stets in Outlaw 11 now veered as suddenly back to where he was supposed to be. I expected pieces of broken metal and other wreckage to start cascading down from our 2,500-foot altitude. The turn back involved a bank angle to the left as well as the movement out of the way. A miracle had happened; no collision had occurred. I had clearly seen the rotor discs almost enmesh; they had become "X's" overlapping for a moment. Norris Marshall, AC of the second platoon lead aircraft that Stets had flown under, had pulled all the pitch he had and gone up as straight as he could manage, thus avoiding the midair between these first and second platoon ships. I was aghast at how close my friend had come to exiting this world right in front of my eyes. It had damned near happened—the worrisome moment I perpetually dreaded about flying in combat with my best friend. Going to war with your buddy is almost like going to war with a family member. It's not to be recommended. The scene had been fairly theatrical, almost surreal. The sky was weirdly colored, and the half-light above the dried out, blond rice paddies far below in the hazy, dry season highlighted this macabre event. We lucked out with this one, and my fine friend from Middlebury was still alive. I was hyperventilating with relief.

Flying these lifts during my last months in-country earned me the nickname of "Chicken Hawk" from the new guys, because I was so rough on all the recently arrived pilots. I wouldn't let them get away with anything, and whoever was flying my aircraft had to fly it as well as I did. My place in formation was trusted, and I wanted no one to be able to determine whether Easty was flying on the controls or someone else was. I wasn't a nice guy in the cockpit; I no longer cared about someone's personal feelings. They could be in a body bag to the States and their family real quick if that was what they wanted. Too many things could go wrong up here, and they were not going to happen to my ship. My EM knew this to be true and had complete confidence in me. I wanted to be the best AC in the platoon, and I believed I was. My crew deserved nothing less from me during this eleventh month of experienced in-country flying, and no peter pilot wet behind the ears was going to screw it up. I was merciless about correcting their flying, and was no wet-nursing baby-sitter. I'm sure that many a warrant who flew in late 1967 does not have pleasant memories of flying with me. But they're also still alive.

A curious event happened to us one day under the command of the new Knight 6. He was a recently arrived company commander who had just been promoted from major to lieutenant colonel. As was usual, we all would wait out his performance and see what kind of stuff he was made of. There was always room for surprises. In this operation, he had the Vietnamese brass in the backseat of his Command and Control aircraft, loaded down with radio consoles so they could talk directly to the ground units slogging through the rice paddies beneath them. General Thi was the commander of the Ninth ARVN Division; he was a tall dandy, of fairly athletic build. In Vietnam, you could buy your rank, and he seemed to be of quite aristocratic origin. Wealth could purchase prestige here, if not a great military mind. The problem for a newly appointed aviation company commander was to avoid getting sucked into the "genius" of the militarily experienced Asian mind in the backseat and maintain some judgment about not getting our ships exploited by someone who did not have a high regard for his troops' lives in the first place. The typical high-ranking Vietnamese officer felt no more about our safety than he did for his own troops, mostly of peasant origin. He might as well have been herding cattle. It must have been hard for these elitists locked in a feudal time to comprehend how Americans felt about the common man who was the backbone of our military machine.

If the ARVN commander could get his troops landed where they would be in immediate contact with the enemy, they would have to fight. It was as simple as that. What difference to him if it took a few helicopters along with the plan? It was not the same math that we Americans were computing with. He had a different take about being in harm's way. So a newly arrived, naive CO could be talked into a risky landing by the lift just to show he was as macho as the Vietnamese counterpart. After all, we were both out to win the war, right? Zestful military leadership and all that.

On this particular day, the LZ in question was in an omega-shaped treeline that also had a .50-caliber in it. What had started out as a small firefight by the troops as they were returning home that afternoon had become a bigger firefight, with some serious enemy weaponry. The Maverick gunships were having a time of it here, and we could see them buzzing about in extreme banks, putting out considerable firepower toward whatever was causing the problem. And there obviously was a big problem; a .50-caliber machine gun is *always* a matter of grievous concern. You didn't want to go in there; you didn't even want to be a gunship pilot that day. Bad medicine, no go there. This was not the place to land a formation of Hueys; you would want to land at least a few hundred yards away for a minimum of safety. There was some very real contact going on. On a day like this, you did not listen to the backseat in a C&C ship; you turned diplomat and saved the lives of the pilots flying all those ARVNs sitting back there in the UH-1D cabin areas. If you wanted contact with the VC by the ground troops, they could walk or crawl a few hundred yards, like the old days when the infantry walked to the battle. Let them close with the enemy on the ground; let's not shoot up a bunch of perfectly good helicopters while doing it. It was the job of a good aviation company commander to insist upon this reality, not to defer to a martinet fop of a Vietnamese general perfectly willing to spill the red blood of American flyboys.

Well, the newly assigned Lieutenant Colonel LeBlanc was not thinking this good stuff at all; he was going along like a dumb elephant with the program being sold to him from the backseat. We knew it, we could feel it. Resonating through our flight was, "Oh, shit, somebody do something to prevent this awful deed from happening." This arrogant man was both naive and insistent. Also duped was the new, green senior advisor to the Ninth ARVN Division. Knight 6 wanted those slicks to land *inside* that omega-shaped enclosure of a treeline, just as the Vietnamese general was dictating. Joe Moffett, as Maverick Lead, stood him up, saying, "No, sir, I am not going to put those slicks in there!" "Good, Joe, good! Don't back down. Stay firm," I was thinking, attentively overhearing the UHF transmissions. This quickly became a game of, "I'm giving you a direct order"; really shitty. It *was* the gun platoon leader's job to inform you that your plan had some holes in it; he was the one who was supposed to guarantee protection and execute suppressive-fire coverage for the incoming lift and get them out alive. Gun-platoon Leads took pride in this. I kept wondering what was going to happen to counteract this new idiot of a Knight 6 and save the day for us slicky pilots. I decided to tune in to channel 3 of the VHF and see what the Mavericks were saying among themselves in this predicament. I suspected it would make good listening.

There on their VHF was the new Delta 6, Colonel Harper himself, cajoling Joe Moffett on his own gun-platoon frequency. I thought this really splendid and indeed interesting. Who else, but I, would have thought to dial in and catch that conversation?

Harper was saying to Maverick Lead: "Do what you gotta do, and I will back you up on the ground with whatever decision you have to reach to get those slicks in there safely and out again OK." Then he told Moffett to give a false set of instructions that Knight 6 could hear over UHF, and give the real message about landing over our FM frequency to Outlaw Lead. Hearing those words, I whooped, and my crew asked what that was about. I told Greenfield and Duane Liebe, my crew chief, to flip up the "3" switch and "listen in on the races!" Gawd, how I loved this job!

Moffett came up on Outlaw FM to Stanley Arnold, *who I knew* had not had not thought to eavesdrop on the Mavericks' frequency, so what he was about to be told was complete news to him! He was a bit perplexed when Maverick Lead told him to disregard the landing instructions he'd be giving him over UHF, and pay attention only to what he was telling him to do *right now* over Outlaw FM.

In his whiny Nebraska accent, Captain Arnold then told the lift over the FM: "Pay no attention, Outlaws, to what you hear over UHF. Only listen to the landing instructions over FM." He transmitted this obediently, but I knew from the quaver in his tone that he still had no idea why he was saying it. His voice registered his confusion. The gunship Lead was going to have the Outlaws land well short of the LZ, approaching a smoke grenade thrown out at the last minute for the landing spot that was a good 500 yards from what Knight 6 specified. "Good work, Joe!" was what I was feeling. "Atta boy, keep a'going." In this soap-opera scenario, Joe Moffett conveyed rather well what he wanted the Outlaws to do, and I was feeling very happy, reassured about my life status. "We are going to live!" I was singing in my heart. Arnold was saying, "OK," and still not getting the why of it.

Moffett then came up on UHF and informed Knight 6 that he had seen the light and would do just as the new commander wanted. "Good boy," LeBlanc purred. "I knew you would see things my way eventually!" This crank thought he was *so* brilliant. I knew, though, that when both got on the ground, LeBlanc would threaten Joe with removal from his platoon's command status; little did he know of Harper's role in this episode.

"Yessir, we'll do it your way after all!" said Joe. Maverick Lead then gave the bogus landing instructions to the Outlaw flight and Arnold rogered OK. The sting was in.

Knight 6 was happy and didn't know what our flying circus was about to unveil. One of the Maverick gunships wheeled in just at the last moment, as planned, and dropped a red smoke grenade at the *right* touchdown spot, and the "Vs" of Outlaws landed precisely where they were supposed to, on the billowing red wisps of the grenades' pungent smoke. Knight 6 went berserk.

LeBlanc hollered, "That's not what I said, that's not what we agreed upon. That's not where they were supposed to land! What's going on down there?"

"Sorry, sir. That's where in my judgment they're safest to land. See you on the ground, sir." Moffett was just *so cool,* brass balls and all that.

"You bet we will. *You can count on it.* I'll see you right away!" screamed LeBlanc. Not that he knew that every single slick in that flight had also kissed him off for good. One bad move like this and his book was closed forever on our account.

As we landed short in the rice paddies, we still could see the gunships in close contact with the firepower of the VC unit owning that omega-shaped treeline to our front. Nothing had improved over the course of the conversation between Knight 6 and Maverick Lead. The place was still impossibly hot, a real death-trap destination for helicopters. We would have been terribly shot up if we'd gone in there.

As we unloaded the ARVN's quickly and departed to the left, over the sound of Knight 6's continuing, raucous protests on the radio, I gave Outlaw 24 everything it had and climbed out. I mean, *really* climbed out! Little Fernald was sitting in the copilot's seat and pestered me about how much was "enough" as we zoomed up into the Delta's air, high above the rest of the flight. All of them labored to do the same thing; they just didn't have a ship like 24 underneath their butts. I had never performed a cyclic climb like I did that particular moment; sometimes you save your best for when you need it the most. I had no apologies at all upon first reaching 2,000 feet and then some; then I decided to level off and not embarrass anyone any further. They were far below. Then came the inevitable humorous call, this one from Stansbury in Outlaw 25, "What are you doing up *there*, 24?" And I sarcastically quipped with a smile in my voice, "Holding my place in formation, waiting for you guys!" There was nothing they could do about it except catch up, of course, and laugh about it. It was quite a while before they did exactly that, and formed up alongside both sides of me in the "V" I had fictitiously constructed in my mind's eye. I wasn't going to die for anybody's fool, and they all knew it. Stansbury said later, "Oh, 24 climbed, . . . oh, *how 24 climbed!"*

We got back on the ground at Vinh Long as we always did, and I knew we would confront the obnoxious Knight 6 at the club soon thereafter. He was already seated there, just inside the door at the Mekong Manor, in all his arrogance. The young pilots walked past him, all very ready to spit in his eye. I knew he had no consideration or comprehension of what he nearly had just done to us. We were so used to such fools. I spoke to him, as I felt an experienced first lieutenant should, but he only replied, "Nothing could have happened to you guys. I was thinking of you. Nothing could have gone wrong. I was thinking of you all the way."

Meanwhile, the battalion executive officer, Major Stoverink, had Moffett on the carpet in the company orderly room, threatening him with a court-martial. It took a while longer before Harper could get there, informing him that such was not going to happen. Nor was Moffett relieved of his position as Maverick Lead.

36

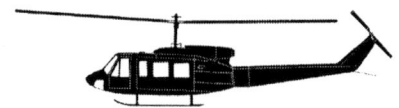

OUTLAW 24 FLIES LEAD

AFTER MONTHS OF ASSISTING NEW PLATOON LEADERS with the tasks of flying Lead, I thought I deserved a crack at doing the job all by myself. Other first lieutenants had done the deed; Jack Payne over in the Knights was doing it all the time. He had just assumed the demanding position because there were so many new captains and majors constantly coming and going in the command assignment of platoon leader. He was just always Knight Lead. As an experienced first lieutenant, you would just get one new Lead trained and he'd be rotated out. You'd have to begin all over again with the new commanding officer and teach him everything you knew for his job. It was a thankless slot, but you did it for the guys behind you. The young warrants were depending on us junior commissioned officers not to let the newly assigned older men screw up our lift flying any more than could be tolerated. As I have stated, we first lieutenants learned to be tolerant, and diplomatic, but we used a firm hand to deal with these career types the Army foisted on us. The success of this interaction was akin to keeping a sore from becoming infected and festering. Sometimes the incoming superior officers were good guys and put up with our protective tactics, and sometimes they didn't catch on. A good man appreciated our efforts and understood the concern behind our actions. If he had any brains at all, he could grasp that he could learn a lot from us.

At any rate, I asked Leuty and O'Kane, who by now was Outlaw 6 himself, if I could be flight Lead before I went home and have the satisfaction of doing the job completely on my own. Needless to say, by this time I was so utterly composed and impressed with my perfection that I was convinced there was no way I could foul up if left completely to my own resources! I would realize later that arrogance is part of developing combat fatigue. At this moment of being in-country going on 11 or 12 months, you almost think you can walk on water. You've seen it all and done it all. You become very rigid and resolute. Everything is in sharp focus, and much has fallen by the wayside. There is a psychological screening going on, a matter of keeping around you only what is important to pay attention to your survival; some emotions are not even present anymore. You will remain in this moment the rest of your life as this sharp identity within yourself. The psychic fatigue or pride of exactly who you are in this development will always stay with you in your mind, even if it's of no further use.

I was raring to go with this prospect, convinced of my abilities and ready to deliver. I found it hard to believe when my superiors looked back at me and said, "Maybe." My response: "Whoa, if you feel that way, then definitely give me a shot at this and I will show you who has been helping out all these temporary platoon leaders over the last few months!" Sighing and rolling their eyes at each other, they said, "OK. We'll give you a mission in the near future, as soon as one comes up that is appropriate for you." Geez, thanks a lot, was my internal reaction to this lukewarm response. I was a lot better than this near-dismissal and wanted to prove it. Of course, I was also deaf to their appraisal of me, which might even have been somewhat accurate.

Stets and Roger Kalinger of the first platoon had already flown Lead together, and I thought it almost funny that the unit thought it wise *to put two first lieutenants together* to accomplish the job. I surmised this to be a slap in the face for all the work we had to do at this rank with our commissioned superiors falling in our laps for their bailouts. Didn't anyone know what we put up with? I guessed not.

I flew Trail that day for Stets; Roger kept silent and off the radios. Joe Moffett thought it was my voice he was hearing over the UHF, so he kept referring to the Lead aircraft as "Dave." He was trying to be very helpful, and I had the giggles in the back of the flight. I'd harass Stets, playing with this overfamiliarity. "Flight's up, *Dave!*" "Trail is down, DAVE!" Stets would come back from up front with a belligerent, "Thanks, JOE!" to continue the comedy. I knew Moffett respected me and wanted to do everything he could for me as Maverick Lead to make the day go better. I considered the whole episode enjoyable.

Within the next few days, O'Kane let me know there was a suitable lift operation coming up, and I could have my wishes come true. I thought, "Swell, I'll do this very well and really show them what I am capable of." After all, a few weeks earlier, I had literally run a division. Leuty and O'Kane could not get off the ground with their C&C ship and had waved me over to take charge of the extraction measures being set up. They said they would overcome their maintenance problems and be up in the air in 15 minutes to take over; I was supposed to just hold the line until then. I said sure, no problem, and took to the air with their maps in my hand. An older major from the MACV ranks got into the backseat with his SOI code book for communicating to the ground troops with their FM radios, and we were set to take over for a while. But, that short while turned into two hours. I put in an air strike, avoided a .50-caliber position, rotated gun crews, and even talked to Col. Harper when Delta 6 came into the operational area. He said, "Unidentified slick flying over the OA, identify yourself." I gave him who I was and explained the difficulty Outlaw 6 was having, at which point he tersely got off the air and headed for the airstrip where Leuty and O'Kane were parked.

I didn't stink up the show too much, but things were getting hectic. We had to keep transferring radio frequencies on the only FM radio we had in the cockpit for the poor major we had in the backseat, but we did fairly alright. In a sweat, he was really getting some "pits" back there, as he had to switch frequencies constantly to talk to those on the ground, who were getting ready to be extracted at the end of the day. (He looked worse for the wear than we did up front: his deodorant must have failed him.) We did accomplish setting up those pickup zones, but geez, putting in airstrikes was a bit over my level of expertise! The Air Force FAC (Forward Air Controller) took care of that, and we enjoyed watching the show. I did the best I could before I got the word to return to the ground; I literally slumped to the turf as I handed over the map to Leuty and O'Kane. They were in considerable mirth, unable to contain their laughter as they looked at me. I asked later, "How'd I do?" O'Kane said it sounded like, "This is Outlaw 24. *Halp!*"

Looking quickly at my face, he next said, "You did all right, Dave. You got the PZs set up OK. That was the basic thing that had to be done." Never mind that I had formations of slicks orbiting out over the China Sea to avoid that .50-caliber position. I had no idea where to put them; they had arrived early, and the troops were not in position to board. The changeover of the gunship fire teams had gone OK, mostly because I just let them proceed with what they were going to do anyway. That was helpful, since they knew what they intended to do with their time in the operational area. It was interesting for a while, and I would always be able to say that as a first lieutenant I had actually run a division for an afternoon, even if it was a Vietnamese division. Not many young officers on the ground ever got that opportunity; all the higher-ranking officers in the chain of command would have had to be dead for the young guys to have the same deal.

The lift assigned me was held near Ben Tre, from an airstrip that we had not used much. From all my military experiences, beginning with ROTC summer camp at Fort Devens, I knew there would be some things that were brand new and could not be anticipated until you were in the command slot. They just pop up and never reveal themselves before you become the commanding officer—almost as if to purposely embarrass you and make your day more complicated. I don't know why these things don't express themselves while you are back there in the ranks, but trust me, they appear like gremlins to ruin your day. I had given the briefing to the platoon the previous night, and I thought things were all prepared, but I realized that complications still could goof me.

I had chosen Freddy Grotenhuis to be my copilot for the day because he was the smoothest of the new pilots who had just come to the platoon. I knew that was a prerequisite if I was going to serve the guys adequately throughout the day. I couldn't have any complaints about Lead flying smoothly if I had Freddy on the controls. I would be doing little flying, just mostly thinking and operating off the map they had given me at the briefing the night before. Maybe I was biting off more than I could chew, but I was anxious for this one brief mission before I rotated home so I could say I once flew Outlaw Lead, instead of just assisting. The guys were supportive, and I hoped O'Kane would be keeping an eye on me from on high in his C&C ship.

We loaded up the ARVNs and I wondered what to do next. I sat there in the ship and realized suddenly that I didn't know the departure time; I only knew when the flight was scheduled to arrive on station and discharge the troops. How do you know when to take off? Someone had calculated the time needed en route, but when were we supposed to leave the airstrip to begin this clock? "Oh, gawd," I thought to myself, "this is really dumb. This is *really dumb.*" In all the times I had coached the Lead officer, I had never had to deal with this minor bit of timing. I sat there.

O'Kane's voice came in my earphones: "Time to take off, Outlaw Lead!" was his helpful command. Yessir, I said to my own brain. Thank God for O'Kane once again. "Outlaws are on the go!" I transmitted outside the ship, and the flight took off to the west. Everybody formed up and we were looking OK. We landed and did the usual things and then went somewhere else to pick up more troops for another LZ. We did almost as well here, but there was a treeline breaking the LZ into two halves, and I computed which side would be the tactical place to land and drop off the troops. Of course, I figured wrong. I chose the near side. Halfway through the approach to the short side, just as we were on very short final to my chosen touchdown point, O'Kane came on the horn again and told me to land on the *far side* of the trees. Freddy had to pull pitch and smoothly transition back to a climb instead of a letdown; I knew this error would infuriate the guys, but we did it. I was annoyed at myself for having calculated wrongly, but it showed me I still had a lot to learn about this game. I was beginning to feel humbled.

We did several other things that day, but nothing really glorious occurred. No major events; I just felt I hadn't done the job to my complete satisfaction, and I don't believe anyone else did, either. Maybe I was better as an independent, single-ship aircraft commander than as a troop leader. I was impressed that being put in a position of command always can put egg on a person's face. It never seems to fail, and there are rare times that a military superior executes all facets of a mission perfectly. So the moment was educational if not superlative. It was probably a good thing to happen to me. Glenn Klutz took a picture of me in Outlaw 24 leading the flight, and that slide from his Canon is still in my collection of Vietnam memories: "There's me flying Outlaw Lead!"

37

THAT MANG THIT CANAL OUTPOST

There was an outpost the VC were always trying to annihilate just to the east of the Mang Thit Canal, very close to where the Battle of Easter Sunday had been fought. It didn't have a name—it was a simple mud fort like all the rest of these Vietnamese-staffed outposts—but it was constantly in great danger. It took a gun team to put in a slick for resupplying this meager garrison of 26 men, because it was literally surrounded by VC in the treelines leading to it. No one ever went in there on a single-ship mission; two birds were the minimum, under the protection of the gunships. This little nondescript place was between Tam Binh and Tra On on the Bassac River, at the intersection of several canals that emptied into the Mang Thit. It was one hostile place; at the time, we didn't know why. The VC knew the strategic value of the Mang Thit, while the Vietnamese did not. For years, the American advisors had not been able to communicate this concept to the ARVN commanders; they could only struggle to hold the post with our help. The outpost guarded the Mang Thit Canal, which was a direct northerly route to Saigon—a shortcut, instead of following the Bassac River all the way out to the South China Sea and then back up the Mekong River. The Vietnamese saw no reason not to use a lot of time moving rice in their sampans all that way over a two-year period; they had no concept in their lives of moving fast to transport rice. The Viet Cong realized this was a short route for a military campaign on their nation's capital. To them, it was valuable.

I was in Sa Dec at the end of a long day when a light colonel approached and informed me that I had been chosen to fly a Corps priority mission. I was to proceed immediately to Tra On and await instructions there. I told him that I had already flown all day and was ready to go home. This wasn't good military utilization of aircraft; it had to be cleared through my aviation company commanders to get an OK. We were used to getting yanked around on the spot by these MACV field forces, and we had to keep a disciplined attitude about their utilizing us any way they saw fit. He came back at me and said it had already been cleared; this was a very important moment and there was no time to waste. I had asked for confirmation, and in a way I got it. There was nothing else to do but comply. I was agitated but had stayed within bounds in my hotheaded discourse with the colonel; he had won, and he knew it. I walked out of the HQ operational room and told my crew we were not going home, not just yet.

It was getting toward twilight when we approached Tra On, where a gunship fire team from the Cobras of the 114th was waiting for us. Jim Parrott was also there in Outlaw 18, and a Soc Trang Tiger ship was parked nearby. I said hello to young Jim and asked what was going on. He said he didn't know much yet. He nodded toward the Cobras, indicating that they might know something. The Soc Trang AC was keeping in the background; he would be used only as a backup if need be. A quiet, dark-haired man, he didn't look like he wanted to get too involved. The agitated MACV major representing the ground command sure did, though. He was all ass-kicking, foot-stomping, in-your-face, with, "We're going to accomplish this mission, Lieutenant," type of stuff. Oh, great, 11 months-plus in-country and now I had this to deal with. Moving past the major, I made contact with the young first lieutenant of the Cobras and asked him what was up. He said we had to resupply the anonymous Mang Thit outpost or those 26 Vietnamese soldiers in it would give up and abandon the fort that night. They were nearly out of ammo and had had no replacements for a month. So far, it hadn't been done; there had been many recent attempts, but they all had failed after being driven off by ground fire from the VC, well in place around the little fort. The Vietnamese were going to quit, that was true.

"Why do you think we can do it?" I asked the tall lieutenant.

"Well, we haven't figured a way in there yet," he replied. "A slick or two was driven off earlier this afternoon while attempting to get in there. They didn't make it. Perhaps we can sneak you guys in there in the dark."

I could see this guy was all gunship pilot; they really ate up this shit. Oh, boy, we get a chance to shoot things up and maybe you slicks can make it in there. Or maybe you can't; all in a day's work with the guns. The tall, handsome Cobra lieutenant looked like an ex–football player. I decided I could trust him, but he had better come up with a good plan. I hadn't heard one yet.

"We've got to go back to Vinh Long and rearm. We'll talk to somebody there and see if we can get some better ideas and permission to use them. Then we'll report back here if we can come up with something," said the strong-looking lieutenant.

"Oh, good. While you're doing that, try to talk to some of my commanders in the 175th and see how they feel about this. I don't know if they've approved of this mission or I've just been told that they have." I very much suspected I was being dealt a hand here with MACV's desperate need to save the outpost. They might have bullshitted me about this thing having my company's approval to get me to do the mission. The lieutenant said OK and took off for Vinh Long. I sure wished I'd been the one going.

While he was away, I took a tongue-lashing from the brazen major. He was insulting my courage, integrity, and everything else he could find in my personal nature to confuse and whip me into a fighting stance. I dealt with him calmly but didn't think he was going to have much to offer. The plan was for me to fly a heavy load of .30-caliber ammo in the olive-drab ammo boxes that look like lunch pails with handles. Jim Parrott was to fly a squad of ARVN replacements just behind me in the two-ship mission. The Soc Trang ship would hang high above us in case one of us, or both, got shot down and needed extraction. The Cobra fire team would execute some kind of low-level plan of approach to get us in there, and fly just behind us and to the side to provide cover. We would wait for their return from Vinh Long to see what that scheme would be. I felt sure they were talking to superiors from both companies at the home strip to get some sound advice on how to pull off this job. I talked to the Soc Trang aircraft commander, who had almost as much time in-country as I did, about whether he thought there was a prospect of pulling off this resupply, and he said he felt the same way I did. Maybe.

The Cobras came back on the air and said they were en route, and they *did* have a plan. The Lead sounded confident, which filled my heart with hope. Maybe they had collectively put their heads together at Vinh Long and proposed a definite idea. As I anxiously awaited their landing, I was gaining confidence by the minute. Meanwhile, I was told I could have Super Sabre jet aircraft from Ben Thuy if I wanted them. Wow, I was getting pretty egotistical. Nobody had ever offered me jet-fighter support before, and I was getting to think this was a very important moment after all. An immense thunderstorm was brewing, which could eliminate this fighter support, but I was to stay tuned and let the FAC know if I wanted this air-strike capability. I told him OK and continued to await the return of the Cobra fire team.

When they landed, I hurried over and asked what their plan was and how many minds had participated in its formation. The young, tall lieutenant said, "Oh, just us. We thought it up on the runway while we were refueling." This wasn't what I had in mind at all, and I asked if any of the superior-ranking officers in either aviation company had been privy to the planning.

"Naw, just us. We thought it up among ourselves. It'll work."

My heart sank as the major watched the expression on my face. He started cranking up with, "Let's get a set of balls here, Lieutenant. You need some courage right now, Lieutenant! Let's get this bird cranked up and start acting like an Army aviator!"

What was this guy? Right out of some basic training camp? I let him know we were going to go and my courage was all right, and in the right place. Helpfully, he climbed in the back to add to the weight of the mound of ammo cans that already would be taxing Outlaw 23 on takeoff. Yes, I had the weakest ship in the platoon under me for this tough mission. My crew were with Outlaw 24 in PE maintenance at this very moment, taking care of the ship during its 100-hour inspection. The crew chief for 23 was meticulous with this ship and had a reputation for being so, but I don't think he thought too well of me yet. I was on his turf, and he kept the aircraft in such a spanking-clean condition that maybe anything would abuse it.

What the Cobras had in mind was for me to fly low-level, nearly blacked out except for my nav lights on steady-dim. I said OK to that. Parrott would follow me a few aircraft lengths behind. I was to follow compass heading instructions as they were given to me by the gunships. They would lead to a major treeline going right to the outpost. The plan was to swoop in over the VC positions before they even knew we had overflown them, settle down within the outpost's perimeter defenses, and discharge the cargo and men. As we took off, the thunderstorm commenced.

I didn't tell the Cobras that my radio magnetic indicators were out. The RMIs are the radio compasses that pivot around on the instrument panel and are far more stable for directional heading than a magnetic compass. This small backup relic is over on the right side of the instrument panel's dashboard, about knee high. Next, we discovered that the tiny light bulb illuminating it was burned out. I put Dean, my copilot, on this with a flashlight. I did think it peculiar that these two devices were out on such a superbly maintained ship. Just coincidence, I figured. I sure needed them to follow the Cobras' instructions over the radio. I decided to give it my best shot and play it cool and confident as we zipped across the nighttime rice paddies, startling those peasants still out there tending their water buffalo or whatever it was they were doing as we buzzed past them. They were probably amazed at seeing such flying fools so close up in their helicopters.

As we headed northwesterly across paddies, I told Dean not to let me deviate even five degrees from that compass heading on which he was holding his flashlight. He didn't. He was calling off any departures from the heading when I told him to stop because he was the only voice I was hearing in my earphones, and I needed to listen to the Cobras. I wasn't using the map at all; I was trusting the Cobras to give me the proper headings as I hurriedly cruised down the treetops of one canal line that would lead to the main one to the outpost itself.

Suddenly the thunderstorm became a complete deluge, and I was having trouble even seeing out the windshield at all. We never turned on the windshield wipers in the Huey, because that just screwed up the Plexiglas something awful. Forever after that, we would have to fly with all those scratches reflecting the sunshine. So, it just wasn't done, and it probably wouldn't have helped very much anyway. The heavy raindrops splattered all over the windshield, and I realized the jet strikes never could have happened. We were on our own to pull this off.

The Cobras gave me the next heading, which was to the southwest, 240 degrees. I was racing across the tops of the trees, and could sense their limbs reaching up to the belly of the Huey. I could intuitively feel their presence and perceive precisely where they were, because I sure couldn't see anything. I was in somebody else's hands at that moment, operating on sheer faith; complete intuition was guiding the ship. Another heading change and the ship sped on toward the outpost with the Cobras behind and even lower than we were. One gunship was on each side of the canal's treeline, flying nearly level with rice paddies on both sides of it. Parrott was following me to my rear and close. The darkness of the thunderstorm was above, pelting rain.

Suddenly the outpost appeared, sooner than I had expected. Four smudge pots marked the landing spot, and I knew there could be no go-around. I screamed, "Flare, One-Eight!" and did the same for my aircraft. Outlaw 23 shot straight up to 100 feet as I went instantly from 80 knots of airspeed to none. With all the deceleration I could muster, there still was no way to keep the Huey from climbing as I zeroed out the airspeed. As we came to a 100-foot hover, I knew there was no possibility we could save the ship. Maybe walk away without a broken back, but no way to land the thing safely. We started losing RPM as the descent began. The needles were now straight up and way out of the green range over at the two-o'clock side of the gauge where they were supposed to be. Dean noticed and screamed, "You're losing RPM!"

"I know it, goddammit!" I shot back. "There's nothing we can do about it!"

As the aircraft approached the ground, I felt for this turf and pulled all the pitch I had, like a hovering autorotation. It worked. The engine made funny "hoom-hoom-hooming" sounds as I pulled off everything still left. We smooshed onto the ground, and it was not even a bad hovering autorotation! Felt just like a good one! The tail boom was resting over a barbed-wire fence, and the tail rotor was chewing up a small palm tree back there. The crew and the cantankerous major were shoving out all the .30-caliber ammo boxes like a shipwrecked crew bailing water from their sinking life raft.

The Cobras were expending all the munitions they had in a blaze of light and thunder. The fire team was rotating round and round on their gun runs' daisy chain, pouring it on the outpost with everything they had. They were also hosing me. Tracers were bouncing up from the ground all around my aircraft, and the immense firepower was lighting up the outpost's fortified walls as though it were a million-candlepower flare drop. Bullets ricocheted off the small fort, and I could imagine all the terrified Vietnamese inside hugging the floor, desperately waiting this one out. Rockets whooshed all around, and one even went right under my rotor disc, between the blades and the ground in front of the cowling. The light was blinding, the noise deafening. Acrid smoke from the exploding ordnance filled the outpost area and drifted toward our aircraft in eerie, multicolored hues through the tracer-lit darkness.

"Stop firing! You're gonna kill me! Cease fire, you're gonna get me, too!"

"Have we hit you yet? Have we hit you?" came back the reply from the lieutenant flying the Cobra fire team Lead.

"No, but you're gonna!" was my response.

"OK, then, if we haven't then we'll keep firing," said the young lieutenant.

Well, there wasn't much more I could do after that but sit there and take it! I was on the wrong end of a gunship attack. The Cobras expended all their ammo in five minutes, and it was an impressive sight to witness, with a carnival-like aura. The night sky was completely lit up with all their rocket and minigun ammo. Rounds were going everywhere, and I don't know to this day which ones were theirs and which might have been the surrounding seven VC automatic-weapons positions helping put on the show. It was garish and ghastly to experience. Finally, my crew said we were empty, and I radioed that I was coming out. I began to pull pitch to get the Huey back up into the sky, gingerly testing what I had to operate with. Everything came loose and still worked. I pulled a section of concertina wire when I came out, but it fell off OK. I climbed out to the pitch-black sky of the southeast, and the Cobras asked where I was at that point.

"What's your location, 23?"

"I'm heading outbound on a heading of 135," I said.

I was noting the quietness of the dark, calm air after the horrendous explosive noise that had engulfed us just seconds ago. I wanted to calm people down after completing our successful mission, and I struck a tone that indicated I knew where I was going.

Dean's eyes were observing me, so he turned on his flashlight and checked the magnetic compass by his right knee. There it was, 135 degrees glued on the little thing. His stunned return look was utmost in its respect; I could sense it across the cockpit. He knew there was no way I could get a glimpse at the device to read this heading. It was way over there, *and* the light was out. I had simply taken a lucky guess, knowing what the numbers were for southeast; that was generally the direction I was climbing out in.

"That was *some* flying, Eastman," he whispered in total awe.

"That was outstanding, Lieutenant! That was outstanding!" The now-exuberant major was backslapping me from the rear of my seat; he was beside himself with excitement and glee. I'd made him happy.

"You deserve the DFC for that, Lieutenant Eastman," said Grant, the door gunner, and I *knew* he knew what he was talking about. He was the most experienced man on the ship other than me. The stocky, black-haired crewman had seen a lot of action, especially when flying with Colonel Dempsey when he was still alive. He also told me at this moment that they had been kicking out a lot of the ammo cans on the way down when we were at that stupendous high hover. That had certainly helped the load at touchdown. I thanked him for that good thinking, lightening the ship's weight.

I couldn't believe we hadn't wrecked the ship, and again I had amazed respect for the Huey D-model. It had saved our lives once more, despite our efforts to beat it up. I called for the Soc Trang ship and asked for his whereabouts. He said he was up at altitude just past my 10 o'clock position. When I looked, I could spot him up against the black night sky. The thunderstorm was over, and we could see again. I told him he was probably released and could go home for the night. He replied he thought so too, and he bade adieu.

"Nice working with ya," was his final call before he switched off.

I landed the major, who was ecstatic about our success. His demeanor toward me had changed completely. I was used to working for these ground-pounders; when you pleased them in executing a mission, they were all smiles. He got out, happy as could be, and we departed for Vinh Long. The Cobras had already pulled off station; Parrott and I were going home together. Jim later informed me that he had done a tight, hard-banked, complete 360 instead of flaring. When he landed, the Vietnamese wouldn't get out of his ship; they were frozen in terror. He had to work hard to get them to exit the aircraft. I was thankful I had only had ammo on board for my tense moments.

Upon landing, and shutting down the old aircraft that had once been mine, I apologized to the crew chief for scratching up the skids. The shiny, black enamel he had just put on showed the scratch marks of the concertina wire we had perched in, and I'd dragged out on takeoff. He said it was all right; he would just paint over it again.

"This used to be my aircraft, you know. I've done a lot of things with it."

"Yessir, I do know that. I heard you used to be the AC of 23."

"Well, sorry again that I scratched it up. You are taking good care of it."

With that, I zippered up my helmet bag and walked off that ramp toward Operations. When I got inside, blinking in the hot lights of the room, I saw the new Outlaw 6, Major "Smokey" Barnett, sitting by the UHF radio with Major Jim O'Neill, who had been promoted to be our new XO. They looked as if they had been listening to the Red Sox game. We had chosen Outlaw UHF as our frequency for the operation; no one else was using it at the time. It never occurred to me that the brass might have been listening in to the whole show.

"You didn't have to do it, East. You didn't have to do it," says Major O'Neill.

"Now you tell me!" I fired back.

Major Barnett, being new to the unit, was looking over at me with considerable respect. I told them both that Sa Dec had said they had given complete approval to the mission. They informed me they had never heard a word of it until they picked up my show on the radio! Wouldn't you know it?

"Well, I guess I gave you your night's entertainment! Now I'm going to get a cold beer!" I picked up my helmet bag and made for the club.

"Go right ahead. You deserve it!" said Major Barnett.

38

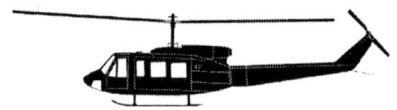

THE MAGNIFICENT SEVEN ARE GOING HOME

I WAS GETTING "SHORT." Homeward bound was actually about to happen to me. I even had a short-timer's calendar made up for my last 30 days, and I was coloring in the footprints of a cartoon character leading to my departure. I had not really anticipated surviving Vietnam, so the opportunity to leave the place seemed foreign to me; I didn't even know if I wanted it. This lifestyle had been thoroughly pleasant for me compared to what had been broadly projected by all those fearing it. I began to understand how a career military officer might feel about outstanding assignments like this. Going home was bringing mixed emotions to me, and I kept quiet about them. I enjoyed too much what we all were to each other. I had lots of friends in both companies. In fact, I had just recorded "Sergeant Pepper's Lonely Hearts Club Band," the new Beatles LP, over in the Knights compound because one of the young warrants had a turntable there. This enabled me to make a crystal-clear copy of the popular album and carry it with me Stateside on my reel-to-reel tape deck. He had been especially helpful at providing a free copy of this marvelously engineered album. I can still see his smile for doing so; he was the same black-haired warrant flying with the Red Knight AC who blew up his ship when landing on the minefield at Chi Lang airstrip. I never let him live that one down.

We would often wander around with a drink in our hands, visiting other units across the Vinh Long compound. It was home to all of us, and a lot of friends existed in those various hooches. There were a lot of high jinks because we were young men. One morning, for instance, I woke up to see something funny on the water tower the base used in purifying water. We were one of the few places in Vietnam that had its own water works; nonpotable water was the rule in most places. The orange-hued tower looked somehow different this particular morning. I put up the Manon binoculars I had purchased for $17 at the Cholon PX and saw what the drunken Mavericks had painted on the tank the previous night. In sloshes of yellow paint, it read, "See Rock City. Outlaws and Mavericks. The Best." Putting down the binoculars, I wondered what the story of this outing would be.

Over at the club, everyone had gotten a view of this lurid accomplishment. There were a few laughs over the incident, but Major O'Kane said it best when he stated, "Now get them drunk enough to go back up there again and paint over it!"

Maj. Robert F. O'Kane left about a month before I did, and when he surprised me down at Can Tho one afternoon, saying that he was leaving that day, I was stunned about the short notice. We'd already had the Outlaw change-of-command party, giving out the plaques, and we'd gotten drunk out of our minds, but I did not know the exact time he was leaving for the States. He was back in his old bumbly sort of understated demeanor, which was not his command stature at all. He was seated in the back of Stansbury's Huey, Outlaw 25, when he leaned over and said, "Good-bye, Dave."

I said something to the effect of what a great pleasure it had been to serve with him, and he just sort of pshawed the whole thing off. I asked him where he was going, and he said, "Rucker. They'll probably make an IP out of me again." With that, they were ready to pull pitch after talking to the tower, and I backed off from the ship.

Standing on the Can Tho apron, I watched as the Huey lifted up to a hover and began taxiing to the active runway. He waved once more from the door gunner's seat, and I returned the gesture.

Then I snapped into the sharpest salute I have ever mustered and held it as the aircraft turned onto the main runway. He waved at my military farewell in jestful embarrassment, but I held the stiff salute until the aircraft was well along on its takeoff and finally became just a dot in the sky as it climbed to the north. Then I turned and walked back to my aircraft, knowing a grand episode had just ended. He was a fine man.

The seven of us who had graduated from flight school class 66-14 decided we would give a going-away party to the rest of the compound that would have no equal. Jack Payne thought up the idea of buying up all the champagne bottles the Delta had to offer, and we were all to do this, purchasing any and all of the bubbly wherever we found it. This started about a week ahead of the party date, and we loaded up the Mekong Manor officers' club refrigerators with the bottles as we procured them. It came to a total of approximately 62 champagnes in various bottles and labeling.

We put up a sign saying that the "Magnificent Seven" were leaving and that a compound-wide party would be held between the two companies and the champagne was on us for the evening. The seven included Troy Tison, Jack Payne, Mike Hershey, Roger Kalinger, Jimmy Redmon, Stets, and me. Come the appointed night, there was not much action around the club, so I went over and hung out with Jimmy Redmon in his Knight hooch room until something developed. Jack got wind of this, called us on the phone, and told us to get over there: "Let's get this thing going!" "OK," I said, and moved out the door to the club.

What started slowly soon picked up some real momentum. I had never seen so many people get so drunk so quickly, all at once. We would pop the cork off a bottle of champagne, pour it out over many waiting glasses, and then open another. Troy thought up the idea of trying to hit the happy-hour bell with the self-propelled cork exploding out of each bottle. He started playing "Dong Tam Control," the voice of the artillery advisory out of the new Ninth Division base on the Mekong just down the river. We had never had artillery firing in the Delta, so it was a new and unique thing to experience. Troy would get the call sign of the new man opening the champagne bottle and scream, "This is Dong Tam Artillery! We have artillery firing from Outlaw 25 to the bell!" Then the person in question would aim the cork at the old Navy bell that was rung only when someone bought a round for everybody in the bar. (If you rang it by accident, or walked into the club with a weapon on, you did the same.) We wanted to hit that fabled bell! As we proceeded through many of the bottles, nobody had hit the brass bell *yet!* The cork would soar right past the bell, and the foaming champagne would quickly flow over the waiting glasses and be emptied once more. After a while, people were completely falling down and broken glasses were littering the floor. New arrivals at the party kept replacing those who no longer could keep their feet. Giggling aviators were flopping around on the floor like turtles. The champagne was beginning to cover the floor, making it incredibly slick for those who couldn't stand up very well anyway. Some of the "Magnificent Seven" began a cancan dance, looking like the Rockettes at their worst. In general, everyone was quite happily drunk and getting worse.

There were still many bottles to go. We had passed the 50-bottle mark, but more aviators were coming through the door and joining the party. I've never seen more people ridiculously drunk at the same time and enjoying themselves to the fullest. Many men remained in a somewhat sitting position because they could no longer attain the vertical. Broken champagne glasses continued to litter the floor, now a few inches deep with spilled beverage. Shards of glass were sticking out of some men's knees and palms. Troy was still bellowing out Dong Tam Artillery advisories, and call signs were still appearing with empty glasses to drain the next opened bottle.

Finally, Stets could stand it no more. Nobody had hit the sacred happy-hour bell with a champagne cork. So he went up and punched "that dumb ol' bell." It flew off its hook and into the arms of some guy from the Navy yard. He looked at this prize, put it under his arm like a football, and ran out the door of the club. Nobody stopped him; we were all in a drunken glaze and not very movable.

At this point, someone threw a red smoke grenade into the club itself. After all the smoke we had landed to, it was amazing what a great amount of smoke could come out of that grenade in close quarters. It billowed and billowed, filling the room with dense, pungent smoke until no one could see. People tried to make it to the door but couldn't find it. I dropped down on all fours, employing a fireman's technique to find the clear air beneath the smoke. I found about 18 inches of visible air there, and I was encouraging others from my drunken state to follow my example. I could see nothing but knees and hairy calves leading down to rubber flip-flops, in great multitudes. But I could also see the door. I was moving towards it, crying, "Follow me!" when the Cobra first lieutenant I'd worked with reached down and grabbed me by the back of my collar, thinking *I* needed some real help.

"I'm OK. I'm trying to help you! I don't need any help!" I hollered up at him.

"You'd better come outside with me; I'll get you to the grass," said the Cobra lieutenant.

The lawn outside the club was filled with escapees from the smoke-grenade attack. Everyone wondered who had thrown the thing. Most immediately suspected the gunship guys, particularly the nearby Cobra gun platoon. Eventually the air cleared somewhat, and we got back inside the club. There were still a few bottles of champagne left in the refrigerator, but the club officers played stern bartender and told us the party was over. I insisted that the champagne bottles belong to us, and they could hand them over if they didn't want anything more to do with our celebration. I got one.

The following day, everything hit the fan. Stets came zipping into my room about 4:30 A.M. and said, "East. East! They're pissed! They are really pissed!" Then he went running back out in the semidarkness. I called after him, "Are they really pissed?" The response came back through the gray stillness, "YES! They are really pissed!" He was talking about "the majors," of course. The two air conditioners in the club had completely burned out, suffocated by the contents of the smoke grenade. All the new white vinyl furniture was now pink. So were the walls. Even the mess side of the wall had been affected by that grenade. We had no idea those things were so potent! That thing had a real knockout punch.

Hershey was put in charge of getting money from the rest of us to pay for the damages. We negotiated what that amount should be and got it down to about $10 or $15 each. The powers-that-be agreed that was sufficient and let it go. Nobody ever again pulled a party like that one at Vinh Long. It remained in everyone's memories for a very long while.

Suddenly, our year's tour of duty in Vietnam had come to a close.

39

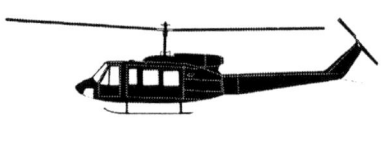

"Deros"

WHEN THE DAY CAME FOR US TO DEPART FOR BIEN HOA for the long flight home, the guys woke me up before they left for the day's mission. I awoke to the racket of all the second platoon pilots lifting me out of my bunk. This totally startled me—coming from a deep sleep—and I was unprepared for their idea of a joke. Suddenly the room was filled with chicken-plated aviators in jungle fatigues, with grins on their faces, all tearing me from my covers in my fuzzy consciousness. I was too surprised to express any feelings adequately, but they had enjoyed scaring the wits out of me. I groggily said good-bye as best I could, and they all went out the door enjoying the fact that they had pulled a good one on me. In my stunned condition, I could hardly react to their affectionate farewell. It just couldn't be true that this was my last day in-country—DROS (date return overseas, or, as we said it, "DEROS").

We ate breakfast at the club and got out our stuff for the trip to Bien Hoa. A bird was waiting out on the Outlaw ramp for our trip up to the other side of Saigon. I was at a loss for feelings. I sat there in the Jeep not really knowing what to do in this state of mind. It was not the mood I had anticipated. Our Vietnamese hooch maids sat there in their funny perching squat while they polished the platoon members' black combat boots and jungle boots. We had all grown close to them; they asked: "You go home now?" I simply nodded my head, and could not even go over and give them a hug good-bye. This was a trifle sad and mysterious for them too, because I used to crack them up with a smooch and an embrace as I left for the ship every day. They knew, or had learned, that I was acting like some gray-flannel-suit commuter from Long Island leaving his wife for the day. We would play this up as a great comedy. They had a funny way of snickering.

"Good bye, dear. Say hello to the kids when they get up. Have a great morning. I'll be home, at say, . . . oh, about five o'clock?"

This always caused them to go into absolute giggles and cackle all over the place. They thought it hilarious to play out some cultural game from the other side of the world, and they would slap me away with ineffectual pushes, understanding the game all the way, They would try to come back with some words of their own, like "good bye, dear, I work too. Yoo goe fly now!" But usually they would break up and couldn't even get through the act; it struck them as oh-so-funny.

This day, I could not even move from the jeep and say good things to them for the last time. They peered at me from their peculiar perching squats as they went on polishing the combat boots. I felt badly I couldn't do something more appropriate.

All that morning, I was remorseful, surprising myself. After all this time of waiting, nothing was as expected .

After such a tremendous year, there was no joy in me for my last day at this special place. I was homesick before I even left Vinh Long. The hooch girls kept observing me as I sat there, and asked again, "You go home today?" I nodded and still couldn't do more. They watched me in sad confusion.

We got to the runway and started counting noses. Stets's girlfriend from the airfield commander's office was there, dressed up in a western-style business suit and carrying a white purse. She and Stets had been very close and had even spoken of getting married. But nothing had been resolved about that matter. Stets's eyes were very tender and hurt. He and Nguyet asked me to take their picture; Hershey joined in to make a threesome. In the slide,

Hershey looks like a typical GI, and has no idea of what the other two are feeling at that moment.

All of a sudden, out of the sky, the whole lift descended upon the Outlaw ramp for refueling! We would have a chance to say good-bye to all those we had flown with over the year and were now leaving behind. Crews hurriedly ran out to shake our hands as others remained on the controls and shut down the ships. The whole second platoon lined up for a shot, with a few from the first platoon in there with them. They looked like a motley crew of assorted personality types. I moved over with my cherished Outlaw 24 crew of Tommy Greenfield and Duane Liebe, and the pride we had of being together is still evident in those pictures. We look very proud of ourselves. I like being the guy I see in those shots with those two good kids. I thanked them for remaining with me until I left; they were going over to the Mavericks due to their being such high quality EM. They had already been accepted, but had pledged to stay as my crew until my departure. They acknowledged my praise and thanks.

All went back to their flight crew business as we climbed aboard Outlaw 18 and took off for the last time. As the Huey lifted high above the Vinh Long compound and airstrip, I asked that the door remain open as long as possible. We circled as we climbed up to 2,500 feet of altitude, and they kept the sliding cabin door back longer than usual. I just kept gazing at the scene below, knowing I would never see it again. I wanted to paint it into my brain, imprinting that familiar runway far below as I would never be able to forget it. I didn't know how anyone else would ever see the place in their life's history, but it would never leave my memory as one of the best young manhood experiences I had ever had. Finally the crew said they *had* to shut the door, and I looked up front at those flying; their heads were crooked back, waiting for me to let them proceed. I nodded and waved my finger at them as a signal. They moved their helmeted heads affirmatively, the doors slid forward, and we went on. I sighed deeply, slumped back in my seat, and watched the EM regard me with some degree of somber fascination. I don't know if anyone else would ever depart Vinh Long with as much sad, heartsick emotion as I did, but I wouldn't be surprised to hear about it. That wonderful moment, this peaking experience of the Vietnam War that was 1966 through 1967, was over.

40

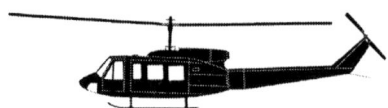

Epilogue

After flying out of Bien Hoa with Jack Payne, and landing in Travis Air Force Base about 18 hours later, we all scattered to the various regions of the United States for 30 days of leave in our hometowns. Some of us then went to Fort Wolters, Texas, to teach in the primary phase of the Army's rotary-wing flight school. Others went to Fort Rucker in Alabama, and we didn't see many of those guys from the unit again. A few more were assigned to Hunter-Stewart in Savannah, Georgia. Thirty-eight of us from the Outlaws eventually were assigned to Fort Wolters, and we had many a beer party; water skiing on Possum Kingdom Lake was the major theme in these fun reunions. Mike Hershey was splendid on one ski behind Tommy Mitchell's red-and-white runabout. Those wives who got along with each other organized the smaller social outings, when we were broken down into three- or four-couple gatherings. For the most part, the women could not understand how come we remained as fascinated with each other's company as we did, always wanting all 38 of the men to be together as often as we could arrange a gathering. Jon Myhre came down from Walter Reed with his crutches for one big Outlaw party at Ray Leuty's; his copilot Jim Martinson was there, too. Compassion and mutual joy reigned that day.

Ever since that time, none of us have ever bonded as effectively with other aviators or various other units. We didn't feel it in our instructor flights, or in the guard or reserve units we eventually joined for the joy of flying the Huey again in our state militias.

Some of us tried commercial work—for the most part, that was a horrid experience—before moving on to better aviation possibilities. Occasionally we would see someone from the Vinh Long crowd in these flying jobs that were in the most boondocky places in the world. Some chopper pilots stayed with it, however, and prospered in due time with the right job. Those who stayed in the service for a career came to realize we had been together at a bright, alive, and vivid moment in the otherwise sordid history of the Vietnam War. Some, such as Jon Myhre, Mike Hershey, Norm Marshall, Bob Millward, and Jim Hardbeck, had two or three tours there. No assignment ever matched that period with the Outlaws. All of us agreed, with 20-20 hindsight, that there was never again a time like we had at Vinh Long in those years of 1966 and 1967. Others, such as Joe Moffett and Mark Howell, spent much of their military careers overseas and therefore avoided a great deal of the hassle between war protesters and veterans that the rest of us encountered.

There are, of course, many stories left out of this recount. WE had to do everything with helicopters that the Air Force was failing to do with close-in air support the old Army Air Corps had been famous for in the past.

When the Air Force was initially still landing at Vinh Long with the Caribous to provide food and supplies, a Caribou hit the tail rotor of one of the parked Hueys alongside the runway. It messed up the Huey from the deck back and tore the de-icing boot on the Air Force's Caribou. Major Casper went down to the runway and looked over the site of the collision. He heard the Air Force pilot say he would be removed from flying status and his career would be ended if this incident got back to his command. Acting as airfield commander, Casper got Bob Millward to look over the damaged Huey. The rotund little major said he could fix it without any report. The Air Force pilot said he could get his maintenance officer to repair the boot without an accident report. The matter was dropped at Vinh Long, but the Air Force never flew any missions into Vinh Long after that. We had to go to Binh Thuy and Can Tho to pick up the stuff they dropped off; meanwhile, food requiring refrigeration spoiled in the sun. At least our mail didn't. We all made do until the runway was rebuilt to their specifications.

We, however, were not without sin, either. In one of the frustrating scenarios during that time, the compound was trying to scrounge up a pizza oven. Another Mikuchonis feat of swapping occurred. I mean, the Mekong Manor needed this to be complete, right? Casper wanted to wait until he could get a CH-47 Chinook to carry the negotiated item down from Saigon. He didn't trust the sling-loading hooks on our Hueys because we never used the things in the Delta. He was legitimately afraid they would fail the mission. Several warrant officers volunteered their ships anyway. One who did, of course with great enthusiasm and initiative, was John Savelli. En route back to Vinh Long, he dropped the oven. It had begun to oscillate, and it is debatable whether he punched it off inadvertently or not. The Mavericks and another slick rushed out in an attempt to retrieve what was left of the oven, in hopes of repairing it. There was a crater where the heavy oven had gone into a rice paddy with a big plop, and buried itself. Or had the VC had beaten us to it? It was quickly gone, and we all speculated about whether the guerrillas had ever gotten it working for their own benefit . . . . VC pizzas in the jungle? Savelli was so embarrassed that he would not land. He circled around and around the Vinh Long airfield at altitude because he could not bear to face the music when he landed. He knew how much shit he'd have to take. All of us on the ground watched him flying around up there until he was nearly out of fuel. Eventually he had to come down and face the ridicule of his friends. His humorous attempt to duck the issue provided more laughs than his failure to fly the pizza oven safely home.

The 1968 Tet Offensive occurred during a few days in late January, two to three months after my departure. It was stunning to see stars on the map of Vietnam behind the leading TV network anchors, as they talked in detail about what was happening in those places that had been our homes for a year. The men of Vinh Long fought the VC at point-blank range. I have never encountered anyone who was involved in that historic surprise attack who did not kill someone very close, and often in hand-to-hand combat. For those over there enduring Tet, the rumors were terrifying as they circulated among the men. What could possibly still happen to these aviators-turned-infantrymen after the night of the initial attack around the Vinh Long runway? It was Ray Novotney who first surprised VC sappers putting satchel charges in the helicopters on the Outlaw ramp. Checking out the aftermath of the first mortar attack, his maintenance Jeep was machine-gunned to a stop; he leapt from it and dove into the water between the main runway and the ramp. Others I knew did the same trick at Can Tho, where waterholes existed along the airstrips.

The airfield commander was killed, along with Sergeant Newton in the second Jeep, as they were bent on investigating the defensive perimeter and damage to the ships parked on the Outlaw ramp; Novotney was not able to wave them off from where he was seeking cover. The new lieutenant colonel was following procedure laid down from the times of Major Casper; the airfield commander was "supposed to report to the command bunker near the airstrip." This was probably the origin of the pile of sandbags that Carson Snow climbed into after his own debacle. It just so happened, however, that during the Tet Offensive the VC who had worked on the compound were already in it; they knew of this command obligation better than the rest of us did. They shot everybody who retreated into this now completed command bunker, even the hangar maintenance personnel. Those men running to its cover had been instructed to do so; it was thought that the VC already inside were friendlies who were panic-stricken and firing on their own American buddies. That naiveté cost some people their lives. Three of the EM sent to the Outlaw ramp soon thereafter heroically cleared the VC from the revetments between the parked ships, where the enemy had been placing Chinese hand grenades in and under the Hueys' fuel cells. One was Gary Cox from Outlaw 11, Stets's old ship. He provided a startling recount of the rescue, and it seems that these crewmen made pretty good infantrymen when given the chance to play Audie Murphy.

A wounded or dead VC was often found on a chopper's pad, a rifle still in his hands. The impromptu grunts/first platoon crew members threw grenades and used their M-60s to get the enemy out of a small bunker at the west end of the Outlaw ramp. Cox reported that more men then came to help pick up the wounded after this job was done. He noted that one of the Mavericks getting cranked up took a direct hit from mortar fire as it started to lift off. Occasional fire erupted continuously from the perimeter. It was a very crazy time, and many performed bravely.

Hearing about the death of Lieutenant Colonel Thompson, the fallen airfield commander, Vance Shearer crawled up to where Major Barnett was huddled with others alongside the wall of our beautiful library and informed Barnett (for some reason known only to Shearer) that the major was now the ranking officer of the compound and as such the new airfield commander.

"I am the ranking officer, I must be the airfield commander," said Barnett.

"Right, you are now the airfield commander," said Shearer, and crawled away.

Then he crawled back and said to "Smokey" Barnett, "Hey, this is just like in the movies, isn't it?"

"Yeah," went the senior major, "it *is* just like in the movies!"

In the end, 16 men were killed, along with a number of injured; the Viet Cong lost 98 killed, with a dozen or so captured. Some got away, but some of those who didn't were found to be Vinh Long compound employees. Gary Cox reported in a letter written many years later to one of our second platoon crew chiefs, Ray Roth, that the group included the Vietnamese woman who ran the PX. She was serving as a VC sergeant. Cox's hooch maid and her 14-year-old son were also among the enemy troops that night. His vivid recounting of that first night's attack is now available on the Outlaw web page. Tin Thanh, the downtown tailor who made our Outlaw and Knight shirts, was found dead up around Sa Dec after the Tet Offensive; he was said to have been a VC colonel during the effort. That sure makes his label in many an Outlaw shirt worth something as a collectible.

A lot of the guys acted like gung-ho combat grunts during those three days, and it was all pretty hairy. We had to wait for them to rotate home to tell us their gory stories. Some pilots DEROS-ed right in the middle of it; they had to scramble on board anything that would take him out of there at Vinh Long. I think some jumped into the maw of a C-130 that was nervously taking off! They eventually joined us at flight school. Then the Tet Offensive veterans fit into the Stateside routine of fishing together with us and going out to dinner in Fort Worth or Dallas and the many other things we found to do in a more peaceful setting. We looked forward to a year of rest, but the country was having none of that in 1968.

As instructor pilots in an isolated Texas Army post, we watched political events that we didn't quite understand spiral upward to a tense climax in the country that year of 1968. (Mineral Wells, Texas, could have been the movie set for *HUD*, or *The Last Picture Show*.) George Wallace, Spiro Agnew, riots in "Bombingham"—after Martin Luther King's assassination, then Bobby Kennedy's which followed soonafter. Earlier, LBJ wouldn't accept renomination when he comprehended the Vietnam War could not be won. Hadn't *we* been the ones through the worst? There seemed to be a hell of a lot happening "out there," and we didn't have an inkling of why it was developing. Students were rioting in city squares and waving the Viet Cong flag—how come? Hadn't that enemy been shooting at us? We began thinking maybe we ought to get out of the Army and find out what was happening in civilian life. As young military pilots all of 21 to 24 years old, we still regarded ourselves as "the young people" of America. We were learning about Janis Joplin, Otis Redding, and Jimmy Hendrix, too. But now it seemed, we were already being displaced by a generation we had yet to know. We began to realize perhaps we had departed this society more than we knew.

We taught many students how to fly helicopters so they could survive Vietnam as well as we had. After a while, the number of these helicopter pilots tripled from the time when we had gone through flight school. Standards were being lowered far too much.

There were three times as many helicopters in units in Vietnam as well. The war built up and then backed down as the country went nuts about its involvement in this little Third World country. Nobody ever asked our opinion about the experience; they just knew we had been at risk doing a dangerous job. We already knew that. It had become our legacy, but we got out of the Army as fast as we could in 1969 following our year or so of flight instructing.

Most of the guys have done very well in life. I doubt the "Vietnam vet stereotype" fits us much, if it fits at all the majority of veterans who very capably survived this obscene war. Hippies thought up that stereotype, I fear. Tommy Mitchell and Jim Parrott are both airline captains, making $200,000 a year flying jumbo jets. Mike Hershey had to buy a Citation jet for his bank; Terry McDowell runs a fine airport in Chattanooga where every spiffy biz-jet in that area wants to hangar. Harvey Persyn is a world-renowned shrimp aquaculture expert whom the Third World will not allow to retire. Dwayne Williams is a superb chief test pilot with Bell Helicopter in Fort Worth. Ray Novotney negotiates the perils of remaining constantly with Boeing; he builds 767s. Jack Mankin supervises the flying of two Lear jets; Ron Petty sells Ruger shooting ammo and gear to the hunting community. Ray Leuty is impossibly busy running the only umpire training school in the country. Colonels Casper, Millward, Meehan, Mark Howell, Jim Huey, and Joe Moffett successfully retired after careers in the Army. Nobody knows where O'Kane is . . . or Stansbury, or Tominey, or Dickie Hyde. Fred Stetson and I are the poorest of the lot, mainly because we choose to be writers of the New England scene. (We'll catch up . . . .) Bob Lakey and Jim Martinson have their own aircraft to play with. Norris Marshall, J.R. Wright, and Andy Keeney have already retired; so have some of the others. The dedicated EM crew members we enjoyed on our aircraft call up from time to time; they're OK, too. Reuniting is joyful; even if taking years to accomplish.

For all the famous helicopter pilots of that Vietnam era,

nobody stands taller than Jerry Daly. If ever there is a movie made about a specific hero of Army Aviation, it should be about him. He was a stalwart of the Soc Trang Vikings for some time, and it's easy to recognize somebody who flew with that outfit then, by their constant referral to his tactics: "Jerry Daly said to do this.... Jerry Daly said never to do that.... Jerry Daly said always to do...." Other flying servicemen, even outside of the Army, who encountered him sometime in combat were deeply impressed. The rest of us just say to these pilots, "Yup, that was Jerry Daly." He survived all the travails of the Vietnam War, even Lam Son 719 at the end. The 1999 Vietnam Helicopter Pilots Association Membership Directory contained an interesting anecdote about the 1972 Easter Offensive by the NVA. This is a bit long even for a Jerry Daly story, but it needs to be told to explain the essence of the man.

The Battle of Loc Ninh in April 1972 was going very badly. The NVA was using tanks extensively, and Cobra helicopters had to engage them with rockets to knock them out. Paris Radar, the flight following service, said, "Attention, all aircraft, this is Paris, on Guard. Loc Ninh is under tank and heavy infantry attack. Any aircraft with armament, please respond." The hunter-killer teams of the Cav units responding had *beaucoup* hours fighting in Lam Son 719 in Laos, but this fighting was more intense than any they had ever seen. In the write-up in the annual 1999 VHPA directory, Ron Timberlake reported on incidents witnessed over the next few days as the Cobra gunships used rockets left over even from the Korean War in this high-threat environment. More than 7,000 communist soldiers were killed in the three-day battle—which occurred when the Americans were mostly tooling down and packing up to go home.

On 9 April, the main battle shifted to An Loc and continued into June. The first tanks killed by helicopters during the Spring Offensive were destroyed by multiple hits from 17-pound HE (High Explosive) warheads fired from extremely close range. Timberlake's story continued:

> Within only a day or two, the rearm pads at Lai Khe and

Song Be had small stocks of 2.75 inch rockets with warheads few of the pilots had seen or used, High Explosive Anti-Tank, or HEAT. Manufacture date of these Korean War–era warheads was 1953, when they were used by fixed-wing attack aircraft. The only upgrade was to mate them to current rocket motors with canted nozzles, instead of motors designed to be fired at high speeds, so these little six-pound warheads were propelled by the same rocket motors as the heavier warheads.

That resulted in impressive velocity and trajectory for pilots accustomed to shooting 17-pound warheads, but terminal effects did not satisfy those who needed the bursting radius of the 17-pounders. Against armor, HEAT usually made deadly little holes, but they were all but useless for other types of targets, so they were not favored by the Cobra pilots in the cavalry troops.

The senior advisor at An Loc did not think the helicopters would have any effect on the Soviet T-54 tanks arrogantly driven by the NVA through the defenses. The Cobras, however, did the deed, the colonel observed: "The Cobras were our salvation." His riveting comments served to attract the attention of every senior Army officer concerning the role that armed helicopters would now have as tank killers forthwith.

Why am I relating this tale that happened well after my departure? Because within days of this significant tank engagement, a newly developed and far more effective antitank warhead was delivered to the attack helicopters fighting near An Loc. Arriving in-country on 15 April with a manufacture date of that very month, the High Explosive Dual Purpose (HEDP) was introduced and combat tested. By actual experience during that month, the warhead was found to be able to penetrate a T-54 series tank from all directions, as promised. On soft targets, it provided the same antipersonnel effects as a normal 10-pound HE warhead, and it was the perfect compromise to engage armor, vehicles, and personnel. Timberlake continued with his directory committee's 1999 historical recount of the "Easter Offensive of 1972 to the War's End":

> The new rounds were accompanied by a field grade officer on temporary duty from CONUS, whose duties included ensuring that the rockets were made available to the correct units, briefing the pilots on the warhead's capabilities, and learning of the results. I briefly met that officer at Lai Khe in April of 1972, and in preparing this history, I was surprised to be contacted by Father Jerome R. Daly, of Saint John's Catholic Church in McLean, VA. That's quite a change of pace for a man whose call sign with the 235th in Vietnam was "Devil 6."

Jerry Daly had been promoted to a direct commission of captain after my tour, and he was a major at this appearance. Some know he has since been ordained as a Catholic priest followng his military retirement. He mentioned in this correspondence that the HEAT round was past its shelf life and displayed a high dud rate, so his team at Picatinney Arsenal had been developing a new warhead with the armor penetration of the LAW (Light Antitank Weapon), and the antipersonnel and soft-target capability of the 10-pound HE warhead. When it was apparent that armor was a threat in this new offensive in the latter part of the Vietnam War, the team produced 1,000 of these new warheads in a four-day period, and Daly accompanied them to combat! He arrived in Vietnam on 15 April and determined that An Loc was where they were needed the most; he accompanied their delivery to Lai Khe. Daly flew combat missions with the F/79th, and he described in detail their engagement with tanks prior to his arrival. In his usual manner, he assessed the antiaircraft fire he experienced: "The anti-aircraft fire around An Loc was continual and impressive. Having been at Lam Son 719 last year, I can say that the fire was as high, and a bit higher around An Loc, as it was around some of the fire bases established by ARVN in Laos."

Later, after my tour, a few of my friends even served with Daly as their CO, including Jon Myhre, but no one I know quite understands his reasons for becoming a Catholic priest after so many impressive tours as a combat helicopter pilot and being honored as Army Aviator of the Year. It apparently is all in his past.

At the year 2000 VHPA convention in Washington, DC, the Soc Trang pilots had a mini-reunion and invited Daly to come in from his McLean, Virginia, parish. As usual, he declined—until the guys threatened to attack the church with gunships if he didn't come, and *then* they said they would all stand in line asking him to hear their confessions, which could take a lifetime. So he relented and came to the 17th annual reunion, his first, where Millward and others had their pictures taken with him. McDonald, Daly's copilot on Easter Sunday, was there.

He reported that their old shot-up D-model, "Viking Surprise," had been sent to the States for rebuilding, remaining in the active Army inventory after repairs. Then it had had served in the New Mexico and Arizona Army National Guard units for many a year as an H-model. In the Stateside retrofitting conversion, 130 hits were counted in ole 64-13670 from its Easter Sunday damage. When it became nonflyable in recent years, the guys obtained it privately as a monument and installed it on a pylon on a mountain in New Mexico. The New Mexico National Guard donated the venerable H-model to the Vietnam Veterans National Monument at Angel Fire. To commemorate what the Huey aircraft meant to the guys in Vietnam as a flying lifeline, Santa Fe architect Ted Luna decided to install it in a "soaring status" mode rather than displaying it grounded on a concrete pad. That Huey's last flight was on 27 July 1994, giving it a total flight time of 12,708 hours. At that July 2000 meeting, Jerry Daly was 70 years old. He had retired as a lieutenant colonel in 1988, the same year the old Huey had been moved from the regular Army to the Arizona National Guard.

By mid-June 1972, the Spring Offensive had been won, in that the NVA attack had been broken and the United States was continuing its withdrawal from the war. The armor battles around An Loc were essentially finished, although the missile war had begun, with surface-to-air missiles starting to be used against our aircraft. It is interesting to note that not a single Cobra gunship lost a tank engagement. Timberlake stated in his article that some Cobra rockets certainly missed their targets, but not one helicopter was destroyed by a tank, or even while engaging a tank. When the SAMs were used against the Cobra air crews, they were costly indeed, but even they could not prevail against the attack helicopter.

When the North Vietnamese walked away from the Paris peace table, President Richard Nixon stepped up the bombing in their country with a more effective target list than had previously existed, and he ordered the mining of Haiphong Harbor. Though late in the game, these actions brought immediate and positive reactions. But even as some of our soldiers fought battles of greater intensity than anyone had experienced previously in the Vietnam War, this country was continuing its policy of standing down entire units and bringing them home. One of them was the 175th Outlaws in 1972. It was almost five years later to the day of the Tet Offensive that the United States, the North Vietnamese, the South Vietnamese, and the Viet Cong—called the Provisional Revolutionary Government—officially signed a cease-fire accord. The political settlement was to follow. More American men died in the period between the end of Tet 1968 and this cease-fire date of 28 January 1973, than all those killed before this time.

It has been more than 32 years since we flew together. There have been so many attempts to duplicate this unique experience in our careers; we've never succeeded. It was the best year of our lives, say all, or at least one of the best. We stay linked by the telephone, and now by e-mail; and we visit each other, if we can make it. But we are so geographically dispersed. We want to travel and see each other as we age. The years go flying by, and the Vietnam Helicopter Pilots Association seems to be the only place to find one another. Never do enough of us show up, though. The beer flows and the Jack Daniels are consumed; no hotel can be adequately equipped for our consumption, it seems. We *do* try to warn them ahead of time. Many of the guys are working on their third wives; some times, I think they've finally found the right one. The women know whom they have in harness, and they have heard most of the stories. For those women who stuck with their men through all the time since Vietnam, there is a term—"O.W.," for Original Wife. We salute them as they do themselves, and I hope this book helps them to know what their husbands went through while they couldn't be with them over there. How nice it would be if we all had survived this intriguing experience well. See you at the next VHPA convention, or perhaps an Outlaw reunion?! We'd better do it soon; we are moving on in years . . . .

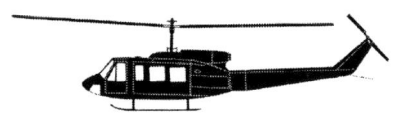

Glossary

AC: Aircraft commander. (If "a/c" is used, it means aircraft.)

AO: Area of operation.

APC: Armored personnel carrier. This lightly armored, tracked vehicle often didn't do too well operating in the muddy rice fields of the Delta, especially crossing canals. South Vietnamese Army units didn't utilize: them effectively in their mechanized infantry units.

Article 15: A reprimand in the military's docket, somewhat in the form of a minor court-martial. It is placed in an individual's personnel folder. Special and Summary Court-Martials are conducted for higher offenses.

ARVN: Army of the Republic of Vietnam. RF/PF's were similar, but even lower in formal military rankings, as these were the local militia in a Reaction Force/Popular Force design.

Ashy-trash: Relatively simple mission assignments usually only involving ferrying supplies and some personnel; usually not very challenging or: dangerous.

AWOL: Absent Without Leave. One step away from Desertion.

B-52: The Strategic Air Command (SAC) long-range heavy

bombers that were used in this war to devastate enemy ground troops and their hidden positions. Absolutely impressive with their tonnage and air strikes. They pulverized the ground in mile-long swathes. You could land a Huey within the width of the craters they created.

BOQ: Bachelor officers' quarters.

B-model: The second model Huey Bell made after the antiquated A-model. Pilots dearly loved it and often considered it the best flying ship of all the Hueys made.

"Big Red One": The First Infantry Division's nickname. Its patch featured a solid red number "1" against an olive-green background.

Branch: An assigned occupational subdivision of the U.S. Army: Infantry, Artillery, Transportation, Armor, Corps of Engineers, Intelligence, Ordnance, Chemical, Signal Corps, and so on.

Bug: Lightning Bug for short. Nighttime illumination missions that revealed the VC transporting themselves and their munitions under the cover of darkness. They were most active then to escape detection.

C-119: The "Flying Boxcar" of WW II fame. Twin-tailed transport airplane.

C-123: Big Air Force fixed-wing; "Provider." Used in short field landings on airstrips with rugged surfaces. The infamous spraying of "Agent Orange" was accomplished with this squat-bodied aircraft.

C-130: Probably one of the most accomplished aircraft in the world. Four engines on the "Hercules" made it a very useful large fixed-wing a/c.

Cadre: A nucleus of trained military men capable of assuming control and training others.

C & C: The Command and Control ship. This bird orbited high above the battlefield, observing all the action and carrying ground commanders in the back seat to accompany the aviation brass flying up front.

CH-47: The Chinook heavy-lift helicopter with two tandem rotor systems. Cargo helicopter was the abbreviation. Several models sling-loaded heavy loads of ammunition for the howitzers they also ferried. They could lift 10,000 pounds; sometimes that was a busted Huey.

Charlie: From the second word in Viet Cong of the military phonetic spelling for VC. Also "Charles."

Charlie model: The 540 rotor system on the C-model Huey. It replaced B-models.

Chicken Plates: Originally just steel plates procured for armor protection; usually chest area. Later were ceramic, bullet proof inserts in wrap-around vests with Velcro attachment strapping. Sat on, worn, placed under seats, etc.

Chicom: Chinese Communist; probably referring to a war trophy commonly picked up as their infantryman's standard issued rifle.

Close Air Support: elf explanatory, be it by fixed-wing or armed helicopter.

CO: Commanding officer. The man in charge, where the buck stops. He is actively present over the battlefield and watchful over all in his charge. He should also have a better idea about anything than any of his subordinates.

Contact: When actively engaged with the enemy in a combat situation.

CP: Command post. Where the brass on the ground plot their progress and scheme about what to do next during the course of the day's battle or operation.

CS: Tear gas. Sometimes dropped out of Chinooks in 55-gallon drums.

CW2: Chief Warrant Officer, Two. The next promotion for a warrant officer pilot.

DA: Department of the Army. When using this term, someone is talking about making direct contact with the Pentagon about personnel matters. As, "I called DA to see what's up."

D-model: The slick helicopter. A stretch version of the original B-model.

Delta: The Mekong Delta; most of the area south of Saigon. IV Corps.

Di-di: Vietnamese for "go-go!" Di-di-ing an aircraft would mean getting away quickly.

DFC: The Distinguished Flying Cross. Every Huey driver probably did something during his tour in Vietnam to be put up for this award; only given to a flight crew in combat. Most came home with one of them.

DROS: When you rotated home, you had a date representing the nearly 365- days you had spent overseas in the Republic of Vietnam. This abbreviation was for "Date Return Over Seas." (That's the way it was spelled it out; we pronounced it: "DEROS".)

DSC: The Distinguished Service Cross. Second only to the Medal of Honor.

Dud: A round that did not go off, short for "did not detonate."

DUSTOFF: The helicopter aero-medical-evacuation ships and personnel. These flying medics landed into the LZ and picked up the wounded crews and infantrymen close to where they had been wounded. Name came from early heroic efforts by one of the Delta's elite helicopter pilots in the begining phases of the war. Supposedly, the rotor wash of the aircraft "dusted off the wounded and corpses" as the ship landed.

EM: Enlisted man. Most Huey aircrews in Vietnam were PFC's or Spec. 4's.

F4: The Phantom jet used by the Air Force, Navy, and Marines in Vietnam as a tactical fighter/bomber. Very dependable, high performance, two seater, with twin engines. Often called a "fast mover."

FAC Forward Air Controller. The guy in the little tiny plane orbiting the target area in a very ballsey way; directs the jet strikes. "Mac the FAC."

.50-Caliber: The heavy machine gun that could create basketball-sized holes in an aircraft. This heavy-caliber machine gun fired with a "pom-pom- pom" sound, and its rounds could travel nearly a mile in a straight line. A very scary antiaircraft weapon to a helicopter pilot.

Fire team: Two gunships flying together as unit, Lead and his wingman, from a gun platoon. A "heavy" fire team would have a third ship with it, usually the "Hog," which had a grenade launcher on the nose and 24 rockets in each pod on either side.

First John: Slang for the first lieutenant officer rank.
Flex kit: The machine gun/rocket pod combination on the sides of a gunship.

FM: Frequency Modulation. The "Fox-Mike" was the radio spectrum in use by the ground troops and between the aircraft within the platoon's lift.

FNG: "F—-king New Guy. Can more politely mean "Frigging new guy."

GCA: Ground controlled approach by radar, which can adjust the pilot on his flight path both laterally and vertically. Coming down out of the clouds, he has to make corrections according to verbal instructions from the guy on the radar screen on the ground at his airfield

Ground-pounder: Another term for the infantry; "grunts."

Hooch: Living quarters; if Vietnamese, sometimes they looked not much more than a straw covered cabana on some tropical isle. For GI's, usually screened, with wood sheathing on the sides, and a corrugated steel roof.

Hotel 3: The Saigon heliport alongside Tan Son Nhut airfield.

Huey: Bell's beautiful flying product for the Vietnam War. See UH-1 below.

IFR: Refers to instrument flight rule conditions; means the weather has turned bad, and the pilot cannot see visually; not necessarily that he has filed a flight plane and intends to fly on instruments in the scud.

IG: Inspector General. When things were going *too* well with an Army aviation unit, the brass had a way of showing up to figure things out.

IOBC: Infantry Officer's Basic Course. The first school young second: lieutenants saw upon entering the Army in the late sixties.

IP: Instructor Pilot; usually rated for one particular aircraft at a time.

KIA: Killed In Action.

Lead: The command slot in a formation of two or more aircraft.

Lifer: Slang term for those enlisted personnel, and certainly some commissioned officers, who are only in the Army for the long haul and a retirement check. Notable for being individuals who never are accountable for very much or unwilling to take a risk in the military sense of action or valor.

LZ: Landing zone. Similar to the term DZ (drop zone) for paratroopers, but here the helicopters are landing the troops in the airmobile concept of operating. They ride in the Hueys to the ground and get out, instead of jumping out of aircraft 1,000 feet up.

M-60: The machine gun of the Vietnam war. It fired belt-fed, 7.62 mm NATO rounds as standard ammo of the Allied forces. Door gunners used it to suppress the enemy when allowed, or to take spontaneous action when defending the Huey.

MACV: Military Assistance Command, Vietnam, established in February, 1962. The oldest assignment for American officers and sergeants advising the Vietnamese troops in country. This went on before these guys even began receiving combat pay in 1962. American military casualties were not even counted before that date. Not the best assignment for a career officer as the war developed. That supposedly was commanding American troops in the divisions engaged with the NVA up north.

Mavericks: The famed gun platoon of the Outlaws. Insignia was a snorting yellow bull with blasts of smoke coming out of both nostrils. Red farmers' kerchiefs completed their unique uniform decorations.

MEDEVAC: This is an abbreviation, but not necessarily a call sign, for aero-medical evacuation by helicopter, or sometimes a large fixed-wing airplane.

MIA: Missing In Action. The person is exactly that, but may be wounded, too.

MOS: Military Occupational Specialty. Your Army job title; numerically expressed.

MP: Military Police. The Vietnamese ones were QC.

NLF: National Liberation Front. See VC below.

NVA: North Vietnamese Army. Very different people than those in the South; almost as much of a difference as in the United States between Yankees and Southerners. The two groups felt that antagonism, too.

O1E: The Bird-Dog; a light observation airplane in use by the Army before the push-pull Cessna aircraft replaced in later in the sixties; the L-19.

OCS: Officers' Candidate School. Each combat arms branch has one.

Officer's Country: EM were not allowed to visit commissioned and warrant officers in their hooches. In some places, small signs alongside walkways indicated these boundaries, which were insisted upon between the officers and the troops. Sometimes the EM crews came over to our living quarters and looked us up anyway; they liked being casual. We didn't.

OH: Observation helicopter, such as an OH-13 or an OH-23. The OH-6 was called a "Loach" because it spelled out "light observation helicopter"; the scouts.

Old man: Traditional military slang for the commanding officer.

Operations: The office for all the assignments and tallying of what the aircraft are going to be doing on their missions. Records of flight time are maintained here. Usually located close to or under the tower.

Orderly Room: The company's administrative command center, where the CO and First Sergeant have their offices. It serves as the CP on the compound, where the Executive Officer works. When you are ordered to report here, you stand erect for the business being conducted.

Outlaw: The call sign of the A/502nd, later renamed the 175th Airmobile Co.

OW: Original wife; a recent term since Vietnam. It refers to those women who are still married to the guy who went over there. Many divorces resulted from the changes the guys experienced on this tour. Any woman who can still put up with us and remain is respected.

PE: Periodic Maintenance. An intense inspection and work period at each 100 hours of flight time.

Peter Pilot: Same as copilot. The young warrant officers who were often only 19 or 20 years old were also called "boy-pilots."

PTSD: Post-Traumatic Stress Disorder. Now heavily researched to try to assess why many Vietnam vets weathered such long-term effects of their combat tour.

PX: Post exchange; the retail aspect of an Army post.

PZ: The pickup zone. The "Poppa Zulu" was where the slicks landed and loaded up the troops during their extraction.

R&R: Rest and Recuperation. A week long vacation to some civilized, affluent destination in the Orient (or in some cases, Hawaii). The best places for the GI's were Japan, Hong Kong, Singapore, and Bangkok. There were also trips to Micronesia and the Philippines. Usually one R&R was awarded during the tour, some guys lucked out by garnering two trips.

RF: Reaction Force. (See "Rat F—k" in text.)

Roger: The compliance signal; also that I comprehend your message to me.

Rounds: Rounds of ammunition expended. Not to be confused with "Round- eyes," a term which was reserved for the only white females in-country.

ROTC: Reserve Officer's Training Corps. The OCS of college boys.

RPG: Rocket-propelled grenade. These were fired at the helicopters from Soviet and Chinese-manufactured, shoulder-held launchers. They were originally designed for anti-tank use, but were frequently used against our infantry's bunkers and our birds with effect.

S3: Operations officer at the battalion level. If this man was operating at the divisional level, he would be a G3. The number "4" was for supply, "5" for XO, and "6" for the CO in the call signs and designation. "1" was personnel and "2" was for intelligence.

SEALS: "Sea-Air-Land Special Operations" guys. Very macho and very athletic to handle all the demands placed upon their physiques for their perilous work. They could parachute out of aircraft, move about on patrol, and be frogmen, too. The Navy's far-out types.

Slicks: The transport helicopters. Carrying only personal weapons and fixed M-60's on pylons at the rear doors, they were deemed "slicked down" compared to the armament of the gunships; therefore the term which evolved early-on in the war.

Slopes: The racist derogatory term for the Vietnamese, because of their slanted oriental eyes. Other terms were Gooks or Gomers.

SOI: The secret code book of all the radio call signs and frequencies in the Corps. Changed monthly, but we suspected Charles had his personal copy as soon as we did. Covered with the Army's famous "green tape" and worn on a string around the neck. The first thing to take from the aircraft, your weapon came second.

STOL: Short-Takeoff-Landing. Groovy, fantastically capable fixed-wings that the CIA commonly had—with which to do the nigh-impossible.

"STORMY WEATHER": The aviator's code name for Cambodia. Though technically a neutral country, it was very dangerous, and no place to stray into accidentally . This term was often used as a tip-off that one had.

TAC-X: Training The last phase of Army flight school at that time when we lived and performed as if we were an aviation company in Vietnam. Mostly the guys played with their survival knives and planned their 30-day leave's activities, while awaiting training flights.

Tet: The Vietnamese New Year. Now forever infamous as that holiday in early 1968 when violent attacks erupted all over Vietnam during the usual truce period. It had never been violated before.

Thermite Grenade: A canister-shaped hand grenade; this incendiary device produces an intense, high temperature fire—hot enough to melt metal, which it is supposed to do. Meant to destroy weapons and equipment.

TI: Technical Inspector. The next echelon up from your crew chief for excellence in determining what is wrong with your helicopter's flying parts. Usually at least an E-6 in rank.

Trail: The last aircraft in a formation, commanded by a second-in-command to follow up Lead's instructions and be his eyes in the rear to ascertain how the flight is doing. Platoon leaders usually alternated flying these two command slots from day to day. Trail was the easier job.

Treeline: Because of the banana trees and coconut palms planted along the canals engineered by the French when they were in Indochina, this vegetation provided cover for VC firing at the approaching or overflying aircraft, so it was crucial to stay away from these during approaches for landing.

UH-1 (A, B, C, D): Various models of the Huey helicopter. The beloved aircraft's nickname came from this "utility helicopter" designation.

UHF: Ultra High Frequency. The radio band in use by the aircraft in most communications with the tower and the company net, and between commands in airmobile operations.

USO: Entertainment provided for the military by contracted musical acts; some were from the States, others from the Philippines or other parts of the world.

VC: The Viet Cong, the National Liberation Front (NLF); the guerrilla force in South Vietnam that was warring against the Saigon government. These Vietnamese felt this institutional regime was the last vestige of colonialism in their country that existed only because of United States military intervention.

VHF: Very High Frequency. Only used for navigation frequencies and between the gunship platoon aircraft. Scratchy sounding.

VHPA: The Vietnam Helicopter Pilots Association. The association open to all pilots who flew helicopters in all the services from the early parts of the war to the end. Largely a reunion group to find sick buddies and enjoy each other once more.

VL: Victor Lima; military phonetic spelling for Vinh Long to shorten radio talk.

VN: Victor November is military phonetic spelling for Vietnamese.

WIA: Wounded In Action

WO1: Warrant Officer. This is the rank bestowed on flight school graduates as their first rank in the warrant officer designation, it leads up to CW-4.

WP: White phosphorous. Often a grenade, used as an anti-personnel weapon. The white-hot pieces of the metal can burn right through a human body. Called "Willie Peter."

XO: The Executive Officer, the second-in-command ranking officer, who tends to administrative matters on the ground to relieve the commanding officer of any such business, or at least to the greatest extent possible. Often the CO is so busy flying as an active leader, that he is too exhausted to tend to these issues and details pushing the troops on the ground.

The"Y": A strong VC headquarters area between Vinh Long and Can Tho. It was easily recognized from the air because several major canal lines converged here. You could get hit at 5,000 feet if you overflew this area.